Baedeker

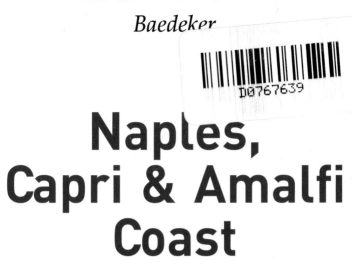

Naples, Capri & Amalfi Coast

www.baedeker.com
Verlag Karl Baedeker

SIGHTSEEING HIGHLIGHTS ★★

The Bay of Naples promises a variety of pleasures: a glittering history, artistic treasures, and gorgeous landscapes. We have put together an overview of the highlights for you here. In addition, there is Salerno – the eternal rival to Naples – and the towns of Benevento and Avellino set in a verdant landscape, not forgetting Sorrento on the peninsula of the same name.

1 ★★ Naples
This lively metropolis has a long and fascinating past, as well as interesting surroundings. Unique archaeological sites in the city and between Pozzuoli and Cumae recall the history of the region, as do world famous museums and a historic city centre that is still buzzes with modern life.
▸ **page 185**

2 ★★ Ischia
Three island pearls grace the Bay of Naples and each one is a world unto itself. Ischia is associated with its healing spas.
▸ **page 172**

3 ★★ Caserta
The Reggia di Caserta is a magnificent palace set in a truly regal park: the Versailles of the south. ▸ **page 155**

4 ★★ Mount Vesuvius
Responsible for terrible eruptions, such as the one in AD 79, which destroyed Pompeii and Herculaneum. Magma continues to bubble and boil 5km/3mi to 7km/4mi below ground, while at 1281m/4202ft, you can look into the sleeping giant's mouth.
▸ **page 327**

5 ★★ Herculaneum
Stroll into the past on streets paved with volcanic stones over 2000 years old: Herculaneum and Pompeii were once thriving cities. Today they are open-air museums of antiquity. ▸ **page 162**

6 ★★ Pompeii
The ruins provide a unique insight into the urban structures and everyday life of antiquity. ▸ **page 265**

7 ★★ Amalfi and the Amalfi Coast
The fantastic panoramic route along the Costa Divina runs a mere 40km/25mi. The serpentine road along the rocky coast on the south side of the Sorrentine peninsula travel through a landscape characterized by terraced lemon groves, ravines and pastel-coloured towns. One of the main sights is the ancient maritime republic of Amalfi.
▸ **page 118**

Agropoli in Cilento
The traditional rhythm of southern Italian can still be experienced along the coast and the interior of the country's second-largest national park

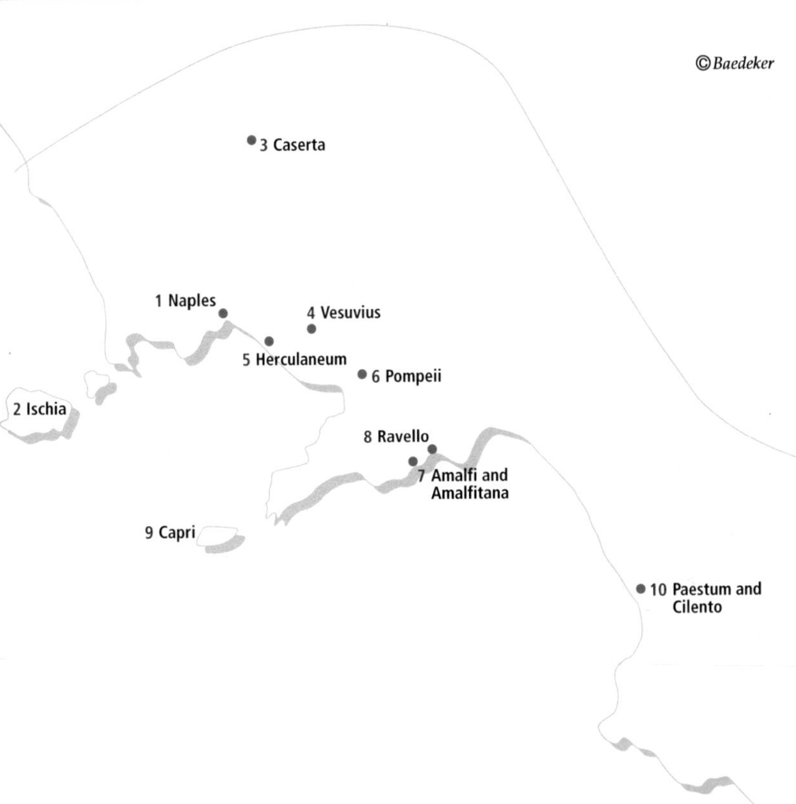

8 ∗∗ Ravello

The magical town with its atmospheric palazzi set in their beautiful gardens lies high above the Amalfi Coast. For many, Ravello has the most beautiful views along the Costa Divina and is an ideal base for mountain hiking in the hinterland.

► **page 301**

9 ∗∗ Capri

This rock in the sea off the Sorrentine peninsula with an area of just 10 sq km/4 sq mi has been attracting exclusive visitors for over 2000 years. ► **page 135**

10 ∗∗ Paestum and Cilento

Three magnificent temples recall the golden age of this Greek town, which is also the gateway to the Cilento region, where forested hills and mountains await with mysterious grottoes and small hilltop villages. The nearby coast with its crystal-clear waters is punctuated by capes reaching out to sea, grottoes, bizarre rock formations and fine sandy beaches, all formed by the combined effects of sea, wind and the rivers. ► **page 245**

BEADEKER'S BEST TIPS

The best of all Baedeker's tips listed in this book have been gathered together here. Experience and savour the Bay of Naples from its best side.

The volcano lover
Naples during the reign of Ferdinand IV in Susan Sontag's historical novel.
► page 30

Overshadowed by Pompeii
Pompeii is the most visited destination of Italian antiquity. Its sister town of Herculaneum is much less overrun, yet just as interesting. ► page 109

Off the tourist track
Small mountain towns and stupendous views in almost total solitude, just a short distance from the much-frequented Amalfi Coast. ► page 124

An ascent with a view
The highest summit on the island can be reached in twelve minutes by chairlift from Anacapri. ► page 138

Gelato al limone
Trying the refreshing lemon ice on the lemon island is a must.
► page 141

Literary cemetery with a view
Forgotten personalities predominate in this, one of the most atmospheric spots on the Bay of Naples. ► page 146

Modern art at the palace
Contemporary art in a Baroque setting: Lucio Amelio's collection in the beautiful rooms of the Reggia at Caserta.
► page 159

Cilento
The southeast of Campania is a nature lover's paradise, while the popular summer resorts of the coast are not far away

Modern art at the castle
Contemporary art in a Baroque setting – Lucio Amelio's collection in the beautiful setting of the Reggia in Caserta.
► **page 159**

A recommendation
Truman Capote once stayed here in Forio's prettiest and most welcoming guest house. ► **page 183**

Personal safety
Naples is no more dangerous than any other major European city if certain precautions are taken. ► **page 185**

Up-to-date information
Stay up-to-date on events, opening times etc. online or in the local press.
► **page 188**

Art on the go in Naples
The Naples underground system has been a much more colourful place since renowned artists were commissioned to design the new metro stations.
► **page 197**

Gods and caffè
Next door to a small altar in honour of Diego Maradona you can get great coffee. ► **page 214**

Bargain hunters beware!
Buying counterfeit designer brands is a very bad idea. Both buyers and seller are punished with heavy fines. ► **page 223**

Learn Italian in Naples
Small classes, committed teachers and a great support programme turn every course into an event. ► **page 225**

Theatregoers please note…
An opera or concert in Naples' Teatro San Carlo is a real experience, even if the tickets are very pricey. It is worth arriving early. ► **page 230**

Vesuvius
The volcano holds death and destruction, but its fertile earth also provides inexhaustible wealth

Pompeii in fiction
The destruction of Pompeii, immaculately researched and well told. ► **page 275**

Fish restaurants with reasonable prices
Excellent fish dishes right next door to the »ancient supermarket« – with moderate prices too. ► **page 290**

Ancient luxury
See how architecture and an elaborate garden landscape in a natural panoramic setting combine to create a work of art.
► **page 326**

Virtual Vesuvius
The latest on Vesuvius and the Phlegrean Fields. ► **page 331**

»Real« mozzarella made from buffalo's milk can only be found in Campania
► **page 80**

BACKGROUND

10 The Mezzogiorno
14 Facts
15 Nature and Environment
17 Population · Politics · Economy
18 *3 D: Mount Vesuvius*
24 History
25 From the Beginnings to the Fall of Rome
27 The Norman, Hohenstaufen, Angevin and Aragonese Dynasties
29 Naples in the 18th and 19th Centuries
36 Naples up to the Present Day
32 *Special: Money, Rubbish and Death*
38 Art and Culture
39 History of Art and Culture (Glossary ►p. 338)
32 *Special: Contemporary Art in Naples*
58 Famous People

PRACTICALITIES

66 Accomodation
68 Arrival · Planning the Trip
71 Beach Holidays
72 Children in Italy
74 Electricity
74 Emergency
75 Etiquette and Customs
75 Festivals, Holidays and Events
79 Food and Drink
81 Health
82 Information
83 Verkehr
88 Literature
91 Media
91 Money
92 Opening Hours
93 Post · Communications
93 Prices and Discounts
94 Shopping
95 Sport and Outdoors
97 Time
97 Transport
101 When to Go

Price categories

► **Hotels (double room)**
Budget: up to 80 €
Mid-range: 80–190 €
Luxury: from 190 €

► **Restaurants (3-course meal without drinks)**
Budget: up to 20 €
Moderate: 20–35 €
Expensive: from 35 €

Naples is every inch the sophisticated metropolis by the entrance to its elegant Galleria Umberto I

▸ **page 185**

TOURS

106 Travelling around the Bay of Naples
107 Tour 1: Caserta – the Italian Versailles
108 Tour 2: Into the Burning Fields
109 Tour 3: On the Miglia d'Oro to Herculaneum and Pompeii
110 Tour 4: The Amalfi Coast and the Sorrentine Peninsula
112 Tour 5: Through the Bay's Green Interior to Benevento
113 Tour 6: Into Magna Graecia to Paestum
114 Tour 7: Island Idyll

SIGHTS FROM A to Z

118 Amalfi and the Amalfi Coast
127 Benevento
135 Capri
136 *Special: Capri Scandals*
150 Capua and Santa Maria Capua Vetere
155 Caserta
162 Herculaneum · Ercolano
172 Ischia
185 Naples Napoli
200 *3 D: San Lorenzo Maggiore*
204 *Special: Wonders Never Cease*
245 Paestum and Cilento
252 *Special: The Doric Temple*
265 Pompeii
276 *Special: A Wonder of the World Defiled*
283 Pozzuoli and the Campi Flegrei
288 *Special: The Goethe Family on Holiday*
297 Procida
301 Ravello
308 Salerno
315 Sorrento · Sorrento
327 Vesuvius · Vesuvio
332 *3 D: Villa Oplontis*

338 Glossary
344 Index
349 List of Maps and Illustrations
350 Photo Credits
350 Publisher's Information

Background

THINGS WORTH KNOWING ABOUT THE BAY OF NAPLES: ITS ECONOMY, POLITICS, HISTORY, CULTURE AND DAILY LIFE

IN THE MEZZOGIORNO

The very epitome of the Latin south, the Bay of Naples has held an irresistible fascination for travellers from northern Europe for centuries. The islands of Capri and Ischia, as well as the Amalfi Coast and Sorrento, have always been highlights of any journey to southern Italy.

Yet Campania – the region bordered by Lazio, Molise, Basilicata, Puglia, and the Tyrrhenian Sea – is so much more than its natural wonders. Crucially, for around 1200 years, from the arrival of the Greeks in Cumae to the fall of the Roman Empire, Campania lay at the heart of Mediterranean antiquity, and all around the Bay of Naples its traces are ever-present. The region's unique archaeological sites are even more significant than those of Rome or Lazio. Key locations for the history of European art and culture are here, ranging from the lost cities of Pompeii and Herculaneum smothered by Vesuvius, to the Greek temples of Paestum, and the legendary Cumae. In addition, there are many smaller archaeological sites in Campania, such as the unique domed architecture of the thermal baths at Baia, or the imperial Villa Oplonti in present-day Torre Annunziata.

Naples *Campania's capital at the foot of Mount Vesuvius*

Naples

Although the southern Italian metropolis of Naples is on the receiving end of numerous prejudices, the capital of Campania is well worth a visit – and not only for its art-historical treasures. Nonetheless, its centro storico (historic centre) is a UNESCO World Heritage site, and the streets of the city centre still follow the original design built during its foundation 2500 years ago. Today, the city's dynamics are sometimes terrifying, but they are easily understood considering the dramatic history of Naples, which lies within sight of Mount Vesuvius, unpredictable in its volcanic activity. Monuments dating from the Middle Ages, the Renaissance and Baroque can make the historic centre seem like a large open-air museum. They include Gothic churches from the time of the Angevin kings, Renaissance buildings constructed by the Aragonese and, most especially, the Baroque architectural treasures of the Spanish viceroys, so characteristic of the Neapolitan cityscape. In the 18th century, during the reign of the Bourbons, Naples and Campania enjoyed a social

← Fresco from Villa dei Misteri in Pompeii

Pompeii
Buried under a blanket of cinders and ash when Vesuvius erupted in AD 79, Pompeii was rediscovered in 1750, including this fresco from the house of Meleagro, which is now kept in the Archaeological Museum in Naples

Vesuvius
During antiquity, Vesuvius was simply known as »the mountain«. Today, the volcano inspires fear and fascination in equal measure and is constantly monitored

Benevento
The 12th-century Arab-Norman cloister can be found in the church of Santa Sofia, built by the Lombards in the 8th century

Capri
Shaped by wind and weather, the Faraglioni stacks in the southeast of Capri are one of the island's emblems

Paestum
The most beautiful temples of Magna Graecia have been defying the ravages of time for over 2500 years

Cilento
One of the most beautiful regions of Italy, with mountains, forests, olive groves, rocky coastlines, sandy beaches, and the sea

and cultural flowering. This period finds best expression in the form of the Reggia de Caserta, the largest palace from the era of absolutism after Versailles and El Escorial. Furthermore, with the art gallery in the Palazzo Reale on the hill of Capodimonte and the National Archaeological Museum, Naples boasts two of the world's most famous museums. The city's greatest attraction, however, is its people. The Neapolitans are as temperamental as they are gracious, and the daily chaos on the streets is usually enthralling rather than frightening, even if it does take some getting used to. There may be plenty of sights in Naples, but really it is a city to live in.

Islands in the Bay of Naples

Ischia and Capri, both beautiful Mediterranean islands, continue to overwhelm visitors with their charms. Ischia's thermal springs have been one of the greatest attractions on the Bay of Naples for the past 200 years, while fashionable Capri is best visited during the off-season. The third island of Procida, on the other hand, still has quiet places to discover and is ideal for a relaxing seaside holiday.

Faith in miracles
The desire for saints and their miracles is met here

More to See

While the Sorrentine peninsula and the Amalfi Coast claim to have the most beautiful coastal road in the world, the hiking routes of the area – between Sorrento and Positano and to the Punta della Campanella – are also second to none. The still very rural provinces of Benevento and Avellino, in Campania's interior, remain almost unknown to tourists. In fact, just a short distance from the tourism centres of the Bay of Naples it is possible to experience an unspoilt Italy that could not be more hospitable. A real insider's tip is the countryside of Cilento, in the southern part of Campania, where endless beaches, crystal clear water and rolling hills ideal for walking make for quite a holiday experience. Wherever you decide to base yourself for a holiday in Campania, there will always be interesting destinations for day trips.

Facts

The Bay of Naples and its Campanian hinterland make up one of the most diverse landscapes in Italy. Mountains alternate with rolling farmland and the famous coastal stretches of the Sorrentine peninsula. Above all, the region is dominated by the twin peaks of Mount Vesuvius.

Nature and Environment

Geographical location

Extending from the western reaches of the Apennines to the Tyrrhenian Sea, Campania is bordered by four other regions of southern Italy: Lazio to the northwest, Molise to the northeast, Puglia to the east, and Basilicata to the southeast. Precisely 50.7% of its territory is mountainous, 34.6% consists of undulating lowlands, and only 14.7% is truly flat. The coast along the Tyrrhenian Sea is defined by the Gulf of Gaeta to the north and the Gulf of Policastro to the south. There are three islands in the Bay of Naples itself: Capri, Ischia and Procida. The fertile earth and beautiful coasts made **Campania felix** one of the most popular and densely inhabited regions of Roman antiquity. The name originally referred to the plain around Capua – the area now known as the »terra di lavoro«, between Capua and Caserta. Meanwhile, the wealth of natural hot springs made the coast between Pozzuoli and Baia one of history's earliest holiday destinations. During summer, at least, much of the Roman Empire's business was managed from there. In fact, owning a country estate in Campania and a villa on the Gulf of Baia, Pozzuoli or Naples was all the rage for the Roman upper class.

Campanian Apennines

Strictly speaking, the Italian peninsula is a large mountainous region set in the sea. It is part of the roughly 1500km/950mi-long **Apennine range** that dominates the Italian landscape between the Po delta and southern Calabria and makes up two thirds of the country. Tectonic movements of the Eurasian and African plates pushed this mountain range out of the earth's crust around 65 million years ago. At the beginning of the Ice Age, two million years ago, the summits of the Apennines were covered by glaciers. The **Monti del Matese**, a chain of mountains reaching up to 2050m/6726ft in the province of Benevento, are spurs of the Campanian Apennines. Even the Sorrentine peninsula and the island of Capri can be considered part of this geological formation. Three permanent rivers flow into the Tyrrhenian Sea: the Garigliano to the north; the Volturno in the province of Caserta; and the Sele, south of Salerno.

Volcanism and bradyseism

The Bay of Naples and the islands of Ischia and Procida have **volcanic origins**, a fact that is memorably underlined by the imposing presence of Mount Vesuvius (► 3D p.18). A volcanic zone stretches from Sicily's Mount Etna, past the Aeolian Islands and through the Bay of Naples, all the way up to Tuscany along the Apennine fault line that includes the coast of the Tyrrhenian Sea. Naples itself lies between two volcanic danger zones: temporarily dormant Vesuvius and the Phlegrean Fields, which include the active crater of the vol-

← Metropolitan flair under a roof of glass and steel: the 19th-century Galleria Umberto I in Naples

cano Solfatara. The most recent research by international volcanologists has also confirmed the existence of a long-suspected giant magma chamber, around 8km/5mi below the earth's surface, running underneath the entire Bay of Naples.

Meanwhile, the phenomenon known as **bradyseism** results in the imperceptibly slow yet constant rise and fall of the earth's crust, especially around the area of the Phlegrean Fields. As long ago as late antiquity, these slow-motion tremors were responsible for the submersion of Baia's coastal strip, and they have been monitored and analyzed in Pozzuoli since 1905. Between 1905 and 1945 the ground there sank by up to 50cm/20in, although it had already risen by 38cm/15in again by 1951. The most dramatic bradyseismic movements recorded so far came in 1970, when the ground at Pozzuoli rose by 85.7cm/33.7in in just two days. Even in distant Bagnoli, the ground rose by 19cm/7in. By the end of 1972, ground levels were an unbelievable 170cm/67in higher than in 1953. Finally, at the beginning of the 1980s, the historic centre of Pozzuoli had to be permanently evacuated due to the constant bradyseismic activity. The ground descended once more between 1985 and 2001, sinking by 90cm/35in, and a certain calm seems to have established itself in recent years, with annual rises of just 1.5cm/0.6in being recorded.

Flora and fauna

The danger signified by volcanic activity is also what ensures the beauty of the Bay of Naples' landscape and the fertility of its earth. Intensive agriculture has been practiced in Campania since Greek and Roman times, and wine is still being cultivated on the slopes of Mount Vesuvius, just as it was 2000 years ago. The heartland of former Campania felix, around Capua, is now an intensive vegetable farming area. Tomatoes predominate, and are harvested towards the end July each year, when mostly family-run enterprises process and tin them. Despite the continued lack of enthusiasm among Italians for nature conservation, there are two **nature reserves** in Campania: the Parco Nazionale del Vesuvio, and the Parco del Cilento e Vallo di Diano. The Italian branch of the World Wildlife Fund (WWF) is also active in protecting the environment here. As long ago as antiquity the **original landscape** of southern Italy was decisively altered when the mountains that were once covered by huge forests were completely logged out by the Romans. Today, holm oaks, centennial pines and shrub-like macchiato predominate on the coastal mountains. The provinces of Benevento and Avellino, on the other hand, still have largely forested mountains. These are regions of large swathes of mixed woodland, with oak and beech trees. Avellino is also the source of Campania's water supply.

Campania's fauna mostly inhabits the Bay of Naples, where a surprising wealth of species is found in the sea. The Naples Marine Institute has been studying the local waters for over a century and exhibits a good cross section of ocean-dwelling species in its famous aquarium. The remote mountains of the Benevento are said to be in-

Houses cascade down to the sea: Positano, on the Amalfi Coast

habited by wolves, while wild boars still forage in the thickets of the protected area of Cilento.

Climate

The ideal months to travel here are April, May and June, as well as the autumn right up to December. July and August are more suitable for seaside holidays, although high temperatures can make excursions onerous and the summer heat bears down oppressively on the streets of Naples. During the months of January, February and March, the illusion of a permanently warm Mediterranean is quickly destroyed. Even if frost is rare, these months can often be rainy, cold and damp. As a consequence the more basic hotel rooms can quickly become uncomfortably clammy, as modern central heating is rarely up to scratch in southern Italy.

Population · Politics · Economy

Population distribution

With an area of 13,595 sq km/5249 sq mi, Campania is not the largest of Italy's 20 regions, but with 426 inhabitants per sq km/1107 per sq mi it is the country's most densely populated (► cont. on p.20) area. The majority of its roughly 5.8 million inhabitants live in the

MOUNT VESUVIUS

Almost affectionately, Neapolitans call their mountain »il scartellato« (the humpback) – yet this is no weakling. The volcano has been dormant for over 60 years, but the next time it erupts, it could well affect Naples itself.

Opening times:
access to the crater summit during summer is from 9am to 6.30pm.

① The crater
The spooky mouth of the present Mount Vesuvius has a diameter of around 600m/2000ft, a circumference of 12km/7mi and is around 200m/650ft deep.

② Along the abyss
Those wearing stout footwear can walk along the crater's edge and risk peering into the abyss of the dormant volcano's mouth.

③ Molten rock at a depth of 5–7km/3–4mi
The magma chamber that the next eruption might expel into the air lies at a depth of around 5km/3mi inside the crater. Around 2km/1mi closer to the crater's edge, a plug »blocks« the crater's mouth.

④ More than destruction
The rapid decomposition of lava into fertile earth has ensured rich harvests of wine, fruit and olives on Mount Vesuvius for millennia. The cooled lava is also a popular building material for new houses.

⑤ Layers upon layers
Bore holes up to a depth of 1300m/4265ft have proved that Mount Vesuvius is at least 400,000 years old. The volcano is actually made of two parts: one of these is the much older Somma crater, which later collapsed; the younger part is the volcanic cone of today's Vesuvius. It is likely that the central cone collapsed during the AD 79 eruption, forming a caldera, which is the edge of the Somma crater. Today's volcano has been building up in that core ever since.

⑥ Move away from danger
Around 550,000 people live in settlements located at the foot of Mount Vesuvius that over the decades have gradually been spreading up the fertile mountain. All are in the line of fire from potential pyroclastic flows and hot showers of pumice and ash. The regional government has developed an evacuation plan. The 150,000 inhabitants of the most endangered zone are to be tempted to move away with financial incentives; so far, this has met with little success. On the contrary, the environmental group »Legambiente« claims that in the past 20 years alone, 50,000 new homes have been illegally constructed in the »red zone«.

Pompeii in the shadow of Mount Vesuvius. A major tourist attraction, two thirds of the city has been excavated up till now

tirrenia

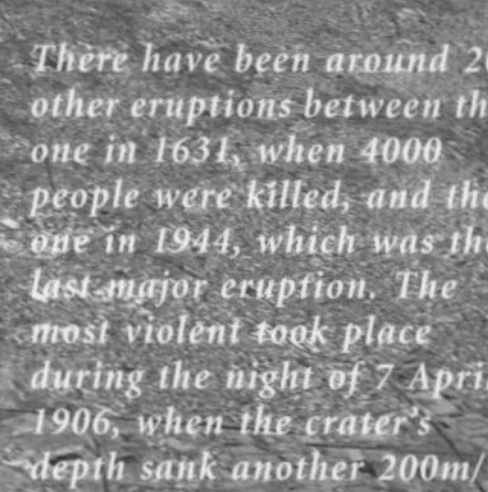

There have been around 20 other eruptions between the one in 1631, when 4000 people were killed, and the one in 1944, which was the last major eruption. The most violent took place during the night of 7 April 1906, when the crater's depth sank another 200m/656ft.

5

4

ıearthed at Pompeii nt Vesuvius prior to ·uption, showing the ith just one summit. planted with vine- ıus, the god of wine, the fertility and the ıature of the region. sumably represented protective spirit, the »Genius Loci«.

©Baedeker

When Vesuvius erupted on 24 August AD 79, the city of Pompeii was buried under 6m/20ft of ash. Many people were caught in the showers of ash and smothered. Later, their bodies decomposed, leaving hollows that have since been filled with plaster.

Local dignitaries inaugurated the first railway up Mount Vesuvius in 1880. However, this practical means of transport was destroyed during the 1944 eruption, and only a few fragments of metal can still be seen around the crater's edge.

A mosaic
portrays Mo
its AD 79 e
mountain
It is dense
yards. Bacc
symbolizes
paradisiacal
The snake pr
the local

urban conurbations in and around Naples and Salerno. The most recent census indicated that the population of Naples, at 983,000, is declining, but the undeclared number of African and East European immigrants without their permesso di soggiorno (permission to stay) is believed to be high.

Government The plebiscite of 2 June 1946 established Italy as a parliamentary republic. It was a very close call in favour of the republic and, of all Italy's regions, Campania came out the strongest in favour of keeping the monarchy (76.5% of votes cast). Christian Democrat regional governments dominated in the decades after the Second World War. Since the 1990s, however, Campania has been ruled by a coalition of the central left. The defeat of Alessandra Mussolini by **Antonio Bassolino** for the post of mayor in 1993 signified a sea change for the region, and he was elected for another term in 1997 with a resounding 72.9% of the vote. Today, he is president of Campania, and his successor as Sindaco (mayor) of Naples was **Rosa Russo Iervolino**, who was elected in 2001. She too, was elected for a second term, taking 57% of the votes, in 2006. **Luigi de Magistris** was elected mayor in 2011.

Economy

A few facts Italy's notoriously inflated administrative structures and opaque bureaucracy hobble Campania's economic prospects in particular.

Refuse problem ► The local authorities are the largest employers. Yet, even **refuse collection**, which employs thousands of people, has long failed to address basic environmentally friendly processing needs. Not a shred of waste separation occurs, even though the region of Campania produces more rubbish than any other in Italy. The rubbish dumps have all been overflowing for decades, and illegal dumping is one of the most profitable businesses of the **Camorra**, as the Campanian mafia are called. They will dispose of everything, even toxic waste, which for decades has been interred in the local countryside without the slightest hesitation. Paradoxically, the construction of modern incineration plants for rubbish has been stymied by the protests of several environmental groups. Most of all, however, it has been obstructed by a corrupt political system dominated by the vested interests of the Camorra.

Unemployment figures hover between 20% and 30%, although the influence of the Camorra and an illegal black economy mean the numbers are unreliable. Youth unemployment in the municipalities around Mount Vesuvius, and especially in Caserta province, stands at 45–60%, with scant prospect of any future employment or career opportunities. The **average annual income** for a family in Caserta province lies at just under €10,000 (as compared with northern Italy, where unemployment stands at under 6% and the average per capita annual income is around €14,000).

Facts and Figures Campania

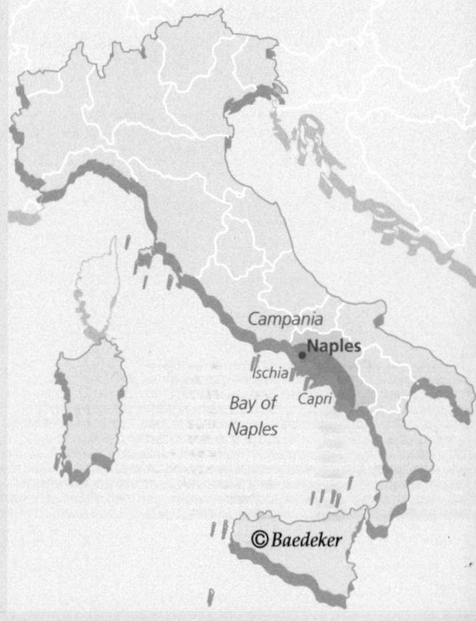

Area and Population

▶ 13,590 km²/5,247 sq mi
5.8 million residents, 426 persons per sq km (1,107 persons per sq mi)

Administration

▶ Campania is divided up into five provinces, which in turn are divided into 551 municipalities.

Government

▶ Campania has been ruled by a moderate-leftist group since the early 1990s. Antonio Bassolino is president of the region (since 2000). The new mayor (sindaco) of Naples since 2011 is Luigi de Magistris.

Name

▶ The name Campania is derived from *campus* (lat. = field). The fertile region with charming landscape was named *Campania felix* (= happy Campania) after Hannibal was finally driven out of southern Italy in the 3rd century BC.

Economy

▶ Unemployment: 20 – 30% (northern Italy: 6%); Family income: just below 10,000 euros p.a. (northern Italy: 14,000 euros)

Universities

▶ six in all in Naples, Salerno and Sannio

PROVINCES OF CAMPANIA

Napoli

▶ Area: 1,171 km²/452 sq mi
Population: about 3 – 3.5 million
2,561 persons per sq km/6,658 persons per sq mi

Salerno

▶ Area: 4,917 km²/1,898 sq mi
Population: about 1.1 million
224 persons per sq km/582 persons per sq mi

Caserta

▶ Area: 2,639 km²/1,019 sq mi
Population: about 880,000
333 persons per sq km/865 persons per sq mi

Benevento

▶ Area: 2,071 km²/800 sq mi
Population: about 300,000
144 persons per sq km/374 persons per sq mi

Avellino

▶ Area: 2,792 km²/1,078 sq mi
Population: about 440,000
157 persons per sq km/ 408 persons per sq mi

? DID YOU KNOW ...?

- Modern basic foods of the Campania were unknown in antiquity. Bread, legumes and garum, a sauce which was made from fermented fish and was the standard spice of Roman cooking, were the basic foods. Like olive oil, garum was available in various levels of quality; fresh fish and meat were luxury.

Industry Campania, next to Puglia, is one of the most highly industrialized regions of southern Italy, thanks to the billions invested by the government in the Cassa per il Mezzogiorno fund. Yet economic development has so far failed and most effort at economic revival in this region has come to nothing. The starkest example of this is the abandoned steel works at Bagnoli, near Naples. In fact, it is **small to medium-sized businesses** that are most significant for the regional economy. The production sites are predominantly textile processing plants run as family enterprises. For example, small municipalities around Mount Vesuvius, such as San Giuseppe Vesuviano, have hundreds of small **sewing workshops**, despite the fact that they have had to compete with the Chinese for some time now. An equally traditional local enterprise in Campania is **small-scale food processing**; the European Union's tinned tomatoes mostly come from the countryside around Naples. **Pasta production** in the factories around Gragnano (near Castellammare di Stabia) is also an important economic factor for the region. Finally, in 2008 the business centre Interporto-Cis was opened near Nola. As Europe's largest and most modern shopping centre and with express railway connections planned in all directions the hope is that Interporto Cis will become an economic hub for the Mediterranean.

Genuine mozzarella is made from buffalo's milk in Campania

Agriculture Agriculture still has a major role to play in Campania and, in the province of Naples alone, 5% of the working population is still employed in this sector. The real figure is believed to be much higher, however, since the tomato and tobacco-growing sector, as well as many other farming activities, largely rely on East European labourers. The feudal landholdings of Campania were all expropriated and divided up in 1860. Today, however, unlike his forebears two generations ago, no landowner can survive exclusively from working his land. These days, the only people left working Campania's once most fertile region, the Terra de Lavoro (Land of Labour), are poorly paid rural labourers. The descendants of the landowners, meanwhile, earn their living in northern Italy and only return to their homeland during the holidays. **Wine growing**, on the other hand, which has been important since antiquity, has experienced a revival in recent years, and is now also significant for exports beyond the region. Wines of certified origin and quality now being produced include Falanghina and Greco di Tufo from the estates on the Irpinia hills. The region around Paestum in southern Campania, meanwhile, is famous for its **mozzarella** made of buffalo milk. However, this is a difficult product to export, as this type of cheese must be consumed fresh. Another industry on the Tyrrhenian Sea that has a tradition going back thousands of years is **fishing**. Today, though, it has been reduced to a local tradition that has long since lost its economic significance for the coastal population.

Tourism

Tourism has been a **substantial source of income** for the Bay of Naples since the 18th century. For example, thanks to its thermal springs, the small fishing village of Pozzuoli virtually lived from tourism as long ago as the mid-18th century. Today, tourism in Campania is a multi-million euro business, though it is almost exclusively limited to the Sorrentine peninsula and the islands of Capri and Ischia. According to the Italian state tourist board ENIT around 4.5 million visitors came to Campania in 2005, though a decline has been noted since. Only Capri has maintained its position as a major tourism destination, while Naples is seeing a decline in bookings. This was initially blamed on the introduction of the euro, but the city's poor image is also responsible. Mainland Bay of Naples simply cannot compete with other European holiday destinations due to a lack of tourist infrastructure, rampant building speculation and environmental pollution. One exception is the nature reserve at Cilento, south of Salerno, which is on UNESCO's World Natural Heritage list.

The Di Viglios have been artisans in Naples for four generations: here with Pulcinella

History

Romans thought of the beautiful fertile land here as »Campania felix« – happy Campania. In the 18th century, the Bay of Naples with its wealth of ancient ruins was declared a romantic arcadia. Centuries of foreign rule, however, have left not only important art-historical traces but also a more complex heritage.

From the Beginnings to the Fall of Rome

7000–2000 BC	Neolithic settlement
From 2000 BC	Immigration of Indo-Germanic tribes
From 900 BC	Native Oscans come under Etruscan influence.
Around 730 BC	Greek colonists found Cumae and settle southern Italy's coast. Magna Graecia is founded.
Around 500 BC	Founding of Naples
474 BC	Defeat of the Etruscans by the Greeks in the naval Battle of Cumae
342–290 BC	Romans conquer Campania
AD 79	Mount Vesuvius erupts. The Bay of Naples continues as a favourite summer residence for the Roman upper class, despite this natural catastrophe.
1st and 2nd cent. AD	Campania's ports lose out to the construction of the port at Ostia, near Rome.
AD 476	Collapse of the Western Roman Empire. Its last emperor dies in Naples.
5th to 8th cent.	Goths, Byzantines and Lombards rule southern Italy.

Early traces

A Bronze Age settlement discovered a few years ago at Nola has been dated to the era around 1800 BC by archaeologists. There is no doubt, however, that the Bay of Naples was inhabited long before then. Prehistoric bone and weapon finds in caves on the island of Capri and ceramic finds on Ischia testify to a long history of settlement. Various tribes migrated to the region now known as Campania early in the second century BC, among them the Oscans, Aurunci and Samnites.
But the most significant impact was made by the Etruscans. Thus, when Greek settlers founded **Cumae** in around 730 BC, the Bay of Naples could already look back on thousands of years of settlement.

Greeks at the Bay of Naples

Initially, with the exception of isolated skirmishes involving the combative Samnites, the various tribes lived in peace here, and Greek

← *Detail from the Arch of Trajan at Benevento. The relief decoration praises Emperor Trajan (AD 98 – AD 117) as Italy's benefactor*

culture did not predominate. Pompeii, Herculaneum and Capua were all Oscan settlements that later came under Etruscan and Greek influence. This was not achieved by force, however; rather it appears to have developed through natural assimilation. Based in Cumae, the Greeks founded additional cities along the coast now known as the Bay of Naples. Thus **Parthenope** (the first incarnation of Naples) and **Dicaearchia** (modern Pozzuoli) were established and, in around 500 BC, the new city of **Neapolis**, today's Naples.

Founding of Naples ►

Paestum and Velia were also part of the Greek colonization process that incorporated the coasts of Sicily and Southern Italy, and were referred to as »Magna Graecia« (**Greater Greece**) from the 3rd century on. Regular trade with all parts of the known European world along with cultural and religious interchange constituted the earliest form of a **globalization** process. With Greek victory over the Etruscans at the Battle of Cumae in 474 BC, the balance of power altered. The pragmatic **Samnites**, motivated less by culture and more by power, also took advantage of this development, conquering Greek, Etruscan and Oscan settlements by mounting attacks from their mountain fortresses. By the end of the 5th century, almost all of Campania was in Sam-nite hands.

Magna Graecia ►

Campania and the rise of Rome

Campania is closely associated with Rome's emergence as a global power. Furthermore, the Bay of Naples and its mainland interior were a decisive factor in the development of the Roman Empire as a whole. Three costly wars had to be fought against the Samnites before Capua could finally be taken in 338 BC. The subsequent rapid construction in 312 BC of the **Via Appia** – the first Roman military highway – then enabled **expansion to the south**. By 194 BC, the Romans were able to construct the **empire's largest port** at Puteoli (present-day Pozzuoli), where the Greek settlement of Dicaearchia had once existed.

Capri: at the heart of empire

The island of Capri was used as the empire's power base between 27 BC and AD 37. **Emperor Augustus** valued the island highly as a summer residence. His successor **Tiberius** even decamped from Rome, making Capri his seat of government. Misenum (Miseno) was expanded to become a **base for the Roman war fleet**. But it was the beauty of the Bay of Naples and its wealth of volcanic **spas** that made this coastal region so popular as a summer retreat for the Roman aristocracy, and Roman bath culture originated here.

Late antiquity and early Christendom

The slow decline of the Western Roman Empire after the division of the empire in AD 395 also augured the **destruction of Campania**, when Goths and Vandals began to attack the ailing world power. The Western Roman Empire finally collapsed in 476, and its last emperor Romulus Augustulus died in exile in Miseno.

In 763, Naples became a **Byzantine dukedom**, despite having successfully beaten off the Germanic Lombards during previous sieges; but

Capua, Benevento and Salerno were all incorporated into the southern section of the Italian **Lombard Empire**. Ravello and Amalfi became independent maritime republics.

The Norman, Hohenstaufen, Angevin and Aragonese Dynasties

1030	Aversa – first Norman duchy in southern Italy
1189	The German Hohenstaufens inherit Norman southern Italy.
1194–1250	Frederick II is Holy Roman Emperor.
1268	His 16-year-old grandson Conradin is executed on Piazza del Mercato. Charles I of Anjou moves his residence to Naples.
1282	Sicilian Vespers. Anjou cedes Sicily to the Catalan House of Aragon.
1442	Alfonso V of Aragon enters Naples and unites the future Kingdom of the Two Sicilies.

Normans and Hohenstaufens

The Norman and Hohenstaufen kingdoms (1030–1266) heralded one of southern Italy's most glorious eras. Enterprise, luck and strategic marriage alliances enabled the Nordic descendents of the Vikings to become the **rulers of southern Italy** and the original founders of the later Kingdom of the Two Sicilies. The Norman mercenary Rainulf Drengot was married to the Duchess of Gaeta and won important military victories against the Lombards. He established the first Norman territory near the Bay of Naples at Aversa, in 1030, which was left to him in fief. The actual conquest of southern Italy, however, took place with papal support after 1091, and was achieved by Tankred de Hauteville and his sons Robert Guiscard and Roger I.

The latter's son **Roger II** went on to become the first King of Sicily, Calabria and Puglia. Only proud and intractable Naples resisted southern Italy's new ruler, holding out until 1139. This magical kingdom was then inherited by the Hohenstaufen ruler Henry VI, who was married to the Norman Princess Constance of Sicily, and afterwards by his son Frederick.

◄ Frederick II

Known as Stupor Mundi (Wonder of the World) the highly cultured Frederick II turned his southern Italian kingdom into an efficient bureaucratic state and founded the University of Naples in 1224. The Italian possessions of the **Holy Roman Empire of the German Nation** included the present regions of Campania, Calabria, Puglia, Abruzzo, Molise, Basilicata and Sicily.

Tavola Strozzi, 15th-century: the return of Ferrantes I's fleet at the port of Naples in 1465 (Museo Capodimonte)

Anjou and Aragon

After the death of Frederick II, the conflict between the Hohenstaufen dynasty and the pope escalated. Pope Innocent IV supported **Charles of Anjou** in his ambition to conquer southern Italy. Angevin troops achieved victory over King Manfred at Benevento, in 1266. Two years later, 16-year-old **Conradin**, the last Hohenstaufen ruler, was executed on Piazza del Mercato in Naples. Thus, with the arrival of the House of Anjou, the **glittering Angevin Gothic epoch** was heralded in Naples and the city was developed into a royal seat. Castel Nuovo and several of the city's most important churches were built during the reign of Charles I. As a result of the Sicilian Vespers – a bloody popular revolt against the French in 1282 – Sicily then came under the rule of the Catalan House of Aragon, although the true start of Aragonese rule of southern Italy is considered to be the splendid arrival of **Alfonso V** in Naples in 1442.

Naples becomes a royal seat ►

Spanish viceroys

The Kingdom of Naples came under the hegemony of the Spanish Habsburg world power in 1503, which heralded the beginning of over two centuries of rule by Spanish viceroys. Naples became Europe's third-largest metropolis and, by the mid-17th century, it had 350,000 inhabitants. Urban building projects, especially the construction of the Via Toledo during the rule of Viceroy **Pedro di Toledo**, permanently changed the cityscape. To accommodate Naples' rapidly increasing population **Europe's first high-rise buildings** were also built. Even the three major catastrophes that occurred in the 17th century – the **eruption of Vesuvius** in 1631, the **Revolt of Masaniello** in 1647 and an outbreak of **plague** in 1654 – could not slow these developments.

Naples becomes a metropolis ►

17th-century catastrophes ►

Naples in the 18th and 19th Centuries

1735	Charles III becomes King of Naples.
1748	First systematic excavations at Pompeii
1759	Ferdinand IV (Il Re Nasone) ascends to the throne.
1799	Parthenopean Republic and the return of the Bourbons
1806–1815	Bonapartist kings rule the Kingdom of Naples.
1816	Restitution of the Bourbon dynasty. Ferdinand IV returns to the throne as Ferdinand I.
1860	The last Bourbon King Francis II flees Garibaldi's troops
1884	Cholera. The cityscape of Naples changes.

Glittering royal seat of the Bourbons

The century of absolutism and the Enlightenment had a more powerful impact on the city than almost any other era. At the same time, a tendency to **romanticize and mythologize** Naples – an impulse that has continued to this day – began with the new passion for travel in the 18th century, although even then visitors were less impressed with the city as a place to live than with its magnificent natural setting. The balance of power among Europe's leading countries was changed by the War of the Spanish Succession (1701–14).

Philip V of the Bourbon dynasty became King of Spain. His son, **Don Carlos**, then ascended to the throne of the kingdoms of Naples and Sicily, replacing the Austrian viceroys.Charles III brought good fortune to the **Regno di Napoli e di Sicilia**. Taking an absolutist approach to his rule, he transformed Naples into a magnificent royal seat. Public buildings were constructed and important transport connections established, while the founding of numerous manufactories led to the early **industrialization** of southern Italy. The construction of the Teatro San Carlo also established Naples as a **European centre for music**. After centuries of rule by viceroys, Charles III was the first king to actually live in Naples. Above all, the discovery of the lost Vesuvian cities of **Pompeii** and **Herculaneum** turned the Bay of Naples into a highlight of any »Grand Tour«. Charles III and his wife, Maria Amalia of Saxony, not only sponsored the excavation of those ancient cities but also used the spectacular finds to promote their kingdom. The world's **first museum of antiquities** was thus established in the palace at Portici.

Charles III ►

Naples becomes a highlight of the Grand Tour ►

Ferdinand IV

Charles III departed Naples in 1759 to become King of Spain. The treaties after the War of the Spanish Succession did not allow for the crowns of Spain and Naples to be claimed by the same ruler, so the king left his 8-year-old son Ferdinand behind as heir to the Naples throne – along with numerous major buildings in an unfinished state.

Ferdinand IV is still a popular figure in Naples, though he commands somewhat less respect. Unlike his father, he was a Neapolitan through and through. Due to a mediocre education, he was poorly equipped to carry out his royal obligations, and furthermore he was married to the ambitious and intrigue-prone Habsburg Maria Carolina. In December 1798 the couple was forced to flee the city under the protection of **Lord Nelson**, sailing to Sicily on an English warship. A month later, French revolutionaries supported by a section of the Neapolitan nobility proclaimed the **Parthenopean Republic**. This utopian assertion of freedom was, however, brought to an end just a few months later, when the king returned. The subsequent mass arrests and executions of the revolutionaries signalled the beginning of the drawn-out end of Bourbon rule in Naples, and the events remain seared into local memory to this day. Many of those executed included members of the high nobility in Naples.

! *Baedeker* TIP

The Volcano Lover

The American author and journalist Susan Sontag recreated Naples under Ferdinand IV in her historical novel *The Volcano Lover*. The protagonist is Lord Hamilton, Britain's ambassador at the court of Naples.

Bonapartist kings in Naples

Napoleonic troops conquered Naples for the second time in 1806, and the royal couple fled to Sicily. This time, their exile lasted a lot longer. Napoleon installed his brother **Joseph** as the King of Naples and, after Joseph became King of Spain in 1808, Napoleon replaced him with his brother-in-law **Gioacchino Murat**.

Murat era

Despite its brevity (1808–15), the era under Murat is considered one of the most successful in the history of the Kingdom of Naples. The decorated military officer married to Caroline Bonaparte reformed the sluggish administrative ministries of the Bourbons. The construction of the **Ponte della Sanità**, which connects the city centre with the hill of Capodimonte, and the building of the **Via Foria** are projects from the time that still define the city today. To save his kingdom, Murat aligned himself with the Austrians in 1814, only to revert back to Napoleon when he unexpectedly returned in 1815. But he met his own Waterloo with the final defeat of his imperial brother-in-law. After having attempted a hair-raising escape, he was executed by firing squad in Calabrian Pizzo on 13 October 1815.

Restoration of Bourbon rule

The return of **Ferdinand IV** and the restoration of the Bourbon dynasty to the throne of Naples brought no pleasure to anyone, except the king, his court, and a few still loyal to the Bourbons. Ferdinand united the Neapolitan and Sicilian kingdoms into the Kingdom of the Two Sicilies (**Regno delle Due Sicilie**) and recast himself as Ferdinand I.

◄ Kingdom of the Two Sicilies

The regime of the last Bourbons (Ferdinand I was followed by Francis I, Ferdinand II and Francis II) was totalitarian, weak, and unable to live up to the challenges of the post-revolutionary decades of the early 19th century. Revolts in Sicily and Naples were brutally crushed.

Garibaldi and the Risorgimento

Garibaldi entered the city of Naples on 7 September 1860, arriving from Sicily. Once the first nationalist thrill of this Italian Liberation Movement had passed, it became clear that the former Kingdom of the Two Sicilies now found itself in a completely changed situation. The new Italy's king was **Vittorio Emanuele II** of the House of Savoy, and Turin, Milan and Rome (designated the national capital) became important economic and political centres of the new Italian state. However the **Mezzogiorno** (Italian: »midday«), along with its capital Naples, was excluded from the upswing associated with the era of industrialization in central Europe. The inexorable decline of the former royal seat into a **problematic city of the south** remains one of Italy's major internal political problems.

◄ Beginning of the end

Cholera outbreak and urban regeneration

The historic city centre's catastrophic hygiene standards led to a cholera epidemic in 1884, which exposed the decline of Naples across Europe. The regeneration and cleaning up of the centro storico shortly afterwards did nothing to solve the underlying problems, but it did significantly change the cityscape, whose **Belle Époque elegance** still feels more French than southern Italian. The harbour dis-

The parliamentary anti-mafia commission estimates that up to 70% of southern Italy's rubbish dumps are controlled by the mafia. In Campania, the region that produces more rubbish than any other in Italy, the legal rubbish depots are all overflowing. The battle to establish new sites stinks to high heaven

MONEY, RUBBISH, AND DEATH

Not a day goes by, it seems, when there isn't a bloody confrontation between Camorra factions in the troubled neighbourhoods of Naples, such as Secondigliano, Scampia, Sanità or the Quartieri spagnoli. The violence has been escalating since 2004 at a rate not seen before, and there are some quarters where entire streets are no-go areas for the authorities. People living there risk a death sentence simply by belonging to the wrong family or because of a misunderstood handshake.

After several years of apparent peace, the Neapolitan version of the Mafia – known locally as the Camorra or »il sistema« – has engulfed the city in an orgy of violence. In 2005, the headlines were dominated by the **power struggle within the Di Lauro clan,** which had been built up by Paolo Di Lauro and his sons in the Scampia neighbourhood during the 1990s. Their drugs cartel earned them an annual turnover in the millions, and the father's arrest left a power vacuum which other members of the clan tried to fill. Paolo's son Cosimo Di Lauro reacted with unimaginable violence and hundreds of people fell victim to it. The war »infected« other Camorra families, who also began to stake out their territories. Yet the Di Lauro clan enjoys broad sympathy, being one of the major »employers« in Naples, and there were celebratory fireworks in Sanità when Di Lauro junior was released without charge, shortly after his arrest, due to a technical mistake.

Roberto Saviano's *Gomorrah*

The Camorra's power remains unbroken, not least because of its annual turnover, believed to be in the region of 16 billion euros – and some estimate it is twice that. An immaculately researched book written from the viewpoint of an insider was published in 2006 outlining in detail the structures of organized crime in the Campania region. This first book

by the young author **Roberto Saviano** became a best-seller, though threats to his life have also ensured that he now lives under police protection, far from Naples. His study shows how the incredible sums made by the Camorra come mostly from the **drugs trade**. In fact, Scampia is one of Italy's largest drug markets, perhaps even Europe's largest one too. Other lucrative income sources are provided by the construction industry, the global sale of fake luxury brands and, of course, protection money. Around 70% of Neapolitan businesses pay »tangente«. Rubbish can also make good money. The Camorra has been in control of **municipal rubbish collection** for years, which is also a reason for its systemic failure. There is no shortage of new blood for the Camorra either: with a youth unemployment figure of over 45%, the Camorra is never short of applicants. This is especially true in the peripheral suburbs of Naples, where it is often the only employer.

History of the Camorra

The deeply ingrained mistrust of state authority all over southern Italy has frequently been explained by a history of constantly changing foreign rulers, which allowed the Mafia to establish itself as **the only permanent local authority**. In Naples, this phenomenon can specifically be traced to the era of the Spanish viceroys during the 16th and 17th centuries. These representatives of the Spanish king were regularly replaced, and only very few of them had any interest whatsoever in the needs of the local territory or of its population. In addition, the aristocracy's move from the countryside to the cities changed rural power structures, so that control of the landed aristocracy's often huge estates went to tenants installed by the owners or to estate managers. Meanwhile, the legend of an early Mafia as Robin Hood style defenders of exploited farmers' rights is questionable. In Naples, at least, the Camorra were able to establish themselves as the true power in the state due to the simultaneously weak and repressive regime of the late Bourbon kings. The earliest mention of the Mafia in legal documentation dates to the mid-19th century, but even then, the context

was not crime, but the nationalist revolutionary movements. Italy's unification during the Risorgimento then sealed southern Italy's fate, turning it into a Third World country even while the Italian north was experiencing its first economic boom.

Those therefore who emigrated to the USA in the late 19th century and early 20th century, brought not only Italian culture and lifestyle but frequently also the Mafia network. Legendary Mafia bosses such as **Al Capone** and **Lucky Luciano** were romantically idolized in Hollywood movies, even long after the criminal background of their organizations, which were run like extended families, could no longer be overlooked.

The Mafia and the USA

The opportunity to become a globally operating shadow force was provided to the Mafia, Camorra and Cosa Nostra by the **Second World War**. The American forces cooperated with the Sicilian Cosa Nostra to facilitate Allied military landings in Sicily and on the Gulf of Salerno, and their middle man was the Mafia boss Lucky Luciano, who was in prison in America. The partnership succeeded and the helpful Mafia was not only rewarded with the repeal of prison sentences, but also with key positions in post-war Italy's economic and political structures. For the Camorra, this was the beginning of their outstanding road to success. With the help of corrupt politicians, they initiated an era of building speculation on the Bay of Naples which not only almost completely destroyed one of the most beautiful cultural landscapes in the world, but also created a dependent proletariat living in the newly constructed high-rise apartment blocks.

The modern Camorra

For the longest time, the black market trade in cigarettes was the staple business of minor Camorristi. But globalization also internationalized trade for the Camorra. Long-standing friendly contacts in South America and newly established relationships in Eastern Europe allowed their business to expand. By the 1980s, the drug

Globalization also internationalized business for the mafia. The high level of potential profits has also increased the level of violence

trade had made a few Camorristi super-rich, even while millions of people all over the world were thrown into dependency and misery. The massive profits to be made also increased the level of violence criminals were prepared to use. In Campania, entire city councils are regularly replaced due to suspicion of Camorra infiltration. For example, during one of Pope John Paul II's last journeys to visit Our Lady of the Rosary in Pompeii, no civic authorities were able to greet him, as the mayor and his officials were all awaiting charges of corruption.

Italy's effort to fight organized crime is being carried out by a number of brave state attorneys and judges. However, their work is undermined by inconsistencies, such as Italy's Prime Minister **Silvio Berlusconi's** attempts to evade prosecution for suspected misdemeanours. Nor has Giulio Andreotti been significantly damaged by his trials exposing his Mafia links: the seven-times prime minister, who defined post-war Italy, avoided punitive measures against him with the help of his Christian Democrat supporters. Even the »mani pulite« campaign of the 1990s, which successfully changed the face of Italian politics by denying power to the Christian Democrats, did not succeed in fundamentally weakening the Mafia and the Camorra.

Consequences for Naples

The continued excesses of Camorra violence have almost entirely wiped out the positive image Naples so carefully fostered during the 1990s. The brief success of establishing the capital of the Mezzogiorno as a city of art and culture has given way, once more, to the negative media coverage of old – a devastating blow for the city. Roberto Saviano's bestseller »Gomorrah« impressively describes the unscrupulous and inhuman Camorra. Tourists visiting Naples, however, do not usually come into contact with the Camorra. Tourism is a profitable business in which the Camorra fully participates: not only does it ensure an income of millions, but it is also an ideal means to laundering dirty money.

trict of **Santa Lucia** was razed to make way for the Lungomare seafront, where several luxury hotels built then still survive today. The port district around Piazza del Mercato did not escape the attention of developers either. In the years following 1900, hundreds of thousands of southern Italians emigrated to America and Argentina.

Naples up to the Present Day

20th century

In retrospect, efforts to prevent the Mezzogiorno falling into poverty by giving it an industrial future appear to have done more harm than good. Northern Italian ignorance, misunderstandings resulting from cultural differences and the Mezzogiorno's complex structures have opened up a **divide between southern and northern Italy** that is getting ever wider. The industrial ruin of the ILVA steelworks founded on the Bay of Naples on the once beautiful coastal strip of Bagnoli is the most depressing example of this early attempt at industrialization.

Naples under Mussolini

In the 1930s, **Mussolini** attempted to transform chaotic Naples into a Fascist metropolis. An entire district was demolished in the historic centre and replaced by administrative buildings and the post office – an area now known as the **Rione Carità**. Another entirely new neighbourhood grew up around the **Mostra d'Oltremare exhibition area** built on the edge of the Phlegrean Fields: the now densely populated **Fuorigrotta**. The German Wehrmacht occupied Naples in 1943 after the defeat of Mussolini and the collapse of the alliance between Berlin and Rome. A furious **popular revolt** between 28 September and 1 October 1943, remembered as »le quattro giornate«, liberated the city of its German invaders. Nevertheless, Allied bombing of Naples, followed by attacks by the German Luftwaffe, severely damaged the city centre. Some parts, such as the church and monastery of Santa Chiara, were entirely destroyed.

Le quattro giornate ►

After the Second World War

Rise of the Camorra ►

While the Sicilian mafia and Neapolitan Camorra could still be considered Robin Hood-style popular bandits during the corrupt and weak rule of the Bourbons in the early 19th century, they had certainly evolved into criminal organizations by the time the Second World War was over. American mafiosi and Camorristi also played a significant role in the Allied preparations for the invasion of southern Italy. The **corrupt relationships between politicians, businessmen and the mafia** created many opportunities during the turbulent post-war years, especially in **building speculation**.

Naples is buried in cement

Founded in 1951, the Cassa per il Mezzogiorno fund pumped over 140 billion euros into southern Italy in the years up to 1997. A fraction of this sum would have sufficed to regenerate the resources around the Bay of Naples, including tourism. Instead a series of catastrophic urban building projects were overseen by notorious mayor **Achille Lauro** (1887–1982) and his successors. The damage that was caused is irreversible. Where once magnificent 17th- and 18th-century villas lined the road between Naples and Portici, there are now a series of depressing suburban settlements. The hillsides of Posillipo and Vomero were also ruthlessly built up. The **building speculation** was most fatal along the coast north of Cumae.

The earthquake of 1980 and its aftermath

On 23 November 1980 an earthquake shook Campania. 3000 people died in the provinces of Benevento and Avellino, and hundreds of thousands were made homeless. It was a catastrophe that focused the world's attention on the **problems of the Mezzogiorno and its capital, Naples**. Scaffolding covered much of the severely damaged historic centre for many years, and some of the emergency accommodations, such as those in Avellino, exist to this day. And yet the earthquake is also seen as the beginning of the much heralded renaissance of Naples. Under mayor **Antonio Bassolino** in the 1990s, Naples became a widely admired model of urban regeneration. Parts of the city centre were pedestrianized and important historic buildings were at last restored. The **Maggio dei Monumenti** was also established. Alongside the reforms begun by Bassolino, numerous private initiatives were undertaken and a renewed self-confidence among Neapolitans emerged. By the time the G7 Summit was held in Naples in 1994, the world's TV viewers were, for the first time, shown a European city with a great past and a hopeful future, rather than the old image of a place marred by criminality and corruption. With the construction of the **Metropolitana** metro system, Naples' transformation to become a modern city was complete.

◄ Rebirth of Naples

Difficult entry into the 21st century

Just a few years after the apparently successful redevelopment of Naples, all the millions invested from the coffers of the European Union appear to have been for nothing. The hundreds of fatalities claimed by the **violent excesses of the fighting between competing Camorra clans** have permanently damaged the city's image. For the time being at least, the dream of a renewed flowering of Campania felix and of Naples as a magnet for tourists has fallen victim to the reality of organized crime – and the Neapolitans are as horrified by this as anyone. The problem of rubbish disposal above all has had a negative effect on the city's image worldwide.

Art and Culture

There are few European regions so rich in art treasures, historic buildings and archaeological sites as Campania. Its 3000-year history of civilization and culture has left a unique legacy. Even among the modern chaos that is life around the Bay of Naples, traces of Greek and Roman antiquity are ever-present.

History of Art and Culture

Cosmopolitan Bay of Naples

Greeks and Romans in Campania

A significant chapter in European cultural history began in the 8th century BC with the foundation of Cumae and the colonization of southern Italy. The Greeks introduced philosophy, theatre, science and the alphabet, as well as their gods, to the Bay of Naples, and an advanced civilization emerged from a lively exchange with the Etruscans. Rome conquered southern Italy during its march to world domination in the 3rd century, incorporating the foreign gods as well as the Greek arts. The **Bay of Naples came to define the cultural landscape of Roman antiquity**.

Temples

The various incarnations of the Greek temple are one of the most significant developments in European architectural history. Even today, many public buildings take their cue from the designs of Greek temple architecture. During the 7th century BC, the original temples made of wood were replaced by stone monuments designed according to the Doric order. The most beautiful examples of this process are found among the temples at **Paestum**. The Romans developed and expanded Greek designs in the construction of their grandiose prestigious buildings.

Necropoli

Greek ceramics and, above all, rare examples of pre-Roman painting are preserved in the necropoli at **Paestum**. In addition to the famous paintings on the slabs of the Tomb of the Diver, the Lucanian tomb paintings also provide valuable insight into a settlement history that ended long ago. Roman necropoli became veritable **cities of the dead**, lining both sides of the highways that led out of the city. One of the most beautiful and best preserved roads is the Via delle Tombe, which runs from the centre of **Pompeii** to the Villa dei Misteri.

Greek ceramics

The potter's wheel was known to the Greeks from the 2nd century BC. The clay container made on the wheel constitutes a ceramic form more common and versatile than any other item of Greek antiquity. It served not only as a container for foodstuffs but was also used for ceremonial purposes or simply as decoration. Such items have survived in abundance as tomb offerings. They are frequently decorated with rich illustrations inspired from Greek mythology and everyday life and, as such, provide a valuable insight into the world of the Greeks. The golden age of ceramic art and decoration was the 6th century BC. The initially black, and then red, decorative art from

← Detail from the bronze doors at the cathedral in Ravello. They are the work of the great Puglian sculptor Barisanus of Trani

Dive into the blue yonder: detail from the Tomb of the Diver (5th century BC, Paestum)

that era enjoyed great popularity as an export item, especially to Etruria, the heartland of the Etruscans. When southern Italy was colonized, Puglia and Campania became important **centres for the production of ceramics**.

Greek sculpture and Roman copies

Greek sculpture has largely survived in the form of Roman copies: most of the bronze originals did not survive the upheavals of the Post Classic period. With a constant eye on posterity, the Romans populated their villas, theatres and public places with sculptures and statues. High-ranking figures and, of course, the Roman emperors and their families were honoured with statues in every town. An Etruscan influence is especially evident in the very precise portrait busts produced by Roman sculptors. One of the most important sculpture collections was in the **Villa dei Papiri** at Herculaneum.

Theatre

While Roman theatres were still made of wood, Pompeii already had an amphitheatre built of stone. Bloody gladiatorial spectacles took place here. The amphitheatre at Pompeii is around 150 years older than the Colosseum. The elliptical design for arenas, however, is a purely Roman one. Greek theatres were built into hillsides where the rising auditorium followed the natural contours of the landscape and the base of the semicircle was closed off by a mighty backstage wall. The **Teatro Grande at Pompeii** was originally also designed in this way by the Greeks. The Romans later followed the design, although their theatres were developed into huge municipal arenas built of brick, such as, for example, the **theatre at Herculaneum**. The theatrical arts flourished around the Bay of Naples as in hardly any other region of the empire. Naples alone had three theatres, while Pozzuoli had a second small theatre in addition to its huge amphitheatre. Capua not only had an amphitheatre, but was also home to the most famous gladiator school in the Roman Empire. Pompeii even had an entire theatre district. The towns of the interior, whether at Nola, Nocera or Benevento, also all had their own theatres. Travelling theatre companies played the smaller »talking stages« or intimate odeons, while the amphitheatres were reserved for the great »panem-et-circenses« spectacles.

Roman architecture

Thanks to the beauty of its landscape and the numerous thermal hot springs, the Bay of Naples was much visited by the Roman upper class during summer. Even today, the ruins of **Roman spas** testify to the comfort of Roman bathing culture. Under-floor heating was a given: known to the Greeks as hypocauston (to heat from below), this type of heating was later also used in private residences. The spa at Baia represents a highlight of Roman architectural history. The invention of **opus caementicium** – a material made of pumice stone and pozzolana, a Roman cement based on volcanic ashes – enabled dome constructions in dimensions that had never been seen before. At the same time, luxurious **summer holiday villas** were built along this paradisiacal stretch of coast. Usually positioned in exceptional locations above the sea, their particular attraction lay in the many terraces that led down to the shoreline. The most famous example is the Villa dei Papiri at Herculaneum. Another familiar design was the **villa rustica**, which was a mixture of landed estate and summer residence. The owner generated income from the sale of produce to the urban areas. The best example of this kind of building, which was often run by military veterans, is the **Villa Regina at Boscoreale**. The **villa urbana** on the other hand, though it also frequently lay at the heart of an agricultural operation, was primarily designed as an elegant summer residence rather than as a farm.

Villa dei Misteri Plan

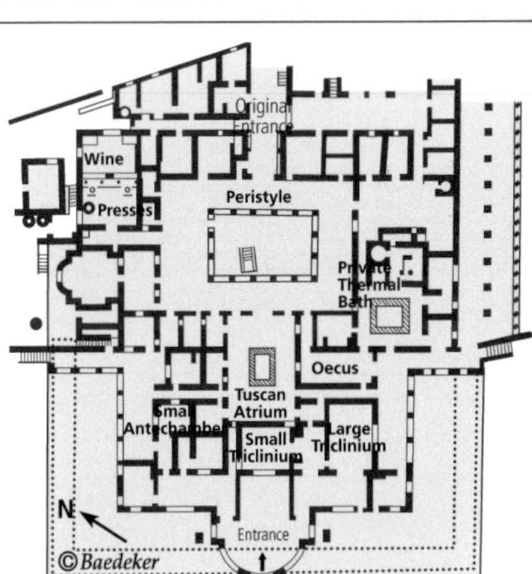

Urban architecture

It is believed that the strictly linear design of Greek cities goes back to the architect and state theoretician **Hippodamos of Milet**. There was a very practical reason why the Greeks designed their cities to such a rigid plan: it made fair distribution of urban real estate and farming land near cities much easier. At the same time, public spaces could be easily delineated. The division of public spaces (for example the agora), sacred spaces (temples) and housing is still very clearly seen at **Paestum**. The Romans took up this system, expanding the city's grid accordingly with two major highways: the Decumanus, which was orientated east-west, and the Cardo, which was orientated north-south.

Forum The Greek agora became the Roman forum: the most important place for public life. **Pompeii** offers a useful example for studying the design and construction of a forum and its major buildings, as well as for learning about the architectural development of Roman houses. In some of Campania's towns, such as Nola and Benevento, the original forums have continued as the focus of urban life there for millennia. In Naples, the forum is partly accessible as an archaeological excavation site, submerged under Piazza San Gaetano and the church of San Lorenzo Maggiore in the historic city centre.

Triumphal arches The triumphal arch is emblematic of prestigious Roman architecture. Victorious field marshals were honoured with these monumental stone buildings, whose construction could only be decreed by the Roman Senate. An outstanding example survives in **Benevento** in the form of Trajan's triumphal arch with its wealth of decorative reliefs. The Renaissance portal at Castel Nuovo also exhibits numerous architectural references to its Greek predecessors.

Roman painting If it had not been for the catastrophe of AD 79, when two thriving cities on the Bay of Naples were smothered in ash, our knowledge of Roman painting would be minimal. Numerous frescoes from over two centuries survived in **Pompeii** and **Herculaneum**, even enabling archaeologists to develop a **stylistic history of the painting of antiquity**. Works of exquisite quality, such as the cycle of frescoes at the **Villa dei Misteri**) can be found alongside run-of-the-mill decorative painting. Occasionally, it is even possible to detect a failed art project, such as at the **Casa della Venere** in Conchiglia. The repetition of subjects is often rather monotonous. However, at that time domestic interior décor was less about artistic quality and more about demonstrating the owner's educational level.

Mosaics Intricate mosaics have also been found. No house in Pompeii or Herculaneum is without its floor mosaics. The most magnificent examples discovered so far were designed for the **Casa del Fauno** at Pompeii, although the most famous example, the **Alexander Mosaic**, was not created by Roman artists. Instead, it was probably prepared in eastern Greece and imported to the Bay of Naples some time around 100 BC, for the purpose of decorating Pompeii's most luxurious

Mosaic from Villa di Cicerone in Pompeii (Archaeological Museum, Naples)

home at that time. Floor mosaics have also survived beyond the towns around Vesuvius. Often, they are all that remains of former buildings that were either destroyed after antiquity or simply became derelict, in which case the floor mosaics were protected by the rubble. The enduring artistic tradition of laying mosaics continued almost without interruption into the centuries of early Christendom.

From Late Antiquity to the Renaissance

Late antiquity

The collapse of the West Roman Empire signified a period of political decline, which however was in no way mirrored by a cultural breakdown. Despite the fact that Christianity, as the new state religion, resulted in the elimination of the old gods, many important features of the Roman World were simply adapted. Furthermore, even though Greek culture, so highly valued by the Romans, no longer fulfilled a significant function during Christian times, it nevertheless remained a strong influence around the **Bay of Naples**. During the 4th and 5th centuries, heathen temples were converted to churches (Pozzuoli, Naples, Paestum), and ancient heathen customs were Christianized. For example, at **Paestum**, the veneration of the goddess Hera continued in the form of the Madonna with the Pomegranate. The Roman basilica that functioned as law court and public meeting place in every urban centre was used as a prototype for religious architecture, eventually defining the nave-and-aisles design of Romanesque churches.

◄ Decline

A fall in population and the loss of engineering and architectural knowledge resulted in the decline of the almost perfect Roman infrastructure of Campania. The roads, aqueducts and coastal drainage systems collapsed. Paestum was submerged and became virtually uninhabitable. Most of the fashionable coastal strip at Baia disappeared into the sea due to bradyseismic activity (►p.16). The global port of Pozzuoli shrank and once again became a fishing village.

Early Christendom

During late antiquity, Naples and especially Cimitile near Nola quickly became centres of early Christendom. Meropius Pontius Anicius Paulinus (AD 355–431), later known as San Paolino, is a highly significant figure in early church history. He invested his immense private wealth to make a **»new Jerusalem« of Cimitile**. The grouping of early Christian basilicas around the tomb of Felix, the former bishop of Nola, became the second most important Italian pilgrimage site after Rome at that time. The remains of the basiliche paleocristiane are a unique example of sacred architecture of the 4th and 5th century. Furthermore, the West's first clock tower or **campanile** was built at Cimitile.

Catacombs at Naples

As early as the 2nd century AD, a complex of catacombs was created in the ancient necropoli outside Naples that is at least as significant for early Christian archaeology as the Roman catacombs. The frescoes at the **Catacombe di San Gennaro** below the Capodimonte hill are sensational. The ceiling fresco of Adam and Eve is possibly the oldest representation of the fall from grace anywhere in the world. The crypt for the early Neapolitan bishops contains a veritable gallery of early Christian painting, dating from the 3rd to the 10th century.

Oldest church in Naples ►

Shortly after the Edict of Milan was issued in 313, Emperor Constantine erected a basilica in Naples, which is now a side chapel of the present Neapolitan cathedral: the **Chiesa Santa Restituta**. Despite many changes, its design and the position of the columns still reflects Constantine's original basilica. The neighbouring **baptistery**, dating from the 4th and 5th century, is a work of art in terms of early Christian design; the artistic virtuosity of its ceiling mosaic is another example of the richness in form and the craftsmanship of the mosaic art of antiquity.

Spolia and the Early Middle Ages

Southern Italy became one big stone quarry after the arrival of the Goths, Vandals and, later, the Lombards. Ancient buildings (particularly the amphitheatres at Capua and Pozzuoli) were either destroyed or systematically dismantled so the stone could be used as building material. The **Neapolitan theatre and odeon** were briefly part of an early Christian **cemetery**, before the ruins were reused to build **residential housing**. Spolia, architectural fragments from buildings of antiquity reused for new constructions, can be found in numerous buildings in Campania, most of them churches. The historic city centre of **Capua** is almost entirely built of material taken from its ancient predecessor.

Romanesque

The 11th century is the era of the **great Romanesque churches** in Campania. Built in 1071, the Benedictine monastery church at Mon-

The frescoes at Sant'Angelo in Formis still exhibit Byzantine artistic traditions

tecassino in southern Latium is a key example of the era's church architecture in central and southern Italy. Early medieval church building became significantly more monumental as new techniques in arch construction made imposing interiors possible. The most common feature of Romanesque buildings is the round arch found in windows, portals and arcades. The flat ceilings of the past were replaced with arched vaults; transepts and choirs were added; and the nave was subdivided by means of a highly structured design of columns and by accentuating individual vaulted sections. A particular feature of Romanesque churches was the façade, whose sculptural art and design was a highly valued component. The building boom during the Romanesque architectural era was fired not so much by religiosity as by economic power and innovative construction techniques. Campania enjoyed a period of unimaginable growth under the Normans during the 11th and 12th centuries. Outstanding sacred buildings of that epoch include the cathedrals at **Salerno** and **Amalfi**, which are witness to the might and wealth of these maritime republics. Romanesque churches were also built in **Benevento** and **Capua**. **Sant'Angelo in Formis** is a perfect example of an 11th-century Campanian church built of spolia: erected on the foundations of a temple, its cycle of frescoes harks back to the Byzantine tradition.

Fine arts

The fine arts also flourished, especially **sculpture**. Romanesque church façades are richly decorated showpieces, populated by demons, mythical creatures and Christian symbols, and designed to impress. Along with their bronze doors and silver candle holders (**Santa Maria Capua Vetere, Salerno**), the wealth of Romanesque churches finds its best expression through the sculptural work of mostly anonymous artists and their workshops. Outstanding examples are the ambo (around 1130) in San Pantaleone in **Ravello** and the relief slabs from around 1200 in the left aisle of the Cappella Santa Restituta in **Naples Cathedral**. A highlight of figural art can also be found on the bridge gates of **Capua**, erected during the reign of Frederick II.

Gothic Gothic architecture arrived in Naples with the French kings from the House of Anjou. Outstripping the Romanesque influence, the Gothic style was an international movement that spread throughout Europe in the 13th and 14th centuries. Its most noticeable stylistic feature is the **verticality of its architecture**. Round arches became pointed ones and the massive stonework was dispersed and replaced by delicate pillars and columns. Large windows were also introduced for the first time. Ribbed vaulting made entirely new spatial effects possible. The delicate filigree stonework of these enormous buildings was supported by the characteristic exterior support buttresses found on Gothic churches. Another typical stylistic element was the rose window in the main façade. In addition to those built by the Angevin kings, Naples also gained large church buildings designed in a specifically Italian form of Gothic by the mendicant Dominican and Franciscan orders. The open hammer beam roofs built of wood instead of stone vaulting are emblematic of Angevin Gothic in Naples. Several of the most important churches in the historic centre have their origin in this golden age of Gothic architectural art. For example: San Pietro A Maiella (1319–43), San Lorenzo Maggiore (1270), Santa Chiara (1310); and in the Mercato district: Sant'Eligio Maggiore (1270).

Artistic citadel of Anjou The construction in 1279 of **Castel Nuovo** as a sea fortress and palace of the Angevin kings made Naples a glittering royal seat. In addition to the French master builders, artists from all over Italy came to the Court of Anjou. The two most important were the Tuscan artist Giotto di Bondone and Tino da Camaino. **Giotto** painted the cycle of frescoes (today destroyed) at Santa Chiara and at Castel Nuovo, while **Camaino** created some of the most beautiful tombs of the early 14th century for the Angevin kings. **Petrarch** often spent time in Naples in his role as papal emissary. He was one of the first to take a systematic approach to exploring the ancient ruins of the Campi Flegrei, where he also visited the presumed tomb of Virgil. **Boccaccio** lived in the city in 1328. He wrote *Decamarone*, a famous portrait of Neapolitan life.

Renaissance The 14th century rediscovered the art and thinking of antiquity and made it its own. Known as the Renaissance (rebirth), this movement was much more than just a style. Humanist philosophers developed a world view founded on ideas, first discussed during antiquity, that placed the individual at the centre of society. Knowledge that had been forgotten for thousands of years was rediscovered and reinterpreted. Artists evolved from being humble labourers to public personalities who saw themselves as pioneers and scientists (such as Leonardo da Vinci). The rational investigation of the world led to revolutionary new knowledge. In painting, the discovery of central perspective was of great significance. Architecture and sculptural art returned to the repertoire of shape and form used during antiquity, inspired in particular by the Roman ruins. The first collections of the art and sculpture of antiquity were also established. Tuscan and Florentine artists, especially, worked at aristocratic courts throughout Italy. In Naples, the Renaissance left few traces, although those it has are outstanding. The earliest example, dating from 1428, is the tomb of Cardinal Brancaccio, designed by the Tuscan artists Donatello and Michelozzo, in the **Chiesa Sant'Angelo a Nilo**. The art of the Renaissance, which dominated all of central Italy, really only reached Naples in 1442 with the arrival of Alfonso V. The monumental triumphal arch at the **Castel Nuovo**, completed in 1471, is one of the most significant examples of Renaissance architecture in southern Italy. The small **Cappella Pontano** (1490–95) commissioned by Giovanni Pontano, who was personal secretary to Alfonso, clearly displays the Humanist leanings of intellectuals at the court of Anjou.

17th Century

Baroque

As with Romanesque and Gothic, Baroque is merely a collective phrase encompassing many stylistic variations that spread across Europe in the 16th century. For example, by the late Renaissance the mathematically precise harmony of proportions familiar during its earlier phase were no longer being held to; instead a sometimes eccentric style known as **Mannerism** developed, which used exaggeration to great effect and later evolved into Baroque. This new era of European art history took its name from the irregularly shaped pearl, La Perla Barroca, and its shapely forms invaded sacred and profane architecture throughout Europe. In southern Italy, in particular, this new artistic taste was frequently responsible for the remodelling of Romanesque and Gothic churches. The theatricality and surprising visual effects of the Baroque and its occasionally excessive decorative style and architectural extravagance found great resonance in Naples. The era known as **Neapolitan Baroque** lasted from the late 16th century to the early 18th century. Ruled by the Spanish viceroys, Naples became one of Europe's major cities, with 300,000 inhabitants. This explosive population growth required significant urban expansion. At the same time, Naples became a **seat of the Counter-Reformation**, and religious orders, such as the Jesuits, commissioned the building of **large churches** (San Paolo Maggiore, Gesù Nuovo) in the city centre. Among the most important architects of the era were **Francesco Grimaldi** (1545–1630), who built the

◄ Naples becomes a metropolis

Cappella del Tesoro in Naples Cathedral, and **Giuseppe Donzelli** (died 1631), also known as Fra Nuvolo, who built the Dominican church of Santa Maria della Sanità. He is also credited with being the inventor of the majolica dome. Another architect working in Naples from 1572 was **Domenico Fontana** (1543–1607), who was responsible for the reconstruction of the Palazzo Reale. The Florentine **Giovanni Antonio Dosio** (1533–1609) worked on San Martino from 1591 onwards.

Glittering 17th century

Despite the eruption of Mount Vesuvius, the Revolt of Masaniello and an outbreak of plague, the 17th century was the **most glittering era in Neapolitan art history**. The short residence of **Caravaggio** revolutionized Neapolitan painting. His so-called chiaroscuro technique, which cleverly played with light and shade in his paintings, was shockingly new not only to his patrons but also to the public and his fellow artists. It influenced numerous Neapolitan artists, including Giovanni Battista Caracciolo, Giuseppe (José) Ribera and, later, Luca Giordano and Francesco Solimena. It seems the city was the natural home for this dramatic style of painting. The Naples-born artist **Luca Giordano** (1632–1705), one of the most productive painters in the history of art, was known as »Luca fa presto« (Luca hurry up!). His almost unimaginably huge oeuvre can be seen in museums and churches throughout Europe. In Naples, his works can be found at the museums of San Martino and Capodimonte, in the churches of San Gregorio Armeno and Santa Brigida, as well as numerous other places. The painter's final resting place was also Santa Brigida. With the possible exception of Luigi Vanvitelli, who was active almost a century later, no other architect had as much impact on the cityscape of Naples as **Cosimo Fanzago** (1591–1678). This northern Italian came to Naples at the age of 17 and quickly proceeded to make a great career for himself. In 1623, he was elected master builder of the abandoned construction site for the Certosa di San Martino,

A masterpiece by Fanzago: Certosa di San Martino

which had been abandoned after the death of Dosios. Fanzago is credited with being the master and inventor of the virtuoso »pietra dura« technique. Ornamental marble inlays made from cleverly cut stone decorate the interiors of his churches to an almost excessive degree. The church that did most to guarantee his fame was **San Martino**, though this incredibly hard-working and detail-obsessed architect also took responsibility for almost all the major building contracts in Naples given out during his time. His canon includes the modernization of the churches of Gesù Nuovo and San Lorenzo Maggiore, the façade at Santa Maria di Costantinopoli, and the new constructions of San Giorgio Maggiore and Santa Maria Maggiore. In addition, Fanzago even found time to design several of the most important palaces in Naples.

18th century

The second half of the 18th century saw Naples become one of Europe's largest building sites once again. Duke of Bourbon Charles III and his successor Ferdinand IV employed the finest master builders of their era in an ambitious plan to turn a medieval city that had largely grown from the design established during antiquity into a modern metropolis of late absolutism. Naples was decisively imbued with a late Baroque stamp by Ferdinando Sanfelice (1675–1748), Ferdinando Fuga (1699–1782), Luigi Vanvitelli (1700–73), and his son Carlo (1739–1821). **Sanfelice** is credited with one of Neapolitan architectural history's unique inventions. His staircases (Palazzo dello Spagnolo, Palazzo Sanfelice, Palazzo Spinelli) transformed the architecture of palaces into a veritable stage set for glamorous social occasions. The world as a stage on which, in the social microcosm of the palace, a variety of characters performed was mirrored in the theatrical school of the Commedia dell'Arte and, later, even in the films of Totò. Sanfelice's staircases can therefore be viewed as more than »mere architecture«; they are an expression of 18th-century Neapolitan life. Meanwhile, Ferdinando Fuga built the city's largest building with the **Albergo di Pover**. The most important architect of Bourbon Naples, however, was **Luigi Vanvitelli**. As the designer of the **Reggia at Caserta**, he created one of the most beautiful staircases in the history of European architecture. Furthermore, he was an ingenious engineer, as proved by the complicated design of the fountains in the park at Caserta. Numerous designs for palaces in the historic centre of Naples were either made by Vanvitelli or his son or were inspired by them. The modern Piazza Dante was also designed by Vanvitelli, when it was known as the Foro Carolino.

Classicism and the Rediscovery of Antiquity

Rediscovery of antiquity

The development of the austere classical style of the second half of the 18th century was wholly inspired by antiquity and would have been unthinkable without the excavations at Pompeii and Herculaneum. This »rediscovered« style was to define European art history

A portrait of the royal family of Ferdinand IV by Angelika Kauffmann (1782/83)

and architecture for decades. In parallel with the early development of archaeology as a science, **»à la pompeiana«** became all the rage in Europe. It was not only architecture and painting that took inspiration from the form and style of antiquity, but also craftwork. The Accademia Ercolanese, founded in 1755, published elaborate books with images of archaeological finds. The tableware produced by the porcelain manufacturers at Capodimonte was embellished with painted scenes taken from ancient ruins, while the interior décor of Vesuvian villas by Miglio d'Oro was often entirely inspired by Pompeian style.

Grand Tour

The Grand Tour is a **cultural and historical phenomenon** that made its mark on the Bay of Naples more than anywhere else. One of the more pleasant obligations of the English aristocracy of the 16th century was to complete their education with an art-historical journey to the Continent. Italy and Greece were among the favoured destinations for these journeys, which often lasted several months. Rome, of course, was a compulsory highlight of any Grand Tour, but with the discovery of Pompeii and Herculaneum the Bay of Naples also became an essential stop on any 18th-century journey to Italy. The European aristocracy not only visited Naples, but also the Phlegrean Fields and the archaeological excavation sites. The Grand Tour was not just an educational trip; it was also for pleasure, and its significance in people's lives is testified to by entire libraries filled with travel journals. It was a phenomenon that ended only with the French Revolution and the beginning of modern tourism in the 19th century.

Foreign artists in Naples

Naples' fame as a European cultural capital set in the midst of an Arcadian landscape of ruins drew numerous artists to the Bourbon court during the second half of the 18th century. The celebrated painter **Angelika Kauffmann** (1741–1807) came to the city on the invitation of Queen Maria Carolina. She painted portraits of the royal family here (one hangs in the gallery at Capodimonte), although she came to prefer Rome as her Italian home. **Anton Raphael Mengs** (1728–79) was the director of the Neapolitan Royal Academy of Art for several years, while **Jakob Philipp Hackert** (1737–1807) spent almost half his life in Naples, employed as court painter by Ferdinand IV. The painters **Joseph Anton Koch** (1768–1839) and **Ludwig Richter** (1803–84) belonged to the Nazarene artistic circle based in Rome, but they were also frequent visitors to the Bay of Naples. Joseph Mallord William Turner, the English artist known as the »painter of light«, was also intermittently present in Naples: his watercolour *The Castel dell'Ovo, Naples, with Capri in the Distance* was painted in 1819. The Amalfi valley with its mills was well known for its magnificent landscapes and picturesque popular festivals and became one of the most painted subjects of 19th-century landscape painting.

Goethe's Italian Journey

From 1786 to 1788 **Johann Wolfgang von Goethe**, the pre-eminent figure of German literature and Germany's greatest lyric poet, travelled through Italy. First published in 1816–17 as *Italian Journey*, his diaries shaped the image of Italy for generations. W. H. Auden, who listed Goethe as one of his »tutors«, translated Goethe's writings on Italy into English. One of the people Goethe encountered in Naples was **Sir William Hamilton**, who as British ambassador enjoyed the trust of the Neapolitan royal couple and was known throughout Europe as a vulcanologist, collector and antiquities dealer. Both *Italian Journey* and the rediscovery of the Blue Grotto by the German painter and poet **August Kopisch** in 1826 mark the **beginning of a longing to visit southern Italy**. As of 1839 the first Italian train service began running between Naples and Portici and soon afterwards travel companies organized by Thomas Cook were able to offer trips to the Bay of Naples at a set price.

Scuola di Posillipo

Around 1820 the Dutch painter **Anton Sminck van Pitloo** (1790–1837) made his studio in Posillipo, a hilltop village near Naples, into a meeting place for young artists. This new school of landscape painters quickly became famous as the **Scuola di Posillipo**. The artists' use of a lighter palette and concentration on plein-air painting was a reaction to the academicism in the work of Neapolitan landscape painters of the late 18th century. The best known representative of the Scuola di Posillipo is **Giacinto Gigante** (1806–1876), whose mostly small-format watercolours in glowing colours today hang in various museums in Naples. J. M. W. Turner, perhaps the most famous English landscape painter, made visits to Naples between 1819 and 1829 and was an important external influence on van Pitloo.

One of the most important Neapolitan painters of the 19th century was **Domenico Morelli** (1826–1901), whose expressive paintings often portrayed historical or literary subjects.

19th century

The decades following the unification of Italy (Risorgimento) are associated with **Historicism** – an era when Neapolitan painting became very kitsch. The repertoire of saccharine subjects, such as the eternal sunsets over the long-disappeared (even then) fishing quarter of Santa Lucia, has stubbornly prevailed on the postcards of Naples to this day. The exception to this 19th-century excess of romance was the cycle of frescoes painted by **Hans von Marées** at the Stazione Zoologica. Designed in 1873, it was quickly recognized as the archetype of Neapolitan romance. As in Wilhelmine Germany, Italian architecture after the Risorgimento was characterized by **nationalism**. Naples saw the construction of the Mergellina, as well as imposing apartment blocks embellished with imaginative stucco façades along major urban roads such as Corso Umberto I and Corso Garibaldi. An impressive example of eclectic and monumental turn-of-the-century architecture in Naples is the Galleria Umberto I opposite the Teatro San Carlo.

Neapolitan songs (canzoni)

»O sole mio«, »Funiculì funiculà« and »Torna a Surriento« are **Neapolitan songs** known all over the world, though the image of the city they inspire is based more on fantasy than fact. The golden era of Neapolitan canzoni was between 1870 and the First World War, which was also the time when Naples enjoyed its final fling as a southern Italian capital of culture and tourism. It was also an era of mass emigration to America, and entire generations of Neapolitans staved off homesickness with these songs. The jolly tune of »Funiculì, funiculà« was even commissioned by the company that ran the Mount Vesuvius cable car. Nevertheless, however popular songs such as »Comme facette mammeta«, or the irresistible »A tazza è cafè« are, they are also entitled to be regarded as part of Neapolitan cultural history. Even right up to the 1950s, the festival of the Madonna di Piedigrotta was really a festival of popular song in Naples.

Neapolitan photography

Born in Frankfurt, **Giorgio Sommer** (1834–1914) moved to Naples in 1857, where he founded his photographic studio shortly afterwards. In the decades that followed, the studio became a great success and Sommer's images of Neapolitan street scenes touched a contemporary spirit that ensured him tremendous commercial success. His photos are more folklore than documentary. However, in addition to his commercial mass-produced images, Sommer also created a body of more sophisticated artistic work. Based in Naples, he travelled throughout Italy, photographing monuments that were gathered in collector's bindings and sold worldwide. His Naples workshop also produced small reproductions of ancient sculptures displayed in the National Archaeological Museum.

Liberty

The **Italian version of Art Nouveau** known as Liberty could be found in all the better neighbourhoods from 1900 onwards. Veritable palaces of the early 20th century can be admired on the Vomero, along Via dei Mille, all around Piazza Amedeo, and also in Mergellina. This uniquely Italian style is much less decorative than eclectic: references from architectural history were mixed with an unabashed joy to create a style never seen before or since. Outstanding examples are the magically playful Palazzina Paradisiello (Via del Parco Margherita 36), dating from 1908–09, and the fairy-tale Castello Aselmeyer (Corso Vittorio Emanuelle 166). Luxurious Liberty villas can also be seen set in their parks along Via di Posillipo, many of them with direct access to the sea. The highly original Palazzo Galli on Via Caracciolo was built in 1925–27, and already exhibits the first stylistic signs of Fascist bombastic architecture.

Fascism and Futurism

Unlike German Fascist architecture, its Italian counterpart can lay claim to artistic significance. A visionary manifesto of Futurism was written by the poet **Filippo Tommaso Marinetti** as early as 1909. His daring theses had great impact on the architecture of the time and, in the early years of Fascism under Benito Mussolini, Futurism was virtually the official state art. In Naples, an entirely new administrative district known as the **Rione Carità** was built in the heart of the city. The most spectacular and daring building of this era still amazes to this day: the **Palazzo delle Poste**/ built between 1933 and 1936, is a stone monument of futuristic vision that celebrated speed, technology and progress in the arts. Meanwhile, in 1937 on the island of Capri, **Curzio Malaparte** built his villa and called it »Una casa come me« (a house like me). It is not only an architectural self-portrait but also a veritable dictionary of 20th-century architecture.

Curzio Malaparte's villa in Capri

From 1971 onwards, Joseph Beuys (1921–86) made his home in Capri (for the peace and quiet) and in Naples (for the eternal chaos). The German artist enjoyed a close friendship with the Neapolitan gallery owner Lucio Amelio

CONTEMPORARY ART IN NAPLES

For a short time in the 1920s, Naples, and in particular Capri, was a centre of modern art. Tommaso Marinetti, one of the leading representatives of Italian Futurism, organized sensational evenings in the theatre of the Quisisana Hotel. In Naples in 1965, Lucio Amelio founded the »Modern Art Agency« – as Galleria Amelio, it was to become one of the most important Italian galleries for contemporary art in the 70s and 80s.

Spending unprecedented amounts of money, Naples has for some years been trying to make a link with its past and become a modern European metropolis. **Two museums of contemporary art**, the PAN (Palazzo delle Arti di Napoli, Via dei Mille 60) and the MADRE (Museo d'Arte Contemporanea Donna Regina, Via Settembrini 79) were opened at the same time. There is a spectacular **new Metropolitana line** up to the Vomero hill. Art displayed in public spaces, be it in the metro stations or on Piazza del Plebiscito, is intended to contribute to the city's cultural splendour. The memory of **Lucio Amelio** is ever-present.

After the earthquake in 1980 the gallerist Amelio, who died in 1994, initiated an exhibition entitled **»Terrae Motus«**. It caused an international furore. Artists such as Joseph Beuys, Andy Warhol, Gilbert & George and Anselm Kiefer exhibited in Naples. One of Beuys' best-known multiples, the *Capri Battery*, has become almost an emblem of that year. Numerous Terrae Motus works can be seen in **Caserta Palace** in an exhibition donated by Lucio Amelio.

The city's art scene

But also beyond Neapolitan cultural politics and its large-scale projects, the art scene in Naples is one of the liveliest in Italy. **Galleria Alfonso Artiaco** took over Amelio's rooms on Piazza dei Martiri a few years ago and exhibits internationally renowned ar-

tists there. The young experimental galleries are still more interesting, such as **Galleria 293** (Via dei Tribunali 293) or **Galleria Franco Ricardo Artivisibile** (Piazzetta Nilo 7). **Galleria Lia Rumma**, one of Naples' oldest galleries, offers an international programme. In a spectacular building above the city the privately run **Fondazione Morra** has established the Museo Nitsch (www.museonitsch.org). Those looking for more examples of Viennese Actionism may like to visit the **Hermann Nitsch Museum-Archive-Laboratory for Modern Art**, housed in the Stazione Bellini, a former electric power station in the centre of Naples. A new addition to the scene is the **Fondazione Morra Greco** (www.fondazionemorragreco.org), which organizes four exhibitions a year. The Morra brothers are collectors and patrons and have been active in the cultural life of Naples for years. Furthermore, there are regular exhibitions of contemporary art in Castel Sant'Elmo and Castel dell'Ovo. Stars of the art scene such as Damian Hurst, Jeff Koons and Richard Serra were invited to present their works in the antiquities collection in the Naples National Archaeological Museum at an exhibition that was quite sensational. Piazza del Plebiscito, too, serves from time to time as a public exhibition space for often spectacular works of art.

The **cultural institutions** of different European countries also make a contribution to the variety of the Naples art scene. Alongside its courses in foreign languages, the British Council (Via Morghen, 36) also organizes numerous art events in the city.

Second half of the 20th century The post-war years on the Bay of Naples were characterized by rampant urban and rural building speculation that did permanent damage, destroying both cityscapes and the countryside. Only the **Centro Direzionale**, built under the aegis of the Japanese architect **Kenzo Tange**, and the 1950s Olivetti building in Pozzuoli can be considered successful examples of modern town planning.

Joseph Beuys, Andy Warhol and Lucio Amelio Thanks to the activities of the Neapolitan gallery owner and collector Lucio Amelio (1931–94), the city became a **centre for contemporary art** in the 1970s and 1980s. Amelio brought artists of international renown to Naples – for example **Joseph Beuys** – who were inspired by the anarchic chaos of the city. The legendary exhibition entitled »Terrae motus«, first shown at Villa Campolieto near Herculaneum, included original work specifically related to Naples made by numerous artists associated with the Galleria Amelio. **Andy Warhol's** painting *Vesuvio* is today exhibited in Capodimonte Palace; and a large number of the paintings and installations can be viewed at the permanent Fondazione Amelio exhibition at the **Reggia in Caserta**. Contemporary art is also to be found underground in Naples, as renowned artists have been designing the metro stations for line 1. A taste of the future »stazioni dell'arte« can be viewed at www.metro.na.it.

The Literati on the Bay of Naples

The Bay of Naples was a favoured destination among artists and intellectuals during the 19th and 20th centuries, due not least to the discovery of the Blue Grotto on the island of Capri. Romantic writers were drawn to the subject: Wilhelm Waiblinger in *The Legend of the Blue Grotto* (1828); Hans Christian Andersen in his semi-autobiographical novel *The Improvisatore* (1835); and Alexandre Dumas père in his travel writing published as *Le Speronare* (1842). Painters and writers alike were inspired by the beauty of the landscape: indeed it is less a question of who was there, more one of who was not.
Among writers, the island of Ischia was even more popular than Capri. The Bavarian King Louis (Ludwig) I eulogized the loveliness of the island and, a few decades later, Hendrik Ibsen wrote his drama *Per Gynt* here. In 1949, Truman Capote stayed for three months and invited not only the island's »most beautiful fishermen, but also the English poet W. H. Auden« to his farewell party. Capote was inspired to write a short story entitled »Ischia«, in which he described the unsullied island idyll he had found.

Capri, island of inspiration From about 1870 until the outbreak of the Second World War the small Mediterranean island of Capri received such a number of famous visitors that it was considered the cosmopolitan centre of the artistic world. However it was perhaps rather the prospect of pleasure than of serious work that lured them here – the great Capri novel is notably absent from world literature. Only Swedish physician **Axel Munthe's** *The Story of San Michele*, a series of overlapping vignettes and reminiscences, has managed to shape the image of Capri for generations. The visitors' books of Capri hotels, many of them still preserved today, read like a veritable who's who of the intellectual elite of the turn of the 19th into the 20th century. The history of tourism on Capri began with the Hotel Pagano, in which the likes of August von Platen, Ferdinand Gregorovius and Theodor Fontane stayed. Friedrich Nietzsche, coming from Sorrento, also paid a visit to the island. As of 1870 the »Zum Kater Hiddigeigei« café served as a meeting place for Capri's foreign visitors: D. H. Lawrence, Maxim Gorki, Walter Benjamin and Joseph Conrad all enjoyed its cosy atmosphere. The strange name of the café, a nod to the predominance of German guests, came from a popular poem by Joseph Victor von Scheffel. The English poet **Norman Douglas**, who died on the island in 1952, is an exception amongst the writers of Capri. His 1917 novel *South Wind* is one of the few works written on the island that are still readable today. Whether the same can be said of the works of Scottish writer Compton Mackenzie, the author of two novels set in the Capri of the 1920s, *Extraordinary Women* and *Vestal Fire*, is debatable. **Curzio Malaparte** achieved literary fame after his death with his novel *The Skin*.

Final flowering

The writer **Elsa Morante** worked on the island of Procida, and film director **Luchino Visconti** spent the summer months at his magnificent villa on Ischia. W. H. Auden fled the seaside tourists early on, but **Graham Greene** remained true to his holiday and working home on Capri, which he regularly visited between 1948 and 1990. The American author and scriptwriter **Gore Vidal** was only able to tear himself away from the spectacular setting of his villa above the sea at Ravello in 2006.

Travel journals and other writing

Many travel journals and letters were composed by travellers to the Bay of Naples from the era of the Grand Tour onwards. Johann Wolfgang von Goethe's *Italian Journey*, translated from the German by W. H. Auden and Elizabeth Mayer, is a journal replete with observations on art and history, the flora and landscape of the region, and the character of the people he met on his journey to Venice, Rome, Naples and Sicily. In *Siren Land*, Norman Douglas writes informatively on the ancient Neapolitan setting, Capri, and Sorrento. One of the most unusual diaries inspired by the area is by the English author **Norman Lewis**, who spent time in Naples as an intelligence officer in 1944 (*Napoli 44*). Finally, in her memoir *Greene on Capri*, Shirley Hazzard not only offers an insight into the celebrated author's personality, but also paints a picture of the island of Capri and the myriad of characters who spent time there.

Famous People

Agrippina the Younger murdered by poisoning, committed incest and cooked up conspiracies. Antonio Bassolino stands for the rebirth of Naples and Sophia Loren was given the freedom of the city of Pozzuoli. Totò is much loved, even 40 years after his death, and Virgil is the most read writer of antiquity. Read about some of the extraordinary characters from the Bay of Naples here.

Agrippina the Younger (around AD 15–59)

Roman empress

Several psychologically challenged emperors ruled the Roman Empire in the first century AD, and **Agrippina the Younger** operated as the éminence grise of these infamous rulers. Caligula was her brother and Claudius, divorced from Messalina, was her uncle and became her husband. Lucius Domitius Ahenobarbus – later known as Nero – was her son. Murder (by poisoning), incest and conspiracy are all attributed to Agrippina. She persuaded the weak Claudius to adopt Nero and disown his own son Britannicus, then had her imperial husband poisoned. In October AD 54, Agrippina finally achieved her goal: her son Nero became emperor. Her victory was short-lived, however, because when Nero fell in love with Poppaea Sabina, the days of her influence at the imperial court were numbered.
It was hate that drove Nero to plot **matricide**. The setting was the Gulf of Pozzuoli. After dining with her imperial son, Agrippina intended to travel back to her villa at Antium by ship, setting off from Baia. But the vessel had been tampered with: the roof of the wheelhouse was laden with lead. It was supposed to look like an accident at sea, but the plan went wrong, and although the ship did sink in the open sea, Agrippina managed to swim back to shore. On Nero's orders, she was then murdered in her villa by the prefect of the imperial fleet, Anicetus, and several of his soldiers. "Aim for my womb!" she is said to have cried, according to Tacitus. The so-called Tomb of Agrippina, near Bacoli, has no relationship with the imperial mother, however. Where her ashes were spread by her maid servants remains unknown.

Sophia Loren (born 1934)

Actress

Whenever **Italy's most famous film star**, who grew up in Pozzuoli as Sofia Scicolone, visits her home town, there is always an explosion of popular excitement. The last time she visited was in 2005, when she was moved to tears while accepting her honorary citizenship. An illegitimate child, she was born into humble social conditions. She almost became Pozzuoli's prettiest primary school teacher, but an ambitious mother and a series of propitious events paved the way to a unique career in film instead. Her second place in the competition to find the »Queen of the Sea« in Naples was followed by winning the competition for »Miss Rome«, which resulted in her meeting the film producer Carlo Ponti – and the rest is movie history. Carlo Ponti made Sophia Loren a film star who, thanks to her genuine talent as an actress, was far more than her famous cleavage. Today, at over 70 years old, she is an **Italian legend**, the mother of two grown-up sons and, since the death of Carlo Ponti in 2007, undoubtedly the most glamorous widow in the world.

← *Totò remains ever-present in Naples, even over 40 years after his death*

Sophia Loren as newly elected honorary citizen of Pozzuoli, beside the regional president for Campania, Antonio Bassolino

Giacchino Murat (1767 – 1815)

King of Naples

There is a room in the Palazzo Reale in which the memory of one of the most **dazzling personalities** in Neapolitan history is especially present: Napoleon's brother-in-law sat behind the Empire-style desk from 1808 to 1815. Murat proudly called himself the »King of both Sicilys« even though his kingdom only consisted of the southern part of the boot (the Bourbon king Ferdinand IV lived on Sicily).
Murat, the later king of Naples, was born in 1767 in rural France as the son of an innkeeper. After breaking off his studies for the priesthood he joined the army and his career took off due to his friendship with Napoleon. But this was certainly not just due to Napoleon's protection. Murat was, as all of his remaining portraits show, a proud, virile, ambitious and fearless man. After marrying Napoleon's younger sister Caroline the French innkeeper's son and the Corsican minor noblewoman became king and queen of a small but especially beautiful kingdom. Their relatively short reign was among the happiest periods in Naples' complicated history. Murat's thoroughly Napoleonic and efficient style of ruling was just as modern as the recently restored Parisian furniture in his study. He modified the pon-

derous Bourbonic burocracy and transformed Naples into a modern European capital. The building projects which he initiated mark the cityscape until today. The tragic of this ambitious and capable king was that his fate was inseparable from that of his imperial brother-in-law. After Napoleon's downfall he made secret treaties with Napoleon's opponents, but fought again at his side after he returned from Elba and wound up – after an adventurous flight to France and Corsica – in Pizzo on the coast of Calabria. But even the queen's jewellery, which was sewn into his uniform, could no longer help him. His arrest was followed by imprisonment in a small castell, an improvized trial and – Ferdinand IV was vengeful – the death sentence. On October 13, 1815 Gioacchino Murat was shot by a firing squad.

Maria Carolina of Austria (1752–1824)

Queen of Naples

The life of this unhappy queen reads like a novel. Her marriage to the young king of Naples, Ferdinand IV, got off to a bad start: her mother Empress Maria Theresa of Austria really wanted to marry off her daughter Josepha, but she died of smallpox shortly before her departure for Italy. Thus the 15-year-old Maria Carolina was sent to the Kingdom of the Two Italies in her sister's place, more or less as second-best. She was received by a childish husband and the all-powerful minister Tanucci, who Charles III had installed as advisor before departing for Spain. Though Maria Carolina was **both intelligent and ambitious, she was not very diplomatic**. The French Revolution and the death of her sister Marie Antoinette at the gallows haunted her. Her first escape from French revolutionary armies was by warship, accompanied by Admiral Nelson. This journey into Sicilian exile was full of drama in itself, with a seasick Nelson, a fatalist King Ferdinand, a stressed Lord Hamilton guarding a priceless art collection, and a mortally ill prince who died at sea. The queen's revenge, after her return from a brief exile, was terrible. Supporters of the Parthenopean Republic – many of them members of the Neapolitan high aristocracy – were executed. Her second and permanent exile in Sicily came in 1806, when she was forced to flee Napoleon's army. Unloved by her royal husband – despite having to endure 17 pregnancies by him and to put up with his mistress – unpopular across Europe, and worn down by intrigues and false hopes, the proud and ambitious queen returned home to Vienna. She died there on 8 September 1824. The only items recalling her life in Naples are a few portraits and, oddly, her bathrooms at the small palace of San Leucio and at Caserta. The almost entirely ruined »Bagno della Regina«, set below the Villa d'Elboeuf in Portici, also dates from her reign.

Padre Pio (1887–1968)

20th-century saint

The most unusual saint's story of the 20th century began entirely without incident during a hike through the lonely Apulian landscape in June 1916. Born in the small village of Peitrelcina near Benevento, the 29-year-old Capuchin monk Francesco Forgione was walking to San Giovanni Rotondo, in the barren Gargano region. He was welcomed at the tiny monastery there by just a handful of monks. 90 years later, San Giovanni Rotondo is visited by around seven million pilgrims annually, and is Italy's most important pilgrimage site after Rome. Francesco Forgione, meanwhile, is better known as Padre Pio, and is today **the most popular saint of the Catholic world**. Where faith is strong, miracles are often seen, and so it was with Padre Pio, whose hands developed stigmata two years after his arrival at the monastery. The Catholic Church considered this miracle to be a step too far, but its repressive measures from 1922 onwards, such as prohibiting Padre Pio from holding Mass, only increased his status as a martyr. In 1933, the Vatican decided to issue a declaration of no objection and, just 34 years after his death, in 2002, **Padre Pio was canonized**. Miraculous healing, his ability to be in more than one place at the same time, his charisma and stern manner are all features of the legends that have grown up around this southern Italian icon. In San Giovanni Rotondo itself, the veneration of Padre Pio is mostly a matter of commerce. The place of his birth, on the other hand, holds one of southern Italy's most beautiful processions in honour of the saint's birthday on 25 May, an event that captivates with its humility and lack of pomp. The Forgione family's rural home at Pietrelcina is also a popular pilgrimage destination.

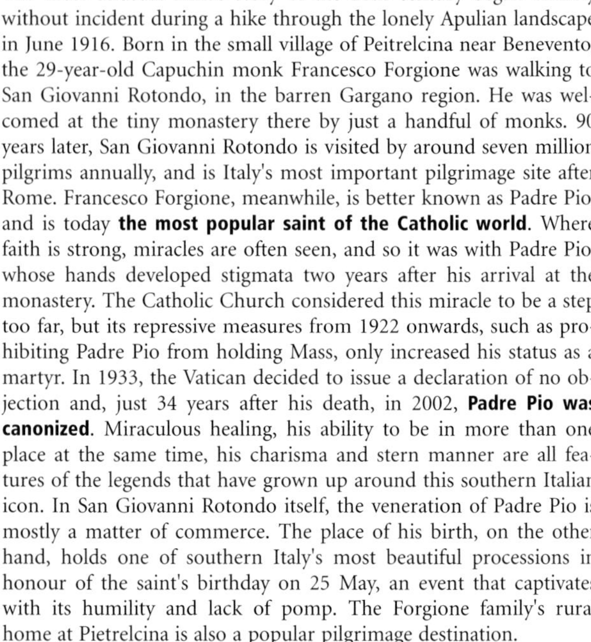

Totò (1898–1967)

Actor

Even forty years after his death, the grave of Naples' most famous actor at the cemetery of Poggioreale looks more like a flower shop than a burial site. Many of the bouquets of flowers left here have loving notes attached to them. **Totò is much loved by all Neapolitans**, no matter what their age or class. The life of this popular actor was as incredible as the action in his films. This illegitimate son of a maid, born into the poor Sanità quarter, was to ascend the social ladder in an incredible way. After his natural father, the impoverished Count of Curtis, officially acknowledged him, Totò allowed himself to be adopted by yet another aristocrat. For several years, he went by a variety of stylish titles, including that of a Byzantine prince. As an actor and comedian, Totò had the ability to express a certain kind of melancholy that could tread the **fine line between tragedy and pathos**, and he was also able to imbue the most absurd film with genuinely philosophical moments. This delicate man with the inscrutable face, who could act out sudden temper tantrums and epiphanies (usually with catastrophic results) was both a genius comedian and one of the greatest tragic actors of all time – for Naples, at least. For no subtitles can ever convey the quick Neapolitan wit and the frequently surreal madness of situation comedy personified in Totò's art, nor his ability to convey a uniquely stoic patience in the face of seemingly inevitable complications. Next to San Gennaro, the actor's strangely irregular face is virtually the emblem for Naples. His film classics include *L'Oro di Napoli*, *Napoli milionaria* and *L'Imperatore di Capri*. Italy's answer to Charlie Chaplin, otherwise known as the Count Antonio de Curtis, would be mightily amused by the capers that have held up the opening of the Totò-Museum, which has been in the offing for years.

? DID YOU KNOW ...?

- The figure of Pulcinella (photo p.1), dressed in white and with a huge nose sticking out from his black mask, is seen everywhere in Naples. His origins possibly go all the way back to the theatre of Roman antiquity, but he certainly enjoyed great popularity by the time of the 16th century. He is a clown born of the Comedia dell'Arte, and his sly and witty ways are capable of twisting any situation to his advantage. His descendants include, among others, the French Pierrot character, the Russian Petruschka, and the English Mr Punch.

Virgil (70 BC – 19 BC)

Author

»Mantua gave birth to me, the Calabrians took me, now Naples holds me; I sang of pastures, fields, and leaders.« Virgil, actually called Publius Vergilius Maro, was a star author in his day and remains **the most-read author of Greek and Roman antiquity**. Born in Mantua in northern Italy, Virgil spent most of his life on the Bay of Naples, having studied in Cremona and Rome. He eulogized the beauty of the countryside in his bucolic poetry like no other before or since. Virgil probably owned a small country estate in the region between Naples and Pozzuoli. The poet was famous for much more than his enchanting verses, however. A witness to the dramatic events that took place after Caesar's murder in 44 BC, of the civil war, and of the breathtaking rise of Gaius Octavius (Caesar's adoptive son and great-nephew), he also wrote famous prose. Octavian's fame as **Augustus** is unthinkable without Virgil, as it the legendary Augustinian epoch of economic growth and peaceful expansion. Virgil's fame has endured for millennia and his presumed tomb in Naples was a popular pilgrimage site for travellers to southern Italy long into the 19th century.

Practicalities

HOW TO GET TO CAMPANIA, FIND THE BEST BEACHES AND GET TO GRIPS WITH NAPLES: RECOMMENDATIONS FOR AN ENJOYABLE HOLIDAY.

Accommodation

Hotels and guest houses

Italian hotels are officially categorized into **five categories**, ranging from luxury five-star hotels to simple accommodations with one star. There are also uncategorized small pensions or guest houses that can be entirely acceptable places to stay. Small hotels without car parks send staff out to help find a parking spot. Hotels with car parks charge extra for a parking space. **Hotel listings** are provided by ENIT offices, as well as by regional and local tourist offices. In addition to hotels, pensions, holiday apartments and holiday houses, you can also find accommodation on farms. The island hotels and on the Sorrentine peninsula normally only accept bookings for **half board or full board** during the high season.

Price categories

- Luxury: from €190
- Mid-range: €80–€190
- Budget: up to €80

for a double room per night without breakfast

Prices

Hotel prices vary, depending on the **time of year**, but are always higher in the large cities. Single rooms cost around 20–25 % less than doubles.

Bed & breakfasts

A **recommended alternative** to hotel accommodation is provided by bed & breakfasts. There are some very good ones in Naples in particular. The main company supplying B&B accommodation is Bed & Breakfast Italia, but there are other reliable providers as well. The accommodation on offer ranges from rooms with shared use of a bathroom to bedrooms in prestigious historic buildings, complete with private bath and terrace.

Agritourism and rural tourism

Agriturismo is the Italian version of **farmstay holidays**. The choice of accommodation ranges from campsites and rooms at a working farm to well-equipped holiday apartments in a rural setting. In addition, there are also often **leisure and sporting opportunities** available, such as tennis, fishing, bicycle rental, hiking or wine tasting. The ideal way to reach these out-of-the-way places is in your own car. Some farms run country restaurants or sell their own products, such as olive oil, honey, jam, meat, sausages, cheese, wine and grappa. Local tourist offices are a good source of information, and Agriturist (based in Rome) also publishes an annually updated guide. Of course there are other sales agents for rural Italian holidays in the UK and North America.

Youth hostels

Accommodation at Italian youth hostels (albergho per la gioventù) requires a valid **international youth hostel card**. During high season, it is highly advisable to have a **reservation**.

IMPORTANT ADDRESSES

AGRITOURISM

▶ **Agriturist**
Corso Vittorio Emanuele II 101,
00186 Roma, tel. 0 66 85 23 42
www.agriturist.it

▶ **Additional information**
www.turismoverde.it
www.terranostra.it
www.vacanzeverdi.com

BED & BREAKFAST

▶ **B & B Italia**
Corso Vittorio Emanuele II, 282
00186 Roma, tel. 0 66 87 86 18;
www.bbitalia.it

▶ **Additional information**
www.anbba.it
www.bb-napoli.com
www.italiabb.com
www.bedandbreakfast.it
www.bed-and-breakfast.it

CAMPING

▶ **Federazione Italiana del Campeggio e del Caravaning**
www.camping.it

HOTELS

▶ **Central reservations**
Tel. 02 29 53 16 05
Numero verde (toll free)
Tel. 8 00 01 57 72 (only in Italy)
www.hotelme.it

▶ **Other addresses:**
www.initalia.it
www.italypass.com
www.familyhotels.com

YOUTH HOSTELS

▶ **Information worldwide**
www.hihostels.com

▶ **Information in Italy**
Associazione Italiana Alberghi per la Gioventù
Via Cavour 44
I-00184 Roma
Tel. 0 64 87 11 52
Fax 0 64 88 04 92
www.aighostels.org
www.hostelitaly.it

▶ **Information in UK**
Youth Hostels Association
Trevelyan House, Matlock
Derbyshire, DE4 3YH
Tel. (0 16 29) 59 27 00
Fax (0 16 29) 59 27 01
www.yha.org.uk

HOLIDAY HOMES

www.cilento-ferien.de
www.italimar.com
www.i-fewo.com

Holiday apartments

There are holiday apartments and houses along the coast, on the islands and in Cilento province that are good value-for-money alternatives to staying in a hotel.

Camping

The most beautiful campsites in Campania are on the Sorrentine peninsula and in southern Cilento. There are also attractive campsites on the islands of Ischia and Procida, but camping on Capri is prohibited. The nearest site to Naples is in Pozzuoli. **Advance reservations** are strongly advised for the high season during July and August. A list of campsites is published by ENIT (► Information), as well as by the Italian Camping Association.

Caravanning, camping wild

Mobile homes and camper vans are generally permitted to spend one night at a car park or rest stop, or by the side of the road, unless the contrary is indicated by a sign. However, **for reasons of safety**, it is better to use campsites. Wild camping is illegal.

Arrival · Planning the Trip

By car

From the UK ►

The quickest way across the English Channel to France is via the Eurotunnel. Passengers drive their cars onto the train, *Le Shuttle*, which covers the distance from Folkestone to Coquelles near Calais in 35 minutes. At peak times there are four trains every hour (tel. 0870 535 3535; www.eurotunnel.com). Drivers can also take their cars across the Channel by ferry.

In summer, in particular at the beginning of August, the start of the holidays in France and Italy, there is likely to be heavy traffic on motorways heading south. Those driving southeast through France can go south to Lyon, then cross the Alps on the E70 to Turin, continue west to Bologna and then head south to Rome and Naples; alternatively take a route further north past Geneva and through the Mont Blanc tunnel to Turin (E25). The coastal road is the E80, which runs from the south of France parallel to the shore of the Mediterranean to Genoa, La Spezia, Livorno and south towards Rome.

From northern Europe ►

Drivers who have been in the Swiss or Austrian Alps or are coming from Germany or other points further north have a number of options.

One is to take the St Bernard Pass, entering Italy at Chiasso, continuing to Milan and then heading south to Naples via Bologna and Rome. Alternatives from Switzerland are the Simplon Pass and St Gotthard Pass. Further east the E45 runs from Munich to Innsbruck and over the Brenner Pass. A toll is payable on this stretch of motorway.

Motorway tolls

►Transport

By rail

Those travelling by train are best advised to take a Eurostar from London to Paris and then a TGV on to Milan, either via southeastern France or via Switzerland (booking online: www.raileurope.co.uk), a journey that takes about 12 hours. There are high-speed rains from Milan to Naples. Alternatively, travel from Paris to Rome overnight on a sleeper train, and then make use of the frequent services from

USEFUL INFORMATION

BY RAIL

► **In London**
Rail Europe Travel Centre
178 Piccadilly
London W1V 0BA
Tel. 0870 8 37 13 71
www.raileurope.co.uk

► **In Italy**
Trenitalia
Tel. 848 88 80 88
(toll-free)
www.trenitaliaplus.com
www.ferroviedellostato.it/
homepage_en.html

BY BUS

► **Eurolines**
Bookings online and in UK through National Express
Tel. 087 05 80 80 80
www.eurolines.com and
www.nationalexpress.com

AIRLINES

► **Aer Lingus**
Tel. 0818 365 044
www.aerlingus.com

► **Alitalia**
Tel. 0870 225 5000
www.alitalia.com

► **British Airways**
Tel. 0844 493 0787
www.britishairways.com

► **Easyjet**
Tel. 0871 244 2366
www.easyjet.com

► **Lufthansa**
Tel. (0845) 606 0320
www.lufthansa.com

ON TO THE ISLANDS

► **Car ferries and hydrofoils**
The maritime routes from Naples and Salerno are well served, with regular car ferries (traghetti) and hydrofoils (aliscafi) departing from Naples (Molo Beverello, Mergellina), Pozzuoli, Sorrento and Salerno for the islands of Capri, Ischia and Procida. Ships also ply the routes Salerno–Amalfi–Sorrento and Naples–Sorrento. VIPs also travel by helicopter, private yacht or the yellow speedboats run by *Taxi del Mare* (tel. 8 18 77 36 00, www.taxidelmare.it). During summer, there are additional speed ferries departing from Positano, Amalfi, Salerno and Castellamare de Golfo. Ships from Naples also head for the Pontine Islands, Cagliari (Sardinia), Palermo (Sicily) and Tunis (Tunisia). Current timetables are published in the daily press, by the tourist of-fices, and on the websites of ferry companies, as well as being posted at the relevant ports as well as at: www.aliscafi.it, www.traghetti.com and www.traghettiamo.it.

Rome to Naples. You must make reservations on many international trains and all Italian long-distance and night trains.

By bus or coach Eurolines run several coaches daily from London Victoria to Paris. Further Eurolines services continue to Milan, and from there on to Naples. The total journey time is about 36 hours.

By air Naples-Capodichino International Airport (► p.190) is served by both scheduled and charter flights.
British Airways flies direct from London Gatwick to Naples, and there is a new direct Easyjet route from Gatwick, too. Easyjet also flies to Naples from London Stansted and, in the summer, from Liverpool. Alitalia offers services several times a day from London Heathrow via Milan and Rome. Aer Lingus flies direct from Dublin to Naples.
The airline offering the most regular connecting flights to Naples from any city outside Italy is Lufthansa, though these services depart from their secondary hub at Munich, which is not so well served by flights from the UK.

Travel Documents

Personal documents The identity cards and passports of EU citizens are often no longer checked. However, since random inspections are carried out at the border and identification is required at airports, all visitors should be able to show their **passports** when they enter the country. Children under 16 years of age must carry a children's passport or be entered in the parent's passport.

Car documents Always carry your driving licence, the motor vehicle registration and the international green insurance card when driving in Italy. Motor vehicles must have the oval sticker showing nationality unless they have a Euro licence plate.

Pets and travel Those who wish to bring pets (dogs, cats) to Italy require a **pet pass**. Among other things, it contains an official veterinary statement of health (no more than 30 days old), a rabies vaccination certificate that is at least 20 days and no more than eleven months old, and a passport photo. In addition, the animal must have a microchip or tattoo. A muzzle and leash are required at all times for dogs.

Customs Regulations

Regulations for EU citizens The European Union member states (including Italy) form a common economic area within which the movement of goods for private purposes is largely duty-free. There are merely certain maximum quantities which apply: 800 cigarettes, 400 cigarillos, 200 cigars, 1 kilogramme of tobacco, 10 litres of spirits, 90 litres of wine (of which a maximum of 60 litres can be sparkling), and 110 litres of beer. Should a customs inspection occur, a plausible explanation for the intended private use of the goods is required.

For travellers from outside the EU, the following duty-free quantities apply: 200 cigarettes or 100 cigarillos or 50 cigars or 250g of tobacco; also 2 litres of wine and 2 litres of sparkling wine or 1 litre of spirits with an alcohol content of more than 22% vol.; 500g of coffee or 200g of coffee extracts, 100g of tea or 40g of tea extract, 50ml of perfume or 0.25 litres of eau de toilette. Gifts up to a value of €175 are also duty-free.

Regulations for non-EU citizens

Travel Insurance

Citizens of EU countries are entitled to treatment in Italy under the local regulations in case of illness on production of their **European health insurance card (EHIC)**. Even with this card, in most cases some of the costs for medical care and prescribed medication must be paid by the patient.

Health insurance

Upon presentation of receipts the health insurance at home covers the costs – but not for all treatments. Citizens of non-EU countries must pay for medical treatment and medicine themselves and should take out private health insurance.

Since some of the costs for medical treatment and medication typically have to be covered by the patient, and the costs for return transportation may not be covered by the normal health insurance, additional travel insurance is recommended.

Private travel insurance

Beach Holidays

There are numerous options for seaside holidays along the extensive coast of Campania, which stretches between the mouth of the River Garigliano to the north and the Gulf of Policastro to the south, as well as on the islands in the Bay of Naples. Many beaches are **not open to the public**, however, and are managed by private bathing institutions (stabilimenti) or hotels, who charge for their services, such as changing rooms, deck chairs and parasols. Many of the bathing spots on Capri and along the mainland coast are not sandy. Instead they are reached by ladders and steps going down to the water. Some beaches can only be reached by boat.

The most beautiful beaches are on the island of Ischia, along the Sorrentine peninsula, and in the province of Cilento between Agropoli and Marina di Camerota. The bathing season runs from the end of May to October (for water temperatures see ►p.101). Swimming near Naples is not recommended because of water pollution, but elsewhere the water quality is very good. Information on water quality can be found at www.feeitalia.org, www.legambiente.org and others).

A nature lover's paradise: Porto degli Infreschi, south of Marina di Camerota

Children in Italy

Long journey The worst thing about an overland journey to southern Italy is the long distance and time required to get there. Once arrived, however, Mediterranean Italy is full of child-friendly attractions. **Bucket and spade holidays** are top of the list, of course, but tours to places where **art, culture or nature await discovery** can also be tailored to children's needs. The mighty Vesuvius volcano, the bubbling slime at the Campi Flegrei, the islands of Capri and Ischia, the picturesque rocky coastline of Amalfi and the lovely beaches of southern Cilento, as well as the remote forests and caves of its hinterland, are all capable of thrilling young people.

Most larger hotels and most campsites in southern Italy have playgrounds. Holiday resorts also offer mini clubs and special children's programmes. An appealing holiday option for families is also the farm holiday (►Accommodation, Agriturismo).

Naples ► Traffic in the bustling port of Naples is chaotic, and parents must expect pavements to be blocked by parked cars and speeding mopeds (Vespas) whizzing by in the pedestrianized city centre. The seaside promenade of Lungomare Caracciolo is closed to traffic only on Sunday mornings, when the place is taken over by Neapolitan families out for a stroll.

SOME RECOMMENDATIONS

► **Naples and its surroundings**
There are many museums and parks with playgrounds, including the Museo Zoologico (Via Mezzocannone 8; daily except Sat, Sun 9am–7pm; closed in August). The municipal park at Villa Comunale attracts visitors with an oceanic aquarium ►p.241.

The Astroni crater in Pozzuoli is a small natural paradise set inside an extinct crater ►p.292.

Leisure parks: Naples has two leisure parks with the usual attractions. Edenlandia (in western Naples: Viale Kennedy 75; www.edenlandia.it) and Magic World, which also has a large aquapark (Giugliano, about 15km/9mi northwest of Naples; www.magicworld.it).

The Città della Scienza is the place to find out how the cosmos was created, or how lightning occurs. The interactive science museum at Bagnoli has plenty of hands-on exhibits as well: »please do touch!« ►p.244.

Daily life during antiquity: men playing kottabos (museum in Pontecagno, p.315)

▸ **Pompeii**
Children can explore the city in the company of a virtual friend: 8-year-old Caius (www.pompeii sites.org).

▸ **Islands and seaside resorts**
During summer, fishermen offer boat tours out of numerous seaside resorts along the coast that are the best way to discover islands and hidden bathing coves, as well as the lovely grottos (►see relevant pages in »Sights from A to Z«). Independent boat trips can also be made in hired boats, including pedalos.

▸ **Cilento**
Cilento is not just attractive for its beaches. The interior has areas of spectacular natural beauty to explore, including the two caves of Grotte di Pertosa (also called Grotte dell'Angelo, www.grotte dellangelo.sa.it) and Grotte di Castelcivita (www.grottedicastelci vita.com; information on location, opening times etc. ►Paestum, Cilento).

Electricity

The Italian grid generally supplies 220-volt electricity. Due to the variety of sockets all visitors, especially who are not from mainland Europe, are advised to take an **adapter** (spina di adattamento).

Emergency

IN ITALY

▸ **Pan-European emergency number**
Tel. 112

▸ **Police**
(polizia) tel. 113

▸ **Fire**
(vigili fuoco) tel. 115

▸ **Ambulance**
(emergenza sanitaria) tel. 118

▸ **Automobile Club d'Italia (ACI)**
(soccorso stradale)
Tel. 80 31 16 and 0 64 99 81
Tel. 1518 (condition of roads)
Tel. 116 (breakdown service)
www.aci.it

▸ **Touring-Club Italiano (TCI)**
(touring servizi)
tel. 0 31 78 46 01 54
www.touringclub.it

AUTOMOBILE CLUBS IN THE UK

▸ **AA**
Tel. +44 (0)161 495 8945
(international enquiries)

▸ **RAC**
Tel. +44 (0)1922 727313
(general enquiries)

INTERNATIONAL
AIR AMBULANCE SERVICES

▶ **Cega Air Ambulance (worldwide service)**
Tel. +44 (0)1243 621097
Fax +44 (0)1243 773169
www.cega-aviation.co.uk

▶ **US Air Ambulance**
Tel. 800/948-1214 (US; toll-free)
Tel. 001-941-926-2490 (international; collect)
www.usairambulance.net

Etiquette and Customs

Tips

Between 5% and 10% of the total bill is commonly left as tip in cafés and restaurants. If paying by cheque or card, it is best to leave the tip in cash separately. In cafés and bars, it is customary to leave the tip on the plate provided for change after paying the bill. Taxi drivers (0.50–1.00 €), tour guides (1–2 €), toilet attendants and room service staff also like to receive tips.

Smoking prohibited

A smoking ban in all public places, including restaurants and cafés, was instituted in January 2005. Only establishments with separate smoking areas can allow smoking.

Permesso, scusi

Even those with no Italian would do well to remember the words permesso and scusi, which are heard everywhere and have many uses. They can be used interchangeably to politely pass someone or walk through a communal area.

Bella figura

Keeping up a certain standard of appearance, as encapsulated by the phrase bella figura, is engrained in the Italian psyche. It is simply unthinkable for most Italian men and women to step outside without looking their stylish best, even if only going to the post office or the market. Tourists strolling around cathedrals in flip flops, viewing art museums in casual shorts or, worse still, walking around the city centre without even a T-shirt on, attract responses from their fastidious hosts ranging from amusement to bafflement.

Festivals, Holidays and Events

Folk festivals

Southern Italy has a wealth of folk festivals, usually with a religious theme. The highlights of the Catholic festival calendar are Christmas and Easter, followed by celebrations of the patron saint days for towns, villages and churches, as well as those for the Virgin Mary. These festivals are often major events and should be experienced at least once: with processions, music and dance, and plenty of food and drink.

Music festivals During summer, there are musical events in almost all the larger towns, including classical, opera, rock and pop music, as well as jazz, ballet and theatre. Current programmes are published in the local press and by the respective information centres. Central ticket sales: www.boxol.it (only in Italian).

PUBLIC HOLIDAYS AND FESTIVALS

PUBLIC HOLIDAYS

► **Nationally**
1 January (New Year: Capodanno)
6 January (Epiphany: Epifania)
Easter Sunday and Monday (Pasqua, Lunedi dell'angelo)
25 April (national holiday: Festa della liberazione)
1 May (Labour Day: Festa del primo maggio)
2 June (national holiday: Festa della Republica)
15 August (Assumption of the Virgin: Ferragosto)
1 November (All Saints Day: Ognissanti)
8 December (Immaculate Conception: Immacolata Concezione)
25 and 26 December (Christmas: Natale)

JANUARY

► **Many places**
celebrate *the end of winter/beginning of spring and carnival.* This is the case in Amalfi and Maiori, as well as in the province of Avellino.

MARCH – APRIL

► **In many towns**
there are passion plays and processions during *»Settimana Santa«* (Easter week). For example, on the island of Procida, in Sorrento, Positano and Amalfi, as well as at Sessa Aurunca.

MAY

► **Maggio dei Monumenti**
During weekends in and around Naples, villas, monasteries, palaces, churches and gardens open their doors to the public. In Salerno this tradition is called »Salerno porte aperte«.

► **Sailing Cup Regatta**
Traditional sailing regatta off the island of Capri

► **Naples**
Festa di San Gennaro: in honour of the city's patron saint, held in the cathedral during the first weekend in May

► **Positano**
Festa di San Vito including fireworks

JUNE

► **Palio delle Quattro Antiche Repubbliche**
The former maritime republics of Amalfi, Pisa, Genoa and Venice take turns celebrating their past greatness with a rowing regatta on the first Sunday in June. The event will be held in *Pisa* in 2010.

► **Benevento**
Premio Strega: literature prize

Good Friday procession on Procida

- **Ischia**
  On the evening before the festival for St John the Baptist (San Giovanni Battista; 24 June), the 'Ndrezzata is performed, a kind of sword dance.

- **Nola**
  A traditional procession by the guild of master craftsmen, the Festa dei Gigli, is held on the last Sunday in June (►p.336).

- **Cava dei Tirreni**
  Disfida dei Trombonieri: history play held at the end of June

JUNE – SEPTEMBER

- **Capua, Caserta, San Leucio**
  Leuciana Festival end of June/ beginning of July: theatre, ballet, and concerts, as well as the traditional festival of silk weavers held during the last weekend in June, at San Leucio (the silk town)

- **Sessa Aurunca**
  Estate Sessana: concerts and a traditional tournament in historical dress

JULY

- **Vietri sul Mare**
  Chamber music concerts in the Villa Guariglia (June–July)

- **Caserta province**
  Teano Jazz, jazz festival, www.teano.org.

- **Baia**
  Opera and concerts in the Antiche Terme Romane (second half of July; www.infocampoflegrei.it)

- **Ischia**
  Sant'Anna-Fesival: procession and competition on rafts; fireworks in the evening

- **Naples**
  Madonna del Carmine on 16 July, with traditional music and the symbolic burning of the spire. Open-air festival with top-name rock stars from Naples, Italy and other countries, held at the Arena Mostra Oltremare

- **Sorrento**
  Procession of boats on first Sunday in July

JULY – AUGUST

Pompeii
Theatre in the historic venue

Procida
Maritime festival

Ravello
Festival Musicale, including Wagner concerts in the park at Villa Rufolo ► p.302

JULY – SEPTEMBER

Pompeii
Classical music at the Teatro Grande

AUGUST

Teggiano Jazz
Jazz festival in early August in Teggiano

Many towns
celebrate Assumption Day 14–15 August. The holiday resorts celebrate this highlight on the Italian religious calendar with folkloric festivals, fireworks and culinary delights.

Altavilla Irpina
Watermelon festival on 18 August

Marina di Camerota
Festival in honour of the myth of Aeneas's landing in Italy

Montevergine
'A juta a Montevergine: thousands of pilgrims meet for a big festival on the eve before 11 September, celebrating the Madonna di Montevergine.

SEPTEMBER

Many places
Ferragosto: Assumption Day (15 August) is the highlight of the Italian summer and a special day throughout Italy.

Caserta Vecchia
Theatre and ballet festival

Marina di Camerota
Le Notti del Mito: the grotto disco Il Ciclope celebrates the end of summer with an amazing party.

Naples
Pop festival; also Festa di San Gennaro, when the city's patron saint's birthday is celebrated with the blood miracle in the cathedral, on 19 September

Sessa Aurunca
Tournament held in medieval costume

SEPTEMBER – OCTOBER

In many places
wine festivals (Festa dell'uva) are held, including exhibitions, processions and feasting.

Avellino
Musica in Irpinia: intenational contemporary music

NOVEMBER – DECEMBER

Acerno
Chestnut festival with parade on horseback (palio)

Cava de'Tirreni
Olive oil festival (November)

Naples and many other towns
Nativity plays and Christmas crib exhibitions

Galdo (near Benevento)
Sausage and polenta festival in honour of Santo Bartolomeo

Food and Drink

Great variety

◄ Local features

In addition to restaurants (ristorante), there are simple eateries known as trattoria, osteria, pizzeria or tavola calda (= warm table). It is not customary to choose a table for yourself in Italian restaurants; diners wait instead for the waiter to show them to their place. A service (servizio) and/or a cover charge (coperto) will sometimes be added to the normal price of the food. Lay the tip on the plate for change separately from the amount on the bill. An important point: except in holiday resorts, many eateries are closed in **August**.

Eating habits

The Italian **breakfast** (prima colazione) often amounts to no more than a cappuccino (espresso with foamed milk), espresso or caffè (strong espresso) with pastries, for instance a small croissant (cornetto). However, hotels are usually geared to the habits of their guests and provide a more or less extensive breakfast buffet. **Lunch** (pranzo) normally consists of an antipasto (starter), primo (pasta, rice or soup), secondo (meat or fish) with vegetables (contorno) or salad (insalata). After that there is a choice between cheese (formaggio), a sweet dessert (dolce), ice cream (gelato) and fruit (frutta). An espresso rounds off the meal, sometimes in the form of a »corretto« (»corrected« with grappa, cognac amaro or sambuco).

- Expensive: over €35
- Moderate: €20–35
- Inexpensive: under €20

for a three-course meal without drinks

The **evening meal** (cena), with the same succession of courses as at midday, is seldom served before 7.30pm (for menus see ►Language).

Cucina italiana

History

According to the Larousse Gastronomique, the bible of French cooking, »Italian cuisine provides the true foundation for the art of cooking in all western European countries«. Its originators were the Romans, who not only took advantage of the abundance of ingredients growing in their own country, but also reworked the culinary artistry of many other countries. Even today, Italian cuisine serves up a very broad palette. In fact, there is no such thing as Italian cuisine. Rather, the cucina italiana is comprised of **regional cooking styles** and is merely a catch-all phrase for a huge variety of regional traditions. These variations depend a great deal on the products characteristic for the different rural environments, and Italians are very attached to their locally produced homemade food.

Campania

Campania's cuisine is like its people: open and uncomplicated. Its distinctive dishes include the huge variety of ever-crisp **pizzas**, and also spaghetti. The number and variety of **pasta** dishes is bewildering. A tiny selection includes fusilli alla napolitana (pasta and tomato sauce), spaghetti alle vongole (spaghetti with mussels), penne alla puttanesca (short pasta tubes with olives and capers) and vermicelli con pomodoro (thin spaghetti in a tomato sauce). Vegetables and cheese are compulsory items on the menu. Genuine **mozzarella** made of buffalo milk is common in northern Campania, between Capua and Sessa Aurunca, as well as in the plain around Paestum. **Fish** is another important ingredient. It is said that fish from the Bay of Naples tastes better because a certain type of algae infuses it with an iodine taste.

Sweets The selection of desserts and pastries (pasticcerie) is huge. Some of the most famous include: sfogliatelle (puff pastry filled with ricotta, candied fruit, vanilla and cinnamon); babà (light pastry dipped in orange water and rum); sciu (small pastry filled with cream and a caramel glaze); and torta caprese (with lots of chocolate and almonds).

Drinks Standard drinks served at all meals include wine (vino) and mineral water (acqua minerale; gassata if carbonated). Beer (birra) is served everywhere – the light Italian version, often along with foreign varieties (birra estera). German, Danish and Dutch beers can all be found. Common non-alcoholic drinks include orangeade (aranciata), lemonade (limonata) and freshly pressed fruit juices.

Wines Excellent **red wines** are once again being produced in Campania, one of the oldest wine-growing regions in Italy. The aglianico grape (especially in Avellino province) produces a full-bodied aromatic red wine. Other important and historic varieties incude aspirinio, biancolella, coda di volpe, falanghina, fiano, forastera, greco and piedrirosso. Only 3% of total production reaches the standard of DOC wines. Of these, the best-known red wine is the falerno del massico produced between Sessa Aurunca, Caserta and Benevento. A good quality **white wine** is made from the fiano grape grown in Avellino; and the Greco di tufo is a refreshing white wine to drink when young and well-chilled. The taurasi, on the other hand, is a heavy tannin-rich red wine from the eastern regions of Avellino. The wines grown on Mount Vesuvius are more for local consumption, as are those grown on Capri and Ischia, and in Cilento province. Locally famous Neapolitan wines include the white asprinio and the lacrimae Cristi (Christ's tears), a dessert wine that also comes from grapes grown on the volcano.

Producers ▸ The most famous wine producers are **Mastroberardino** from the Atripalda/Avellino region (taurasi, fiano, greco di tufo, and a few excel-

? DID YOU KNOW ...?

- The Margherita pizza was invented in 1889 using the national colours of green (basil), white (mozzarella) and red (tomatoes), to honour unified Italy's first queen.

lent table wines) and **Cantina Villa Matilde** from Cellole near Sessa Aurunca (both red and white falerno del massico). The Greco di Sant'Agata dei Goti produced by **Azienda Agricola Mustilli** enjoys a good reputation. This family enterprise between Caserta and Benevento also offers holiday accommodation; see www.mustilli.com). **Cantina D'Ambra Vini** from Ischia specialises in white wines, such as the biancolella, as well as various collector's red wines. The red wines produced by **Tenuta Montevetrano** in San Cipriano Picentino, near Salerno, are also highly prized, not least because of the small quantities produced. Table wines (vino da tavola) are served open, and come in carafes of one litre (un litro), half a litre (un mezzo litro) or a quarter of a litre (un quarto litro). High-quality wines are uncorked at the table.
Among the better-known **spirits** are **liqueurs** such as nocillo, made with walnuts, cinnamon, cloves and nutmeg. Another speciality is strega, from the province of Benevento. Also popular are centerbe, a herb liqueur from Montevergine, and limoncello, the sweet lemon liqueur from the Amalfi Coast.

Wine labels

The variety of different types of wine in Italy is rather confusing, but it also makes things interesting. The wines served by the carafe in simple restaurants are rarely of high quality. Labelled bottles are one step up, as Italian law distinguishes and controls labelled wines in three categories. Most of Campania's wines are table wines (VDT, vini da tavola), whose labels provide no information on grape varieties used, origin or year of production. The next step up are IGT wines, which do indicate the grape or source. The highest quality wines are the DOC wines from verified sources, but they only make up 2% of Italy's wine production.

Health

Pharmacies, medical care

Pharmacies (farmacia) can be recognized by a red or green cross on a white background. They are normally open Mon–Fri 9am–12.30pm and 4pm–7.30pm. When they are closed, they all display a notice giving the address of those chemists running an emergency service (farmacie di turno). **Emergency medical care** during the night (8pm–8am) and on public holidays is provided by the Guardia Medica notturna e festiva. Emergency doctors and first aid (pronto soccorso) are provided by hospitals (ospedali), but also, among others, by the White Cross (Croce Bianca), the Green Cross (Croce Verde) and the Red Cross (Croce Rossa Italiana), whose addresses are listed on the first pages of any public phone book (avantielenco). Dentists can also be found in the yellow pages of the phone book under the heading »medici dentisti«.

Information

IN AUSTRALIA

► **ENIT**
Level 4, 46 Market Street
Sydney NSW 2000
Tel. 02 92621666
Fax 02 92621677
Email:
italia@italiantourism.com.au

IN CANADA

► **ENIT**
175 Bloor Street E. – Suite 907
South Tower
Toronto M4W 3R8
Tel. 1 416 9254882
Fax 1 416 9254799
Email:
enitto@italiantourism.com

IN THE UK

► **ENIT**
(Italian state tourist board)
1, Princes Street
London W1B 2AY
Tel. 020 7408 1254
Fax 020 7399 3567
Email:
italy@italiantouristboard.co.uk

IN THE USA

► **ENIT**
630, Fifth Avenue – Suite 1565
New York NY 10111
Tel. 1 212 2455618
Fax 1 212 5869249
Email: enitny@italiantourism.com

12400, Wilshire Blvd. – Suite 550
Los Angeles CA 90025
Tel. 1 310 8201898
Fax 1 310 8206357
Email:
enitla@italiantourism.com

IN ITALY

► **ENIT (Ente Nazionale Italiano per il Turismo)**
Via Marghera 2–6
I-00185 Roma
Tel. 06 4 97 11
www.enit.it

► **Easy Italia**
ENIT service number:
Tel. 039 039 039
Daily from 9am until 10pm at local rates, also in English. Along with up to date travel tips there is help for any problem imaginable.

► **Assessorata Tourismo – Regione Campania**
Via Santa Lucia 81, 80132 Napoli
Tel. 08 17 96 29 01,
fax 08 17 64 82 80;
www.turismoregionecampania.it
www.in-campania.it
Addresses for the local tourist offices are given in the relevant chapters in »Sights from A to Z«.

EMBASSIES IN ITALY

► **Australian embassy in Rome**
Via Antonio Bosio 5
Tel. 06 85 27 21
www.italy.embassy.gov.au

► **British embassy in Rome**
Via XX Settembre 80A
Tel. 06 422 00 001
www.britishembassy.gov.uk

► **British consulate in Naples**
Via dei Mille, 40
80121 Napoli NA
Tel. (0039) 081 423 8911
E-mail Info.Naples@fco.gov.uk

- ▶ **Canadian embassy in Rome**
  Via Zara 30
  Tel. 06 44 59 81
  www.canada.it

- ▶ **Embassy of the Republic of Ireland in Rome**
  Piazza Campitelli 3
  Tel. 069 697 91 21
  www.ambasciata-irlanda.it

- ▶ **New Zealand embassy in Rome**
  Via Zara 28
  Tel. 06 441 71 71
  www.nzembassy.com

- ▶ **United States embassy in Rome**
  Via Vittorio Veneto 119
  Tel. 06 4 67 41
  www.usis.it

INTERNET

- ▶ **www.italiantouristboard.co.uk**
  www.italiantourism.com
  The official ENIT websites provide a wealth of information on accommodation, museums, and travel within Italy, as well as a calendar of events and the latest news.

- ▶ **www.comune.napoli.it**
  www.napolinapoli.com
  www.inaples.it
  Lots of information for Naples and the events programme *Qui Napoli* available as a download

- ▶ **www.portanapoli.com**
  www.provincia.salerno.it
  Information on the Amalfi Coast and Salerno

- ▶ **www.welcometoitaly.com**
  Descriptions in English of museums and accommodation

- ▶ **www.beniculturali.it**
  www.museionline.it
  Plenty of information in Italian on museums, cultural events and exhibitions

- ▶ **www.italiamia.com**
  A good source of links and background information

Language

Intonation

The accent is normally on the second-to-last syllable. When it is on the last syllable, an accent is used, as with città. Accents are also used to indicate other exceptions.

◀ Pronunciation

c, cc before »e, i« similar to »ch«, as in church. For example, dieci. Otherwise, it is hard, as in car or cow.
ch, cch as in car.
g, gg before »e, i« like »g« in general. Example: gente
gl like »lli« in million. Example: figlio
sc before »e, i« like »sh« in shut. Example: uscita
sch like »sk« in skip. Example: Ischia
sci before »a, o, u« like the English »sh«. Example: lasciare
z like »ds« in pads.

Concise Italian Language Guide

Numbers

zero	0
uno	1
due	2
tre	3
quattro	4
cinque	5
sei	6
sette	7
otto	8
nove	9
dieci	10
undici	11
dodici	12
tredici	13
quattordici	14
quindici	15
sedici	16
diciassette	17
diciotto	18
diciannove	19
venti	20
ventuno	21
ventidue	22
trenta	30
quaranta	40
cinquanta	50
sessanta	60
settanta	70
ottanta	80
novanta	90
cento	100
centouno	101
mille	1000
duemille	2000
diecimila	10 000
un quarto	1/4
un mezzo	1/2

At a glance/Travelling

Sì/No	Yes/No
Per favore/Grazie	Please/Thank you
Non c'è di che	It's a pleasure
Scusi!/Scusa!	Excuse me!
Come dice?	Pardon?
Quanto costa?	How much is it?
lo scontrino	bill
una ricevuta	receipt
il conto	bill
a sinistra/a destra/diritto	left/right/straight ahead
vicino/lontano	near/far
Quanti chilometri sono?	How far is it (in kilometres)?
Vorrei noleggiare ...	I want to rent…
... una macchina/una bicicletta	... a car/a bicycle
... una barca	... a boat
Scusi, dov'è ...?	Excuse me, where is ...?
la prossima fermata	the next stop?
la stazione centrale	the main railway station?
la metro(politana)	the underground?
l'aeroporto	the airport?
il bagno	the toilet?

Ravello's Villa Cimbrone: the »Terrace of Infinity«

all'albergo	the hotel?
Ho un guasto.	My car has broken down.
Mi potrebbe mandare un carro-attrezzi?	Would you send me a breakdown vehicle?
Scusi, c'è un'officina qui?	Is there a garage here?
Dov'è la prossima stazione di servizio?	Where is the next petrol station?
benzina normale	leaded petrol
super/gasolio	super/diesel
deviazione/senso unico	diversion/one-way street
sbarrato	closed
rallentare	drive slowly
tutti direzioni	all destinations
zona di silenzio	no car horns
zona tutelata inizio	start of the no-parking zone
Aiuto!/Attenzione	Help!/Watch out!
Chiami subito ...	Please quickly call ...
... un'autoambulanza/la polizia	... an ambulance/the police

Accommodation

Scusi, potrebbe consigliarmi ...?	Can you recommend
... un albergo/una pensione	... a hotel/a guest house?
Ho prenotato una camera.	I have a room reservation.
È libera ...?	Do you still have ...?

... una singola/una doppia	... a single room/a double room
... con doccia/bagno	... with shower/bath
... per una notte/settimana	... for one night/for a week?
... con vista sul mare	... with sea view
Quanto costa la camera ...?	How much is the room ...?
... con la prima colazione?	... with breakfast?
... a mezza pensione?	... with half board?

At the doctor's or the chemist

Mi può consigliare un buon medico?	Can you recommend a good doctor?
Mi può dare una medicina per ...	Please give me medication for ...
Soffro di diarrea.	I have diarrhoea.
Ho mal di pancia/testa.	I have a stomach ache/headache.
... mal di gola/denti	... a sore throat/toothache
... influenza/tosse/la febbre	... flu/cough/temperature
... scottatura solare	... sunburn

Menu

prima colazione	**Breakfast**
caffè espresso/caffè macchiato	small black coffee/ with a little milk
latte macchiato	small coffee with lots of milk
caffè latte	coffee with milk
caffè decaffeinato	decaffeinated coffee
cappuccino	coffee with foamed milk
tè al latte/al limone	tea with milk/lemon
tè alla menta/alla frutta	peppermint/fruit tea
cioccolata	hot chocolate
pane/panino/pane tostato	bread/bread roll/toast
burro	butter
salame/prosciutto	sausage/ham
miele/marmellata	honey/jam
iogurt	yoghurt

antipasti	**Starters**
affettato misto	mixed cold meats
anguilla affumicata	smoked eel
melone e prosciutto	melon with ham
vitello tonnato	cold roast veal with tunafish sauce

primi piatti	**Pasta and rice dishes, soups**
pasta/fettuccine, tagliatelle	pasta

gnocchi	small potato dumplings
polenta (alla valdostana)	cornmeal porridge (with cheese)
vermicelli	thread noodles
minestrone	thick vegetable soup
pastina in brodo	meat broth with thin noodles
zuppa di pesce	fish soup

carni e pesce	**Meat and fish**
agnello	lamb
ai ferri/alla griglia	from the grill
aragosta	crayfish
brasato	roast meat
coniglio	rabbit
cozze/vongole	mussels/clams
fegato	liver
fritto di pesce	baked fish
gambero, granchio	prawns
maiale	pork
manzo/bue	beef
pesce spada	swordfish
pollo	chicken
rognoni	kidneys
salmone	salmon
scampi fritti	fried shrimps
sogliola	sole
tonno	tuna
trota	trout
vitello	veal

verdura	**Vegetables**
asparagi	asparagus
carciofi	artichokes
carote	carrots
cavalfiore	cabbage
cicoria belga	chicory
cipolle	onions
fagioli/fagiolini	white beans/green beans
finocchi	fennel
funghi	mushrooms
insalata mista/verde	mixed/green salad
lenticchie	lentils
melanzane	aubergines
patate/patatine fritte	potatoes/chips
peperoni	green pepper
pomodori	tomatoes

spinaci	spinach
zucca	pumpkin

formaggi	**Cheese**
parmigiano	Parmesan cheese
pecorino	sheep's cheese
ricotta	cream cheese

dolci e frutta	**Desserts and fruit**
cassata	slice of ice cream roll with candied fruit
coppa assortita	mixed ice cream
coppa con panna	ice cream with whipped cream
tirami su	dessert with mascarpone cream
zabaione	egg white dessert
zuppa inglese	biscuit drenched in liqueur with vanilla cream

bevande	**Drinks**
acqua minerale	mineral water
aranciata	orangeade
bibita	non-alcoholic drink
bicchiere	glass
birra scura/chiara/alla spina	dark beer/light beer/draught beer
birra senza alcool	alcohol-free beer
bottiglia	bottle
con ghiaccio	with ice
digestivo	digestif
gassata/con gas	carbonated
liscia/senza gas	non-carbonated
secco	dry
spumante	sparkling wine
succo	fruit juice
vino bianco/rosato/rosso	white/rosé/red
vino della casa	house wine

Literature

Fiction **Giambattista Basile**, *The Tale of Tales*, Wayne State Univ. Press, 2006 – A collection of earthy and humorous Neapolitan fairy tales for children.

Truman Capote, *The Dogs Bark* – Capote's short story »Ischia« describes the magic of that island in 1949.

Ann Cornelisen, *Torregreca: Life, Death, and Miracles in a Southern Italian Village*, Steerforth Italia, 1998 – Arriving in an impoverished region south of Naples in 1959 to establish a nursery school, a single, young Protestant woman quickly becomes the object of gossip. A beautifully written social document on Cornelisen's adopted home and its people.

Luciano De Crescenzo, *Thus Spake Bellavista*, Picador, 1989 – A classic of Neapolitan literature and still worth reading, despite the clichés.

Dominique Fernandez, *Porporino: Or the Secrets of Naples*, Morrow, 1976 – Colourful novel set in the 18th-century era of the castrati.

Robert Harris, *Pompeii: A Novel*, Random House Trade Paperbacks 2005 – A fine historical novel set in the shadow of Mount Vesuvius, whose eruption is imminent. This exciting page-turner also features some well-researched volcanology.

Robert Harris, *Pompeii*, Arrow 2004 – Top class thriller.

Dan Hofstadter, *Falling Palace: A Romance of Naples*, Vintage, 2006 – This personal story focusing on the beauty of the city was highly praised by the critics.

Giuseppe Tomasi di Lampedusa, *The Leopard*, Panther paperback, 1996 – No one else has described the collapse of Bourbon rule in southern Italy better than this author. His novel was turned into a movie by Visconti, in 1963, with Burt Lancaster in the lead role.

Norman Lewis, *Naples '44 – An Intelligence Officer in the Italian Labyrinth*, Carroll & Graf, 2005 – A war diary that manages to be as amusing as it is shattering. It is the harsh truth of one man's year in wartime Naples.

Curzio Malaparte, *The Skin*, Picador, 1988 – A bitter-sweet portrait of Naples in the 1940s and a brilliant declaration of love to the city and its inhabitants.

Susan Sontag, *The Volcano Lover: A Romance*, Penguin, 2009 – A historical novel set in 19th-century Naples with Lord Hamilton as protagonist.

Baedeker TIP

The Sopranos

The American TV series »The Sopranos« is one of the most interesting series of recent times. The storyline follows two generations of a »normal« Italian immigrant family going about their criminal business and keeping up with their Neapolitan roots. The successful series offers a scrupulously observed portrait of organized crime (2005, Warner Home Video, 6 DVDs).

Non-fiction

Joanne Berry, *The Complete Pompeii*, Thames & Hudson 2007 – This well-illustrated guide to the ancient town is excellent.

Raffaele La Capria, *Capri and No Longer Capri*, Nation Books 2001 – A lovely piece of travel writing on Capri.

Joseph Jay Deiss, *Herculaneum: Italy's Buried Treasure*, Getty Publications 1989 – This vivid portrayal of life in Pompeii's sister city includes a detailed account of the ancient Villa dei Papiri, on which the present Getty Museum in Malibu is modeled.

Anthony Everitt, *Augustus: The Life of Rome's First Emperor*, Random House 2006 – A lively retelling of the life of the Roman emperor who ruled from Capri.

Johann Wolfgang von Goethe, *Italian Journey*, Penguin Classics, 2004 – Goethe's travel journal marks the beginning of the German fascination with Italy.

Shirley Hazzard, *Greene on Capri: A Memoir*, Farrar, Straus and Giroux 2001 – Not only an insight into the celebrated author's personality but also a portrayal of the island of Capri and the myriad of characters who spent time there.

Shirley Hazzard, Francis Steegmuller, *The Ancient Shore: Dispatches from Naples*, Chicago, 2009 – A collection of the best of Hazzard's writings on Naples, along with a *New Yorker* essay by her late husband, Francis Steegmuller.

Roberto Saviano, *Gomorrah: Italy's Other Mafia*, Pan, 2008 – A journey through the realms of the Camorra's economic and power structures.

Alwyn Scarth, *Vesuvius: A Biography*, Princeton University Press, 2009 – These accounts of each of the volcano's known eruptions are not only of interest to geologists, they are also a good read for the layman.

Oliver Taplin, *Greek Fire*, Cape, 1990 – This book shows to what extent Greek antiquity still influences the present.

Food and drink

Anna Teresa Callen, *My Love for Naples: The Food, the History, the Life*, Hippocrene Books 2007 – An informative recipe book incorporating history and a real passion for Naples.

Nikko Amandonico, Amanda Borri, *La Pizza: The True Story from Naples*, Mitchell Beazley 2005 – Food lovers' account of the history of pizza and Naples, with photographs and recipes

Media

Radio and television

The public service radio station Radiotelevisione Italiana (RAI) runs several national radio and TV channels (RAI Uno, Due, Tre). In addition, there are numerous private and commercial radio and TV companies. Hotels catering to an international clientele normally offer cable TV.

Newspapers

Italy's major newspaper is *La Repubblica* (liberal), followed by *Corriere della Sera* (conservative). Important regional papers are *Il Mattino* and *Il Giornale di Napoli*. ***Qui Napoli***, a monthly magazine in English and Italian, is very informative for visitors to Naples. It is available free in many hotels and at tourist information offices. Major international news publications in English can also be found in Naples and the larger holiday resorts.

Money

Euro

Since 2002 the euro has been the official currency of Italy.

Currency regulations

Citizens of EU members countries may import to and export from Italy unlimited amounts in euros.

Banks

As a rule banks are open Mon–Fri 8.30am–1pm and 2.30pm/3pm–4.30pm. On days before holidays (prefestivi) the banks close at 11.20am.

◄ ATM machines, debit cards

Cash is available at ATM machines round the clock by using credit and debit cards with a PIN. Credit cards have limits.

◄ Loss

Loss of a card must be reported immediately.

◄ Credit cards

Most international credit cards are accepted by banks, hotels, restaurants, car rentals and many shops. While Visa and Eurocard are common, American Express and Diners Club are not accepted everywhere.

Receipts

In Italy customers are required to request and keep a receipt (ricevuta fiscale or scontrino). It can happen that the tax authorities (guardia della finanza) will ask to see receipts.

i EXCHANGE RATES

- 1 € = 1.34 US$
  1 US$ = 0.74 €
  1 £ = 1.18 €
  1 € = 0.84 £

CONTACT DETAILS FOR CREDIT CARDS

In the event of lost bank or credit cards you can contact the following numbers in UK and USA (phone numbers when dialling from Italy):

- **Eurocard/MasterCard**
  Tel. 001 / 636 7227 111
- **Visa**
  Tel. 001 / 410 581 336
- **American Express UK**
  Tel. 0044 / 1273 696 933
- **American Express USA**
  Tel. 001 / 800 528 4800
- **Diners Club UK**
  Tel. 0044 / 1252 513 500
- **Diners Club USA**
  Tel. 001 / 303 799 9000

Have the bank sort code, account number and card number as well as the expiry date ready.

The following numbers of UK banks (dialling from Italy) can be used to report and stop lost or stolen bank and credit cards issued by those banks:

- **HSBC**
  Tel. 0044 / 1442 422 929
- **Barclaycard**
  Tel. 0044 / 1604 230 230
- **NatWest**
  Tel. 0044 / 142 370 0545
- **Lloyds TSB**
  Tel. 0044 / 1702 278 270

Opening Hours

Museums

Museum opening times **vary according to season**. Opening times for the larger establishments can be found in the relevant chapters under »Sights from A to Z«. For the most up-to-date information, check with the local **tourist office**. In general, museums are closed on Mondays (the Archaeological Museum in Naples closes on Tuesdays). On all other days, museums are normally open 9am–1pm, and some are open 3pm/4pm–7pm. The last admission is often 30 minutes before closing time.

Churches

The larger churches are normally open 7am–noon/12.30pm; some also open in the afternoon from 4pm–7.30pm. Many churches are only open during religious services.

Excavation sites

Archaeological sites are usually open daily, from 9am until sunset.

More information

Banks ►Money, post offices ►Post · Communications, shops ►Shopping, petrol stations ►Transport.

Post · Communications

Italian post offices only handle letters and packages (Mon–Fri 8.30am–1.30pm, Sat 8.30am–noon); **stamps** (francobolli) can also be purchased in tobacconists (tabacchi). Sending a postcard or letter within the EU currently costs €0.65. Post offices

Almost all public telephones function exclusively with telephone cards (scheda or carta telefonica), which can be purchased in bars, tobacconists and newsagents. What were once **area codes, including the zero, are now an ordinary part of Italian phone numbers.**. The exceptions to this rule are the emergency phone numbers, as well as commercial and mobile phone numbers. Numbers beginning with 800 are toll-free. Telephoning

The use of mobile telephones from other countries is generally problem-free in Italy. The two most frequented telephone networks are Telecom Italia Mobile (number 2 22 01) and Omnitel Pronto Italia (number 2 22 10). If you spend much time in Italy, it may be worth buying a prepaid chip of Telecom Italia Mobile (TIM). ◂ Mobile phones

AREA CODES AND INFORMATION

TELEPHONE CODES

▸ **From other countries to Italy:**
+39 (followed by the old area codes including the zero)

▸ **From Italy**
to other countries: 00 followed by the country code, e.g.
to Australia: tel. 0061
to the Republic of Ireland: Tel. 00353
to the UK: 0044
to the USA: 001

▸ **Directory enquiries**
Inside Italy tel. 412
Outside Italy tel. 176

Prices and Discounts

EU citizens under the age of 18 or over the age of 65 frequently enjoy free admission to tourist sites. 18–25-year-olds are also advised to ask for student or youth reductions. Entrance fees

A useful means to saving money is the Campania Artecard, a **tourist card** valid between 3 and 7 days. Depending on the combination chosen, it is possible to visit almost all museums and excavation sites in Naples and in the region of Campania either for free or for half price. The card is available at tourist offices, railway stations, airports, in museums and at many hotels (www.campaniaartecard.it). ◂ Campania Artecard

WHAT DOES IT COST?

Three-course meal	Simple meal	Double room	Cup of coffee	Petrol per litre
from €20	from €8	from €60	€1–2	approx. €1.40

Shopping

Coral, crib figures and other souvenirs

Every town and village in Campania has its own traditional handicrafts. A speciality in **Naples** is the porcelain from Capodimonte, as well as traditional figurines made of plaster and clay for Christmas cribs. Modern personalities are also portrayed as small figures. In Torre del Greco, jewellery is made of **coral**, precious stones and seashells. Sorrento is known for its **inlaid wood craftwork**, where artisans create small pieces of furniture and other items using this highly skilled decorative technique. Bastions of **ceramic craftwork** include Vietri sul Mare (Amalfi Coast), Agropoli (Cilento) and Ischia, as well as inland Cerreto Sannita, San Lorenzello, Caserta and Cassanno di Sessa Aurunca. Products range from vases and crockery to majolica tiles. Cava de'Tirreni specializes in ceramic tiles.

A centuries-old tradition in Amalfi and Tramonti is the production of **hand-made paper**. Positano is renowned for its light and colourful **summer fashions**, as well as for hand-made sandals. **Silk** is still woven in San Leucio (near Caserta), occasionally still using 18th-century weaving stools. Imaginative **perfumes** are made from local flower essences on the island of Capri.

? DID YOU KNOW ...?

- Beware of buying fake designer goods as the sale of imitation commercial goods is prohibited in Italy. Heavy fines are imposed on both vendors and buyers – and that includes tourists.

Antiques markets

Several places have antiques markets where, with a bit of luck, one or two interesting souvenirs can be found. Markets in Naples include the one on Via Caracciolo, on the 3rd and 4th weekend of the month; and in Salerno on the Piazza Alfano, every 2nd weekend of the month. A flea market can also be found every Sunday on the Corso Malta in Naples.

Culinary souvenirs

Culinary souvenirs are popular. Typical regional products include pasta from Torre Annunziata, Cicciano and Gragnano; high-grade olive oil from the hills of Salerno and from the Sorrentine peninsula;

the unique mozzarella di bufala from Agerola, Mondragone, Vico Equense, Castel Volturno, Battipaglia and Paestum; sweets; (vacuum packed) cheese specialites from the Monti Lattari; and Campanian wines and other delights, such as **limoncello** or nocino (lemon or walnut liqueur), which taste just as good back home.

Shop opening times are normally Mon–Sat 8am/9.30am– 1.30pm and 4.30pm–7.30pm/8pm; many shops are closed on Monday morning, except food stores (alimentri). In holiday resorts, opening times are geared according to the season.

Limoncello also tastes good as a digestif liqueur back home

Sport and Outdoors

Sporting nation

Italy is an enthusiastic sporting nation, especially when it comes to football. Almost all the larger hotels in the seaside resorts have **tennis courts** that can also be used by non-residents. The primary activities on the coast are swimming, surfing, and other water sports, though football pitches and (beach) volleyball courts can also be found. Information on many other sporting provisions can be found through special events organizers and local tourist offices.

Cycling

The best options for both relaxed cycle touring and extreme mountain biking can be found in Cilento. Bikes are available from almost all hotels and rural tourism accommodation. Information is available from regional and local tourist offices, as well as from organizations such as Touring Club Italiano (TCI, Corso Italia 10, 20122 Milano, tel. 0 28 52 63 04).

Hiking

Campania offers a wealth of hiking regions, including the islands of Capri and Ischia (with Monte Epomeo), the Amalfi Coast (with its ancient footpaths and donkey trails), the Sorrentine peninsula (with Monte Lattari and Monte Faito, as well as the thermal springs of Castellammare di Stabia), and the province of Cilento, where the sea and the mountains lie in close proximity. Guides to hiking routes are published by the tourist office. Maps with hiking paths are published by the Club Alpino Italiano as well as foreign publishers.

Horse-riding

The Cilento region is an excellent place for wonderful horse-riding excursions. Some rural tourism outfits keep horses for their customers. Information is available from local tourist offices.

Sailing, surfing and diving

There are sailing, surfing and diving schools all along the coast and on the islands. The waters around Ischia and Capri are especially popular among divers, as are those of the Sorrentine peninsula and of the Cilento coast with its many grottoes (near Marina di Camerota, Palinuro and the Palinuro peninsula). Diving among the remains of Roman villas at Baia to the west of Naples is a unique experience. Many places have boat rentals, but a sailing or motor-boat licence is mandatory. The gorges of the Calore river in Cilento are good for kayaking.

Fishing ►

No permits are required for fishing at sea. Fishing in lakes and rivers does require a permit, which can be purchased at the relevant administrative offices (check with the local tourist board) or from the Federazione Italiana Pesca Sportiva (tel. 0 27 74 01).

Time

Italy is in the central European time zone (CET), one hour ahead of Greenwich Mean Time. For the summer months from the end of March to the end of October European Summer Time is used (CEST = CET+1 hour).

Transport

By Car

Motorway tolls

A toll is normally charged for the use of motorways in France, Austria, Switzerland and Italy. In France it can be paid either in cash or by credit card (but not with a Maestro card) at the »CB« counter. The so-called **»vignettes«** for Austrian and Swiss motorways are available from tobacconists, post offices and local automobile clubs, and automobile clubs can supply them in other countries. They are also sold at petrol stations near the border crossings. In Italy, motorway (autostrada) tolls (pedaggio) can be paid in cash, by credit card or with a Viacard. The Viacard is obtained from automobile clubs, ACI offices at the border crossings, at motorway toll stations (»Punto Blu«), in tabacchi, and at motor-

i Speed limits

- Within urban areas, cars, motorbikes and mobile homes up to 3.5 t: 50kmh/31mph; outside urban areas, the speed limit is 90kmh/56mph on country roads and 110kmh/69mph on dual carriageways; the maximum speed limit on motorways (autostrada) is 130kmh/81mph

	Amalfi	Aversa	Benevento	Capua	Caserta	Cumae	Herculaneum	Naples	Paestum	Pompeii	Pozzuoli	Salerno	Sorrento
Amalfi	-	85	96	103	100	90	56	69	74	39	84	25	41
Aversa	85	-	101	17	19	26	32	17	122	45	25	74	67
Benevento	96	101	-	114	97	115	98	97	116	100	110	74	129
Capua	103	17	105	-	13	47	44	49	126	57	45	84	84
Caserta	100	19	97	13	-	45	36	20	120	62	44	90	80
Cumae	90	26	115	47	45	-	30	18	128	49	6	78	71
Herculaneum	56	32	98	44	36	30	-	9	94	10	25	45	40
Naples	69	17	97	49	20	18	9	-	116	28	15	57	50
Paestum	74	122	118	137	120	128	94	116	-	78	124	37	106
Pompeii	39	45	100	57	62	49	10	28	78	-	43	29	28
Pozzuoli	84	25	110	45	44	6	25	15	124	43	-	72	65
Salerno	25	74	74	84	90	78	45	57	37	29	72	-	66
Sorrento	41	67	129	84	80	71	40	50	106	28	65	66	-

way services and petrol stations. (Information of the condition of roads and costs of tolls are available at www.auto strada.it.)

Petrol stations
◄ Opening hours

Petrol stations are usually open 7am–noon and 2pm–8pm; motorway petrol stations are open 24 hours a day. At weekends, during lunch breaks, and at night, many petrol stations only offer self-service.

Traffic violations incur very heavy fines in Italy. Carrying petrol in a spare canister is prohibited. Traffic on the major road always has **right of way**. The relevant sign is a white or yellow diamond shape with red or black-and-white lining. The general rule is that traffic coming from the right has right of way. On mountain roads, the traffic coming uphill has right of way. Trains always have right of way. The **blood alcohol limit (BAC)** is 0.05%.

Helmets are mandatory for motorbikes over 50cc. **Dipped headlights** must be used outside urban areas, even in daylight. Note that **during rain**, the speed limit on motorways drops to 110kmh/69mph. **Luminous waistcoats** must be carried in all vehicles in Italy, for use during vehicle breakdowns. Private towing on motorways is prohibited. In case of a breakdown, foreign vehicle and motorbike users are towed to the nearest workshop by the Automobile Club d'Italia (ACI). Should your car be written off after an accident, contact Italian customs authorities to ensure you are not charged import tax on the vehicle.

◄ Vehicle breakdowns

IMPORTANT ADDRESSES

RAIL

Trains in Italy

The Rail Europe Travel Centre in London can give details on rail services in Italy (►p.69).
The Italian state railways provide information under the heading of Trenitalia, www.trenitalia.com (►p.69).

Suburban trains for Naples

Ideal for day trips, *tickets* can be purchased at station ticket booths or in any FS office with the Trenitalia logo. Note: tickets must be validated prior to travel by inserting them into the yellow machines on platforms.
The *Circumvesuviana* travels from Naples (underground railway station at Corso Garibaldi; first stop is Piazza Garibaldi) via Pompeii, Herculaneum, Castellammare di Stabia and Vico Equense to Sorrento.
Tel. 08 17 72 24 44; www.vesuviana.it. The *F.S. Cumana* and *F.S. Circumflegrea* lines, which join at Torregaveta, connect Naples (Stazione Monte Santo) to its western suburbs, including Pozzuoli, Baia, and Cumae. Tel. 08 17 35 41 11; www.sepsa.it

Metrocampania Nord-Est covers the routes of Naples-Caserta-Piedimonte Matese, Naples-Benevento, and Naples-Aversa. Tel. 08 17 34 52 68; www.metrocampanianordest.it

BY BUS

In Naples

►Sights from A to Z, p.189

Outside Naples

Timetables can be checked on the internet at www.italybus.it and www.orariautobus.it. Most of the blue long-distance buses depart from the bus station at Piazza Garibaldi or from the airport at Capodichino:
SEPSA (tel. 08 15 42 97 84; www.sepsa.it) for the Campi Flegrei.
CTP (tel. 08 17 00 11 11; www.ctpn.it) for Aversa and Caserta.
SITA (tel. 08 15 52 21 76; www.sitabus.it) departs from Via G. Ferraris (southeast of Piazza Garibaldi) and from Piazza Immacolatella Vecchia (north of Stazione Marittima) for Pompeii, Salerno and Sorrento, via the Amalfi Coast.
Curreri (tel. 08 18 01 54 20; www.curreriviaggi.it) for Sorrento.

BY SHIP

A network of ferry routes (traghetti = ferries; aliscafi = hydrofoils) connects the towns, cities and islands of the Bay of Naples all

Circumvesuviana *Most Important Stations*

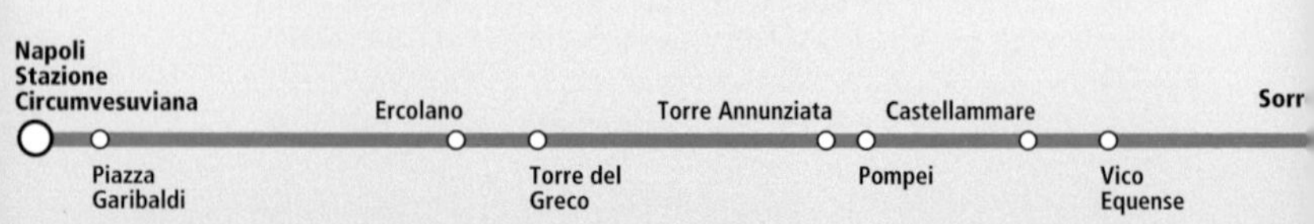

year round. The service is very crowded during high season and advance purchase of tickets is recommended.
Metro del Mare ►p.101

Selected addresses:
AliLauro (Molo Beverello, Mergellina)
www.alilauro.it
Caremar (Molo Beverello, Pozzuoli)
www.caremar.it
Metro del Mare (Molo Beverello, Mergellina)
www.metrodelmare.com
Navigazione Libera del Golfo (Mergellina)
www.navlib.it
SNAV (Mole Beverello, Mergellina)
www.snav.it

HIRE CARS

► **Avis**
Tel. 199 100 133
www.avis.com

► **Budget**
Tel. 800 472 33 25
www.budget-italy.com

► **Europcar**
Tel. 800 014 410
www.europcar.com

► **Hertz**
Tel. 019 213 112
www.hertz.com

VEHICLE BREAKDOWN ASSISTANCE

► **see p.97**

Parking

City centre car parking spots are a rarity. All parking restrictions (zona tutelata INIZIO = no-parking zone) should be scrupulously heeded. Curb stones painted white, or white parking outlines indicate free parking; yellow ones indicate parking spaces are limited to the exclusive use of certain drivers, such as the disabled; blue curb stones and parking outlines indicate parking fees are in operation. Parking tickets are either bought at the roadside machines or from the nearest tobacconists, in which case they are scratch cards (»gratta e sosta« = »scratch and park«).

Car theft

Rule number one when parking your car: never leave anything in the car, and certainly not anything valuable. The glove compartment should be emptied and left open and the car radio should be removed, if possible. Ideally, cars should be left in **secured car parks** or in a garage overnight. Should the worst happen, always report it to the police. This is essential for the processing of any insurance claim.

Hire cars

To rent a car in Italy, drivers must be at least 21 years old and have held their **national driving licence** for a minimum of one year; they also need a credit card. The international car hire firms have offices in all the larger cities and can take advance reservations from abroad, which often work out cheaper. Local car hire firms in Italy are found in the telephone book under »Noleggio«.

By Bus and Rail

Rail transport

Most of Italy's railway network is served by the state railway companies, such as Ferrovie dello Stato (FS) and **Trenitalia**. In addition, there are several private railway companies. Timetables are published by FS.

There are a variety of trains: regional slow trains, interregional express trains and Espresso trains, which are high-speed trains. Travel on Intercity, Eurocity, Eurostar and Pendolino (a luxury high-speed train) requires seat reservations and a supplement is also charged on the price of tickets.

The daily traffic along the Amalfi Coast: patience and driving skill is required

Single (andata) and return (andata e ritorno) **tickets** are sold for the first (prima) and second (seconda) class.

International rail tickets are valid for two months after the date of issue, and the journey can be interrupted as often as the traveller wishes. The validity of tickets bought in Italy is as follows: for distances up to 50km/30mi, one day; for greater distances, three days. Return tickets are issued only for journeys of up to 250km/150mi. On the day of travel the tickets must be stamped in one of the machines that are placed on the platforms.

Reductions ▶

There are ticket price reductions for those over 60 or under 26 years old, as well as for families.

By bus

Timetables ▶

Almost all towns and holiday resorts can be reached by public bus services. Timetables (orari) are published in the daily press and also displayed at tobacconists and at kiosks, where tickets can also normally be purchased. There is a severely restricted bus service on Sundays and public holidays.

By Boat

Travel around the Bay of Naples

A network of ferry routes connects the towns, cities and islands of the Bay of Naples all year round. The service is very crowded during high season and advance purchase of tickets is recommended. The latest timetables are published in *Qui Napoli*, the daily press, and on ferry company websites, and they are also available at tourist offices and at ports. Ferries (traghetti) and hydrofoils (aliscafi) depart from the Molo Beverello (Stazione Marittima), near the Piazza Municipio, for the islands of Capri and Procida, as well as for Sorrento. The ferries for Sicily and Tunisia also leave from there. Porto Mergellina only services routes to the islands and Sorrento using hydrofoils. The shortest sea route to Procida and Ischia is from Pozzuoli.

◄ Metro del Mare

The route between Bacoli to the north and Sapri to the south is served daily by the Metro del Mare in July and August; also at weekends only from April to June, and in September. Major stops enroute are Napoli Beverello, Sorrento, and Salerno.

When to Go

Climate and when to travel

The relatively warm Mediterranean and the high position of the sun ensure that Italy's coasts enjoy a very mild climate. The average summer temperature lies at 26°C/79°F; in winter it is 11°C/52°F. Most **rainfall** occurs between October and May. Mountainous regions suffer from landslides. Between December and the end of April, the highest mountains also have snow cover. In general, western Italy is damper than eastern Italy.

◄ Ideal time to travel

The **summer months**, between mid-June and mid-September, are dry and very warm, but temperatures rarely exceed 40°C/104°F. The most beautiful time of year for a journey to southern Italy is **spring** and **early summer** (mid-April–mid-June). That is when the macchia flowers and even the driest regions become green. Swimmers need to be tough, though, as the Mediterranean Sea warms up only very slowly. Another very nice time to travel is **late summer and early autumn** (end of August–beginning of October): although the flowers have usually already disappeared by then, the landscape offers beautiful autumn colours instead. July and August should be avoided if at all possible, as these are the traditional holiday months for Italians. Not only are these the hottest months of the year, but also the most crowded, since the Bay of Naples, its islands, and the Sorrentine peninsula are very popular holiday destinations for both Italians and foreigners. Many of the smaller hotels and most of the campsites are only open from the beginning or middle of April until the beginning of October. Many museums, restaurants and other tourist attractions are closed during the so-called **Ferragosto** (mid-August), unless they are major holiday destinations in themselves.

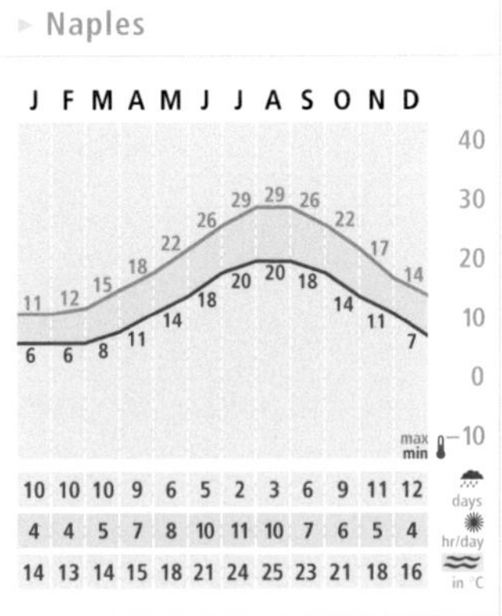

Tours

EXUBERANT NAPLES, PRETTY COUNTRY TOWNS, COASTAL ROUTES AND LONELY MOUNTAIN ROADS: SUGGESTIONS FOR EXPLORING THE BAY OF NAPLES

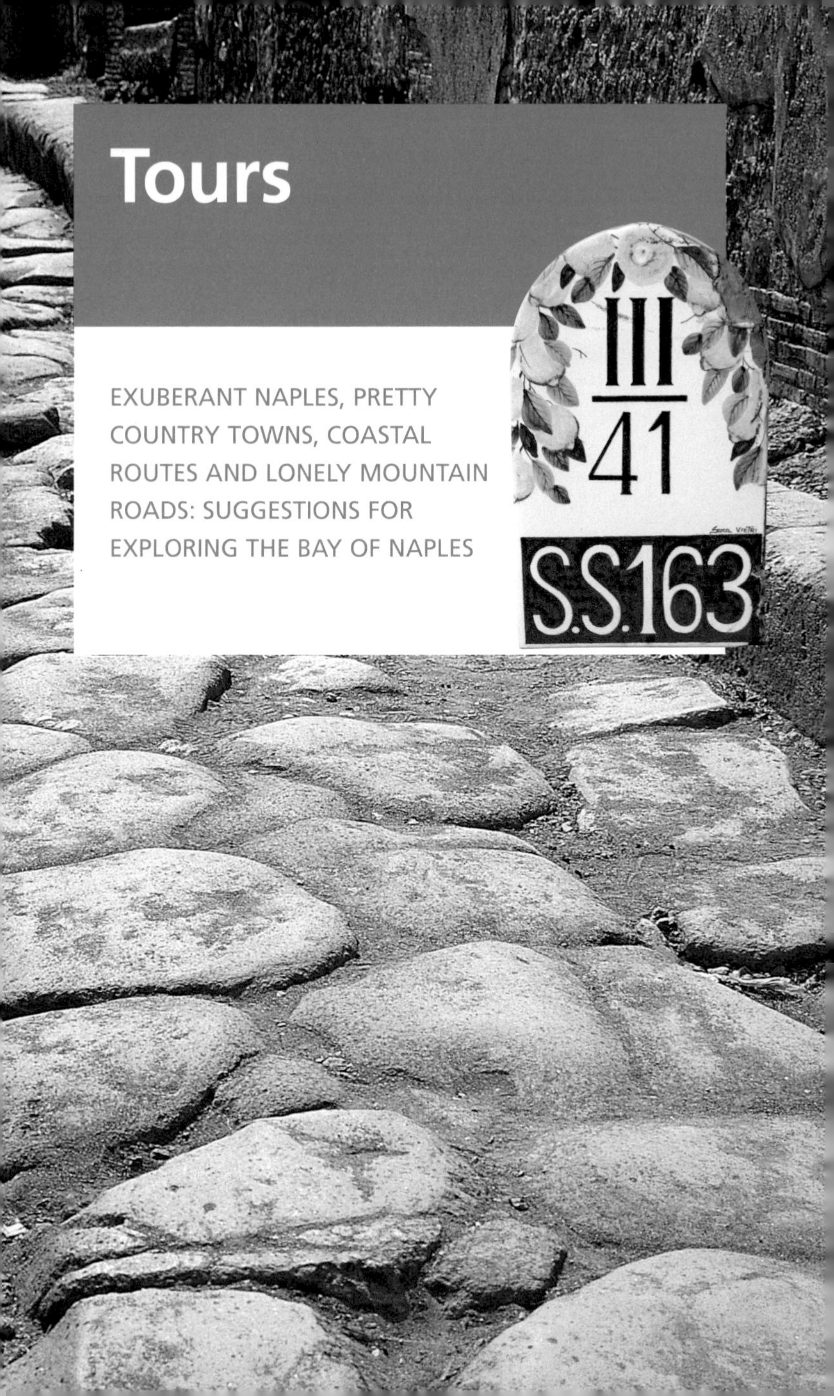

TOURS AROUND THE BAY OF NAPLES

Seven tours – four of them day trips out of Naples – explore the bay and its hinterland.

TOUR 1 **Caserta – the Italian Versailles**
Charles III's residence outside Naples is the largest building in Italy. Medieval Casertavecchia and Ferdinand V's utopia at San Leucio are also worth a detour. ▸ **page 107**

TOUR 2 **Into the Burning Fields**
The Phlegrean Fields, the legendary landscape of Greek and Roman antiquity, the amphitheatres at Rione Terre and Pozzuoli, and in particular the archaeological parks at Baia and Cumae are among the finest sights around the Bay of Naples. ▸ **page 108**

TOUR 3 **On the Miglia d'Oro to Herculaneum and Pompeii**
During the 17th and 18th centuries, it was Campania's most beautiful road. Today, it leads into the more complex environment of the Mezzogiorno, but the excavation sites at Herculaneum, Torre Annunziata and Pompeii are still world famous. ▸ **page 109**

TOUR 4 **The Amalfi Coast and the Sorrentine Peninsula**
This is a route of spectacular panoramic views and the archetypal images of romantic Italy embodied in places such as Sorrento, Positano and Amalfi. In addition, a bucolic landscape laced by hiking paths also offers breathtaking views. ▸ **page 110**

TOUR 5 **Through the Bay's Green Interior to Benevento**
The Campanian hinterland is off the beaten track for tourists. Away from busy Naples and the seaside resorts, the Monti del Sannio region of the Bay of Naples is not only a wonderful hiking area but also home to Benevento, one of the area's most beautiful towns. ▸ **page 112**

TOUR 6 **Into Magna Graecia to Paestum**
Time runs to a different tack in the land of the water buffalo, while the temples at Paestum have dominated a unique cultural landscape for over 2500 years. Cilento's beautiful beaches and green hilly interior are also very inviting. ▸ **page 113**

TOUR 7 **Island Idyll**
Fashionable Capri and the »green island« of Ischia are synonymous with beautiful scenery and bubbling hot springs. But the little island of Procida is also worth more than just a day trip. ▸ **page 114**

← Pavement in Pompeii over 2,000 years old

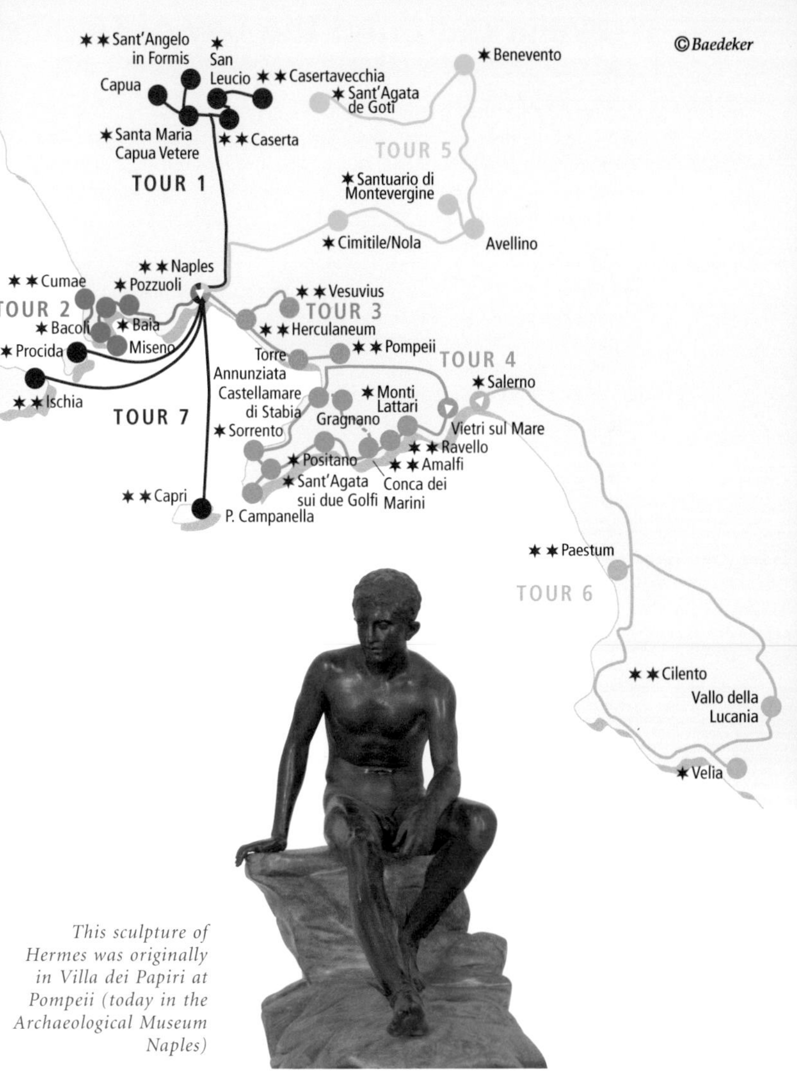

This sculpture of Hermes was originally in Villa dei Papiri at Pompeii (today in the Archaeological Museum Naples)

Travelling around the Bay of Naples

The Bay of Naples, a dream destination Despite Italy's artistic wealth and its lovely countryside, the Bay of Naples and its interior are a place apart. Magnificent coastal stretches combine with rural mountain landscapes, and it is not only Greeks and Romans who have made their mark on the region's impressive cultural heritage.

Options Those with a steady nerve who are keen to explore both the famous and the not-so-famous sights of Campania's busy and chaotic capital are well placed in Naples. Almost all destinations around the Bay of Naples can easily be reached by public transport from Naples. On the other hand, those looking for virtually untouched nature are better off in Benevento or the interior of Cilento. The combination of nature and sea is best on the islands in the bay and at the resorts along the Cilento coast.

Transport The question of transport depends very much on your travel expectations. A (hire) car is likely to be more of a hindrance than an ad-

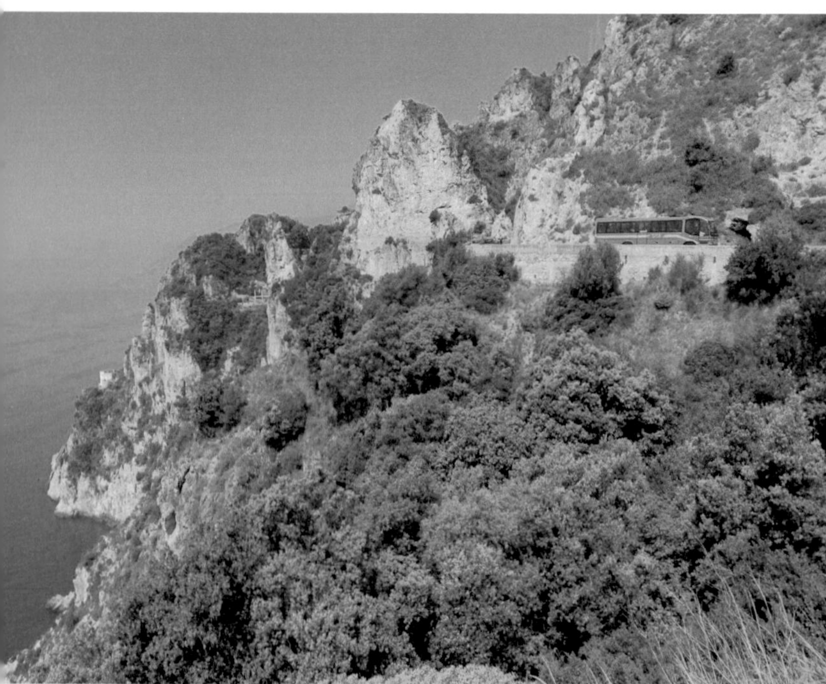

Travelling along the famous Amalfitana route

vantage if staying in Naples, on the islands, along the Amalfi Coast or on the Sorrentine peninsula: southern Italian driving style, the heavy traffic, and the frequently appalling state of the roads make driving a real challenge. It is also worth taking into consideration that most destinations can easily be reached by public transport. A car is really only an advantage for exploring the interior of Cilento, where it will enable better access.

Tour 1 Caserta – the Italian Versailles

Start and finish: Naples **Length:** 115km/72mi

Late Baroque magnificence in the Reggia di Caserta, medieval Casertavecchia and classical San Leucio provide variety on this tour. Those with extra time can continue to nearby Capua.

Departing from ❶✱✱ **Naples**, ❷✱✱ **Caserta** is reached by taking the A 1 in the direction of Rome (exit Caserta north). This is where King Charles III built his **Reggia**, the royal residence far beyond the gates of his capital. The impressive palace is worth a visit, and the extensive park and the intimate English Garden are also nice places for a stroll. From Caserta, the SS 87 leads to nearby ❸✱ **San Leucio**. The signage is excellent and a visit to the old silk factory and summer residence are worthwhile. From San Leucio, there is the option of a detour up to ✱✱ **Casertavecchia**, driving along a very serpentine road. The little town with its medieval centre is very popular with the people of Naples, especially at weekends. From Caserta, the SS 7 leads to ❹✱ **Santa Maria Capua Vetere** and its famous amphitheatre. ❺✱✱ **Sant'Angelo in Formis** is also not far away. Medieval ❻**Capua** is barely 5km/3mi from Santa Maria Capua Vetere, and is worth an excursion in its own right.

Tour 2 Into the Burning Fields

Start and finish: Naples **Length:** 105km/66mi

The Campi Flegrei, a legendary landscape of Greek and Roman antiquity, lie to the west of Naples. The amphitheatre and the Rione Terra at Pozzuoli and the archaeological parks at Baia and Cumae are among the finest sights around the Bay of Naples.

Setting off from ❶ ✶✶ **Naples**, take the the panoramic coastal road via **Mergellina** and **Posillipo** as far as Bagnoli. The industrial ruin of the former steel works is one of Naples' many unsolved problems, although the interactive natural sciences museum at **Città della Scienza** is worth visiting. Lively ❷ ✶ **Pozzuoli**, with the volcanic cone of **Solfatara**, its impressive amphitheatre and Roman Macellum is especially worth visiting at weekends, when the archaeological excavation site of Rione Terra is open to the public. The route follows the Gulf of Pozzuoli and continues in a great arc in the direction of Baia, an interesting drive that involves travelling through the **Arco Felice** on the ancient cobblestones of the Via Domitiana. This stretch of coastline, the most elegant section of Campania felix during the time of the Romans, is often referred to as the »Côte d'Azur« of antiquity. Most of the remains of the former spa in the Parco Archeologico di Baia have disappeared into the sea. The fortress above ❸ ✶ **Baia** offers unique views and has a very worthwhile archaeological museum. Immediately behind the fortress, the road descends to the pretty settlement of ❹ ✶ **Bacoli**. Only the amazing cisterns of the **Piscina mirabilis** and the **Cento camerelle** remain from Roman Bauli.

Spiaggia di Miliscola at ❺ **Miseno** is today's most popular bathing site for Neapolitans. An enchanting moated castle can be found on the small **Lago Miseno**, built by Carlo Vanvitelli. Nearby, **Monte di Procida** provides a sensational view onto the Bay of Naples and the islands of Ischia and Procida. Heading north, the road leads to ❻ ✶✶ **Cumae**. The beautifully located archaeological park there exhibits the remains of a Greek acropolis. The return drive to Naples is via the Tangenziale (toll). Nature lovers can stop off for lovely walks in

DON'T MISS

- The city of Naples
- The amphitheatre and remains of the Macellum: the ancient market of Puteoli, today Pozzuoli
- The beautifully located archaeological park at Cumae

complete solitude in the nature reserve inside the extinct Astroni crater (take the Agano exit, then follow the signs).

Tour 3 On the Miglio d'Oro to Herculaneum and Pompeii

Start and finish: Naples **Length:** 74km/46mi

Pompeii and Herculaneum are the Bay of Naples' world-famous archaeological attractions. Also included on the tour is Poppaea's villa at Torre Annunziata.

This tour is aimed at visitors with their own transport. The direct route to the archaeological sites on the Bay of Naples is via the A 3, which runs between Naples and Salerno. However, those who are also interested in the complexities of contemporary Naples should take the following route. It begins with the road that heads out of ❶ ✶✶ **Naples** in a southeasterly direction, beginning at the port as Via Reggia di Portici, after which it becomes Corso San Giovanni a Teduccio before turning into the SS 18. Faded 18th-century palaces can be spotted just beyond San Giorgio a Cremano, surrounded by even more derelict apartment blocks dating from the post-war years. The palaces are all that is left of the days when this route was better known as the **Miglio d'Oro**, Campania's most glorious route at the base of Mount Vesuvius. Now, this former Golden Mile displays all the misery that is southern Italy's reality today. In fact, it was only ruined by building speculation in the 20th century, when it fell victim to the mass demolition of the Neapolitan aristocracy's summer palaces and their parks to make way for new housing. What remains of the **Ville Vesuviane** houses offices and municipal departments, if they have not been converted into housing for the impoverished. In **Portici**, the main road leads straight through the courtyard of the former summer palace of the Bourbon kings, which is now used as an agricultural college. The Herculanese Museum, one of the most recent additions to the array of mu-

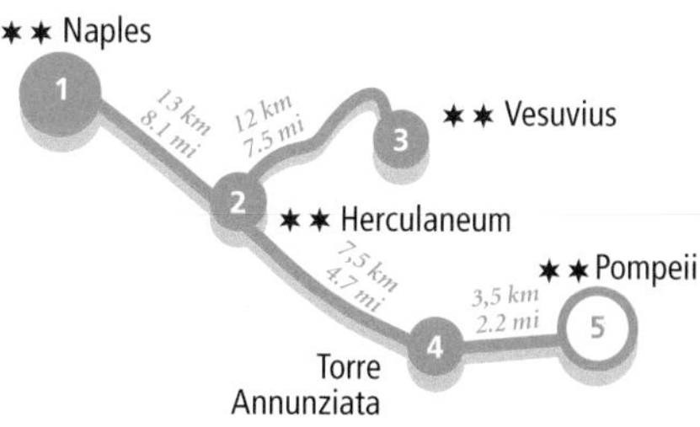

! Baedeker TIP

In the shadow of its famous rival

With around 3 million visitors annually, Pompeii is Italy's most visited destination dating from antiquity. Much less crowded, yet just as interesting, is the less famous Herculaneum.

seums on the Bay of Naples, is also here (►p.171). A short distance beyond Portici are the archaeological excavations of ❷ ✶✶ **Herculaneum**, as well as **Villa Campolieto**, which is one of the few Vesuvian villas to have been restored. There is a well-signposted road leading from Herculaneum up ❸ ✶✶ **Mount Vesuvius**, Naples' emblematic mountain. Continuing on the SS 18 through densely built-up areas, ❹**Torre Annunziata** is reached along with the imperial ✶ ✶ **Poppaea Villa**, the finest of all the ruined villas of antiquity on the Bay of Naples (follow the signs to Villa Oplontis). From there, follow the signs for Pompei Scavi on to the ancient city of ❺ ✶✶ **Pompeii**. The best return route is on the A 3, which connects Salerno with Naples, as traffic jams are common on the SS 18.

Tour 4 The Amalfi Coast and the Sorrentine Peninsula

Start and finish: Vietri sul Mare

Length: approx. 140km/160 km (87mi/100mi)

The SS 163 was blasted out of the rock along the steep coastal cliffs in the mid-19th century. Today, the Amalfi Coast or Costiera Amalfitana is among the most beautiful panoramic routes in Italy. The best way to enjoy these winding stretches of road is to entrust yourself to the skills of the local bus drivers: those who would prefer not to do without their own car will need expert driving skills and a great deal of patience. All efforts are rewarded by sensational views, though, and the SS 145 on the Sorrentine side is less narrow and serpentine.

❶**Vietri sul Mare** lies right on the ✶ ✶ **Costiera Amalfitana** (SS 163), and connects with several of the most beautiful places in southern

Positano's houses climb uphill between the sea and the mountains

Italy. Don't miss cliff-top ❷ ✶✶ **Ravello**, a highlight of any tour of the Amalfi Coast. ❸ ✶✶ **Amalfi**, the oldest of the former maritime republics, lies right by the sea, as does ❹ ✶ **Positano**, which was discovered by artists at the beginning of the 20th century. At ❺ ✶ **Sant'Agata sui due Golfi**, the SS 145 and then a series of smaller country roads lead into the southwestern tip of the ✶ **Penisola Sorrentina**. A lovely detour can be made to the viewing point at **Punta Campanella**, though the last stretch must be covered on foot. Park your car in the little village of Termini at the foot of Mount Costanzo (485m/1591ft). The SS 145 then continues via the legendary city of ❻ ✶ **Sorrento** and the pretty ✶ **Vico Equense** to ❼ **Castellammare di Stabia**. Its heyday as a seaside resort is long gone, but the ancient villas above the town are still worth a visit. To get there, follow the signs for Gragnano and then Scavi archeologici. The return drive is quickest via the A 3, which runs between Salerno and Naples. An alternative longer route is via Gragnano on the SS 366, the Strada Statale per Agérola, which crosses ✶ **Monti Lattari**. This stretch goes through virtually untouched nature and passes lonely hillside villages before rejoining the hustle and bustle of the Amalfi Coast at Conca dei Marini.

Tour 5 Through the Bay's Green Interior to Benevento

Start and finish: From Naples to Sant'-Agata de Goti **Length:** 150km/94mi

Campania's interior has hardly been touched by tourism and is ideal for the more adventurous traveller. Far from the madding crowd that is Naples and the seaside resorts along the coast, it is possible to go on wonderful walking tours in the Monti del Sannio, and the provincial capital of Benevento is also interesting.

The A 16 in the direction of Avellino is easily reached via the urban highway in 1 ✶✶ **Naples**, known as the Tangenziale. Those with a bit of extra time and an interest in early Christian history should visit the basilicas in 2 ✶ **Cimitile** near**Nola** (exit Nola). The restored historic centre of pleasant 3 **Avellino** is a nice place for a stroll. On the other hand, the serpentine road up to the ✶ **Santuario di Montevergine** (clear signage) is an absolute must. After Avellino, the SS 88 leads through the hilly landscape of the **Irpinia** region before reaching the provincial capital, 4 ✶ **Benevento**. The interior of Campania is ideal for pleasant excursions into the **Monti del Sannio**, which was the original settlement area of the pugnacious Samnites, who once caused Rome so much trouble. Northeast of Benevento, the birthplace of Italy's most important saint, **Padre Pio**, can be found at **Pietrelcina**. Halfway between Benevento and Caserta, you will come across the charming 5 ✶ **Sant'Agata de Goti**.

Tour 6 Into Magna Graecia to Paestum

Start and finish: From Salerno to Paestum

Length: 170km/106mi

Paestum, in southern Campania, is frequently the last stop on a journey to this region, though it is a shame to give it no more time than a day trip. The temples are really at their best at sunset, once all the tourist buses and day trippers have left. The Cilento countryside is also worth exploring.

At the Battipaglia exit on the A 3 heading out of ❶ ✶ **Salerno** begins the famous **SS 18**, which connects Naples with Calabria. The route leads to the ruins of ancient Poseidonia, through the flood plain of the Sele river. To the north of Paestum, reached via a clearly signposted road, lies the **Santuario di Hera Argiva** with its worthwhile museum.

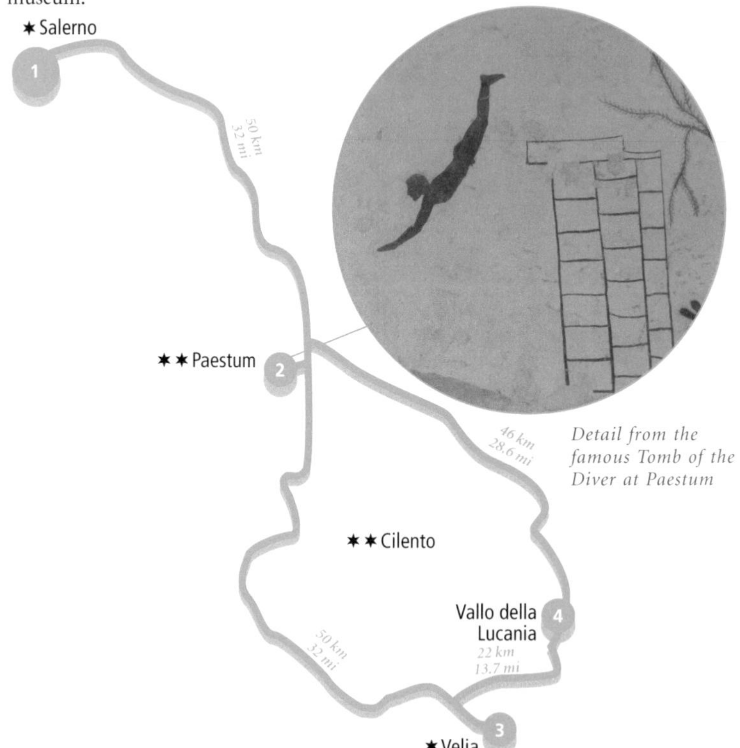

Detail from the famous Tomb of the Diver at Paestum

The hilltop town of Roccadaspiede in the Cilento

❷✶✶ **Paestum** itself is one of the most impressive archaeological parks in Campania and has no less than three temples. Meanwhile, the ✶✶ **Cilento** coast, with its sweeping beaches and reliably clean water, is a real paradise for bathers. Ancient ❸✶ **Velia** is also reached via the SS 18, or alternatively via the coastal 447. The town is only rarely visited by the tour-group buses. At ❹ **Vallo della Lucania**, the route turns back towards Paestum on the SS 18. Vallo is also a good base for a drive into the ✶ **Parco Nazionale del Cilento e Vallo di Diano**, a UNESCO natural heritage site. Independent travellers who enjoy getting off the beaten track away from mass tourism can explore the Cilento hinterland further, with its forests, rivers and unsullied mountain villages.

Tour 7 Island Idyll

Start and finish: Naples

Journey time: Depending on the point of departure and the vessel, about 1 hour

The decision on how long to stay on the islands will depend on individual schedules, but none (with the exception of Procida) can really be explored during a day trip.

The famous island of ✶ ✶ **Capri** is connected to Naples, Sorrento and Positano by regular ferry routes. The transportation of private vehicles is only permitted to local island inhabitants, but most people get around the island on foot, by bus or by taxi. Capri is dominated by nature and, away from the tourist towns of Capri and Anacapri, it makes for wonderful walking. Staying at least one night is highly recommended.

✶ ✶ **Ischia** can by reached by ferry from Naples or Pozzuoli. The bus services on the island are so well-run that visitors can really dispense with their own vehicles. The largest of the islands in the Bay of Naples, Ischia is famous for its numerous hot springs and well-tended beaches. The island is also a great place for nature, with plenty of beautiful walking to be done. Footpaths head into the bucolic mountain world of the island's interior from the busy little tourist spots of Ischia Porto, Forio and Casamicciola. Wonderful views over the bay can be enjoyed from the footpaths on Mount Epomeo.

Tiny ✶ **Procida** is the insider's tip for the Bay of Naples. This island should definitely not be visited with a car. The island's narrow roads require nerves of steel – and a distinctly Italian driving style. Without a car, Procida guarantees a romantic island experience that does not have to be shared with hordes of other visitors. The handful of beaches has room enough for everyone and only gets overly busy in August. For the classic Mediterranean seaside holiday, Procida is ideal, and it can even be a rewarding place for a quiet day trip.

CANTIERI DEL MEDITERRANEO

Sights from A to Z

THE VIBRANT METROPOLIS OF NAPLES IS THE STARTING POINT FOR A TRIP INTO THE PAST. FIND REST AND RELAXATION IN THE VERDANT HINTERLAND AND ON BEAUTIFUL BEACHES.

★★ Amalfi and the Amalfi Coast

F 5

Region: Campania
Altitude: Sea level
Province: Salerno
Population: 5500

Constructed in 1840, the 40km/25mi-long coast road between Vietri sul Mare and Positano is arguably one of the most beautiful panoramic roads in the world. Spectacular views make the drive a fantastic experience, but one which also requires a fair amount of concentration on the part of the driver. It was from here that the former maritime republic of Amalfi dominated trade in the southern Mediterranean between the 9th and 11th centuries.

History

The reasons why are clear at a glance. As in the case of Venice and Genoa, the lack of interior land forced the inhabitants to focus on the sea. Today, the setting of the **town flanked by rocks** is still impressive. Like Venice, Amalfi was also a tightly organized trade empire with an elected doge at its helm. A **Mediterranean network of outposts spanned the world**, guaranteeing profitable long-distance trade. The city's territorial sphere of influence was, however, limited to the area of today's Costiera Amalfitana and parts of the Sorrentine peninsula. Whilst Venice would dominate world trade for centuries, the heyday of the maritime republic of Amalfi, founded in 920, came to an end some 150 years later, in 1073, when Robert Guiscard conquered the city. It also never recovered from the 14th-century seaquake that sunk large parts of Amalfi beneath the sea.

← *Overlooking Naples from the Vomero hill*

VISITING AMALFI

INFORMATION

AAST Amalfi
Corso delle Repubbliche Marinare 27, 84011 Amalfi, tel. 0 89 87 11 07
www.amalfitouristoffice.it

AAST Positano
Via del Saracino 4,
84017 Positano, tel. 0 89 87 50 67
www.aziendaturismopositano.it
www.positanoline.it

GOOD TO KNOW

Transport
In the summer, the SS 163 (Amalfitana) is often very busy. This narrow, winding road has few lay-bys, whilst in the towns parking spaces are both hard to come by and expensive. Public transport is a much more relaxing way to travel to the region and move around within it. Amalfi's bus station at the harbour is the central hub for the Amalfi Coast.
Boats: from Easter to October ferries run from Salerno to the Amalfi Coast (Maiori, Minori, Amalfi, Positano); during summer boats connect the Amalfi Coast with Capri, Sorrento and Naples. From Amalfi and Positano there are boat trips along the coast (look for the information booths of

the boat and shipping agencies at the harbour).

Shopping

Amalfi: at Arte e Carta di Rita Cavalieri (Via Casamare), visitors can not only buy handmade paper but also see it being made following ancient traditions. The Pasticceria Andrea Pansa (Piazza del Duomo 40) offers candied lemon and orange peel alongside enticing delizie al limone and handmade chocolates.

Positano: the »Dolce Vita« at the end of the 1950s marked the birth of the »Moda di Positano« fashion; the traditional lace-trimmed linen dresses can still be bought in various boutiques around the Santa Maria Assunta church. In the same way as in Sorrento and on Capri, expensive leather sandals are made by hand here too.

Cetara: in Cetara, small fish factories still produce the fish sauce condiment highly valued by the Romans as garum. Just a few drops of this colatura di alici are enough to lend dishes a unique flavour.

Duomo di Sant'Andrea in Amalfi

EVENTS

The Good Friday processions in Amalfi and Positano are full of atmosphere. Since 1955, the four former maritime republics of Amalfi, Pisa, Genoa and Venice have been pitting their rowing skills against each other at the ***Palio delle Quattro Antiche Repubbliche Marinare***. The races are to be held in Amalfi again in 2012 and in 2016 (usually on the first Sunday in June). The race is accompanied by a fancy-dress party. On 15 June Positano celebrates the ***Festa di S. Vito***, while between 25 and 27 June Amalfi honours its patron saint Sant'Andrea with processions and large-scale firework displays, with the bishop blessing the sea and the fishing boats. On 29 June, the fishing village of Cetara holds a boat procession honouring its patron saint San Pietro.

SPORT AND OUTDOORS

Water sports: Positano, Amalfi and Cetara have extensive pebble beaches, while Maiori has a long sandy beach. In summer changing cubicles, deck chairs, parasols and showers are available. Whilst water quality is good, currents or heavy rain can make the sea cloudy. The craggy limestone coast, with sea caves and an enduring diversity of fauna, make the Costiera Amalfitana a rewarding diving spot; there are dive stations in Positano, Praiano and on the Sorrentine peninsula. Cetara and Erchie are favourite spots with windsurfers.

Hiking: a network of old tracks criss-crosses the terraced mountain slopes above Amalfi and Positano. Pick up free hiking maps and tips from the tourist information offices at Amalfi, Agerola (www.prolocoagerola.it), Positano and Ravello. There is more information at www.carteguide.com and www.sulsentierodeglidei.it.

WHERE TO EAT

► Expensive

Amalfi • La Caravella
Via Matteo Camera 12
Tel. 0 89 87 10 29, www.ristorantela caravella.it; Jan–mid-Nov, closed Tue. Located towards Positano. A high-class culinary experience with prices to match.

► Moderate

Marina di Praia • Alfonso a Mare
Via Praia 6, tel. 0 89 87 40 91, www.alfonsoamare.it; mid-March–early Nov. This terrace restaurant above the small fishing harbour, with a well-kept hotel above, is a Costiera classic.

Atrani • 'A Paranza
Traversa Dragone 2
Tel. 0 89 87 18 40; closed Tue
This long-established fish restaurant is worth the walk (!) from Amalfi.

Amalfi • Pizzeria Donna Stella
Salita Rascica, tel. 33 83 58 84 83
Apr–Nov closed Mon, the rest of the year closed Sun.
Cosy pizzeria and cucina run by Stella and her daughters Lorenza and Germana. Sitting pretty on the lush terrace, it is easy to feel far removed from the hustle and bustle of nearby Piazza Duomo.

Montepertuso • Il Ritrovo
Via Montepertuso 77
Tel. 0 89 87 54 53, 0 89 81 20 05
March–Dec, closed Wed
Home-grown vegetables from the garden, grilled chicken, kid goat and lamb, and rabbit roasted in the oven.

Cetara • San Pietro
Piazza San Francesco 2
Tel. 0 89 26 10 91
March–Dec, closed Tue
Here, the best ingredients from mare e terra (sea and earth) come together in surprising combinations, but always with plenty of panache. The terrace is a good vantage point to follow what's happening on the corso.

► Budget

Amalfi • Da Baracca
Piazza dei Dogi
Tel. 0 89 87 12 85
Feb–Dec, closed Wed
Both tourists and locals appreciate this family-run trattoria with its pretty glass veranda on Amalfi's market square.

Pogerola • Trattoria da Rispoli
Via Riulo 3
Tel. 0 89 83 00 80
closed Thu This is a tasty refuelling spot after a short outing or a hike in the Valle delle Ferriere. Ask about the dishes of the day. The restaurant can be reached by bus from Amalfi or on foot on the terraced path.

WHERE TO STAY

► Luxury

Amalfi • Luna Convento
Via P. Comite 33, tel. 0 89 87 10 02 www.lunahotel.it. Amalfi's top hotel on the eastern edge of town used to be a convent in the Middle Ages. The visitor's book reads like a who's who of the well-to-do cultural aristocracy. Breakfast is taken in the former cloisters, and the restaurant and pool are located in the Saracen tower.

Atrani, on the Amalfi Coast, even has a small beach

Positano • Palazzo Murat
Via dei Mulini 23, tel. 0 89 87 51 77
www.palazzomurat.it; March–late Oct. Former summer residence of the Neapolitan king and Napoleon's brother-in-law Joachim Murat. Today, travellers with no royal connections but who don't need to watch the budget can also afford the luxury of this stylish hotel and top-class restaurant. On summer evenings concerts are held in the romantic courtyard.

▶ Mid-range

Amalfi • B & B Residenza del Duca
Via Mastolo II Duca 3, tel. & fax 08 98 73 63 65
www.residencedelduca.it
Charming place to stay on the fourth floor of a palazzo on Piazza dei Dogi. Roof terrace with views, perfectly quiet.

Amalfi • Centrale
Largo Piccolomini 1, tel. 0 89 87 26 08
www.hotelcentraleamalfi.it
Closed Jan. Friendly hotel on the cathedral piazza. Some of the spacious rooms have a view of the cathedral, while everyone can enjoy the beautiful views from the roof terrace.

Praiano • Le Sirene
Via S. Nicola 10, tel. & fax 0 89 87 40 13
www.lesirene.com; Easter–early Nov. Friendly B&B, signposted from the S. Gennaro church and only accessible on foot. Utterly peaceful and with spectacular views of Positano at sunset. Steps lead down to the sea.

Vettica Maggiore • Villa Bellavista
Via Rezzola 45, tel. & fax 0 89 87 40 54
www.villabellavista.it; Easter–late Oct. Family-run B&B, about 50 steps below Piazza S. Gennaro. Sun until late evening and with a little luck the sun can even be seen sinking near Capri. Small parking lot

▶ Budget

Atrani • A'Scalinatella
Piazza Umberto I 5–6, tel. 0 89 87 14 92
www.hostelscalinatella.com
Youth-hostel style accommodation with atmosphere. Some nice

apartments with kitchenette are available too.

Positano • Ostello Brikette
Via G. Marconi 358, tel. 0 89 87 58 57
www.brikette.com; mid- March–Nov.
Even cash-strapped travellers can enjoy a nice few days here. Squeaky-clean rooms and dormitories with good beds, a bar, sun terrace and useful travel advice.

Furore • Sant'Alfonso
Via Sant'Alfonso 6
Tel. & fax 0 89 83 05 15
www.agriturismosantalfonso.it
Welcoming agriturismo farm accommodation in a former convent attached to the nearby church of Sant'Alfonso, with the »Walk of the Gods« right outside the front door. Good restaurant upon request. Can be reached either by private car or SITA bus on the Amalfi–Agerola route, or by climbing some 500m/1640ft on an old stairway from the SS 366.

Vettica Maggiore • Villa Bellavista
Via Rezzola 45, tel. & fax 0 89 87 40 54
www.villabellavista.it
Easter–late Oct
Family B&B some 50 steps below Piazza S. Gennaro. Enjoy the sun here till late evening, and with a bit of luck you can even watch it sinking into the sea at Capri. Small car park.

What to See in Amalfi

With its inhabitants supposedly numbering 50,000 (including the coastal towns), medieval Amalfi in its heyday was a densely populated town. On **Piazza Flavio Gioia** outside the centro storico stands a statue of the inventor of the compass. Porta Marina leads directly onto **Piazza Duomo** with its spectacular flight of steps leading up to the cathedral.

✶ **Duomo di Sant'Andrea**

Dedicated to St Andrew the Apostle, this place of worship is an impressive monument to the history of Amalfi, with the cathedral, the cloister and the interesting Museo Diocesano (Nov–Feb daily 10am–12.45pm, 2.30pm–5.15pm, March–May and Oct daily 9am–7pm, June–Sept daily 9am–8pm). Today little remains of the former building, which was probably erected at the time the republic was founded and saw many subsequent extensions. The façade collapsed in 1861 during an earthquake and was reconstructed somewhat liberally between 1875 and 1894; that was after an early 18th-century redesign in the most banal Baroque style had already ruined the original Arab-Norman interior. All that remained was the **campanile**, built between 1180 and 1276.

✶✶ Bronze doors ►

Of greatest interest in terms of art history are the bronze doors, with scenes from the life of St Andrew. Cast in 1066 in Constantinople, where the church founder Pantaleone di Mauro from Ravello had a flourishing trading post, they are the first doors of this kind in southern Italy. The Cloister of Paradise is like something out of an Arab fairy tale. Dating from 1266–68, it is the most beautiful testimony to the former greatness of Amalfi. Delicate double columns

Chiostro del Paradiso ►

support intricate pointed arches. This stylized depiction of nature in stone surrounds a small Mediterranean garden with palm trees where the Amalfi aristocracy had themselves buried in earth imported from the Holy Land.

Most day trippers head straight for Amalfi's Corso, Via Lorenzo di Amalfi and Via Capuano. However, it is a good idea to stroll further on to the **Valle dei Mulini**. Here, if ambient sound levels permit, the subterranean rivulet of Canneto can be heard burbling underneath. The many famous paper mills, which became a popular symbol of picturesque ruin in the 19th century, have long gone. Amalfi was the first Italian town to produce paper, which secured the town a small monopoly in terms of Mediterranean trade, though it was otherwise insignificant. A **paper museum** in a former mill serves as a reminder (Via delle Cartiere; Tue–Sun March–Oct 10am–6.30pm, Nov–Feb 10am–3.30pm).

Detail from the bronze doors at the cathedral of Sant'Andrea

Museo Civico

A museum in the Amalfi town hall tells of the local history. The most valuable exhibit, and also the most interesting, is the *Tavole Amalfitane*. This 13th-century copy documents the older *Tabula Amalfitana*, one of the earliest legal texts on seafaring (Palazzo Comunale, Piazza del Municipio; Mon–Fri 8am–2pm, 3–8pm, Sat 8am–2pm).

Arsenale della Repubblica

The Arsenale della Repubblica is what remains of the medieval shipyards where Amalfi's trading fleet was built (Piazza Flavio Gioia; daily 9.30am–12.30pm, 4pm–7pm).

★★ Costiera Amalfitana

One of the world's most beautiful roads

The road simply denoted as the SS 163 on the map belies the attractions of one of the most beautiful stretches of highway in the world. Running between sky and sea along the foothills of the **Monti Lattari**, the road not only offers breathtaking views, but is in itself a marvel of road construction. Before the SS 163 was built, the main access to the towns along the Amalfi Coast was by water, while inland they were connected by a system of mule trails and stepped

Baedeker TIP

Off the beaten track

Those much sought-after but elusive places that are off the main tourist trail can still be found today along the Costiera Amalfitana. The mountainous back country of the Monti Lattari is excellent for hikes on well-developed and sign-posted trails. Small mountain towns and stunning views in near-complete solitude show a completely different, authentic side of the well-worn Amalfi Coast.

paths, some of which have been developed into hiking trails. The slopes of the Monti Lattari (Milk Mountains) have been cultivated agriculturally for centuries. The fields are mainly small, but with their terraces reaching into the rocks, they support vines, lemons and olives.

Amalfi was not on the »Grand Tour« itinerary for travellers, but in the first decades of the 19th century the dramatic rock landscape of the Valle dei Mulini became a favourite motif for artists. The real discovery of the Costiera Amalfitana as a tourism area occurred in the second half of the 19th century. The climate, relatively mild even in winter, and the beauty of the landscape turned towns such as Amalfi and Ravello into favourite destinations for the top ranks of the Anglo-American upper classes. Whilst it was sophisticated summer visitors who took refuge in the coastal towns – chiefly Positano – during the 1950s, the mass tourism of more recent decades has also left its mark here.

Vietri sul Mare

In sunlight the whole town, the start or end point of the Amalfi Coast, lies resplendent in the colours of its traditional ceramic products, which are sold mainly along Corso Umberto I. A small **ceramics museum** outside the town (follow signs in the direction of Raito; Museo Provinciale della Ceramica, Toretta di Villa Guariglia, Raito; Tue–Sun June–Sept 9am–1pm, 4pm–7pm, Oct–May 9am–1pm, 3pm–6pm) gives an introduction to ceramics production. Vietri was famous most of all for its floor tiles, exported throughout Campania. The supposition that Vietri sul Mare is truly of Etruscan origin is still open to question and remains unsupported by archaeological evidence.

✶ **Cava dei Tirreni**

Situated a few miles inland from Vietri sul Mare, Cava dei Tirreni is a small town well worth visiting. The arcaded passageways lining the corso are a reminder of the former wealth of the town, a market and trading centre in medieval times. The town's significance stems from the Abbazia della Santissima Trinità in the Corpo di Cava district (5km/3mi from Cava dei Tirreni). Founded in the 11th century, this abbey became one of the most powerful in southern Italy thanks to endowments and privileges, and is said to have controlled 500 monasteries. The abbey's trading fleet used Vietri sul Mare as a harbour, with the imported goods being handled in Cava dei Tirreni. The wealth accumulated in this way was invested in a library and extension to the monastery. Its manuscripts and valuable book miniatures

✶ Abbazia della Santissima Trinità ►

A restaurant is now housed in the former Saracen watchtower at Maiori

make the former **one of the most significant monastic libraries** in Italy. The 18th century saw the renovation and restoration of the complex, lending it a completely Baroque appearance today. Visitors can see the medieval cloisters, the impressive Lombard cemetery and splendidly furnished rooms of the monastery (Via Badia di Cava; daily 9am–12.30pm, 4pm–6pm by appointment, tel. 0 89 46 39 22).

Torri saraceni

At the entrance to Cetara stands the first of the so-called torri saraceni, characteristic of the whole of the southern Italian coast. The establishment of countless such towers, erected in sight of each other, created an early warning system intended to protect the population from the pirates regularly pillaging the coast.

Maiori

Maiori and Minori – two small towns named after the rivers Regina Minor and Maior – are much visited resorts in summer. Their exposed position on the rocky coastline might be exceedingly picturesque, but it brings dangers with it: in 1954, both towns were partly destroyed by a huge mudslide. Their reconstruction, carried out very much with the expanding tourism sector in mind, has resulted in Maiori in particular losing some of its charm. Have a look though at the **Chiesa S. Maria a Mare**, with its typical majolica dome and pretty flooring in the crypt. 3km/2mi away, set high up in a rock face, is the uniqueBadia di S. Maria di Olearia. In the 10th century Byzantine monks built a monastery in a natural grotto here, which owes its name to a nearby oil mill. With their frescoes, the three chapels – built one above the other in different period styles and extended in

✶

◄ Badia di S. Maria di Olearia

later centuries – are well worth taking a look at (Oct–April Sun 4pm–6pm, May–Sept Fri, Sat, Sun 4pm–7pm).

Minori ✶ Villa Romana ► Minori, with the ruins of a Roman villa marittima, possesses one of the rare reminders of ancient history along the Amalfi Coast. Whilst the original owner of the extensive villa complex is unknown, the luxury of the interior decoration, in particular the unusual triclinium (dining room), which is arranged as a nymphaeum (sanctuary dedicated to water nymphs), is reminiscent of Roman villas on the Bay of Naples. A small **antiquarium** houses finds from the villa, amongst them fragments of sculptures and ceramics (Piazzetta Pompeo Troiano; daily 9am to one hour before sunset).

✶ **Atrani** A romantic highlight of the Amalfi Coast, little Atrani (pop. 950) boasts the **Chiesa San Salvatore de'Bireto** church, where the doges of Amalfi were elected. Whilst it is a separate municipality, Atrani really belongs to Amalfi. Here, in a bewildering array of alleyways and squares and »scalinatelle« (small sets of steps connecting houses with each other), the entire Eastern allure of Amalfitan architecture is displayed on an area of only 0.2 sq km (less than a tenth of a square mile). Until its destruction by the Pisans, Atrani was the favourite dwelling place of Amalfi's aristocratic families. Alongside the Chiesa San Salvatore de'Bereto (founded in 940), the town is dominated by the **Chiesa S. Maria Maddalena**, dating from the 13th century and given a Baroque makeover in 1771. Only a rocky ledge separates Atrani from Amalfi. This very cliff supports one of the most famous hotels of the Costiera Amalfitana, the **Luna Convento**. The former monastery was converted into a hotel as early as the beginning of the 19th century. Henrik Ibsen wrote *Nora* here in 1879.

✶ **Vallone di Furore** Between **Conca dei Marini** and **Praiano**, the Amalfi Coast shows its dramatic side. The Vallone di Furore (Gorge of Fury) is the most spectacular gorge along this part of the coast. A lift takes visitors from Conca di Marini to the Grotta dello Smeraldo, which was only discovered in 1932. The **stalactite cave** bears comparison with Capri's Blue Grotto, with the light coming in through openings under the surface of the water making for fantastic colour effects. From Conca dei Marini a road leads up into the hills to Agerola. The Sentiero degli Dei, the**Path of the Gods**, which at a height of 638m/ 2093ft is one of the most beautiful hiking paths in the world, begins (or ends) in the Bomerano district. The hike, taking 3 to 4 hours, is difficult in parts (solid footwear required!), and leads to Positano.

✶ Grotta dello Smeraldo ►

✶ ✶ Sentiero degli Dei ►

✶ **Positano** Positano (pop. 4000) divides opinion. For some, this is one of the most beautiful places on the whole of the Amalfi Coast, while others bemoan that it has been completely **given over to tourism**. In any case, the development from small fishing village to positively chic holiday resort is remarkable. The pastel-coloured houses, built vertically into the rock face of the **Monte Sant'Angelo** and connected by countless sets of steps, are much admired. In the decades before the Second World War, Positano was a favourite place for artists and intellectuals to spend their holidays. Today it is mainly day trippers who throng past the town's numerous boutiques. Even so, Positano has remained extraordinarily exclusive, with some of the most expensive hotels in all of Italy catering to an elegant summer clientele. The beach- and summer-wear sold here has become a trademark of the town. Positano is a all sea views and picturesque alleyways; art history enthusiasts will enjoy the **Chiesa Santa Maria Assunta**, especially its campanile with the relief of a sea monster in the wall, which probably dates from Lombard times.

? DID YOU KNOW ...?

- The »Li Galli« group of islands off Positano used to have illustrious owners. It was here that the Russian dancer and choreographer Leonid Massine founded a ballet academy, and from 1979 onwards, Rudolf Nureyev spent the summer months on the largest of the three islands. When the dancer died in 1993, private investors bought Li Galli. For a while now the Italian state has attempted, through the courts, to reclaim the right to buy Li Galli, in spite of the fact that it didn't exercise it at the time of the sale. The Galli islands are said to be the seat of the mythological Sirens, who lured passing seafarers to their deaths with their enticing songs.

★ Benevento

G 2

Region: Campania **Province:** Benevento
Altitude: 115m/377ft **Population:** 63,000

Visitors who are not put off by the rather unattractive outskirts of Benevento, with its motorways, tenements and all kinds of architectural atrocities, can discover a wealth of well-preserved art and monuments in a historically interesting town.

History

Mythology points to **Diomedes**, a Greek warrior supposed to have washed up in the Sannio after the destruction of Troy, as the founder of the Benevento. Archaeological finds, however, suggest it was founded by the Samnites in the 8th century BC. Maloenton, as they called it, with its strategic position on a hill between the rivers Sabato and Calore, quickly became an important town of the Samnite empire. It was here that the Romans suffered a substantial defeat in 321 BC at the hands of Samnite warriors, who were described in ancient sources as fearless and tough fighters. In 275 BC, however, Roman soldiers were victorious against the Molossian king Pyrrhus near Benevento. As a Roman colony, Beneventum was connected directly with Rome by the Via Appia (Appian Way) and became an important trading post for southern Italy. In the Post Classic period, Benevento's strategic position made it important to all the invaders penetrating this immense but crumbling empire. Of those, the Lombards prevailed and expanded Benevento into the capital of their southern Italian duchy. After a short Norman intermezzo, the town came into the sphere of influence of the Pope as early as 1077. It belonged to the **Vatican** until 1860, which explains some of the extraordinarily splendid buildings along Corso Garibaldi. In 1943, an Allied bomb attack destroyed 65% of the town, whilst the disastrous 1980 earthquake, with its epicentre in nearby Avellino, placed the entire region in a state of emergency for years. The reconstruction of the centro storico has, however, been carried out in an exemplary manner.

? DID YOU KNOW ...?

- The victories of the general from Epirus against the Romans resulted in such loss of life and proved so pointless in the end that they effectively amounted to defeats and have entered common parlance as »pyrrhic victories«.

City of witches The reason why Benevento is known as the city of witches becomes ominously clear on foggy winter days when the Sannio mountains appear particularly bare and archaic – think the mountains of the Scottish Highlands. A reminder of these ancient pre-Christian myths is a herbal liqueur sold in many shops in Benevento under the name »strega« (witch).

VISITING BENEVENTO

INFORMATION

EPT Benevento
Via Nicola Sala 31
82100 Benevento
Tel. 08 24 31 99 38
Fax 08 24 31 23 09
www.eptbenevento.it
www.comune.benevento.it
www.provincia.benevento.it

EPT Avellino
Via Due Principati 32 A,
83100 Avellino, tel. 08 25 74 73 21
www.eptavellino.it

EVENTS

'A juta a Montevergine: one of the oldest celebrations in Italy is re-enacted near Avellino. By 11 September, the eve of the Festa della Madonna di Montevergine, the pilgrims arrive in Ospedaletto. The night before the ascent of the holy mountain ('a juta) is given over to partying, an echo of the Bacchanalian rites of the cult of Kybele (www.santuariodimontevergine.com).
Città Spectacolo: film and theatre festival (tel. & fax 0 82 42 18 48, www.cittaspectacolo.com) in the first half of September, with open-air performances in the ancient theatre of Benevento.

WHERE TO EAT

► Expensive

Avellino • Antica Trattoria Martella
Via Chiesa Conservatorio 10, tel. 0 82 53 21 23; closed Sun eve and Mon. This trattoria in the old town has been upholding the culinary traditions of

the Irpinia for over 70 years. Game, hearty meat dishes and vegetables.

► Moderate

① ***Cotton Club***

Via De Vita 16, mobile no. 34 93 82 72 26; evenings only, closed Tue and all of August.

This tiny trattoria in a side street of Corso Garibaldi serves traditionally prepared products of the Sannio and dishes inspired by the owners' culinary expeditions through southern Italy.

② ***Nunzia***

Via Annunziata 152, tel. 0 82 42 94 31; closed Sun

Osteria in the Old Town near Piazza Roma. Home-made pasta and hearty vegetable soups are amongst friendly Signora Nunzia's tasty and filling dishes.

► Moderate

Sant'Angelo dei Lombardi • Alle Sorgenti dell'Ofanto

Contrada San Guglielmo

Tel. 08 27 21 51 20; closed Mon.

Benevento Map

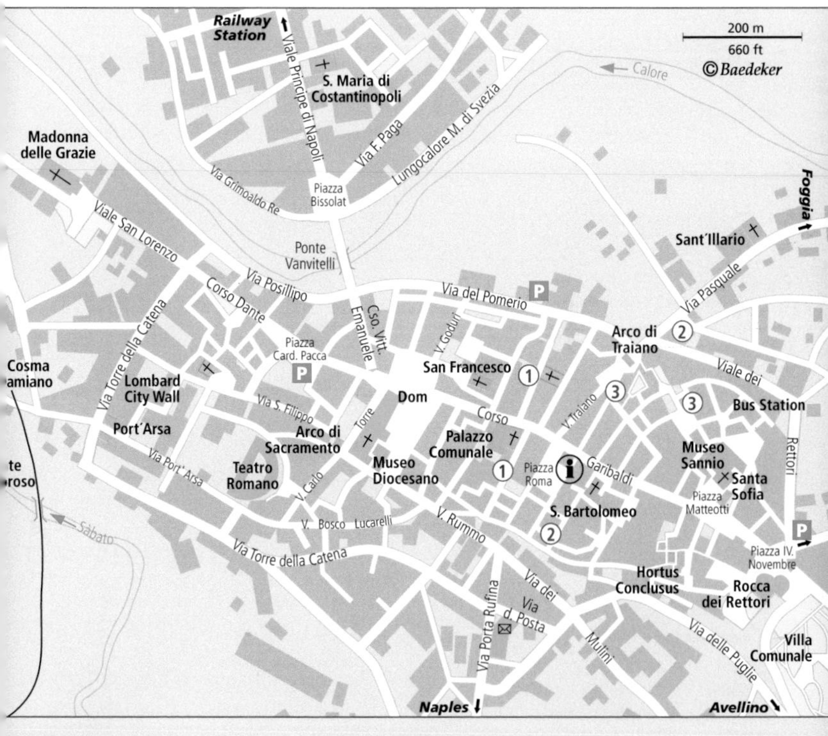

Where to eat
① Cotton Club
② Nunzia
③ Traiano

Where to stay
① Le Stanze del Sogno
② Villa Traiano
③ Albergo della Corte

Worth a trip, and not just for the medieval Abbazia del Goleto. Right in front of the restaurant are the best cheeses in the Irpinia are sold, along with good wines. 45km/28mi east of Avellino.

③ ***Traiano***
Via Manciotti 48
Mobile tel. 34 62 87 32 32; closed Tue eve
Family trattoria at the Arch of Trajan serving hearty Sannio cuisine – this is the real thing. In the evenings there is wood-fired oven pizza.

Sant'Agata dei Goti • Il Barbaro
Via Riello 4
Tel. 08 23 71 77 14;
Nice trattoria; serves homemade pasta and wood-fired oven pizza in the evening. Go to Gelateria Normanno at Via Roma 65 for an ice cream afterwards.

WHERE TO STAY

► Mid-range

Melizzano • Mesogheo
Contrada Valle Corrado 2
Tel. 08 24 94 43 56
www.mesogheo.com
Comfortable rooms in a masseria farmhouse at the foot of the Camposauro, halfway between Telese Terme and Sant'Agata dei Goti. Good food.

Sant'Agata dei Goti • Agriturismo Mustilli
Piazza Trento 4
Tel. 08 23 71 74 33
www.mustilli.com
Quiet rooms, spacious and stylishly furnished in a palazzo in the centre of town. The excellent restaurant serves the award-winning Mustilli wines. Cookery classes also on offer. 50km/31mi southwest of Benevento.

Telese Terme • Grand Hotel Telese
Via Cerreto 1, tel. 08 24 94 05 00
www.grandhoteltelese.it
Imposing Belle Époque building in a park outside town on the road to Castelvenere. Substantial breakfast buffet and good cuisine. In the summer, a refreshing bath can be taken in the spa gardens of Telese, where the sparkling water bubbles in open-air pools at a pleasant 20°C/68°F. 30km/18mi northwest of Benevento.

② ***Villa Traiano***
Viale dei Rettori 9
Tel. 08 24 32 62 41
www.hotelvillatraiano.it
Closed Aug. Elegant early 20th-century villa, centrally located near the Rocca dei Rettori.

► Budget/Mid-range

① ***Le Stanze del Sogno***
Piazzetta De Martini 3
Tel. & fax 0 82 44 39 91
Mobile no. 33 84 60 33 59
www.lestanzedelsogno.it
Tiny B&B run by a young cooperative in the heart of the Old Town. Tastefully furnished rooms with kitchenette. Each guest gets his own key.

Sant'Angelo dei Lombardi • Goleto
Contrada San Guglielmo
Tel. 08 27 21 52 15
www.ilgoleto.it
This well-kept albergo in the immediate vicinity of the famous medieval abbey is run by a dedicated young team. Honest local cuisine. 45km/28mi east of Avellino.

③ ***Albergo della Corte***
Piazza Piano di Corte 1
Tel. & fax 0 82 45 48 19
Tiny, friendly family-run albergo between the Arch of Trajan and Santa Sofia. Public car park and garage.

Triumphal arch in honour of Trajan

What to See in Benevento

Benevento's central **Corso Garibaldi**, cutting through the centro storico, follows the course of the Via Appia and is among the most beautiful pedestrian areas in Campania. The town's main sights lie to either side of the corso.

The **duomo** on the piazza of the same name was founded as early as the 8th century, extended in the 13th century in Romanesque style, and almost completely destroyed in 1943 during an Allied air raid. The highly impressive main façade and the campanile have been restored, whilst the modern east façade unobtrusively refers to its predecessor. The famous bronze doors were restored a few years ago and visitors can see them at the **Museo Diocesano**. At the moment, the small museum with the remains of a crypt is open by prior appointment only. Recent archaeological excavation work below the floor of the central nave kept the cathedral closed until spring 2009.

More sights

The **Arco di Sacramento**, right behind the cathedral, on Via Carlo Torre, is a ceremonial arch probably dating from the time of Hadrian. It has been stripped of its marble cladding and all that remains are the niches where the statues of the emperor used to stand. From here it is just a few steps to the **Roman theatre**. During summer, there are occasional performances here (Piazza C. Ponzio Telesino; daily 9am to one hour before sunset).

◄ Teatro Romano

🕒

★★ **Arco di Traiano**

The triumphal Arch of Trajan was built in AD 114–119 and is unique in that its marble decoration was not dismantled and destroyed in the Post Classic period. The iconography celebrates the emperor as a benefactor; in the relief in the archway, for example, he brings peace and distributes food to the poor. The occasion for the construction of the triumphal arch, which has a height of 15.6m/51ft (arch height 8.6m/28ft), is likely to have been the inauguration of the Trajan Way (Via Traiana), which used to lead from here to Brindisi. The Via Traiana leads back into town and onto **Piazza Roma**, where there are a number of imposing 19th century buildings.

Piazza ★

◄ Santa Sofia

Also on Corso Garibaldi, Piazza Santa Sofia – with its church of the same name and the Museo del Sannio – was only laid out in 1809. The church was built as early as 760 by the Lombard dukes Gisulfo II and Arechi II and served as the actual **Lombard court church**, not least because of its proximity to the ducal palace, today's Rocca dei Rettori. An earthquake in 1688 wrought considerable havoc, whilst the subsequent Baroque makeover completely »ruined« the church building. The original architecture was reconstructed as far as possible in the 1950s. Today the church is open in the mornings and again from 5pm. Of the original building, the circular domed structure with 16 ancient columns remains, as well as the apses (recesses) to the left and right of the altar, which contain fragments of fresco paintings. Standing some way from the church, the **campanile** has two stone tablets proudly telling the story of Benevento. One shows the extent of the old Samnite empire between the 6th and 4th centuries BC and the second shows the extent of the Lombard duchy.

Museo Sannio
✶
Cloister ►

The museum (Tue–Sun 9am–7pm) is worth visiting, if only for the cloisters of the former 12th-century monastery, which surpass all notions of a medieval, Arab-Norman paradise garden. Ornate capitals are supported by 47 columns, whilst the cloister exhibits spolia from Roman and Lombard times. The ground-floor Isis Hall displays holy artefacts from the Temple of Isis, »Lady of Benevento«. Also on display are Samnite ceramics, as well as Roman sculptures and architectural fragments.

✶
Rocca dei Rettori

Diagonally opposite the museum lies the Palazzo del Governo, seat of Benevento's provincial government. The old seat of power is right next to it: the Rocca dei Rettori (1321) was built as a residence for the papal governor on the foundations of an earlier Lombard and Roman construction. The building houses the offices of the provincial government, as well as rooms for temporary exhibitions.

Hortus Conclusus

Mimmo Paladino, an artist of international renown, has established a permanent sculpture gallery in his home town, which is mounted as a hortus conclusus – i.e. an »enclosed garden« – in the former monastery of San Domenico (Piazza Guerazzi; Mon–Sat 9am–1pm, 3pm–7.30pm, Sun 9am–1pm).

Ponte Leproso

Lying a little outside the town centre, but only a few minutes on foot from the Roman theatre, the Ponte Leproso across the Sabato was once part of the Via Appia, the north-south axis to which Benevento owed its significance.

Around Benevento

Pietrelcina

Pietrelcina, a nice little town 10km/6mi northeast of Benevento and birthplace of **Padre Pio** (► Famous People), has been attempting to turn itself into a site of pilgrimage. The residence of the Forgione family receives many pilgrims, whilst the saint's birthday, on 25 May, is celebrated with a procession.

Its name recalls the mid-6th-century founders: Sant'Agata de Goti

★ **Sant'Agata de Goti**

Also in Benevento province but equally accessible from Caserta, Sant'Agata de Goti occupies a singularly elevated position. The town, described in some travel guides as »enchanting« or at least »picturesque«, does indeed merit such admiration. The medieval appearance of the town has been most impressively preserved and a stroll along Via Roma to the cathedral is enough to inspire anyone. The many restaurants are frequented, particularly at weekends, by visitors from Benevento, Caserta or Naples, who appreciate the old-fashioned charm of this little town as much as its cuisine. Among the numerous churches worth visiting is the **Chiesa di San Menna** with its extraordinary mosaic floor. The **duomo** and its piazza combine into a work of art reminiscent of Capri's Piazzetta. The small town owes its name to its Goth founders (around 550).

Irpinia

Large areas of the landscape around Naples have been contaminated by toxic waste and have come to resemble a scene from a science fiction film in which even the ancient Greek settlement of Cumae could easily be missed. But the province of Avellino has a beauty that never fails to entice. The land of the Irpinia region, with the Montevergine and the Monti Picentini, ranks among the most fertile areas of Campania. Furthermore, the springs in these mountains provide the metropolis of Naples and a number of other Campanian municipalities with water. Irpinia is a veritable **paradise for nature lovers**. Whilst lacking in tourist infrastructure, the area does provide for the most beautiful excursions.

Avellino The friendly provincial capital (pop. 57,000; 348m/1142ft) in the Campanian hinterland is not at all touristy, having been almost completely destroyed in the 1980 earthquake. After being successfully rebuilt, Avellino's modern, cheerful and well-kept appearance now seems almost reminiscent of towns in northern Italy. The commercial and administrative centre with its elegant Corso Vittorio Emanuele forms the focal point of the still rural landscape of **Irpinia**. An early Samnite-Roman settlement was destroyed during the civil wars of Sulla and founded anew under the name of Abellinum. This outpost of the Roman Empire – one of the many settlements for war veterans which came straight from the drawing board – kept being damaged by earthquakes, and was destroyed several times during the Gothic wars. The town's subsequent conquest by the Lombards, in 571, again led to it being re-founded, this time on a hill to aid defence. A few remains of the old Roman town were found in the 1920s, in Avellino's neighbouring town of **Atripalda** (Museo Archeologico, Piazza Umberto I; daily 8am–2pm, 4pm–8pm). The Lombard town was the core from which today's Avellino evolved. Also dating from Lombard times, the **fort** was rebuilt in the 18th century. Following the 1980 earthquake, the original 12th-century cathedral was reconstructed the way it would have looked after 19th-century alterations. The highlight of Avellino is the **Museo Provinciale Irpino** (Corso Europa; Mon–Sat 8.30am–1.30pm, Mon, Thu also 4pm–7pm). The archaeological collection shows numerous finds from all the settlement phases of the Irpinia region, amongst them rare wooden votive statues.

? DID YOU KNOW ...?

- Campania has still not completely recovered from the major earthquake of 23 November 1980, which claimed 3000 lives and left half a million people homeless. The epicentre was near Avellino and in the hills of Irpinia whole towns collapsed within seconds. Campania's beauty and its wealth of art treasures were suddenly subject to worldwide media attention. This natural disaster was therefore a turning point in the history of southern Italy: without the earthquake the fresh political start in the 1990s, under Antonio Bassolino, might not have happened in the same way.

★ **Santuario di Monte Vergine** Montevergine, above Avellino, is one of the most important places of pilgrimage in Campania. A 13th-century image of the Virgin Mary credited with working miracles established the fame of the church, situated at an altitude of nearly 1270m/4170ft. The church's origins go back to the early 12th century; it was rebuilt in the 18th century, whilst today's basilica only took shape between 1952 and 1961. It is thought that a temple dedicated to Cybele already stood here during antiquity. A visit to the **Sala delle Offerte** in the new basilica, with its hundreds of votive images, can be a moving experience. The images are no longer painted, but the photographs dedicated to the Virgin, often decorated or displayed in silver frames, are equal testimony to the continued vibrancy of Montevergine as a spiritual place.

★★ Capri

D 5

Region: Campania
Surface area: 10.4 sq km/4 sq mi
Population: 13,400
Province: Napoli
Altitude: Sea level–589m/1932ft

Possibly the most famous island in the world, Capri is one of those places at the Bay of Naples where a little advance preparation is very worthwhile to avoid disappointment. During arrival, nerves of steel are also a distinct advantage. That said, travellers can nevertheless enjoy spectacular nature in near total solitude along with the many other wonders on this enchanting island, despite the »turismo di massa« lamented even by the Caprese themselves.

Advice

During high season, Capri and Anacapri, the two towns on the island, are completely overrun. Masses of day trippers tag along behind guides, who try to keep their flock together on the way along Via Camerelle, or cluster in front of Villa Munthe in Anacapri. Most don't realize that beautiful strolls await them just a few paces off the beaten tourist track. The roughly one-hour walk from Piazza Umberto I up to the ancient Villa Jovis is an experience by itself that shows the island off from its best side.

History

The landscape of Capri is one of the few on the Bay of Naples that is not of volcanic origin. The topography that has made the island famous consists of sheer rock faces plunging almost vertically into the sea, and the remarkable difference in altitude between east and west. Until some 10,000 years ago, before the ocean floor level began to sink, this barren limestone rock was connected to the mainland. It was already relatively densely populated in **Palaeolithic times** because of its many grottoes and caves. In the Grotta delle Felci and near the Quisisana hotel, in particular, several prehistoric tools and weapons have been found, as well as a great variety of fossils. Little is known about the pre-Greek settlement of Capri; it is certain however – and confirmed by finds of imported goods, such as ceramics and the volcanic ore obsidian – that as far back as the 4th century BC, the trading post of Capri formed part of a network of early shipping links. In the middle of the 8th century BC, Greek colonists settled the island, believed to owe its name either to the Greek word kapros (wild boar) or the Roman capra (goat). The Romans knew Capri as **Goat Island**, and the Punta Tragara (from the Greek tragarion = goat stable) is a reminder of its original agricultural use. Owing to the barren soil, the island would not have allowed for much more than goat rearing. Very little architectural evidence remains of the Greek settlement. From the back, a few houses in the Via Longano – visible

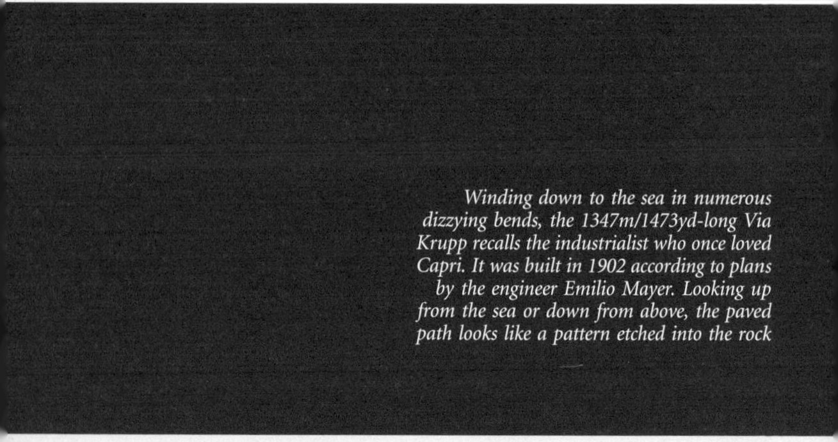

Winding down to the sea in numerous dizzying bends, the 1347m/1473yd-long Via Krupp recalls the industrialist who once loved Capri. It was built in 1902 according to plans by the engineer Emilio Mayer. Looking up from the sea or down from above, the paved path looks like a pattern etched into the rock

CAPRI SCANDALS

The island of Capri has been associated with erotic excesses since the era of Tiberius. Yet even Roman historians and writers, such Suetonius and Tacitus, cannot always be believed. Gossip, especially sexual intrigue, has been bolstering sales for millennia.

The German industrialist **Friedrich Alfred Krupp** was caught up in a scandal during his Capri sojourn at the turn of the 19th century. Enchanted by the island, he dreamt of a simple life and ocean research, but his close relationships with hairdressers, fishermen and farm labourers attracted the attention of a contemporary star journalist from Naples. Edoardo Scarfoglio proceeded to vilify Krupp with a singular press campaign throughout Europe, accusing him of (unproven) homosexual misdemeanours perpetrated on the local island youth. Krupp did not survive the scandal, committing suicide in 1902.

A similar result was achieved by a series of articles written by the journalist Matilde Serao, Scarfoglio's wife and co-founder of the Neapolitan daily newspaper *Il Mattino*. She covered **Oscar Wilde's** stay in Naples, publishing a series of highly defamatory articles about him under a pseudonym, in which she described him as a danger to male youth. Only recently released from prison in England, Wilde had joined his feckless and unreliable lover Lord Douglas in Naples. They rented a villa at Posillipo, travelled to Capri and Taormina on Sicily, and waited in vain for monies to arrive from England. Serao's articles rubbed salt in his wounds and Wilde departed for Paris a disillusioned man. He died just a few months later.

The stories about **Count Jacques d'Adelswaerd-Fersen** are shrouded as much as anything in clouds of opium. A French poet, dandy and heir to millions, his Villa Lysis was located directly below the ancient villa once owned by Tiberius. His home was a

Fin-de-Siècle temple dedicated to the youthful beauty of the male form. A life-size bronze statue of **Nino Cesarini** stood in the park that spread out before the open-air stairway: the Roman newspaper salesman and occasional construction labourer stood in full classical nakedness. Officially, he was the count's personal secretary. The luxurious villa contained a smoking room dubbed the »opiarium« by the daily *Il Mattino*, and the orgies that are said to have taken place there are legend on the island.

A frequent guest at the Villa Lysis was **Wilhelm von Plüschow**, a relation of Wilhelm von Gloeden, resident at Taormina (Sicily). Both were successful photographers of nudes. Their images of naked boys in a variety of settings inspired by antiquity encouraged the north European fantasy of sensuous innocence.

The Hamburg artist **Chistian Wilhelm Allers** – known as »Bismark-Allers« to his Wilhelmine contemporaries – pursued his models as much as his art while on the island. He kept a jolly bohemian crowd at his villa. Studio portraits of the artist show him holding his sketchbook in the company of sparsely clad youths. In 1903, Allers only avoided his imminent arrest by the island police by making a hasty escape.

The literature on Capri is full of anecdotes about eccentrics and sex maniacs, and the island's many grottoes have provided the classic setting for tales of orgiastic scandal ever since the days of **Tiberius**. Yet Capri's biggest scandals are all in the distant past, their veracity questionable. These days, at least, Capri is far too expensive and exclusive to provide unstable hedonists refuge from the harsh realities of life. *Il Mattino*, however, continues to report on the island's big and insignificant stories each summer, just as before; and Capri's photographers turn even the most average tourist into a VIP as they go on their summer evening search for exclusives on the Piazzetta.

from the upper platform of the funicolare (cable car) – show the remains of a city wall integrated into today's buildings. The wall probably used to surround the Greek acropolis. The Scala Fenicia is much more impressive. Until 1874, the **Phoenician Stairs**, over 800 steps hewn into the rock, were the only connection between Capri and Anacapri. The stairs actually do date back to the time of their Greek builders. The ascent, covering an elevation of 200m/650ft, begins near the Palazzo a Mare near Capri, and ends in front of Anacapri's old city gate. For centuries, all goods headed for Anacapri were transported via these stairs.

Scala Fenicia ►

Capri: island of emperors

Between 29 BC and AD 37, the small island of Capri was the political centre of the Roman Empire. According to Strabo, **Octavian, later to become Emperor Augustus**, first set foot on the island in 31 BC and immediately fell in love it, acquiring Capri from Naples in exchange for Ischia in 29 BC and making it an imperial demesne.

It was Octavian and his successor **Tiberius** in particular who turned the private imperial property into an official residence, establishing twelve villas and expanding the many natural grottoes into nymphaeums. Imperial Capri was not only a well-developed island, its character was also transformed by a highly artificial coexistence of landscape and architecture side by side. Whilst Octavian Augustus visited the island regularly up to his death in AD 14, Tiberius actually retreated entirely to Capri for the last ten years of his life, feeding numerous speculations on the part of his contemporaries. According to Suetonius and Tacitus, the main reason behind the move was Tiberius' allegedly highly debauched sex life – the emperor finding in Capri the very place to sate his desires. However, the imperial retreat was primarily an affront to the Roman senate. Though Tiberius spent his time far from the capital, he governed the empire no less efficiently from Capri. After his death in AD 37, the island remained imperial property but rapidly lost its status. From the 2nd century AD onwards, Capri was merely a luxurious place of exile for members of the imperial family who had fallen out of grace, and later it sank into complete oblivion. In the Middle Ages, the island fell to a series of the various dynasties ruling in southern Italy, but due to the barrenness of its soil and the poverty of its inhabitants it never played a major role. Until its dissolution, a **Carthusian monastery**, founded in 1371, was the largest property owner and employer on Capri.

! *Baedeker* TIP

An ascent with a view

From Anacapri, a chair lift takes visitors up to the highest point of the island in twelve minutes: with Capri lying at their feet, on clear days the views reach across the whole gulf right into the Cilento region (Via Caposcuro 10, tel. 08 18 37 14 28, www.seggioviamontesolaro.it). At 589m/1932ft, Monte Solaro can also comfortably be climbed on foot from Anacapri. A bar with deckchairs welcomes weary walkers at the summit.

Marina Grande: port for the ferries and hydrofoils

◀ Archaeological excavations

Only a few ruins remain of the twelve imperial villas, but they are very impressive. In addition to **Villa Jovis**, most notably there is the **Palazzo a Mare** near Marina Grande, as well as the ruins of **Villa di Damecuta** lying above the Blue Grotto. For centuries, the ancient buildings served as quarries for stone and were systematically looted in the 18th and 19th centuries. Methodical excavations and scientific explorations of the ancient ruins were only undertaken in the 20th century.

The beginnings of modern tourism

Until the mid-19th century, Capri, unlike Ischia or the Phlegrean Fields, did not really figure on travellers' checklists for visits to the Bay of Naples. In its raw wildness, the chalk cliff rising steeply from the sea did not appeal to the aesthetics or ideas of beauty prevalent in the 18th century. It took the **discovery of the Blue Grotto** by the German poet **August Kopisch** in August 1826 to turn Capri into the most famous island in the Mediterranean. The »discovery« of the Grotta Azzurra by Kopisch and his artist friend Ernst Fries was, however, more of a cleverly engineered PR stunt on the part of inn owner Giuseppe Pagano. The boat trip organized by Pagano and the stage-managed discovery of the grotto, which in truth was already known to the Caprese, marks a significant watershed in the cultural history of travel. The effusive Kopisch turned out to be the ideal ambassador to wax lyrical back home about the natural beauty of the

VISITING CAPRI

INFORMATION

AAST
Piazzetta I Cerio 11, 80073 Capri
Tel. 08 18 37 53 08, fax 08 18 37 09 18
www.capritourism.com.

Uffici Informazioni • Information offices
A map of Capri (1:10,000) can be bought here, with town maps of Capri and Anacapri:
Marina Grande (harbour pier)
Piazza Umberto I, Capri
Via G Orlandi 19 A, Anacapri

GOOD TO KNOW

Transport
Ferries/Hydrofoils: from Sorrento, hydrofoils (aliscafi) and charming old-fashioned ferries (traghetti), from Naples/Porta Calata di Massa and Molo Beverello ferries, from Naples/Mergellina hydrofoils fast ferries, plus in summer additional fast ferries from Positano, Amalfi, Salerno and Castellamare del Golfo. Boats dock at Marina Grande on the northern side of the island. The way up to Capri town from here is on foot via stone steps, or by cable car, bus or taxi (current timetables in daily papers and on the websites of the AAST and the ferry companies).

Getting around the island
By car: between spring and autumn, only islanders may use their cars. However, it is easy enough to get around on foot or by funicolare (cable car), island buses or taxis. Secure long-term car parks are available in Naples and Sorrento. Not all hotels are accessible by taxi though, meaning that visitors have to haul their luggage for the final stretch or have it carried by a porter (facchino).

Shopping
Capri's exclusive shopping streets, Via Camerelle and Via Vittorio Emanuele, celebrate »la bella figura«, while Carthusia entices with lemon perfumes made according to an old monastic recipe (Via Matteotti 2, Via Camerelle 10, Via Axel Munthe 28 and Anacapri). La Conchiglia is an enterprising small publisher with bookshops (Via Le Botteghe 12 and Via Camerelle 18), while La Parisienne was already tailoring Capri trousers decades ago for the likes of Maria Callas and Jacqueline Kennedy (Piazza Umberto I, Via Camerelle 8 and Via Vittorio Emanuele 26). Otherwise, limoncello lemon liqueur and handmade sandals make classic Capri souvenirs.

Sport and outdoors
Capri has no sandy beaches, and most of the few bathing bays are administered by bathing establishments (stabilimento balneare). One of the most beautiful places to swim is the ***Bagno La Fontelina*** on the Punto di Tragara (with restaurant). It takes around 45 minutes to get from Capri down to the cliffs with a view of the Faraglioni stacks. The return journey is made in small boats to Marina Piccola. Standard sightseeing propositions include trips around the island (1–2 hrs) and boat trips into the Blue Grotto. The boats leave from Marina Grande. If possible, visit the Blue Grotto in late morning, when the sun shines directly into the underwater cavity, illuminating the cave with an intense blue light.

EVENTS

14 May: Festa di San Costanzo with a procession to Marina Grande and a big firework display in the evening.
On 13 June Anacapri honours San

Antonio di Padova with a procession and spectacular pyrotechnics.
The *Settembrata Anacaprese* in the first week of September is a rustic festival celebrating the grape harvest with colourful processions.

WHERE TO EAT

► Expensive

Anacapri* • ① *Add'ò Riccio
Via Gradola 4
Tel. 08 18 37 13 80; mid-March–Oct
Fresh and superbly prepared fish served in a spectacular cliff location above the Blue Grotto. This friendly and unpretentious terrace restaurant also has its own small baths (stabilimento balneare).

Anacapri* • ② *Da Gelsomina
Via Migliera 72
Tel. & fax 08 18 37 14 99; March–Dec
Fine country and fish cuisine, 30 min on foot from Anacapri, ideal for working up an appetite. Cosy guest rooms with nice views are also available (see below).

Capri* • ③ *Le Grottelle
Via Arco Naturale 13
Tel. 08 18 37 57 19; Easter–late Oct
Romantic terrace restaurant a few hundred metres away from the Arco Naturale. Fantastic location, good food – and steep bills. In bad weather three tables are placed in a cave, hence the name.

Capri* • ④ *Da Gemma
Via Madre Serafina 6
Tel. 08 18 37 04 61
March–Dec; closed Mon
Wonderfully cosy trattoria/pizzeria where Graham Greene used to dine (photos of famous diners adorn the walls). The antipasti buffet has an extensive selection. In the summer, diners sit on a glass-covered veranda, while in the winter the pizza oven stokes up the temperature in the vaults.

► Moderate

Capri* • ⑤ *Lo Sfizio
Via Tiberio 7/e
Tel. 08 18 37 41 28, closed Tue, in winter only Sat and Sun
Family-run trattopria that is also frequented by locals; on the way to Villa Jovis. Good vegetable antipasti, grilled chicken and in the evenings also pizza

Capri* • ⑥ *La Savardina da Eduardo
Via Lo Capo 8
Tel. 08 18 37 63 00; closed Tue
www.caprilasavardina.com
Cosy garden restaurant just before Villa Jovis, between the grapevines and the lemons. Most of the ingredients that go into everything from the antipasti to the dolci come from the garden, while the fish is caught by an uncle. The Tarantino family also runs the Ristorante-Albergo Belsito (see above).

► Inexpensive

Capri* • ⑦ *Pulalli
Piazza Umberto I 4
Tel. 08 18 37 41 08
Closed Tue.
Wine bar and ristorante with a

! *Baedeker* TIP

Gelato al limone

Make sure to taste the refreshing lemon ice cream on the islands of lemons! The best places are Chiosco Veneruso on the Piazetta, where tourists have refreshed themselves since the 1920s, Buonocore in Via Vittorio Emanuele, where there are often long lines, or at Il Gelato al Limone before embarking at the harbour.

The Piazzetta is also known as the »Mediterranean's theatre of the world«

fantastic terrace right above the piazzetta (reached by a few steps alongside the clock tower). Another mini terrace with views of the Bay of Naples, offering tasty snacks and a good selection of wines.

WHERE TO STAY

▶ Luxury

Capri* • ① *Quisisana
Via Camerelle 2,
Tel. 08 18 37 07 88
www.quisi.com
This grand hotel opened in 1845, initially as a sanatorium, hence the name. With gourmet restaurant, beauty centre, two pools and plenty to please the well-to-do traveller.

▶ Mid-range

Anacapri* • ② *Da Gelsomina
Via Migliera 72
Tel. & fax 08 18 37 14 99
www.dagelsomina.com
Easter–early Nov
Popular family restaurant (see above) offering quiet, comfortable guest rooms with views of Ischia and the sunset. Pick-up from Anacapri with luggage can be arranged. There is also a small pool.

Capri* • ③ *La Prora
Via Castello 8, tel. 08 18 37 02 81
www.albergolaprora.it; Apr–Oct
Attentively run quiet B&B in a part of town above the piazzetta with winding alleyways. Views of Capri or the sea from rooms 11 and 20.

Capri* • ④ *Villa Sarah
Via Tiberio 3/A
Tel. 08 18 37 78 17
www.villasarah.it
Late March–late Oct. Stately villa quietly located in a large garden on the way to Villa Jovis. It has stylishly furnished rooms with balconies, and a small pool. In the summer breakfast is taken on the terrace.

▶ Budget

Anacapri* • ⑤ *B & B Maruzella
Via Lo Funno 15
Tel. & fax 08 18 37 27 68
Mobile phone 33 33 38 12 97
maruzzella.capri@email.it
The Capri experience beyond the glamour and mass tourism: the large veranda of the Biba family's farmhouse opens onto the Bay of Naples, surrounded by an organically cultivated vegetable garden and vine pergolas. On request, Signora Maria will cook for her guests.

half-forgotten little island. Within a few decades, Pagano's inn had become a flourishing hotel and dirt-poor Capri a **legend of late Romanticism**.

In the **1950s** the hitherto fairly exclusive Capri was developed into a destination for mass tourism. Popular it songs like »Isle of Capri«, recorded in 1957 by no less than Frank Sinatra himself, placed the island firmly in the popular imagination. Today, in peak season, up to 15,000 day trippers arrive daily, sometimes stretching the capacities of Capri to breaking point.

What to See in Capri

Capri town, Piazzetta

From the Marina Grande, where all ferries and hydrofoils dock, it is only a few minutes by cable car up to Capri town (pop. 7200, the larger of the two island communities) and **Piazza Umberto I**, or just »Piazzetta« for short. This square has been eulogized from time immemorial, referred to as the salon of Europe or the Mediterranean's theatre of the world. A flight of steps leads up to the **Chiesa Santo Stefano**, a Baroque church constructed at the end of the 17th century following Neapolitan models. Its campanile, standing slightly apart, is the symbol of Capri. The floor around the main altar is worth seeing; it was laid in 1759 using fragments of marble from Villa Jovis. The marble floor of the adjacent rosary chapel also dates back to antiquity. Opposite the 14th-century **Palazzo Cerio** was the residence of the island's historian Edwin Cerio. Today, it shelters a sleepy, picturesque museum with finds from nearly all periods of Capri's long history, as well as the extensive library bequeathed by Cerio (Centro Caprese Ignazio Cerio, Piazzetta Ignazio Cerio 8/A; Tue, Thu, Fri 4.30pm–8pm, Wed, Sat 9.30am–1pm).

Via Vittorio Emanuele

The centre of Capri is compact and at first glance appears to consist mainly of luxury boutiques. There are, however, a few places of cultural-historical significance. Thus, between 1870 and 1929, Via Vittorio Emanuele 27/29 (where the Italian luxury label Ferragamo now sells its elegant products) was the legendary **Café Zum Kater Hiddigeigei**. This is where all the illustrious visitors to Capri used to congregate. Today's **Hotel La Palma** just a few paces along (Via Vittorio Emanuele 39) is the original source of the story of Caprese hospitality. From 1826 onwards, **Giuseppe Pagano** entertained the European artists and writers who came to Capri following the discovery of the Blue Grotto. **Via Camerelle**, with its exclusive shops, leads to the **Quisisana hotel**, built by a Scottish doctor in around 1860 as a tuberculosis sanatorium and today one of the most luxurious hotels in the world.

Giardini di Augusto ★

Via F Serena and Via Matteotti lead to the Giardini di Augusto. The park, with its stupendous **views** of the sea and the **Faraglioni** (the famous trio of limestone stacks off Capri), was a gift from German industrial baron **Friedrich Alfred Krupp** (1854–1902). Via Krupp is

◄ Via Krupp

Capri Map

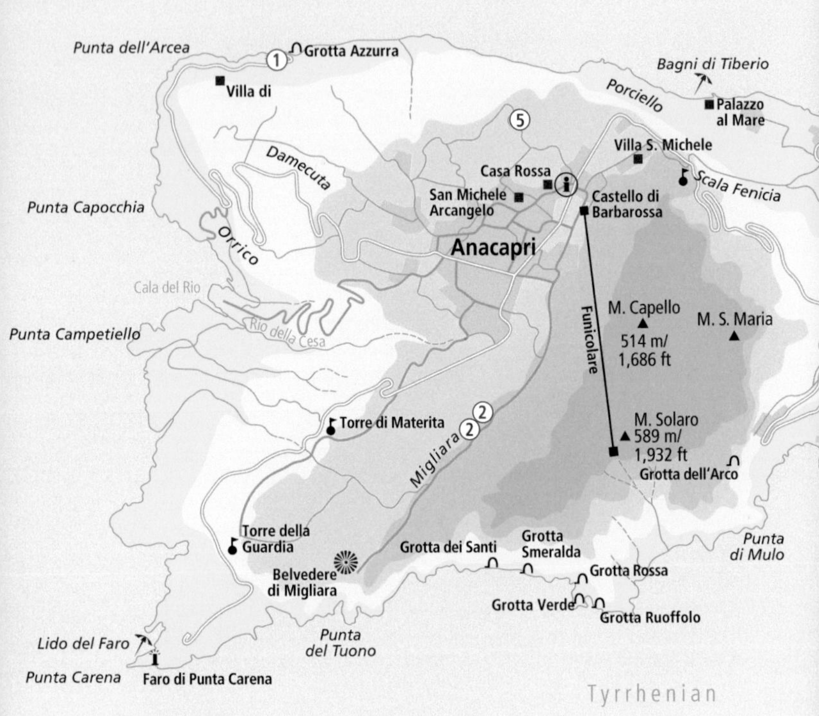

spectacular, winding down to the small harbour of Marina Piccola. Restored a few years ago, this is the road that the patron of the arts had built on his beloved Capri.

★ Certosa di San Giacomo

Close by, the Certosa di San Giacomo is Capri's most important sacred building. The monastery was established for the Carthusian order from 1371 onwards and, until its secularization under Joseph Bonaparte (the older brother of Napoleon and king of Spain, Naples and Sicily), was the island's real centre of power. Today, the former refectory exhibits paintings by the German painter **Karl Wilhelm Diefenbach** (Tue–Sun 9am–2pm).

★ Viewing points

From the Quisisana hotel, typical signposts made from colourful painted ceramics point to **Punta Tragara** or further along to the **Arco Naturale**, two viewing points whose beauty has long made visitors to Capri go weak at the knees.

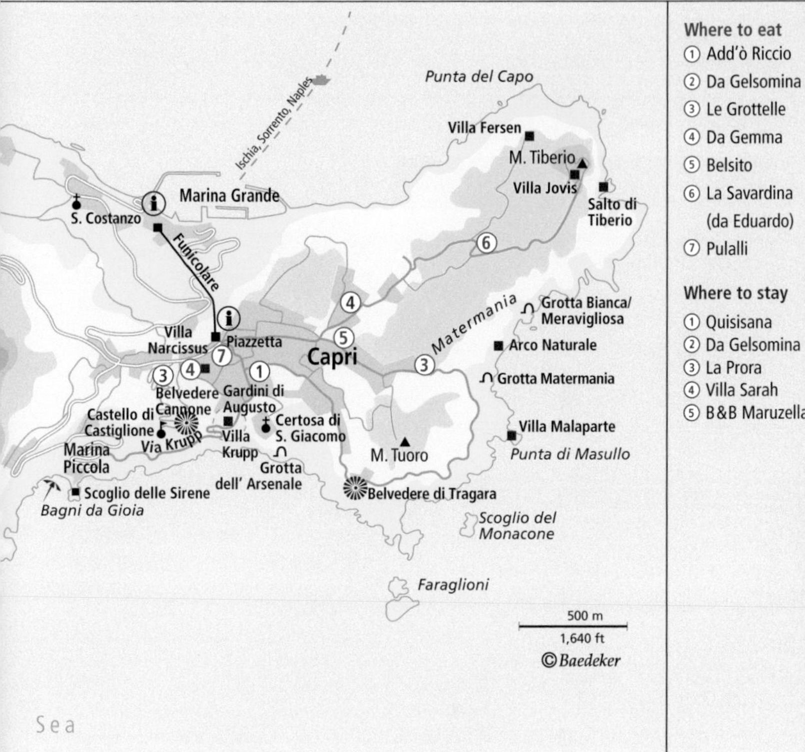

★ **Villa Malaparte**

Further along the route to the **Grotta Matromania**, one of the island's many natural caves, visitors can glimpse one of the most daring buildings in the history of modern Italian architecture. The villa of the German-Italian writer Curzio Malaparte (1898–1957), real name Kurt Erich Suckert, a writer, politician and journalist with a highly chequered biography, is famous the world over. Thanks to Malaparte's excellent contacts with the political elite, construction of the villa began in 1938, in a nature reserve – following designs by architect Adalberto Liberà and Malaparte himself – on the **Punta di Masullo**, a rocky ledge above the sea. Although Malaparte intended to bequeath the villa to the People's Republic of China, it belongs to the Ronchi family foundation and cannot be visited. But just the sight of this compact, bright-red building (10 x 54m/33 x 177ft), with its spectacular flight of stairs up to the roof terrace, makes this stroll worthwhile. It was here that Jean-Luc Godard shot his film *Le Mépris* in 1963.

✶✶ Villa Jovis, Palazzo di Tiberio

A none-too-strenuous stroll of about an hour leads from the Piazzetta to **Monte Tiberio**, in the northeast of the island. The mountain's rock walls, rising steeply 334m/1096ft out of the sea, hold the ruins of one of the largest imperial villas of the Roman Empire (Viale Amedeo Maiuri; daily 9am to one hour before sunset). For eleven years, Villa Jovis was the residence of Tiberius, who reigned over the empire from here. Named after the **god Jupiter** (»Giove« in Italian), the villa covered an area of nearly 7000 sq m/75,350 sq ft. Its unique location with a panoramic view over the entire Bay of Naples makes it seem less like one of the usual villae maritimae and more like a sea fortress.

The core of the complex is formed by four mighty **cisterns**, with the villa spreading out around it on different levels. The quantity of water required by the particularly lavishly equipped thermal baths alone must have been enormous. The cisterns had a capacity of over 8000 cubic metres (over two million US gallons). On the southern side of the ancient building, parallel to the entrance area with its generous atrium and various reception rooms, there used to be a series of luxurious **bathing rooms** following the model of Roman thermal spas of the time. The utility wing to the west housed a kitchen, storerooms and accommodation for the imperial servants across three levels. **Tiberius's private rooms** were in the northern part of the building. It was via a ramp that he would reach a footpath hewn into the rock, which arguably has views unrivalled anywhere in the world. The current state of the ruins is the result of an archaeological dig in the 1930s, carried out under Amedeo Maiuri. The theory that there was another storey above the central cistern owes more to conjecture than actual proof. The island legends surrounding the infamous **Salto di Tiberio**, the rocky overhang from which the emperor, in moments of arbitrary cruelty, is said to have had his victims flung down 300m/985ft, are also not particularly credible. The image of the unloved emperor painted by the authors of classical antiquity, such as Tacitus, is distorted to the extent that he is hardly recognisable.

! *Baedeker* TIP

Literary cemetery with a view

One of the most atmospheric places in the entire gulf is the cemetery for »non-Catholics« (cimiterio acattolico). Founded in 1879 by the English and German expatriate colony, the cemetery is a part of cultural history. Most of those buried here are long forgotten now: artists, intellectuals, outsiders and adventurers as well as victims of lung disease and suicides are gathered here, amongst them **Norman Douglas**, the author of German-Scottish descent who wrote a few classics of Italian travel literature.

✶ Villa Lysis

In 1905, the French poet and heir to a millionaire's fortune, **Jacques d'Adelswaerd Fersen**, had his Capri residence built in a fanciful late-classical style. This is where, together with Nino Cesarini, a former newspaper seller and construction labourer from Rome, Fersen celebrated a life devoted to beauty and drugs, which he terminated with

Villa Jovis Plan

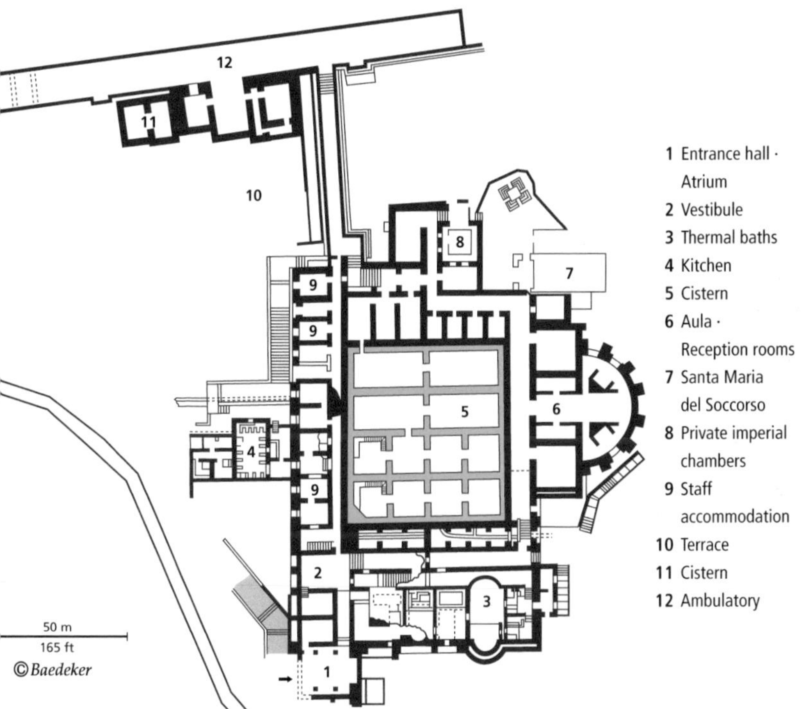

1 Entrance hall · Atrium
2 Vestibule
3 Thermal baths
4 Kitchen
5 Cistern
6 Aula · Reception rooms
7 Santa Maria del Soccorso
8 Private imperial chambers
9 Staff accommodation
10 Terrace
11 Cistern
12 Ambulatory

a deliberate overdose in 1923. Villa Lysis was a cultural centre until recently. At present it is for sale and not open to the public.

Anacapri

The other island community

Whilst Capri is given over entirely to the world of the rich and famous, Anacapri (pop. 6200) is trying to preserve its small-town image. However, even here the sheer volume of day trippers often makes the old-world island romanticism seem somewhat like a stage set. The rivalry between Capri and Anacapri is part of island folklore. It was not until 1877 that the first road link was opened between the two villages; before that the **Scala Fenicia** had been the sole, arduous connection (►History).

✶ Villa San Michele

The centre of Anacapri tourism is **Piazza Vittoria**. From here a path leads to Villa San Michele, a famous sight turned decades ago into a legend by a novel. The Swedish doctor **Axel Munthe** (1857–1949) is one of the main protagonists of local Caprese history. The fashionable doctor, militant animal rights activist and not particularly modest writer landed a worldwide bestseller with *The Story of San Michele*. From 1896 onwards, Munthe had a gleaming white house built on the ruins of an ancient villa and the remains of a chapel (May–Sept 9am–6pm, Oct, Apr to 5pm, Nov–Feb to 3.30pm, March to 4.30pm). The interior of the villa is a captivating jumble of antiques, devotional objects and Roman finds, with a famous stone sphinx on one of the terraces. Due to an eye condition, Munthe was not able to enjoy his light- and sun-filled villa for long, retiring in 1910 to the nearby **Torre Materita**.

Castello di Barbarossa ► Lying above the Munthe villa, the so-called Castello di Barbarossa, a ruined castle dating from the 12th century, owes its name to the Turkish pirate Caireddin Barbarossa, who destroyed the castello in 1535.

More sights in Anacapri

Anacapri's charm is entirely dependent on the tides of day trippers disembarking from coaches. This makes the late afternoon a propitious time for a stroll through the Old Town, centred on **Piazza Armando Diaz**. An idyllic area, with its quiet alleyways and little whitewashed houses, the **Le Boffe quarter** is located southeast of the piazza, behind the Santa Sofia parish church.

✱ Casa Rossa ► Also recommended is a visit to the Casa Rossa (Via Giuseppe Orlandi, daily 11am–1pm and 6pm–9.30pm, closed Mon mornings). The pseudo Norman-Arab style edifice built from 1876 by the American colonel and amateur archaeologist John Clay MacKowen exhibits numerous architectural and decorative fragments dating from antiquity.

San Michele Arcangelo ► The church of San Michele Arcangelo, built in 1719 to a design by **Domenico Antonio Vaccaro**, is worth a visit for its majolica floor in particular. Whilst the latter was only finished in 1761, it probably dates back to a design by Vaccaro (who also played a major part in the construction of the Chiostro delle Maioliche in Naples' Santa Chiara church). The vibrantly coloured floor shows the expulsion of Adam and Eve from paradise by the archangel Michael. The view from the organ loft is particularly fine (Piazza San Nicola; Apr–Oct daily 9am–7pm, Nov–March 10am–3pm).

✱ **Grotta Azzurra**

No less paradisiacal is the walk from Anacapri, taking about an hour, past the remains of the ancient **Villa di Damecuta** to the Blue Grotto. A **tourist attraction of worldwide fame**, the grotto has also come to represent an almost mystical level of natural beauty. However, especially for Capri day-trippers, a visit to the karst cave (30m/100ft high, 54m/177ft long and 15m/50ft wide) tends to be anything but romantic. After approaching by motorboat from Marina Grande, visitors change into smaller rowing boats in front of the opening to the cave proper – but only if the sea is calm. The visit to this wonder of the world is then usually disappointingly short and, due to the high number of other boats, can almost never really be enjoyed undisturbed. Nevertheless, on sunny mornings the light effects in the grotto are overwhelmingly beautiful. The sunlight entering through an opening deep down below sea level gives the water an amazing blue tint and seems to lend any object dipped into the water an instant silver coating. During antiquity, the grotto was a nymphaeum and probably connected by a subterranean passage with **Villa di Damecuta** above, a summer residence belonging to Tiberius (Via Amedeo Maiuri; daily 9am–2pm). The villa was only excavated from 1937 onwards, after having served as a stone quarry for nearly 200 years. Situated directly above the Blue Grotto and connected with it by means of a stairway cut out of the rock, **Villa di Gradola** consists of the remains of another ancient villa maritimae. Many of the finds dug up in the 19th century were reused during the construction of the Casa Rossa.

◄ Visiting the Blue Grotto: best on sunny mornings!

✶ **Monte Solaro**

South of Piazza Vittorio lies the valley station of the Seggiovia chair lift, which takes visitors up to Monte Solaro (589m/1932ft) in just a few minutes. On foot, the ascent takes about an hour. The views from Capri's highest elevation are stunning.

The much-praised Blue Grotto in the northwest of Capri

Capua and ★ Santa Maria Capua Vetere

D 2

Region: Campania
Altitude: 36m and 25m/118ft and 82ft
Province: Caserta
Population: S. Maria Capua Vetere: 31,000; Capua: 19,000

These two towns in the Campanian interior have been separate municipalities for a long time, but their common history is evident everywhere.

★ Santa Maria Capua Vetere · Ancient Capua

History

In the 4th century BC, Santa Maria Capua Vetere, ancient Capua, was the largest town in Campania, but by the early Middle Ages it had descended to the level of an insignificant village. The Appian Way, the first and most important of all Roman military roads, is today a tranquil provincial road leading through the town.

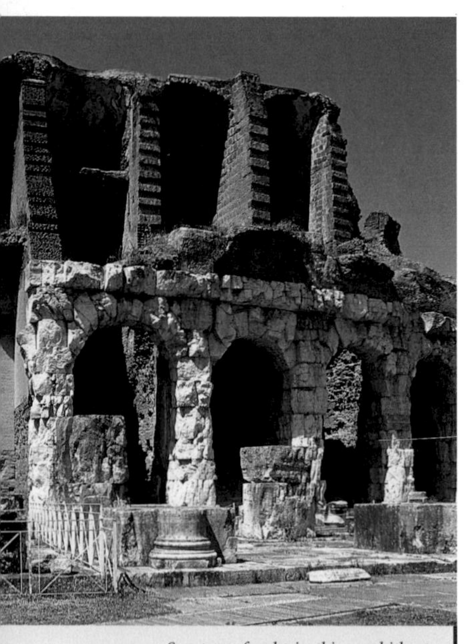

Spartacus fought in this amphitheatre

Originally an Oscan settlement, Capua was Etruscan in the 6th century BC, then Samnite and, after an extended struggle, became a Roman colony in 338 BC. The construction of the Via Appia connected Rome with the southern provinces and made Capua an important base for Roman expansion policy. The town was famous for its amphitheatre and adjoining gladiator school where **Spartacus**, a slave from Thrace, is said to have started the revolt named after him. However, Capua was destroyed as early as 456 by the Goths, and in 841 it was ravaged by the Saracens to the extent that the town could no longer be maintained. Today's Capua was founded 5km/3mi away in a bend of the Volturno river by Lombards in 1856.

★★ Anfiteatro Campano

It was mainly due to its dimensions that the second-largest amphitheatre in Italy after the Roman Colosseum withstood the ravages of time. Whilst now a ruin, a lot of stone having been taken for other uses over the centuries, the construction built under Emperor Hadrian is still impressive (located in the northwest of the town, Piazza 1 Ottobre; Tue–Sun 9am to one hour before sunset, in the winter months to 4pm). Measuring 170 x 140m/185 x 153yd, the theatre held some 50,000 people and had lower floors reminiscent in their ingenious design of the amphitheatre at Pozzuoli. A small museum displays decorative fragments from the theatre and has a permanent exhibition on the **world of the gladiators**. Standing near the amphitheatre on today's Via Aldo Moro is the **Arco di Adriano** from the time of Hadrian; the Via Appia once passed through here.

◄ Museo dei Gladiatori

✶ **Mithraeum**

In 1922, a mithraeum dating from the 2nd century AD was discovered in Santa Maria Capua Vetere (visits by request; enquire at the amphitheatre or museum; Via Morelli). The subterranean sanctuary dedicated to the Persian god Mithras escaped the destructions of the Post Classic period and is well preserved. Gods of foreign religions such as Isis, Serapis or, in this case, Mithras reached southern Italy via the international port of Pozzuoli. The **cult of Mithras** was particularly popular with Roman legionnaires; though the details of its rites are now almost entirely **unknown**. Of central importance was the killing of a bull by the god, often interpreted as an act of creation. The followers of Mithras were initiated into the mystery in seven steps. The Capuan mithraeum is an L-shaped vault with its main section decorated by frescoes. The central motif of the paintings, which have not yet been fully deciphered, shows Mithras killing the bull.

A key scene from the Mithras cult: the killing of the bull

Museo Archeologico

The Museo Archeologico dell'Antica Capua was established in a historical palazzo in 1995. Dating from the late Middle Ages, the building occupies the site of the old forum. Laid out over ten rooms, the collection illustrates the history of Capua from its Oscan foundation to the town's Romanization in the 4th century BC. The Samnite warrior graves are decorated with expressive frescoes reminiscent of the tomb paintings in the museum at Paestum (Via Roberto d'Angiò 48; Tue–Sun 9am–7pm).

Reminders of the Roman past can also be found in some of Capua's churches. In **Santa Maria Maggiore cathedral** ancient columns were reused, and the **Chiesa di San Erasmo** was called »in capitolio«, as it was built on the ruins of the capitol.

VISITING CAPUA

INFORMATION

Pro Loco di Capua
Piazza dei Giudici 4
Tel. & fax 08 23 96 27 29
www.capuaonline.com
www.cittadicapua.it

EVENTS

Carnevale: Capua calls itself »la città che ride« (the town that laughs) – for over 100 years carnival has been celebrated here for a week every spring. *Teatri di Pietra:* from late July to mid-August in the amphitheatre of Santa Maria Capua Vetere and in the other ancient theatres of Caserta province, such as Teano or Sessa Aurunca, Greek drama, Roman comedies and contem-porary works are performed (tel. 08 23 79 57 32 www.teatridipietra.org). *Mitreo Film Festival:* in mid-December short films by young talent are shown in Santa Maria Capua Vetere's Teatro Garibaldi (www.mitreofilmfestival.it).

SHOPPING

Agricultural produce from the Campania felix is laid out behind the cathedral in Capua every morning Tue–Sat; on Mondays, there is a weekly market at the Largo Porta Napoli.

WHERE TO EAT

► Moderate

Capua • ① Osteria dei Nobiluomini
Piazza De Renzis 6
Tel. 08 23 62 00 62
www.osteriadeinobiluomini.it. Closed Sun eve and Mon
Old Town restaurant with modern ambience, creative regional cuisine and a good wine list. During summer there are tables on the piazza.

Santa Maria Capua Vetere • Ninfeo
Traversa Cappabianca
(opposite the law courts)
Tel. 08 23 84 67 00; closed Sun eve
Chef and sommelier Antonio Leonelli upholds the traditions of Campanian cuisine. Home-made pasta, fish and meat dishes.

Capua • ④ Gelateria La Paletta d'Oro
Via Gran Priorato di Malta
Tel. 08 23 62 19 54; closed Tue
Legendary ice cream temple near the cathedral

► Inexpensive

Capua • ② Romano
Corso Appio 34–36 (Piazza Medaglie d'Oro), tel. 08 23 96 17 26; closed Tue
Whilst the vaults of this family trattoria might have lost a little of their charm during a recent refurbishment, the cuisine has not suffered in the process at all. Pizza served in the evenings too. Attracts a younger clientele.

Baedeker recommendation

Capua • ③ Ex Libris
Corso Gran Priorato di Malta 25
Tel. 08 23 96 20 97;
www.architempo.it, www.palazzolanza.it
closed Mon. Arts in the palazzo: Maria Teresa runs a literary café with ristorante in the house of her ancestors (Thu, Fri, Sat eve and Sun lunch), as well as a bookshop and a small bed & breakfast.

Santa Maria Capua Vetere • La Spelunka
Via Pietro Morelli 9, closed Tue
Tel. 08 23 84 47 78
Nice restaurant in a garden of orange

Capua Map

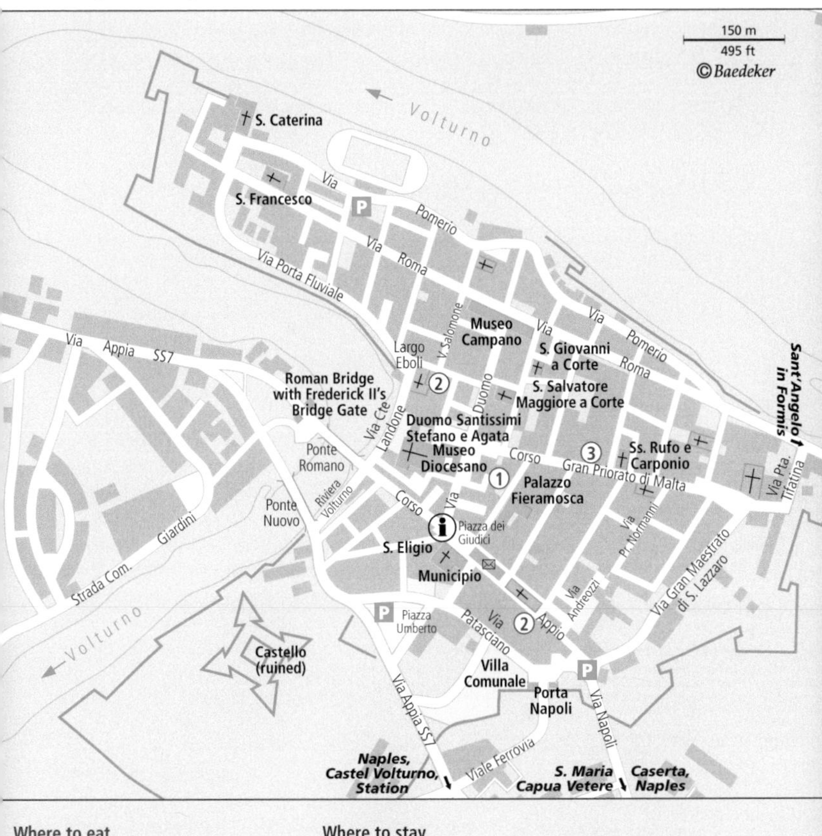

Where to eat
① Osteria dei Nobiluomini
② Romano
③ Ex Libris

Where to stay
① Masseria Giò Sole Agriturismo
② Seminarium Campanum

trees near the archaeological museums. Local cooking, meat from the grill

WHERE TO STAY

► Mid-range

Capua* • ① *Masseria Giò Sole Agriturismo
Via Giardini 31 (direction of Brezza)
Tel. 08 23 96 11 08
www.masseriagiosole.com
The Pasca di Magliano farmhouse lies 1km/0.6mi west of Capua on the northern banks of the Volturno. Cosy guest quarters in the former utility rooms. In the evening, guests can take advantage of a room with a fireplace. Tasty country cuisine with organic ingredients. With patio, pool, bikes for guests and a farm shop.

Around Santa Maria Capua Vetere

Just outside the town in the direction of Caserta lie the so-called **carceri vecchie** on the left side of the ancient Appian Way. Popularly believed to have been a gladiator's prison in the Post Classic period, this is one of the largest Roman tombs in Campania. Further along in the direction of Caserta, to the right this time, rises **La Canocchia**, another ancient tomb monument from the 2nd or 3rd century AD.

Capua · Medieval Town

History

Modern-day Capua was founded by the Lombards on the site of the Roman Casilinum, the river port of ancient Capua. This »new« town was built from the remains of the old one, so that today's Capua effectively consists of many reused building materials from the former capital of Campania felix. Alongside Benevento, Capua was one of the most important towns of the Italian Lombard empire. In 1076, Normans conquered the town, while the Hohenstaufen king Frederick II established the famous bridge gate at this strategically important spot in his empire. During the Second World War, Capua's historic centre was heavily damaged during bombing raids by Allied squadrons.

What to see in Capua

The centro storico, a monument to southern Italy's medieval history, is small and largely restored, with the main sights easily reached on foot. **Corso Appio**, with its Roman bridge across the Volturno (reconstructed after the war), was ancient Casilinum's main thoroughfare, whilst today's Piazza del Giudice was possibly the small Roman town's forum. Seven large relief heads from the amphitheatre of old Capua are built into the wall of the Municipio's façade.

✶ Duomo Santissimi Stefano e Agata

Founded in 856 by the Lombard Bishop Landolf, the cathedral was rebuilt in the 12th century, given a Baroque makeover in the 18th century, and destroyed in 1943. During reconstruction, the interior was recreated in Romanesque style. Note the 13th-century Easter candelabra standing to the right of the main altar. The atrium with columns from ancient Capua escaped destruction, while the Lombard campanile has also withstood the passage of the centuries.

Remnants of the past

Capua's biggest attractions are the ubiquitous remains from Roman, Lombard, Norman and Hohenstaufen times. A stroll around the town soon reveals columns with mighty capitals and fragments of sculpture built into walls and in courtyards. The Norman **Castello delle Pietre** (not open to the pubic) also consists mainly of ancient spolia. Capua's most famous structure, the bridge gate of **Frederick II** (1234–39), was destroyed in the Second World War. It had already been partly dismantled as early as the 16th century, when Charles V had the town wall reconstructed. All that remains are the octagonal pediments. A part of the rich **sculptural decoration** can be seen at the Museo Campano.

Bridge gate of Frederick II ►

The **Museo Campano**, in the Palazzo Antignano at the end of Via Duomo (entrance on Via Roma), is well worth visiting. It contains some spectacular exhibits, such as the Roman mosaics from the temple dedicated to Diana Tifatina, today's church of Sant'Angelo in Formis. The **matres matutae** – female figures with babes-in-arms, hewn from tuff stone (some larger than life) – are the votive offerings of an old Campanian fertility cult. The **sculptural decoration** of the Hohenstaufen bridge gate alone makes the visit worthwhile. The German historian and Nobel Prize winner Theodor Mommsen put together an extensive catalogue of the preserved Roman inscriptions in Capua, from 1880 onwards (Via Roma 68; Tue–Fri 9am–1.30pm, Sun only to 1pm).

Symbol of fertility: one of the »Matres«

★★ Caserta

E 2

Region: Campania
Altitude: 68m/223ft

Province: Caserta
Population: 80,000

The Reggia di Caserta, centre of the vibrant provincial capital at the foot of Monte Tifata, is one of the largest castles ever built by a European monarch during the period of absolutism.

★★ Palazzo Reale · La Reggia

Opening hours:
Wed–Mon
8.30am–7.30pm
last admission: 7pm

Charles III of Bourbon inherited from his great-grandfather – French King Louis XIV – not only a passion for hunting, but also for building. Following the example of Versailles, a new residence was established far from the cramped and overcrowded capital of Naples. This posed a severe challenge to the man commissioned to build it, **Luigi Vanvitelli**, the greatest architect of Neapolitan Baroque. In order to provide the castle and the huge park in particular with water, the Acquedotto Carolino was designed to bring drinking water from the springs of Monte Taburno all the way to Caserta, a distance of 41km/25mi. The construction of the Carolino Aqueduct, much admired at the time, is said to have cost as much as the entire

Central feature of the Reggia: Vanvitelli's magnificent staircase

A perpetual construction site ▶

castle. The foundation stone was laid on 20 January 1752, the king's 36th birthday. Saluting soldiers marked the outline of the future castle, and Vanvitelli's foundation stone bore the inscription: »May this house and its threshold endure as long as the Bourbon dynasty, until this stone flies up into the air!«

In the end, Caserta castle did not prove very propitious for the Bourbons. When Charles III left Naples in 1759, the complex was still a construction site. After the death of Vanvitelli in 1773, his son Carlo took over the construction management. However, the original plans were never fully implemented. No central dome was built; nor were the four corner towers. Planned as a square, the extension of the building to a rectangle to accommodate the king's demands for more space was to the detriment of Vanvitelli's façade design. Furnishing the rooms also took far into the 19th century. Ferdinand II and his family were the only people to really live here.To this day, the dimensions of one of the largest castles of European absolutism – along with the Spanish Escorial and Versailles in France – are still astounding: covering 44,300 sq m/476,841 sq ft (of which 16,000 sq m/over 172,000 sq ft are taken up by the four interior courtyards alone), the castle has a façade 247m/810ft wide and sides of 184m/603ft in length each. Over 1200 rooms, 1741 windows, two mighty staircases, 30 ancillary flights of stairs and a theatre with a rear stage wall that could be opened towards the park allowing very special effects, make this residence a unique monument of European architectural history.

La Reggia in figures ▶

Son of the Dutch-born painter Gaspar van Wittel, architect Luigi Vanvitelli (1700–73) did much to shape the appearance of 18th-century Naples. However, the construction of the castle at Caserta became his life's work.

◄ The architect Luigi Vanvitelli

The Reggia in the 19th and 20th centuries

In 1860, the Bourbons left Naples and, from then on, the House of Savoy became the supplier of kings for a united Italy. Rome, Turin and Milan became the centres of the new kingdom. Since 1921, the Reggia has been owned by the state. For a short time, in 1943, it was the headquarters of the Allied forces in the Mediterranean; in 1945, one of the documents of surrender was signed by the German Wehrmacht here. The restored royal apartments have been open to the public since the 1950s. In 1994, the throne room saw a ceremonial dinner in honour of the heads of state participating in the G7 Summit. The staircase and vestibule of the first floor served as a backdrop for some scenes in the *Star Wars* films: the Reggia was last rented by the American director George Lucas in 2005. Only a very small proportion of the rooms can be visited. In addition to being a museum, the Reggia houses municipal authorities, the offices of the Soprintendenza (archaeological supervisory body), and a military academy, the Scuola Aereonautica.

VISITING CASERTA

INFORMATION

EPT
Palazzo Reale, 81100 Caserta
Tel. 08 23 55 00 11, www.eptcaserta.it
Info Point Turistico
Viale G. Douhet 2a; tel. 08 23 32 11 37
www.casertaturismo.it

GOOD TO KNOW

Shopping: in and around San Leucio some silk manufacturers are still in operation. They use age-old designs to make curtain and upholstery fabrics, plus fabric wall-coverings (showrooms on Piazza della Seta and Piazza Scuderia).

Hiking in the Oasi di San Silvestro: the preservation of 76ha/188ac of magnificent evergreen oak forest on the hill bordering the Reggia park, to the north, can be put down to Ferdinand IV's passion for hunting. The World Wildlife Fund organizes guided walks through the nature reserve (Via Giardini Reali 1 bis, 1km/0.6mi from San Leucia in the direction of Castel Morrone; tel. 08 23 36 13 00, www.laghiandaia.info; Mar and Oct until mid-Nov 11am and 3pm, April–July and Sept 10.30am and 5pm; free admission for WWF members).

EVENTS

Leuciana Festival: in July, the Real Belvedere of San Leucio complex becomes the stage for a renowned theatre and music festival (www.leuciana.org). ***Settembre al Borgo:*** in early September, the historical town centres of Casertavecchia and San Leucio provide a charming backdrop for this international theatre, ballet and music festival (www.settembrealborgo.it).

WHERE TO EAT

► Moderate

San Leucio · Antica Locanda
Piazza della Seta 8/10 A
Tel. 08 23 30 54 44,
www.ristoranteanticalocanda.com
Closed Sun eve and Mon
Elegant speciality restaurant in the centre of town, its tables decked out with the finest silk brocade. There are mouth-watering pasta dishes, whilst the winter menu features dried cod, roast pork and salsicce (sausages).

Casertavecchia · Gli Scacchi
Via Sant'Annunziata 5
Tel. 08 23 37 10 86, closed Mon–Wed
Owner Gino Della Valle and his wife Marilena display great enthusiasm for rediscovering traditional recipes, and they are also not averse to culinary experiments. In a verdant spot outside the centre of the Old Town near the large car park.

Le Colonne
Via Nazionale Appia 7/13
Tel. 08 23 46 74 94, closed Tue
The finest cucina casertana home-cooking in a gem of an Art Nouveau building 1km/0.6mi west of the Reggia. Buffalo ricotta and mozzarella are some of the classic ingredients used here, while the roast buffalo braised in Aglianico wine is also recommended.

Casagiove · Le Quattro Fontane
Via Quartiere Vecchio 60
Tel. 08 23 46 89 7, closed Sun
Trattoria in the Casagiove part of town west of the Reggia. Popular with locals and highly rated by the Slow Food movement. Rustic cuisine with hearty seasonal soups.

► Inexpensive

Angelica Caffè & Self Service
Palazzo Reale, tel. 08 23 35 58 68, closed Tue
Pleasant, modern caffè-bar serving tasty pasta and salads at lunchtime.

WHERE TO STAY

► Mid-range

Amadeus
Via Verdi 72, tel. 08 23 35 26 63
www.hotelamadeuscaserta.it
Comfortable, small albergo within walking distance of Reggia and railway station.

Jolly
Viale Vittorio Veneto 9
Tel. 08 23 32 52 22
www.jollyhotelcaserta.it
Dependable fare within walking distance of railway station and Reggia.

Castel Campagnano · Castello Ducale
Via Chiesa 3, tel. & fax 08 23 86 30 31
www.castelloducale.com
Ferdinand IV's former hunting lodge with a view of the Matese Hills. Elegant rooms and pool. Organic wine is aged in a tuffstone cellar and served with regional sausage and cheese.

► Budget/Mid-range

B & B Galileo Galilei
Via Galilei 12, tel. 08 23 27 93 35
Mobile no. 33 92 64 61 77, bb_galileo-galilei@libero.it – 19th-century palazzo on a road intersecting with Corso Trieste, some 800m/875yd east of the Reggia. The rooms are reasonable and Livia Messina has good tips for her guests. Public car park and good-value trattorias nearby.

► Budget

Casertavecchia · Caserta Antica
Via Tiglio 75, tel. & fax 08 23 37 11 58
www.hotelcaserta-antica.it
Laid-back, quiet hotel in a green setting, 500m/550yd east of the little town. Good restaurant and pool.

Tour of the Reggia

★★ Vanvitelli's staircase

Vanvitelli's staircase is the heart of the castle. Decorated with precious marble, the stairway leads into the first floor's octagonal vestibule. The three figures in alcoves in the central wall symbolize the monarch flanked by allegories of power and merit. The ceiling fresco (1769) shows Apollo surrounded by the circle of the seasons. The **vestibule**, another work of late Baroque architectural art, gives access to the court chapel as well as the royal chambers. At the request of Charles III, the chapel (consecrated in 1784) was designed in the style of the castle at Versailles.

Baedeker TIP

Modern art at the castle

Lucio Amelio, the legendary Neapolitan gallery owner (1931–94), wanted to bequeath his collection of contemporary art to the city of Naples. When the gesture was met with a friendly refusal, the city being concerned about follow-up costs, the art works went to the city of Caserta. Today, the Reggia presents the collection (with works by Joseph Beuys, Tony Cragg, Keith Haring, Anselm Kiefer, Gilbert & George, etc.) under the title »Terrae Motus«. Even visitors not too enamoured of modern art should take a look at the particularly beautiful exhibition rooms.

Caserta was conceived not just as a royal residence. Rather it was a place to hold the entire apparatus of government. The first of the large **state rooms** (Sala degli Alabardieri, Sala delle Guardie del Corpo) still go back to Vanvitelli's designs. The ceiling frescoes from the last decades of the 18th century glorify the House of Bourbon. The bust of Ferdinand IV on one of the console tables was sculpted by **Antonio Canova**. The **Sala di Alessandro**, connecting the east and west wings, owes its name to the ceiling fresco by Mariano Rossi (1787) showing the marriage of Alexander the Great. Two parlours from Napoleonic times dedicated to Mars and Astraea lead to the **throne room**, the largest room in the castle. The ceiling fresco shows the laying of the foundation stone of the Reggia in the presence of the royal couple. A frieze with 44 medallions showing the Sicilian-Neapolitan kings runs along the wall.

Royal apartments

The continuation of the tour leads through the royal apartments, whose furnishings are of more interest to the study of cultural history than the history of art itself. The floors with hand-painted Neapolitan tiles are extraordinary, while the so-called »finto legno« (fake wood), which gives the appearance of a wooden floor, is most unusual. The bedrooms of Gioacchino Murat and Ferdinand II, complete with their original furniture, are worth taking a look at, as is the latter's bathroom with an ostentatious marble dressing table.

◄ The east wing

From the Sala di Alessandro, the tour carries on into the apartments of the **east wing**. The veduta (vista paintings) seen on entering the Sala della Primavera are by the Neapolitan court painter **Jacob Philipp Hackert**, and the ceiling fresco showing an allegory of spring was

The water flows down a 78m/256ft cliff, constructed especially

painted by Antonio Dominici (1779). The succeeding rooms are dedicated to the seasons. The mantelpieces are decorated with sumptuous vases from the famous German Meissen porcelain manufactory. The gouaches hanging on the walls of the small study used by Ferdinand IV are by Hackert. Next are the private dwellings of Queen Maria Carolina. Sister of Marie Antoinette, she had her rooms decorated in the Neapolitan version of the Louis XVI style. In the Sala Ellittica, an exceptionally large **nativity scene** is on display all year round. Most of the figures date back to the second half of the 18th century.

✶✶ Castle Grounds

Opening hours:
Nov–Feb
8.30am–3.30pm
March, Sept, Oct
8.30am–5pm
April to 6pm
May, Aug to 6.30pm
June/July to 7pm
(last admission:
one hour before
closing time)

Vanvitelli's genius is also shown in the castle's park, whose incredible dimensions demonstrate the Bourbon kings' claim to absolutist power. Due to its size, the park is less conducive to strolling than to **horse-drawn carriage rides**. There is also a coach connecting the castle with the great cascade.
Following the tastes of the time, nature was transformed with mathematical precision into an artificial world for the senses. The 3km/1.8mi-long central axis offers a view, seemingly stretching into infinity, of a landscape entirely subjected to the royal will. This line of perspective running into the far distance is structured by pools and smaller cascades, with the silvery shimmer of the central waterfall at its end. The waterfall's monumental scale only becomes apparent close-up. In the groups of figures to either side of the great cascade the **sculptural decoration** follows a strict programme inspired by Ovid's *Metamorphoses*, depicting Actaeon transformed into a stag by Diana.

Not far from the great cascade, the path leads to a seemingly natural spectacle – which is no less artificial. On the suggestion of Lord Hamilton, the English ambassador to the court of Naples, Queen Maria Carolina had an **English garden** laid out here, with a ruined temple, exotic plants, secluded little paths, an open-air theatre and a cryptoportico (covered passageway) based on the Pompeian ruins. (Note that the garden closes an hour earlier than the park.)

★ ◄ Giardino inglese

Around Caserta

Lying in the hills above the Reggia, 2km/1.2mi from the castle park, San Leucio is both a pretty resort and a complex to marvel at. From 1779 onwards, Ferdinand IV had his **personal utopia** built here: Ferdinandopoli was intended as an idyllic counterpoint to the regimented life at court. The king decreed his own constitution, had houses built for his subjects and founded a silk factory, one of the few successful ventures of his reign. The clients of local silk firms today include Buckingham Palace and the White House. Together with the Royal Palace at Caserta and the Aqueduct of Vanvitelli, the San Leucio complex is on the UNESCO World Heritage list. Over the past few years, the Real Fabbrica di San Leucio has been sumptuously restored and today serves as a **museum of early industrial history**. In the **Belvedere**, the castle proper, it is the interior courtyard that is most worth seeing (Wed–Mon, in the winter months 9am–6pm, last guided tour 5pm; in the summer months 9.30am–6.30pm, last guided tour 5.30pm).

★ **San Leucio**

★ ◄ Real Fabbrica di San Leucio

The little town of Casertavecchia on the slopes of Monte Virgo is a popular destination for Neapolitans, not least because of its restaurants. The town owes its enchanted sleeping-beauty quality to the way Caserta grew up around the Royal Palace. The old settlement was abandoned, leaving its picturesque appearance intact. This original Caserta (the appendage »vecchia«, meaning old, was added only in 1819) was established in the 8th century by the Lombards and became a bishopric in 1113. The ruins of the castle, which originally had six towers, give an idea of the town's importance in the early Middle Ages. The cathedral of San Michele, dating from the time of the first bishops, is an impressive example of Romanesque architecture. The 13th-century pulpit, parts of the floor and the ancient columns crowned by pretty capitals are all especially noteworthy. The domed basilica exhibits Arab-Norman influence, while the freestanding **campanile** (1234) is the town's symbol.

★★ **Casertavecchia**

★ ◄ San Michele

In the early Middle Ages an earlier building stood here, on the ruins of a Roman temple dedicated to Diana. The Benedictine monks of Montecassino had today's basilica erected from 1072 onwards. Their abbot, Desiderius, is represented on the left-hand side of the apse fresco. He is portrayed as benefactor, with a model of a church in his

★★ **Sant'Angelo in Formis**

Medieval atmosphere at Casertavecchia

hands. The vestibule with its five Arab-style pointed arches is unusual, while the **unique frescoes**, predominantly showing scenes from the Old Testament, are still entirely influenced by the Byzantine style. The columns and capitals are ancient, with the partly preserved floor also probably originally from the Roman Temple of Diana. The church is dedicated to the archangel Michael (Via Luigi Baia; daily 9.30am–12.30pm and 3.30pm–7pm).

★ Acquedotto

Near the town of **Maddaloni**, an aqueduct in excess of 500m/550yd long crosses the Valle di Maddaloni. It is the most spectacular part of Vanvitelli's water supply line.

★★ Herculaneum · Ercolano

E 4

Region: Campania
Province: Napoli
Altitude: 44m/144ft
Population: 55,500

This ancient town is overshadowed not only by Mount Vesuvius but also by its much-visited sister town of Pompeii. Yet the excavations are no less fascinating here.

It is the intimate scale of the archaeological area and the ancient houses – in many details actually better preserved than at Pompeii – that make a visit absolutely worthwhile. Ercolano (called Resina up to 1969) is a lively little town, and buses up to ►Mount Vesuvius also leave from here.

History

Heracles (called Hercules by the Romans), the mythical Greek hero, is said to have founded the town. Scientific research suggests the earliest settlement was in the 5th century BC. It was probably at this time that the streets were first laid out in a grid pattern. After periods of Oscan and Samnite dominion, the town came under Roman influence in the 3rd century BC. In 89 BC it was conquered as a consequence of the Social War waged by the Campanian towns against Rome and became a Roman municipium. In contrast to Pompeii, Herculaneum was no commercial centre, its inhabitants living mainly from fishing. Herculaneum was greatly expanded during the Augustine era. The small town's unique position on the Bay of Naples made it an increasingly wealthy residential suburb of Naples, but 24/25 August AD 79 sounded the death knell for Herculaneum too. Unlike Pompeii, however, Herculaneum was not covered by a layer of ash, volcanic lapilli stone and pumice. Rather, it was buried under a boiling avalanche of mud and lava, which preserved organic material such as wood and textiles in a unique way, allowing even the second storeys with their wooden beams to survive in some of Herculaneum's houses.

◄ From wealthy residential suburb to a pile of ruins

VISITING HERCULANEUM

INFORMATION

Ente Ville Vesuviane
Corso Resina 283 (Villa Campolieto)
80056 Ercolano
Tel. 08 19 24 45 32
www.villevesuviane.net
Brochures and event listings for the Festival delle Ville Vesuviane.

Ufficio Turistico
Via IV Novembre 82/84
Tel. 08 17 88 12 43
www.comune.ercolano.na.it
Tourist office on the route from the Circumvesuviana station to the excavations.

Info-Point
Corso Resina 6, tel. 08 17 32 43 38
www.pompeiisites.org
At the entrance to the excavation site.

TRANSPORT

By car: traffic jams are not uncommon on the A3 motorway. Take the

Baedeker TIP

Antiquity – below ground and futuristic

The famous Villa dei Papiri is currently closed for renovations. The Museo Archeologico Virtuale (MAV, Via IV Novembre 44, tel. 08 11 19 80 65 11, www.museomav.com, Wed–Sun 9am–5pm) breaks new ground by using sophisticated multimedia technology to simulate time travel into the archaeological past.

exit for Ercolano-Portici and carry on towards the sea following signs to Ercolano Scavi. There is a secure fee-paying car park near the archaeological site. From Ercolano, a panoramic road leads up to ►Mount Vesuvius. *By bus:* the ANM 255 bus runs between Naples/Piazza Garibaldi and Torre del Greco, passing Portici and Ercolano. From the Ercolano/Circumvesuviana station, take the EAV bus up to ►Mount Vesuvius (Unico tickets). *By train:* the easiest way to get to Ercolano from Naples or Sorrento is on the Circumvesuviana/Ercolano-Scavi station; from there, it is only 10 minutes on foot to the archaeological excavations at Villa Campolieto.

EVENTS

Festival delle Ville Vesuviane: from spring to autumn, concerts and theatre performances take place in the classical Vesuvius villas (Ente per le Ville Vesuviane; advance ticket sales in Naples, c/o box office, Galleria Umberto I, tel. 08 15 51 91 88; www.boxofficenapoli.it).

WHERE TO EAT

► Moderate

① ***Antico Ricupo***
Ripa di Quaglia 10
Tel. 08 17 77 74 62
www.anticoricupo.it; open evenings and Sun noon, closed Mon
This family-run agriturismo restaurant in the middle of an orchard is located on a turn-off from the Vesuvius main road. Honest country cooking.

② ***Viva Lo Re***
Corso Resina 261
Tel. 08 17 39 02 07; www.vivolore.it; closed Sun, Mon
Culinary treats inspired by Mount Vesuvius and its seasonal produce. Sophisticated presentation in a comfortable atmosphere a stone's throw from Villa Campolieto. There is a B & B with 3 lovely rooms attached.

WHERE TO STAY

► Luxury

① ***Miglio d'Oro Park Hotel***
Corso Resina 269
Tel. 08 17 39 99 99, 08 17 77 40 97
www.migliodoroparkhotel.it
Erected in the mid-18th century and set in a huge park, the villa is resplendent again today, housing a conference centre alongside magnificent rooms and suites. Located just a few steps away from the excavations and Villa Campolieto.

► Mid-range

Torre del Greco · ② Albergo Casa Rossa
Via Mortelle 87
Tel. & fax 08 18 83 15 49
www.casarossa1888.it
The restaurant of the same name has been here since 1888, whilst the tourist restaurant on Via Vesuvio 42 (3.2km/5.3mi from A3 motorway, exit »Torre del Greco«, with excellent pizza from a wood-burning oven, delicious pasta primi and solif fish dishes as well as a dream view of the Gulf of Naples)) is more recent. In 2005, the Pinto family complemented their main hotel with a well-kept little beach hotel. Nearly all the rooms have views of the bay and a veranda. From the A3, take the exit marked »Torre Annunziata Nord«, Circumvesuviana station »Leopardi«.

► Budget/Mid-range

Portici · ③ Villa San Gennariello
Via Madonelle 5
Tel. & fax 08 17 76 12 20
www.villasangennariello.com
Small, charming B & B in a Vesuvius villa at the top end of the castle park. The sun terrace offers fantastic views of the volcano.

Herculaneum was smothered by the eruption of Vesuvius in AD 79

A discovery that stirred the world

In 1710, Emanuel-Maurice de Lorraine, **Prince d'Elboeuf** and an officer serving the Austrian viceroys, built himself a summer villa on the small harbour of Granatello at Portici. Purely by chance, he heard about the marble finds made by a farmer in Resina, today's Herculaneum. It took d'Elboeuf about nine months to clear out the town's ancient theatre – for this is what had been found – almost entirely intact. **Systematic excavations** then began in 1738 by order of King Charles III. Due to the vast quantities of mud, tunnels were dug first to expose the buildings underground. Preserved as if in a time capsule, the Roman town quickly became one of the most famous places in Europe. The intellectual elite of the time flocked to the Bay of Naples to walk down the steps of the theatre. Open-air excavations in Herculaneum only started in 1828. Substantial parts of ancient Ercolano, amongst them the forum with the public buildings, lie beneath the modern town. The very well-preserved theatre is also hidden at a depth of up to 26m/85ft below Corso Resina.

The victims of the catastrophe

While it was assumed for a long time that all the inhabitants of Herculaneum had been able to save themselves, excavations in the area of the ancient beach, from 1982 onwards, proved otherwise: below the suburban thermal baths over 250 skeletons were found in the old boat chambers. Probably hoping to flee across the sea, a group of people from the most diverse social backgrounds had gathered there.

★★ Scavi d'Ercolano

Corso Resina 6

Opening hours: Apr–Oct daily 8.30am–7.30pm (last admission: 6pm) Nov–March to 5pm only (last admission: 3.30pm)

With a population reckoned to have been just 3–4000, Herculaneum was much smaller than Pompeii. Furthermore, only a third of the town has been exposed, so that a stroll through its compact grid of streets is a much more accessible and rewarding experience than a first encounter with Pompeii. Just outside the main entrance there is a **view** revealing the full extent of the burial of the ancient town, as well as the difficulties in exposing it: Herculaneum lies before the visitor like a huge construction site. Easily visible to the right is the **Decumanus Maximus**, one of the town's main streets. A modern bridge crosses the ancient palestra, where the town's youth practised sports, before the path carries on in a wide arch to the entrance proper. However, the recommended option is to take the subterranean path (access near the pavilion, which hires out audio guides).

Terrace of Nonius Balbus

From here, steps lead up to the old town and onto a terrace which would have given extensive views across the sea. It was at this prominent place that ancient Ercolano honoured its esteemed citizen, the Roman senator and proconsul Marcus Nonius Balbus. The funeral altar and the reconstructed statue honouring Balbus survive.

★

Terme Suburbane ►

Right next to it is the entrance to the Terme Suburbane, excavated from 1927 onwards. The luxury of the fittings and interior decoration makes them an elegant work of architectural art. The obligatory rooms for any ancient thermal baths are grouped around a two-storey atrium. Some of the marble floors, as well as the sumptuously decorated stucco ceilings and walls, are very well preserved. The thermal spa was restored after the earthquake of AD 62, probably by order of M. Nonius Balbus. They featured the hitherto unheard-of glass windows in the caldarium (warm bath), affording panoramic views over the sea.

Casa dei Cervi

Right at the beginning of Cardo V, look out for the Casa dei Cervi (House of the Deer), on the left-hand side. Named after its garden sculptures, it probably belonged to a former slave of Q. Granius Verus. Alongside beautiful mosaic floors and some well-preserved frescoes, it is above all the garden that tells of the luxury once enjoyed here. The **sculpture of a stag being attacked by dogs** – now replaced by a copy – is among the most famous finds made at Herculaneum.

★

Casa del Rilievo di Telefo

It is probable that M. Nonius Balbus was also the owner of both the Casa del Rilievo di Telefo and the Casa della Gemma opposite. Taken together, they cover 1800 sq m/19,375 sq ft, making them amongst the largest properties in Herculaneum. The House of the Relief of Telephus had three storeys and owes its name to an **artwork showing the myth of Telephus**, son of Hercules (the mythical founder of the city). Don't miss the atrium with a marble relief slab (oscilla) hanging between the columns. These reliefs, mostly bearing Dionysian imagery, were used to protect houses and their owners from harm.

The Casa della Gemma preserves one of the most original pieces of graffiti from antiquity. A certain Apollinaris, doctor to Emperor Titus, wrote on the wall of the latrine: »Apollinaris medicus Titi Im- ✶ **Casa della Gemma**

Herculaneum Ercolano Plan

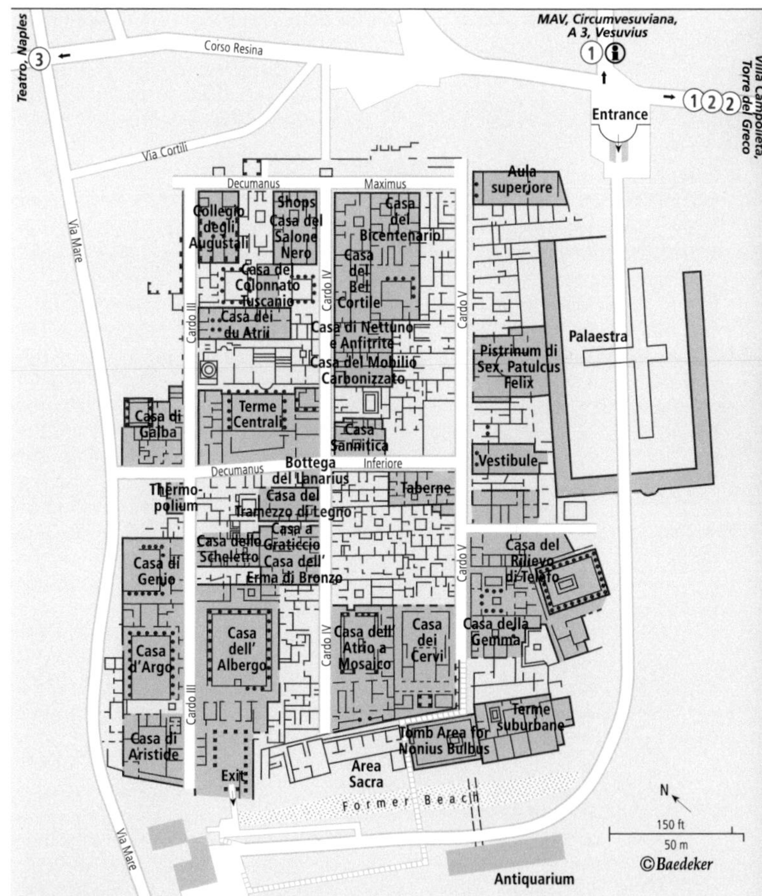

Where to eat
① Casa Rossa 1888 al Vesuvio
② Viva Lo Re

Where to stay
① Miglio d'Oro Park Hotel
② Albergo Casa Rossa
③ Villa San Gennariello

peratoris hic cacavit bene«, thus recording for posterity the news of his successful bowel movement.

Palestra In the lower half of Cardo V, to the right, lies the palestra, dating back to Augustine times. Though it is only partly excavated, the unusual dimensions of the building are remarkable.

Pistrinum di Sex. Patulcius Felix The Pistrinum di Sex. Patulcius Felix is a bakery built into the group of buildings forming the palestra. A signet ring excavated here revealed the name of its owner. The stucco phalluses, which were supposed to protect the business from the evil eye, are a conspicuous feature. The 25 bronze baking pans were once used to bake flatbreads. Opposite the palestra, at the crossroads with Decumanus Inferiore, lie three thermopolia – ancient fast-food outlets.

Saved at the last minute

- Until recently, the Scavi di Ercolano were in a similarly lamentable state to those at Pompeii. Crumbling frescoes, collapsing walls and groundwater were threatening the ancient ruins. But right at the last minute an American computer firm stepped in to save the day. Over the next few years the Herculaneum Conservation Project, financed by the Packard Humanities Institute, will invest over one hundred million dollars in the preservation and restoration of the ancient town.

✶ Casa Sannitica Also on the Decumanus Inferiore, right next to the Casa del Gran Portale with its magnificent entrance, is the Casa Sannitica. Dating from the 2nd century BC, the casa once occupied a whole insula (block), even before the garden belonging to the house was also built on. The atrium, a typical example of old Italic living, is the building's focal point as well as its architectural highlight. The atrium's clever trompe-l'oeil gallery is particularly impressive. Painted mock architecture and purely decorative columns suggest a balcony, but one which is actually only open at one side. After the earthquake of AD 62 part of the building was converted into apartments, which explains the addition of stairs with a separate entrance. All styles of **Pompeian painting** (► p.268) can be found in this house.

✶ Terme Centrali Situated diagonally opposite on Cardo IV, the **women's section** of the Terme Centrali takes up half an insula; access to the men's thermal baths is via Cardo III. The baths have their origin in the second half of the first century BC and were remodelled following the earthquake. The vestibule with its fluted, arched ceiling is wonderfully preserved. The black and white floor mosaic shows a triton (god of the sea) surrounded by all kinds of marine animals. The rooms that were the exclusive preserve of the men, the **Terme Maschili**, are larger and their sequence followed the classic layout of a Roman thermal spa – apodyterium (changing room), frigidarium (cold bath room), tepidarium (warm bath room) and caldarium (hot bath room). Here too a triton surrounded by dolphins adorns the tepidarium's floor mosaic.

Along Cardo IV

To the right hand side of Cardo IV, in the direction of the Decumanus Maximus, lie a few noteworthy houses. Many of the ancient wooden pieces of furniture that make Herculaneum a site of such extraordinary archaeological interest were found in the **Casa del Mobilio Carbonizzato**.

✶ ◄ Casa di Nettuno e Anfitrite

The neighbouring Casa di Nettuno e Anfitrite is one of the most beautiful houses in the ancient town. A wall mosaic in the triclinium (a dining room used in summer) showing Neptune and Amphitrite gave the house its name. The nymphaeum, with its opulent mosaic decoration taking up the eastern side of the room, is particularly unusual.

◄ Bottega

In the same house, an **ancient shop** was preserved, including the wooden bookshelves holding the amphorae. The collapsed ceiling gives a glimpse into the mezzanine floor where the shop owner used to live, and where the bronze foot of a bed can be seen.

✶ **Casa del Salone Nero**

Diagonally opposite is the spacious Casa del Salone Nero. The twenty wax tablets (the notepads of the ancient world) found here yielded the name of the owner of the house as L. Venidius Ennychus. The house, with vestibule, tablinum and peristyle, is a typical town residence of Augustine times. The eponymous »black hall« features virtuoso paintings in the Roman »Style IV«.

Shops

Some shops can be found at the crossroads with the Decumanus Maximus. In the **Bottega del Plumbarius**, a blacksmith's workshop, various tools have been preserved, along with parts of an intermediate wooden floor. Right next door is the **Bottega ad Cucumas**. A few steps away, the **thermopolium** was another »snack bar« offering hot food (Greek: thermos = warm).

Casa del Bicentenario

The name of this building refers to the 1938 bicentennial celebrations of the first organized excavations. A famous fresco in the tablinum shows **Pasiphae and Daedalus**. Pasiphae, wife of Minos, fell in love with a bull. In order to win the animal's heart she asked Daedalus to build her a life-size wooden cow, which she climbed into. The fruit of this amorous adventure was the Minotaur.

✶✶ **Collegio degli Augustali**

According to an inscription, the **College of the Augustales**, at the crossroads of the Decumanus Maximus and Cardo III was founded by the brothers A. Lucius Proculus and A. Lucius Iulianus. Originally built as a meeting place for the Augustales, a priesthood dedicated to the cult of Augustus during the emperor's lifetime, the building later saw changes, as evidenced by Style IV paintings. The walls of the cella (a small chamber usually containing a cult image or statue) preserve frescoes with scenes from the Herculean myths . The guard of the Augustales' college did not survive the eruption of Mount Vesuvius. His skeleton was found on the bed in the small room to the right, behind the cella.

◄ See photo p.170

Casa d'Argo Located at the end of Cardo III, the Casa d'Argo is one of the most interesting houses in Ercolano. The whereabouts of the eponymous fresco showing Argus guarding the nymph Io, transformed into a cow by Zeus, is unknown. Most of the previously well-preserved upper floor was destroyed during the 1828 archaeological excavations. In the same way as the neighbouring **Casa di Aristide**, the House of Argus documents the early archaeological history of Herculaneum. Look out for the generous peristyle (columned hall) with its grooved pillars. A second, smaller peristyle has some tunnels from Bourbon times. The block of buildings opposite the House of Argus, called the **Casa dell'Albergo**, was probably not a hotel but a stately villa, which was converted into a rental house after the earthquake.

Hercules battles for the love of Deianeira with the river god Acheloos

With its excellently preserved wooden door, the **Casa del Tramezzo di Legno on Cardo IV** is unmissable. If necessary, the door folded like a screen to separate the semi-public atrium from the more intimate tablinum. The rings at the door would have held oil lamps.

Casa a Graticcio The best example of an urban house for several families is the Casa a Graticcio. The timbered house (opus craticium) forms a contrast to the surrounding town villas. The reconstructed top floor balcony resting on brick pillars gives an idea of the way the town would have looked. Various entrances and stairs connected the flats with the street. At the corner of Cardo IV/Decumanus, the **Bottega del Lanarius** was the workshop of a draper with a wooden press to smooth out the fabrics.

★ **Casa dell'Atrio a Mosaico** At the lower end of Cardo IV, at the same altitude as the Casa dei Cervi and also once occupying a fantastic panoramic location above the sea, lies the Casa dell'Atrio a Mosaico. The glass veranda in the extensive gardens was a rare luxury.

★ **Villa dei Papiri** Not far from the area of the archaeological excavations lies Villa dei Papiri, one of the most famous ancient villas on the Bay of Naples.

Swiss mining engineer Karl Weber studied villa between 1750 and 1761 using a system of tunnels. The luxurious building contained not only a collection of bronze and marble sculptures but also a Greek library with over a thousand charred but still readable **papyrus scrolls**. The owner of the villa, which extended down to the sea across a series of terraces, was **Lucius Calpurnius Piso Caesoninus**, father-in-law to Julius Caesar. In the hope of also finding a Latin library, new excavations were carried out in the 1990s. Whilst they did not yield any libraries, the archaeologists discovered sculptures, mosaics and fragments of frescoes.

Opening hours: Visits by prior appointment only, Sat, Sun 9am–midday www.arethusa.net

✶ Ville Vesuviane

Miglio d'Oro

A particularly deplorable consequence of the decline of Naples after 1860/61 is the dilapidation of one of the most beautiful streets of the 18th century: the **Miglio d'Oro** (Golden Mile) between San Giovanni a Teduccio and Torre del Greco, with its magnificent Baroque villas, was equalled only by the famous Palladio villas that flank the Brenta Canal between Venice and Padua. Founded in 1971, the **Ente per le Ville Vesuviane** has registered 121 17th- and 18th-century villas, but until now it has been possible to rescue only a handful. Even in their ruined state or converted into apartment blocks, however, these palaces still exude some of their former glory.

✶ ◄ Reggia di Portici

Between 1738 and 1752, Charles III had the Roman architect Antonio Canevari build him a summer residence in Portici. Despite concerns about the dangerous proximity to the volcano, the new royal palace turned out to be the most magnificent on the Bay of Naples prior to the construction of the Reggia in Caserta. With the Neapolitan nobility following their sovereign's lead the **Miglio d'Oro** quickly took shape, flanked by palaces and parks. The palace came under state ownership in 1860. Today it houses the **seat of the agricultural faculty** and one of the most recent museums on the Bay of Naples. A visit is worthwhile for the rooms alone, in which both Goethe and German art historian Winckelmann admired the first finds from Herculaneum and Pompeii. The collection is almost completely virtual. There are video projections, perfectly staged photographic installations, a model of the ancient theatre of Herculaneum and, in numerous display cases, documents and books on the history of the excavations of the buried Vesuvian towns (Via Università 100; tel. 08 15 80 83 90; daily 9am–4pm).

◄ Herculanense Museum

Italy's first railway

On 3 October 1839 the »Vesuvio« locomotive steamed from Naples to Portici accompanied by a jubilant population. Recently restored, the historic station of Granatello (today Portici) is a stop on the **Circumvesuviana**, the line that connects the Vesuvian towns. Situated towards the town in the direction of Naples, the **Museo Ferroviario di Pietrarsa** uses historic carriages and locomotives to document early railway history (Via Pietrarsa, signposted; re-opened in 2007).

Villa Campolieto This palazzo was built by Luigi Vanvitelli in 1763–73 for the Duca di Casacalenda. A textbook example of good restoration and owned by the Ente per le Ville Vesuviane, the building today houses concerts and exhibitions (Ercolano, Corso Resina 283; Mon–Fri 10am–1pm).

Villa Favorita Built by Ferdinando Fuga for the aristocratic Gravina family, this villa was inaugurated in 1768 with a feast in the presence of King Ferdinand IV of Naples (later Ferdinand I, king of the Two Sicilies) and Maria Carolina, his queen. Impressive remains suggest a park with auxiliary buildings which used to extend down to the sea (Ercolano, Via Gabriele D'Annunzio 36; Mon–Fri 10am–1pm).

Villa delle Ginestre With a cholera epidemic decimating the city of Naples in 1837, the poet Giacomo Leopardi spent a few months in this villa and wrote *La ginestra*, one of the most famous poems in Italian literary history (Torre del Greco; Tue–Sun 10am–1pm).

Torre del Greco This town (pop. 90,000; west of Herculaneum) has experienced the dangers of living close to a volcano more often than any other community near Mount Vesuvius, suffering in practically every eruption and being almost entirely destroyed on several occasions. No traces are left of its ancient past. Torre del Greco owes its name to the towers erected along the coast by Frederick II to protect it from the Saracens. It became world famous for the **workmanship of its handcrafted coral artefacts**. Whilst this tradition has not quite died out, the corals have had to be imported for a long time now due to the pollution of the local sea. Two museums display examples of coral workmanship, chiefly jewellery (Museo del Corallo, Piazza Palomba 6; 9am–12.30pm, closed Sun, tel. 08 18 88 11 360; Museo Liverino, Via Montedoro; visits by appointment, tel. 08 18 81 12 25).

Coral museums ►

★★ Ischia

B 4

Region: Campania
Area: 46 sq km/18 sq mi
Population: 56,000
Province: Napoli
Altitude: Up to 788m/2585ft

Thanks to its thermal springs and lush vegetation, Ischia – also known as the »green island« (Isola Verde) – is one of the Bay of Naples' top tourist destinations. A safe distance from the big city, it is nevertheless easy to reach the major attractions such as Pompeii, Capri or Sorrento during day trips, and is therefore an ideal base for a relaxed holiday.

History Despite its proximity to the volcanic Phlegrean Fields, the island of Ischia developed separately from the mainland. **Monte Epomeo** is

The castle hill with the Castello Aragonese

not itself a volcano but rather a giant mound of debris left by a prehistoric volcano under the sea. Nevertheless, a complicated interaction of volcanic activity and tectonic plate movements kept the island unstable for millennia. The last volcanic impact was as long ago as 1301, although frequent earth tremors continued into the 19th century. This unstable foundation, however, is also the reason for the existence of the island's thermal springs.

Like its neighbour Capri, Ischia attracted human settlement as long ago as the early Stone Age. During the Bronze Age, there was a settlement near Castiglione, and some of the ceramics made there were exported. The arrival of the first Greeks was historically significant. They founded **Pithekoussai** in the 8th century BC and turned the island into a centre for the production of ceramics. During Roman times, Ischia was of little importance. The emperor Octavian Augustus swapped the island of Ischia for the island of Capri, and it was the latter island that subsequently became a centre of Roman power for several decades. During the Middle Ages, Ischia was the setting for numerous military confrontations between a series of Neapolitan rulers. After a volcanic eruption in 1301, the island remained uninhabited for some time. The doctor and philosopher Giulio Iasolini published a book entitled *De Rimedi Naturali Che Sono Nell'Isola Di Pithecusa; Hoggi Detta Ischia* (Of the natural remedies on the island of Pithecusa, today known as Ischia) in 1588, but the island's status as a **fashionable spa resort** was not established until the 18th century, when the construction of the first medicinal spas was instituted by Doctor Francesco Buonocuore. The thermal baths above Ischia Porto were also patronized by the Neapolitan royal family, who turned the island into one of their many summer residences on the Bay of Naples by having a royal villa built there.

◀ The first Greeks

Tourism Ischia was a dream destination for travellers in the 18th and 19th centuries, before even Capri and Sorrento. The island's thermal springs and paradisiacal landscape made it a **top choice for European seaside tourism**. But the earthquake of 1883 cut short Ischia's career as a holiday resort. It was only after the Second World War that Ischia, alongside the Adriatic resort of Rimini, rose to become one of the most popular destinations for holidaymakers, especially Germans. However the uncontrolled development that followed was not necessarily good for the island, and the dramatic decline in visitor numbers during the 1990s severely dented Ischia's status as spa paradise. In more recent times, Ischia's somewhat dated 1950s charm has been redeveloped according to the motto »less is more«, with an emphasis on top-end tourism, and the island is once again attracting visitors, including Italians. The numerous nightclubs, especially in Ischia Porto and Ischia Ponte, positively burst with Neapolitans in party mood during July and August.

Green island ► A good deal of the charm of the »green island« lies in the variety of its Mediterranean flora. The fast pace of life along the coast contrasts with the island's peaceful interior, where traditional farming still marks the rural villages in the mountainous areas. The most important salt-water and thermal spas are located on the north coast, at Ischia Porto, Casamicciola and Lacco Ameno. The island's capital is Ischia, which is virtually a conglomeration of Ischia Ponte (with its Castello Aragonese) to the east and Ischia Porto to the west. The western coast, with the popular Spiaggia di Citara beach, is dominated by the town and municipality of Forio. On the mountainous southern coast lies the little town of Sant'Angelo and the Spiaggia dei Maronti, one of the most famous beaches on the Bay of Naples. The island's interior is dominated by the 788m/2585ft-high **Monte Epomeo**.

What to See on Ischia

Ischia Porto and Ischia Ponte Landscape paintings from the early 19th century still portray today's tourist centre, which consists of **the two districts of Ischia Porto and Ischia Ponte**, as virtually uninhabited: just a few whitewashed fishermen's cottages set in lush green surroundings on the edge of a volcano crater filled with water. In those days, what was then called **Lago del Bagno** was not significant for tourism; only the Neapolitan royal family resided during summer in the splendid isolation of their **Villa Reale** above the lake. Nowadays these buildings are much altered and used by the military. They are not open to the public. The basic thermal baths between the harbour and town were extended in 1845 and redesigned once more in 1880. Today they are known as the **Antiche Terme Comunale**. To facilitate easier access for the royal family, in 1853 Ferdinand II had the crater's edge broken down on the Mediterranean side and the shallow lake dug out to create a harbour.

VISITING ISCHIA

INFORMATION

AACST
Via Sogliuzzo 72
80077 Ischia
Tel. 08 15 07 42 11, fax 08 15 07 42 30
www.infoischiaprocida.it.
Information on neighbouring Procida also available here.

The island's official tourist office is in Ischia Porto, right by the Aliscafo landing quay (Via Iasolino 7, tel. 08 15 07 42 31).

www.ischia.it
www.phitecusa.com

GOOD TO KNOW

Transport

Ferries/hydrofoils: car ferries (traghetti), high-speed ferries (traghetti veloce) and hydrofoils (aliscafi) depart for Ischia Porto, Casamicciola and Forio from Naples/Molo Beverello; hydrofoils for Ischia Porto and Forio also depart from Naples/Mergellina; car ferries travel from Pozzuoli to Ischia Porto and Casamicciola. Hydrofoils and tour boats travel to neighbouring Capri during the summer, as well as to the Pontinian Islands (schedules available from AACST, in the daily press, and on the internet; tickets are bought directly at the harbour).

Getting around the island

The island almost suffocates in holiday traffic during summer. Thanks to a good network of bus routes, however, there really is no need for a car. All the island's settlements can be reached by SEPSA buses and there are taxi stands and car-hire firms all along the coast. The three-wheeler micro taxis are an interesting mode of transport (negotiate a price prior to the journey!).

Shopping

Ischia's ceramics have a tradition thousands of years old and the family business of Fratelli Menella at Casamicciola is itself over 500 years old. A range of ceramic products, from kitsch to art, is available in almost every town and village on the island. Culinary souvenirs are also popular.

Sport and outdoors

Thermal pools are a basic component of many hotels on the island. Fun in the water and wellness programmes can be enjoyed without limit at the thermal gardens (giardini termali) such as chic Negombo on San Montano Bay to the west of Lacco Ameno; alternatively, try the extensive Poseidon Gardens near the beach at Citara south of Forio. Locals prefer the Nitrodi springs (open all year) at Baranco, and the open-access Sorgeto cove, south of Panza, which can be reached either via a narrow road and steps leading out of the settlement or by boat taxi from Sant'Angelo). Nature lovers and romantics prefer the island's oldest thermal pools, set in the Cavascura ravine above Maronti beach, where Romans once bathed in hot tubs cut out of the rock.

Beaches: Ischia's finest *spiaggia* is the Baia di San Montano, located to the west of Lacco Ameno. Alternatively, wave breakers protect the child-friendly Spiaggia del Fungo, the local beach at Lacco Ameno. Forio also attracts visitors with the sandy Spiaggia di San Francesco, Cava dell'Isola and Citara beaches. Hot springs bubble into Sorgeto Bay below Panza. Maronti beach in the south of the island is over 3km/2mi long. At Ischia Ponte, the Spiaggia di Cartaromana offers hot springs in the sea, as well as fine views of the Castello Aragonese fortress.

The ancient *trade routes* on the island are slowly being developed as footpaths (for example, in the municipality of Barano d'Ischia). A classic hiking route is the ascent of the island's highest peak, Monte Epomeo. Geologist Aniello Di Iorio offers year-round geology and volcanology tours: tel. 08 19 30 58; www.eurogeopark.com).

EVENTS

Good Friday in Ischia Ponte: nightly lantern processions.
Corsa dell'Angelo: in Forio, the statue of an angel is carried by runners between the Madonna and her risen son.
Between 16 and 18 May at Lacco Ameno the miraculous arrival of Santa Restituta is celebrated with a procession and fireworks.
Forio celebrates its patron saint, San Vito, between 14 and 16 June.
On 26 July each year at Ischia Ponte, nocturnal boat processions and a large firework display are held in honour of Santa Anna.
On 29 September celebrations are held at Serrara San Michele Arcangelo.
In the weeks prior to Christmas, cribs are displayed everywhere and on the morning of 25 December a traditional fish market is held at Ischia Ponte and Forio.

WHERE TO EAT

► Expensive

Ischia Porto • ① Alberto a Mare
Via Cristoforo Colombo 8
Tel. 0 81 98 12 59; mid-March–Oct.
www.albertoischia.it
This romantic restaurant with a terrace above the Lungomare seafront has been synonymous with fresh fish for over 50 years.

Forio • ② Il Melograno
Via G. Mazzella 110, tel. 0 81 99 84 50
www.ilmelogranoischia.it; closed Mondays and mid-March–Dec. Set in a beautiful villa, this restaurant is an excellent choice for elaborate Ischian seafood dishes served with first-class wine. During summer, tables are set in the shade under ancient olive trees; during winter diners eat by an open fire.

► Moderate

Forio • ③ Da Peppina di Renato
Via Montecorvo 42
Tel. 0 81 99 83 12; closed Wed and March–Oct
www.trattoriadepeppina.it
Rural but elegant trattoria in the hills above the SS 270. The tough drive is rewarded by views overlooking Citara beach and tasty Ischian country cooking served with good open wines.

Baedeker recommendation

Barano • ④ Il Focolare di Loretta e Riccardo D'Ambra
Via Cretaio al Crocefisso 78
Tel. 0 81 90 29 44
Closed Wed and Jan–Nov.
The d'Ambra family serve the very best of their culinary art in their roadside restaurant located between Casamicciola and Fiaino (SEPSA buses stop by the door). Truly the best of home cooking! Fresh vegetables, lamb, island rabbits and snails are just some of the ingredients used to delight the taste buds. During late summer and autumn, fresh porcini are a special treat.

Serrara • ⑤ *L'Arca*
Via Ciglio 144
Tel. 0 81 90 42 26, closed Tue.
Charming trattoria in a typical tuff stone house and with a fabulous view. The Monaco family serves its customers tasty pasta dishes, island rabbit and, in the evenings, pizzas too.

► Inexpensive

Ischia Ponte • ⑥ *Da Gaetano*
Via M. Mazzella 58
Tel. 0 81 99 18 07, closed Wed and during February.
Crisp Neapolitan pizzas, gluten free if requested.

Sant'Angelos • ⑦ *La Dolce Siesta*
Via Vallone di Cavascura
Tel. 0 81 99 03 65; closed Easter–Oct.
A friendly place at the entrance to the Cavascura ravine, only accessible on foot. Delightful antipasti and skewered meat, as well as fritto misto, fish soup and coniglio all cacciatora (rabbit).

WHERE TO STAY

An overview of the more than 400 places to stay on Ischia is provided at www.ischiahotels.it. Value for money offers can also be found at www.ischialastminute.it.

► Luxury

Forio • ① *Mezzatorre Resort & Spa*
Via Mezzatorre 23
Tel. 0 81 98 61 11; www.mezzatorre.it
Easter–end of Oct.
Elegant suites housed in the historic lighthouse high above the bay of San Montano; also stylish rooms in pavilions set in the extensive pine grove. Saltwater pool, sports facilities, thermal baths – and a helicopter landing pad!

► Mid-range

Ischia Ponte • ② *Il Monastero*
Castello Aragonese 3
Tel. & fax 0 81 99 24 35
www.albergoilmonastero.it
Easter–end of Oct.
Comfortable »monastic cells« in this former convent of the Poor Clares on the fortress peninsula. Superb views of Ischia from this lofty spot.

Forio • ③ *Umberto a Mare*
Via Soccorso 2
Tel. & fax 0 81 99 71 71
www.umbertoamare.it.
Beginning of April–end of Dec.
Quality guest house and renowned fish restaurant immediately below the pilgrimage church of Santa Maria del Soccorso. Tastefully decorated rooms with stunning views of the sea and sunsets.

Forio • ④ *Semiramis*
Via G. Mazzella 236
Tel. & fax 0 81 90 75 11
www.hotelsemiramisischia.com;
April–beginning of Nov.
Friendly pension set in a large garden above the beach. Breakfast served. The Poseidon Gardens are within walking distance. A thermal spring heats the pool and ensures warm rooms during cooler times of year.

► Budget

Forio • ⑤ *Di Lustro*
Via F. di Lustro 9
Tel. & fax 0 81 99 71 63
► Baedeker Tip p.183

Panza • ⑥ *Pensione Casa Gennaro*
Via Provinciale per Sant'Angelo 60
Tel. 0 81 90 71 18, Easter–end of Oct.
Charming family-run pension with views across the vineyard terraces to the sea. The ingredients for »Mamma« Viola's cooking come directly from her garden and animal pens. Buses stop directly outside.

Ischia Map

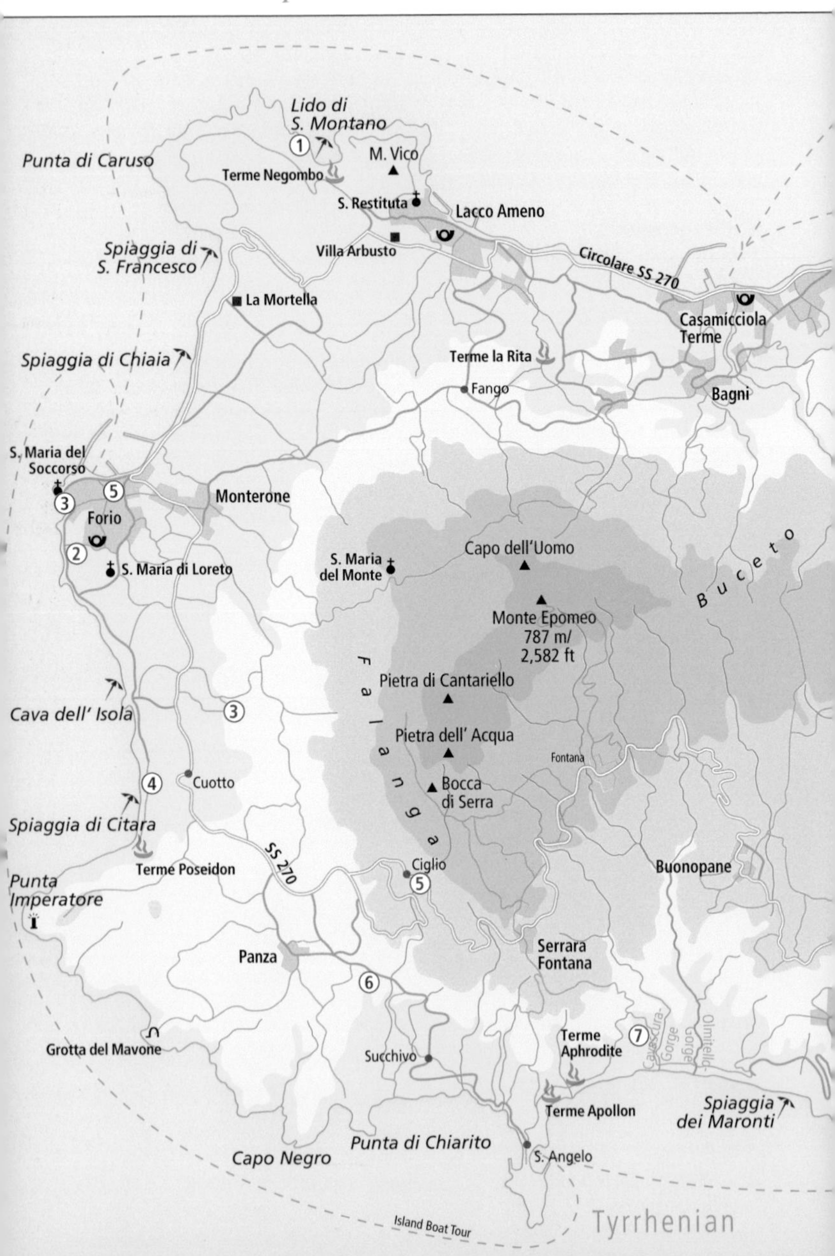

Lido di S. Montano
1
M. Vico
Punta di Caruso
Terme Negombo
S. Restituta
Lacco Ameno
Villa Arbusto
Spiaggia di S. Francesco
Circolare SS 270
La Mortella
Casamicciola Terme
Spiaggia di Chiaia
Terme la Rita
Fango
Bagni
S. Maria del Soccorso
5
3
Monterone
Forio
2
S. Maria di Loreto
S. Maria del Monte
Capo dell'Uomo
Buceto
Monte Epomeo 787 m/ 2,582 ft
Falanga
Pietra di Cantariello
Cava dell' Isola
3
Pietra dell' Acqua
Fontana
4
Cuotto
Bocca di Serra
Spiaggia di Citara
Terme Poseidon
SS 270
Ciglio
5
Buonopane
Punta Imperatore
Panza
Serrara Fontana
6
Grotta del Mavone
Terme Aphrodite
7
Cavascura-Gorge
Olmitello-Gorge
Succhivo
Terme Apollon
Spiaggia dei Maronti
Punta di Chiarito
Capo Negro
S. Angelo
Island Boat Tour
Tyrrhenian

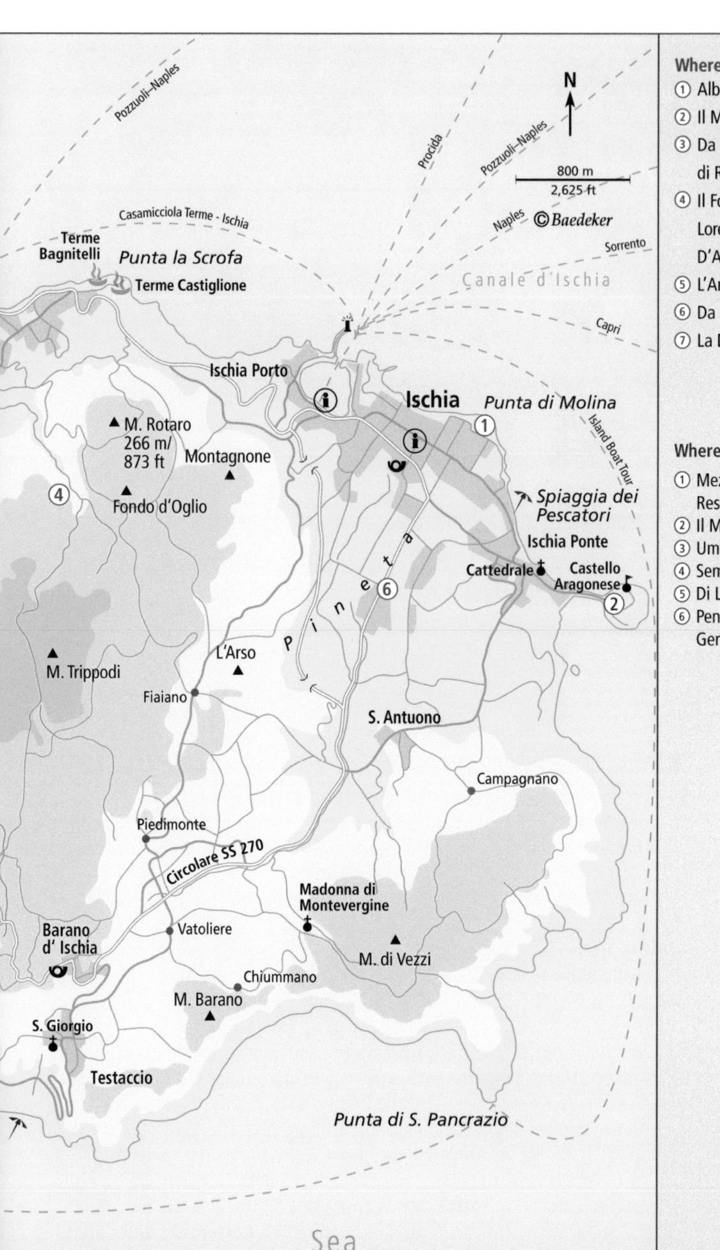

Where to eat

1. Alberto a Mare
2. Il Melograno
3. Da Peppina di Renato
4. Il Focolare di Loretta e Riccardo D'Ambra
5. L'Arca
6. Da Gaetano
7. La Dolce Siesta

Where to stay

1. Mezzatorre Resort & Spa
2. Il Monastero
3. Umberto a Mare
4. Semiramis
5. Di Lustro
6. Pensione Casa Gennaro

The harbour of Ischia Ponte, on the island's east coast

Castello Aragonese

Ischia's most significant secular building spent several centuries as a picturesque ruin before its owners had it restored and opened most of it to the public. The building complex is now a **much-visited sight** on the island, and during summer it is also the setting for many cultural events (Piazzale Aragonese; daily 9am to one hour before sunset; closed in Jan). The place was first mentioned in public records in the 11th century. Charles of Anjou had it developed into a fortress, but its present appearance is the result of major extensions to the castle commissioned by Alfonso V in 1439. He also had a dam built to connect the castello with the island. In this way, he created not only a strategically ideal defensive post for Ischia but also a refuge for the island population, which regularly had to contend with pirate attacks. Ischia was also protected by numerous lookout towers. The Castello Aragonese was a walled town within the castle gates, complete with homes, churches and monasteries. The English fleet destroyed the fortification by cannon fire in 1799 and again in 1809, from which time the ruins served only as a prison. Today, an elevator carries visitors up to the castle, though it is much nicer, if more exhausting, to ascend on foot. The ruin of the **Cattedrale della Santa**

Maria Assunta is certainly picturesque. The building was founded around 1300 and redesigned in Baroque style in the 18th century, but much of the building collapsed in 1809. The crypt, with a few frescoes dating from the 14th century is worth taking a look at. In 1509, Ferrante d'Avalos and Vittoria Colonna (1492–1547) got married here. Vittoria was the **most famous inhabitant of the Castello Aragonese** and a major personality in 16th-century Italy. The princess, a legend in her own lifetime, turned her island residence into a glamorous artistic and intellectual meeting place. An adored friend and muse of Michelangelo, she spent her final years in Rome. The Chiesa dell'Immacolata (1715) once formed part of the **convent of the Poor Clares** founded in 1575. The unusual nuns' mortuary in the crypt has spooked many an Ischia visitor over the years – the Poor Clares were not buried, but left to rot sitting on stone benches. The convent was dissolved in 1810, though the mummified bodies were only removed to their final resting place in recent years.

◄ Vittoria Colonna

◄ Chiesa dell' Immacolata

✱ **Ischia Ponte**

Ischia Ponte, immediately opposite the castle, initially developed as **Borgo del Celso** in the 16th century, gradually merging with Lago di Bagno (Ischia Porto). There are two important churches in this town: the Chiesa della Madonna della Scala was redeveloped into the new **episcopal church of Santa Maria Assunta** after the cathedral on the castle hill collapsed in 1809. the church's original construction goes back to the 14th century, but it was remodelled in joyous Baroque style, with beautiful stucco work, in the 18th century. The left aisle contains a remarkable 13th-century crucifix. Diagonally across from the church stands the Chiesa dello Spirito Santo, where the patron saint of Ischia and its fishermen, San Giovan Giuseppe della Croce, is venerated.

Casamicciola

Next to Ischia Porto, this busy little town has the island's other main **harbour** and it is also the most important **thermal spa centre**. The ruins of a Roman bath house below the Terme Belliazzi prove that the plentiful bubbling hot springs here were already in use during Roman times. Unfortunately, the name of Casamicciola is not only associated with health and wellness, but also with a terrible natural disaster: the entire town was flattened by an earthquake on 28 July 1883. 2313 people died when 1200 houses were destroyed. »Ischia has forever ceased to exist,« announced the world's press, and Ischia was wiped off the tourist map for decades afterwards. The island did not recover its role as a holiday destination until after the Second World War.

◄ The Casamicciola earthquake

✱ **Lacco Ameno**

Lacco Ameno was another much-visited and fashionable bathing resort prior to the earthquake in 1883, when it was almost entirely destroyed. The stylish atmosphere of this little town today is a legacy of the 1950s, when it was briefly a popular summer retreat for the Italian film world and the cosmopolitan literary figures associated with the publisher Angelo Rizzoli. A few **classy hotels**, such as the Regina Isabella, are testament to more glamorous times, now long disappeared.

The true significance of Lacco Ameno really lies in its history. This is where Greek settlers first trod on Italian soil in the 8th century BC: colonists from the island of Euboea founded the first Greek settlement of **Pithekoussai** on Mount Vico here. This was also the base from which the Greeks set out to found Cymae, the present-day Cumae.

Excavations at Lacco Ameno

The necropolis on the Bay of Montano and the few remains of Pithekoussais on Monte Vico were excavated by the German-Italian archaeologist **Giorgio Buchner** in 1952. His discoveries contributed important information regarding the Greek colonization of southern Italy and the growth of Magna Graecia.

✶ Museo Archeologico Pithecusa

The most significant archaeological find at Lacco Ameno was the so-called **Nestor's cup**, which is now exhibited at the Museo Archeologico Pithecusa (Villa Arbusto, Via Angelo Rizzoli 210; Tue–Sun 9.30am–1pm, 4pm–8pm; during winter 3pm–7pm).

The discovery of this cup, which dates from the 8th century BC, electrified the archaeological world at the time because its three-line inscription is considered to be **one of the earliest examples** of the Greek alphabet found anywhere in the world. Furthermore, the direct reference to *The Iliad* proves how widespread and popular Homer's poetry must have been, even so soon after its transcription in the 8th century BC.

Museo e Scavi Santa Restituta

Just a little of the **Roman settlement** at Lacco Ameno survives to be viewed underneath the Chiesa della Santa Restituta. An early Christian construction is evidenced in the remains of walls that were probably a Roman cistern or bath house. In addition, there are numerous small finds from the Greek and Roman era exhibited at the museum (April–Oct Mon–Sat 9.30am–12.30pm, 5pm–7pm; during winter 4pm–6pm, mornings only on Sun).

Other sights in Lacco Ameno

Lacco Ameno's emblem is the rock in the sea known as the **Fungo** (mushroom), whose strange appearance – as if it were a modern art sculpture – is the result of centuries of erosion by wind and water. Another relic of the era when this town was known as Heraclium to the Romans is the herm (stone post with carved head) of the font in the **Chiesa Santa Maria delle Grazie**. The image of Hercules carved into the stone gives rise to the legend that he founded this settlement along with various others around the Bay of Naples, including Herculaneum.

Fango ► Overlooking Lacco Ameno is the small hamlet of Fango, whose famous **medicinal mud** has given its name to the much-prized Fango mud bath products sold all over the world.

✶ **Monte Epomeo**

One of the attractions of an Ischia holiday, much written about in the literature, was once the evening donkey ride up Monte Epomeo to watch the sunset from its summit. Today, visitors travel by bus as far as the village of **Fontana**, from where they can comfortably explore further on foot. In fact, the hiking opportunities on **Ischia's central mountain** are varied, and also worthwhile for the quiet landscapes and wonderful panoramic views. An unusual attraction can be explored at Bosco di Falanga, where the **Case di Pietra** were carved out of the tuff stone. These cave homes, complete with windows and doors, were still inhabited in the early 20th century.

Forio

The charm of this little town on the west coast arises from its well-preserved historical character, though it becomes hopelessly overrun during the summer months. In the 16th century, families who had grown wealthy on wine growing built fine town houses here. The best preserved can be seen in the vicinity of the Torrione, one of the Saracen towers by the harbour. It is also worth climbing the Torrione itself for the beautiful views and the permanent exhibition of work by the painter **Giovanni Maltese**. The tower was built around 1480, and was part of a total of 12 watchtowers designed as the local defence system against Turkish pirates (Museo Civico Maltese, Via Torrione; open afternoons on Mon, Wed–Fri).

Baedeker TIP

A recommendation

The Di Lustro family runs what is probably the prettiest and friendliest guest house in Forio. Comfortable rooms, good home cooking and a sensational roof terrace are all part of the appeal. Truman Capote was taken with the place when he stayed here in 1949; he even immortalized the head chef, Gioconda Di Lustro, in his short story about the island (►p.177).

✶ **Santa Maria del Soccorso**

Built in typical island style (►p.300), the whitewashed 16th-century Chiesa della Santa Maria del Soccorso is reached via an impressive stairway. The church enjoys a spectacular location on a terrace above the sea. The majolica decoration is a notable feature. The tiles, very moving in their simplicity, portray the Stations of the Cross. Also striking are the poor souls shown burning in hell. The church interior is refreshingly plain, with a charming collection of votive offerings in the shape of ships left by Forio's sailors and fishermen in thanks for salvation from maritime accidents. Soccorso means »help« in Italian, hence the name of the church.

Other sights

The 17th-century Chiesa Santa Maria Visita Poveri can be found at Piazza Municipio, but Forio's main church is actually on Corso Umberto, where fishermen from Ancona are said to have founded the **Basilica di Santa Maria di Loreto** in the 14th century. The cult of the Madonna di Loreto spread throughout Italy during the late Middle Ages. The basilica was remodelled in the 16th century and redecorated from 1780 to 1885, with the result that its stucco decoration is some of the finest among Ischia's churches. In contrast, the rather unimpressive façade dates from the 19th century and the mosaic was designed by Eduard Bargheer. At the upper end of Via Roma stands the **Chiesa di San Vito**, which is Forio's oldest church. Its origins go back to the 14th century, but later rebuilding has left no trace of the original building. A remarkable item in the sacristy is a silver statue of Saint Vito, which is said to have been designed according to a model made by the famous Neapolitan sculptor Giuseppe Sammartino.

Villa La Colombaia ► A short distance outside Forio lies the Villa La Colombaia, which was once the summer home belonging to film director **Luchino Visconti**. During the 1950s and 60s, he entertained his famous guests here. Today, the villa functions as a cultural centre, where the Fondazione Visconti also runs a small museum dedicated to its founder.

La Mortella A sight genuinely worth seeing is **La Mortella Garden** located between Forio and Lacco Ameno. It was developed over many decades by the English composer William Walton, who died in 1983. A foundation now maintains the exotic flora of this paradisiacal garden, and also supports young musicians, who regularly give concerts here during the summer months (Via F. Calise 39; April–mid Nov; Tue, Thu, Sat, Sun 9am–7pm; www.lamortella.it).

★ Giardini Poseidon The Giardini Poseidon located south of Forio enjoy legendary popularity on Ischia. Set right next to the **Spiaggia di Citara**, the extensive **thermal spa** is immaculate as well as offering a variety of heated pools, saunas, and steam baths – all maintained to the highest modern standards. The section of beach attached to this establishment is an added attraction for holidaymakers (April–Oct daily 8.30am–7pm; www.giardiniposeidon.it).

Sant'Angelo Sant'Angelo, on Ischia's southern coast, was discovered by artists during the early 20th century, who fell for its charm in the same way they fell for Positano on the Amalfi Coast. Its charm is characterized by the typical island architecture of its painted houses stacked over one another, and also by the picturesque small fishing harbour that epitomizes Mediterranean island life. A spectacular natural adjunct is the **La Roia peninsula**, which is only just connected to the village by
La Roia ► a narrow causeway of sandy beach. The Aragonese tower there is not open to the public, but the village makes a good living from its beaches, thermal pool gardens, boutiques and restaurants.

★ Spiaggia dei Maronti The Spiaggia dei Maronti stretches east for just under 3km/2mi from Sant'Angelo and is one of the most beautiful beaches anywhere on the Bay of Naples. There are also fascinating volcanic phenomena to see, similar to those at the Phlegrean Fields. The sea is warmed by hot thermal springs in a few places and even the sand has varying temperatures.

★★ Naples · Napoli

D 3/4

Region: Campania
Altitude: 10m/33ft

Province: Napoli
Population: 983,000
(metropolitan area: 3.5 million)

Naples, the capital of South Italy, is one of western Europe's most complex cities. The combination of high unemployment, the ever-present Camorra, environmental destruction and a Kafkaesque bureaucracy has resulted in Stendhal's »most beautiful city in the world« declining into a virtual slum by the sea. Nevertheless, a look beyond the flapping washing lines, chaotic traffic and centuries of clichés reveals a city worth exploring for its wonderful art treasures and, not least, for the amiability of its inhabitants.

Between myth and reality

»Naples is not a city… it is a world unto itself,« wrote the author Curzio Malaparte in his novel *The Skin*, and travellers as long ago as the 18th century understood the city more as an experience of chaos than as a place to live. Today, it is harder than ever to set out to discover Naples without preconceptions, not least because of the re-emergence of organized crime making the international headlines. A promising rebirth in the 1990s under the leadership of Mayor Antonio Bassolino has already withered. The phrase »see Naples and die« has for a long time had different implications than originally intended – it is uncomfortably close to bloody reality. However, the media coverage of the city's complicated economic and social realities is hardly fair. Naples is, of course, far more than Camorra, corruption and deprivation. Italy's liveliest theatre and music scene can be found here and, in addition to the official programme of contemporary art, the city is also home to a flourishing alternative art and music scene.

Personal safety

Naples is no more dangerous than any other major western European city. The hot spots for its urban problems lie well beyond any tourist routes, in districts such as Scampia and Secondigliano. It is nevertheless advisable to take special care of handbags and camera equipment while exploring the historic city centre on foot. The centro storico and neighbourhoods such as Sanità and Quartieri quickly empty of people after sundown, which can make them seem a little spooky. Cars should not be left by the side of the road but parked in authorized car parks with attendants.

Despite its 2700-year history, Naples is far from being a museum. The centro storico might be a UNESCO World Heritage site, but it is also a densely populated microcosm with close-knit communities and a daily life that is largely played out on the streets, as visitors will discover when they venture away from the tourist attractions.

The centro storico in Naples

The **Naples of antiquity** was one of many flourishing cities of Campania Felix, but by no means the largest (► p.25). Naples only developed into a royal residence and glamorous metropolis with the arrival of the Angevin kings in the 13th century, after which it was the capital of the kingdom of South Italy under a changing roster of rulers right up until the unification of Italy in 1861. The city's troubles began as early as the rule of the last Bourbon kings, however. The impact of unification and the shift of political and economic status to northern Italian cities is something from which Naples and the Campanian region have yet to recover. In theory, the city's location on the beautiful Bay of Naples and its many historical buildings and art treasures should make it an obvious tourist destination. However, Naples' negative urban image and inadequate tourism infrastructure have retarded development in this sector. Visitor numbers to the city are on the increase, but only due to day-trippers coming from other destinations such as Sorrento, Ischia or the Amalfi Coast.

City Walks

Opening remarks

The seething street life and heaving traffic can make Naples seem confusing at first, but its historic city centre is surprisingly small and ideally explored on foot. The Vomero neighbourhood can also be reached by three or four cable-car routes (► p.188). **Via Toledo is one of the city's main arteries** and a useful orientation point. Together with its extension, Via Pessina, it connects the National Archaeological Museum to the north with Piazza del Plebiscito and the Royal Palace to the south. A visit to Naples is not complete, however, without a trip to quarters such as Sanità, and a ride up the Vomero hill. Via dei Tribunali and the Spaccanapoli running parallel have been major thoroughfares of the present-day centro storico since

Centro storico ►

antiquity. This is where the most important churches are found, along with the excavation site under San Lorenzo Maggiore, which contains Greek and Roman remains of particular interest. North of Piazza Cavour, a short distance from the National Archaeological Museum, lies the typically Neapolitan quarter of Sanità. The main sights of this buzzing district include Baroque city palaces and the catacombs of San Gaudioso. The Ponte della Sanità leads to the Royal Palace of Capodimonte, with its world famous art gallery, and the nearby catacombs at San Gennaro are virtually a museum of early Christian painting in themselves. Piazza del Mercato near the central railway station, which played such a significant role in the city's history, was somewhat cut off from the centro storico during urban regeneration projects in the late 19th century. The narrow huddle of lanes in the Mercato quarter stands in stark contrast to the skyline presented by the modern office district of Centro Direzionale. The southern section of Via Toledo ends in the pedestrian zone around the elegant Piazza del Plebiscito with the Palazzo Reale and the Teatro San Carlo. Immediately opposite the majestic Galleria Umberto I lies the notorious Quartieri spagnoli quarter. The Neapolitan middle classes reside a safe distance from the chaotic city centre on the mound of Vomero. A ride up is highly recommended for the Belle Époque charm of this district and, most especially, for the **phenomenal view** of the city from the San Martino monastery. The elegant part of Naples, which can even be described as chic, begins west of Piazza del Plebiscito along Via Chiaia. Early 20th-century town houses, luxury boutiques and a suitably classy public provide a very different picture of the city than that seen in the newspapers. One of the most beautiful roads in Naples is the Riviera di Chiaia, which begins at the Castel dell'Ovo and the Villa Comunale park. Even though it is now densely built-up, Posillipo hill is still one of the top places to live in the city.

◄ Sanità and I Vergini

◄ Piazza Garibaldi, Centro Direzionale and the Mercato quarter

◄ Toledo and Piazza del Plebiscito

◄ Vomero

◄ From Pizzofalcone to Posillipo

Highlights *Naples*

The best view of Naples
The Belvedere of the Certosa di San Martino offers the best view of Naples.
► **page 237**

Centro storico
Enchanting majolica monastery gardens, imaginative pastori in the street of Christmas creches, a trip into the past, magnificent churches and chapels, historic city palaces as well as inviting street cafés in the heart of the city
► **page 194 – 218**

Great art
Consummate Greek and Roman art in the Museo Archeologico, one of the most important collections of paintings in Italy in the Capodimonte Museum as well as early Christian art in the catacombs
► **page 215, 221, 219 – 220**

Royal Naples
Via Toledo, Naples' real main street, Palazzo Reale, Galleria Umberto I and Castel Nuovo
► **page 223 – 234**

VISITING NAPLES

INFORMATION

AAST Napoli,
Piazza del Plebiscito 1 (Palazzo Reale), 80132 Napoli, tel. 08 12 52 57 11, fax 0 81 41 86 19; www.inaples.it
www.napolinapoli.com
www.portanapoli.com

Tourist information offices:
Piazza del Gesù Nuovo 7/8
Via San Carlo 9 (Galleria Umberto) and Via Santa Lucia 107
Mon–Fri 8.30am–7pm, Sat and Sun 9am–2pm

EPT
Piazza dei Martiri 58
www.eptnapoli.info
Information is also available at the central railway station/Piazza Garibaldi (near track 23)
Mon–Sat 8.30am–8pm

! Baedeker TIP

Up-to-date information

Events programmes, opening times and travel timetables can all be found in the city's daily newspaper *Il Mattino* (www.ilmattino.it); also in the local edition of *La Repubblica* (www.napoli.larepubblica.it) and in the monthly brochure *Qui Napoli*, published by AAST Napoli (internet version at www.inaples.it).

TRANSPORT

Car parks
Parcheggio di Interscambio Autosilo Brin (Via B. Brin) between Piazza Garibaldi and the harbour, and also near Mergellina harbour, at Autorimessa Mergellina (Via G. Bruno 112) and Autorimessa Sannazaro (Piazza Sannazaro 142).

Uniconapoli ticket
Available at newspaper stands and tobacco shops, this ticket is valid on the metro and on all municipal buses and cable cars. It needs to be validated prior to use.

Metro Napoli/funicolare
There are two underground metro lines (Metropolitana) in Naples, which operate services every 10–20 minutes between 6am and 11pm.
Linea 2 is Italy's oldest metro service and mostly travels above ground, connecting Naples with Pozzuoli.
Linea 1 connects the northern suburbs and the Vomero hillside quarter with the centro storico. The lines cross at the »Museo-Cavour« stop. Metronapoli also runs the four cable car services (funicolare): three of them connect the lower city with the Vomero and Posillipo hills; the Mergellina route connects the harbour with Via Manzoni (www.anm.it).

Buses/trams
The orange *ANM* municipal buses are often overcrowded and make only slow progress through the city centre. Most of the blue *long-distance buses* set off from Piazza Garibaldi and the main railway station: SEPSA services the towns around the Campi Flegrei; CTP goes to Aversa and Caserta; the blue SITA buses set off from Via G. Ferraris (southeast of Piazza Garibaldi) or from Piazza Immacolatella Vecchia (north of Stazione Marittima), heading for Pompeii, Salerno and, via Sorrento, to the Amalfi Coast.

Taxis
Authorized taxis in Naples are white and display the city's emblem. Tariffs are available at the airport, the railway

Naples Metro Map

Metro Line 1	F1	Funicolare di Mergellina	Capolinea bus
Metro Line 2	F2	Funicolare di Chiaia	Parking
Metropolitana servizi regionali	F3	Funicolare centrale	aliscafi
Station	F4	Funicolare di montesanto	
Station for changing metro lines			

F1–F4: Funicular

Trenitalia stations
Circumvesuviana stations
Cumana stations

station, in tourist offices and at hotels, and they are also displayed in the taxis themselves.

Trains

Naples' central railway station, *Stazione Centrale F.S.*, is on Piazza Garibaldi. Regional trains from Rome also stop at Stazione Mergellina. The city's suburban trains double up as ideal mode of transport for day trips around the Bay of Naples. For information on the various routes please see ►p.98.

Ships

► Practicalities, p.100

Air travel
The ***Aeroporto Internazionale di Napoli Capodichino*** (www.gesac.it) lies 8km/5mi from Piazza Garibaldi and the central railway station. Take the blue Alibus or yellow ANM bus no. 3S via Piazza Garibaldi to reach the city centre at Piazza Municipio/Molo Beverello (buy tickets on the bus).
Curreri buses travel six times daily via Vico Ecquense to Sorrento (buy tickets on the bus). SITA buses head for Salerno.

EVENTS · ENTERTAINMENT

Maggio dei Monumenti
All of Naples and hordes of tourists set off between the last week in April and the first week in June to see the sights normally closed to the public. Attractions including museums, churches, castles and many other venues open their doors at this time. *Il Mattino* publishes a weekly events programme.

Festa di San Gennaro
The first weekend in May and on 19 Sept, ►Baedeker Special p.204

Napoli Teatro Festival
The international theatre festival has earned a place in the European cultural calendar. The venues are at least as exciting as the programmes. The whole thing is organized by the ever-changing European Ensemble (www.teatrofestivalitalia.it).

Theatre · Opera · Concerts · Jazz · Film
The world famous Teatro di San Carlo (Via San Carlo 98F, tel. 08 17 97 24 12, www.teatrosancarlo.it) is closed in July and August.
The Teatro Nuovo presents experimental theatre (Montecalvario 16 Tel. 0 81 42 59 58; www.nuovoteatro nuovo.it).
Napoli jazz can be heard in the Around Midnight (Via Bonito 32 A) and in the Otto Jazz Club (also Neapolitan folk, Salita Cariati 23 A).
The ensemble Pietà dei Turchini performs 17th and 18th century music to perfection early evenings. Tickets available 1 hour before concerts begin (Via Santa Caterina da Siena 38, www.turchini.it).
The city and surrounding province also organizes a Jazz Festival between June and September (www.circuito jazz.it). Advance tickets can be purchased c/o the box office (Galleria Umberto I 17, tel. 08 15 51 91 88, fax 0 81 40 15 88; www.boxofficeclub.it).
Current Italian and international movies at budget prices from mid-July to early September at the open-air cinema festival Accordi e Disaccordi in Parco del Poggio near Capodimonte Park (Metro 1 Colli Aminei, www.accordiedisaccordi.com).

Going out
Students like to go out in the centro storico, while the more chic meeting places are in the Chiaia district and on the Vomero hill. The latest tips on the nightlife scene are best found on the internet and by reading flyers displayed in copy shops and music stores. The sandy beach at Arenile di Bagnoli, in the northern sector of the city, becomes an open-air dance spot during the summer months. The coolest nightclub in Naples is the Freezer Stereo Bar (Centro Direzionale Isola G 6) in the office district behind the central railway station. The jazz venues Around Midnight and Otto Jazz Club enjoy cult status (►see above).

Football
»Forza Napule! Jammo Ja'!« The most sacred place in Naples next to the cathedral is the San Paolo football

stadium. Games take place every Sunday afternoon between September and June (advance tickets from c/o Azzuro Service, Via F. Galeota 17, Fuorigrotta, tel. 08 15 93 94 45, www.azzuroservice.net).

GOOD TO KNOW

Campania Artecard
Cash can be saved when visiting museums and archaeological sites by buying a Campania Artecard. Tickets can be valid for three or seven days and there are further reductions for young people. The card is for sale at the airport, at railway stations, in museums, at many hotels, and sometimes in kiosks (www.artecard.it).

City tours
The hop-on-hop-off buses run by City Sightseeing Napoli pass all the main sights; one route goes as far as the Capo Posillipo. The main terminal bus stop is on Piazza Municipio in front of the Castel Nuovo (tel. 08 15 51 72 79; www.napoli.city-sightseeing.it).

Nicola Prisco (mobile no. 34 05 92 13 54; www.quovadisnapoli.-net) and his cosmopolitan friends take families and small groups off-the-beaten track in Naples and the surrounding area.

Shopping
Markets are an authentic place to enjoy local culture, for example, those in the Quartieri spagnoli and around Piazza Pignasecca. The epitome of a Neapolitan market can be found at Porta Nolana near the main railway station. In the Chiaia district, on the other hand, the shoppers are rather more refined. Some streets in the city centre are the domain of just one trade, such as the Christmas crib makers on Via San Gregorio Armeno. Some of the city's best ***bookshops*** can be found by the Port'Alba, while the only women's bookshop in southern Italy can be found near Piazza Bellini. A huge selection of books, CDs and DVDs is offered by Feltrinelli on Piazza dei Martiri. Beautiful prints and gouache paintings can be found in the ***antiques shops*** along Via Santa Maria di Constantinopoli and in Bowinkel at Via Santa Lucia 24, as well as at Piazza dei Martiti 24. Umbrellas have been produced by the Talarico family at Vico due Porte a Toledo 4b (a small side street off Via Toledo) since 1860. High fashion is best found along Via Toledo (for example, in Fusaro) and in the Chiaia district. The most famous tie maker in Naples is Marinelli at Riviera di Chiaia 287; customers include Bill Clinton. All the top designer brands can be found near Piazza dei Martiri, on Vial Calabritto and Via Filangieri, while Cilento & Sons on Via Medina 61a has been serving the aristocracy and higher echelons of society since 1780. Recommended sources of antiques and second-hand goods are: Renato Rivieccio, Mobili e Oggetti del Passato, Via dei Tribunali 363 (Palazzo Spinelli), and Giuseppe Gavitone, I Ricordi del Cuore, Via Santa Maria di Costantinopoli 123.

Figurines on Via Gregorio Armeno

WHERE TO EAT

See numbers 1–12 on the ►boxed map of Naples city centre on the separate large map and also the detailed maps on pages 196, 224 and 239.

► Expensive

① *Da Dora*
Via F. Palasciano 30
Tel. 0 81 68 05 19; closed Sun.
No insider's tip anymore, but still a good bet for the best fish dishes. Very busy.

② *Stanza del Gusto*
Via Constantinopoli 104
Tel. 0 81 40 15 78; www.lastanzadelgusto.com; closed Sun and Mon
Two steps from Piazza Bellini, a great experimenter of Campanian cuisine, Mario Avallone is at work in this restaurant. At street level the Squisitezze also serve tasty tidbits to a glass of wine at noon.

③ *Terrazza Calabritto*
Piazza Vittoria 1
Tel. 08 12 40 51 88; closed Mon
Excellent vegetable antipasti and fish dishes.

► Moderate

④ *Europeo di Mattozzi*
Via Marchese Campodisola 4
Tel. 08 15 52 13 23; closed Sat and Sun
The traditional home cooking here is not only appreciated by the local students.

⑤ *La Cantina di Triunfo*
Riviera di Chiaia 64
Tel. 0 81 66 81 01; closed Sun
Changing daily menu of the very best quality. The numerous wine bottles along the walls are not just decoration!

⑥ *Ristorante Al 53*
Piazza Dante 53, tel. 08 15 49 93 72
Locals appreciate the creative vegetable dishes at the central restaurant. The antipasti are virtually a full meal on their own.

⑦ *Taverna dell'Arte*
Rampa S. Giovanni Maggiore 1/A
Tel. 08 15 52 75 58; closed Sun
Charming restaurant in the historical university district. Alfonso Galotti has a penchant for the cuisine of the 17th century, when Neapolitans were still known as »mangiafoglie« (leaf eaters).

► Inexpensive

⑧ *Da Angela*
Salita S. Anna di Palazzo 25
Tel. 0 81 40 14 95; closed Sun and Mon
This trattoria, run by women, is just a stone's throw away from the famous Pizzeria Brandi.

⑨ *Da Michele*
Via Sersale 1/2
Tel. 08 15 53 92 04; closed Sun.
The most traditional Neapolitan pizzeria. Pizza classics such as marinara and margherita are served at unpretentious marble tables for as long as the supply of dough lasts. Long queues at night.

⑩ *Gastronomia L.U.I.S.E.*
Via Toledo 266, tel. 0 81 41 53 67;
and Via S. Caterina a Chiaia 68 (Piazza dei Martiri)
Tel. 0 81 41 77 35.
Excellent fast food (tavola calda) can be found at these two venues.

⑪ *Pizzeria Starita a Materdei*
Via Materdei 27
Tel. 08 15 57 36 82; closed Mon.
Renowned for its delicious pizza fritta and Sophia Loren, who played a scene here in the 1960s movie *L'Oro di Napoli*. Around a 15-minute walk from the Museo Archeologico.

⑫ ***Trattoria da Giovanni dal 1936***
Via Soprammuro a Portanolana 9/10
Tel. 0 81 26 83 20; closed Sun
The third generation of the same family runs this authentic fish trattoria located in the heart of the Mercato di Porta Nolana.

WHERE TO STAY

See numbers 1-11 on the ►boxed map of Naples city centre on the separate large map as well as the detailed maps for ►Where to eat.

► Luxury

① ***Grand Hotel Parkers***
Corso Vittorio Emanuele 135
Tel. 08 17 61 24 74
www.grandhotelparkers.com. This luxury hotel on the Vomero hill has been popular with well-to-do travellers from all over the world since 1865. Superb views over the city and the Bay of Naples. Beautiful roof terrace.

② ***Costantinopoli 104***
Via S. Maria di Costantinopoli 104
Tel. 08 15 57 10 35
www.costantinopoli104.it. A courtyard oasis just a few steps from the Archaeological Museum. Modern accessories add that extra touch in this Liberty palazzo. The roof terrace has a solarium and there is a tiny pool in the garden.

► Mid-range

③ ***Hotel del Real Orto Botanico***
Via Foria 192
Tel. 08 14 42 15 28
www.hotelrealortobotanico.it
Well-kept establishment just a few steps away from the Archaeological Museum and the centro storico, the metro stop »Piazza Dante«, and the Botanical Gardens. Nice roof terrace.

! *Baedeker* TIP

Cioccolato, caffè e sfogliatella

Italy's finest espresso can be savoured in Naples. For example at the Mexico (Piazza Dante 86); at the Gambrinus (Via Chiaia 1–2), located between Piazza Trieste e Trento and Piazza del Plebiscito; or at the Carolina (Piazza Carolina 18) just a little further on. Enticingly fragrant sfogliatella pastries are served alongside your coffee at La Sfogliatella Mary (Galleria Umberto I 66). The city's most exclusive chocolate maker Gay Odin has several outlets in the centro storico as well as an ice-cream parlour on Via Benedetto Croce.

④ ***Parteno***
Lungomare Partenope 1
Tel. & fax 08 12 45 20 95
www.parteno.it
Bed & breakfast in the same area as the local luxury hotels, but with a great deal more charm.

⑤ ***Terminus***
Piazza Garibaldi 91
Tel. 08 17 79 31 11
www.starhotels.it
This hotel near the main railway station is favoured by business travellers and groups. The comfortable rooms have double-glazed windows.

⑪ ***Hotel Piazza Bellini***
Via Constantinopoli 101
Tel. 0 81 45 17 32
www.hotelpiazzabellini.com
Frsh breezes and comfortable, quiet rooms in an old palazzo two steps from Piazza Bellini.

► Budget

⑥ ***Bellini***
Via S. Paolo 44 (corner Via Tribunali)
Tel. 0 81 19 32 35 62 96
www.hotelbellini.net

! *Baedeker* TIP

Rooms with added insight

The bed and breakfast boom has reached Naples. Upper-class apartments, palazzi and former monasteries are opening their doors to overnight guests, and often visitors enjoy all the comforts of a hotel at a fair price combined with a personal touch and an insight into the everyday life of their Neapolitan hosts (www.bb-napoli.com, www.rentabed.it).

Good choice for a bed in the centro storico. Car parking for an additional fee.

⑦ ***Chiaro di Luna***
Via Santa Teresa degli Scalzi 118
Tel. 08 15 49 88 99, 33 98 10 73 70
www.chiarodiluna-napoli.it
Friendly B&B near the Museo Archeologico on the road heading towards Capodimonte.

⑧ ***Europeo/Europeo Flowers***
Via Mezzacannone 109/C
Tel. & fax 08 15 51 72 54
www.sea-hotels.com
Two hotels under the same roof in the university district, just a few paces from Piazza San Domenico.

⑨ ***Ostello Mergellina***
Salita della Grotta a Piedigrotta 23
Tel. 08 17 61 23 46
www.ostellionline.org.
The city's official youth hostel located in a utilitarian building above Mergellina station.

⑩ ***La Casa del Monacone***
Piazza Sanità 14
Tel. & fax 08 17 44 37 14
www.casadelmonacone.it
A favourite place in the authentic Sanità quarter: beautiful rooms and one self-catering apartment housed in a former convent. The early Christian Catacombe di San Gaudioso are in the attached church.

Centro Storico, Spaccanapoli and the Museo Archeologico

Lively open-air musuem

The **historic centre of Naples** is among the highlights of any visit to the city. The anarchic charm of the centro storico – a UNESCO World Heritage Site since 1995 – and its palazzi and churches combine into what is a very lively open-air museum. Meanwhile, the Museo Archeologico Nazionale is not far away on the northern borders of the city centre (►p.215).

Piazza Dante

Via Pessina leads to Piazza Dante, once a square beyond the city walls known as Largo del Mercatello. Today it is one of Naples' central squares. It was redesigned by Luigi Vanvitelli for Charles III in the second half of the 18th century, when it was turned into the **Foro Carolino**.

Museo Nitsch

The beautiful rooms of the former electrical works nearby now house a museum dedicated to the Austrian performance artist Hermann Nitsch. In the context of the genuine wonders on display in

A look into the city's history: remains of the Greek city wall on Piazza Bellini

Naples, however, his works seem rather banal (Fondazione Morra, Vico Lungo Portecorvo 29/d; Wed–Mon 10am–7pm).

Piazza Bellini

Constructed in 1625, the Port'Alba leads from Piazza Dante to Piazza Bellini, one of the most appealing squares in Naples, complete with a memorial to the composer. Be sure to cast an eye around the small area containing remains of the Greek city walls, discovered during road works in the 1950s.

Galleria L'Accademia di Belle Arti di Napoli

Running parallel to Via Pessina, Via Santa Maria di Constatinopoli leads from Piazza Bellini back to the Archaeological Museum. The route leads past the Art Academy, founded by Charles III, which has been housed in the San Giovanni church of the former convent here since 1864 (Mon–Fri 10am–2pm). A museum was installed on the second floor in 2005 with a focus on 19th-century Neapolitan painting, including work by Giacinto Gigantes and others belonging to the **Scuola di Posillipo**.

Via Santa Maria di Costantinopoli

Except for the Chiesa Santa Maria di Costantinopoli, all the churches along this street have been closed since the earthquake in 1980. They are only opened to the public during the Maggio dei Monumenti, when significant sacred buildings, such as the **Chiesa della Sapienza** and the **San Giovanni Battista delle Monache**, can be viewed. Another route from Piazza Bellini is to take Via San Pietro A Maiella past the city's music school. The **Conservatorium**, housed in a section of the convent that belongs to the neighbouring Chiesa San Pietro a Maiella (beautiful cloister), also contains the Museo Storico Musicale. The museum has a worthwhile collection of historic musical instruments, sheet music, and items relating to famous composers (Accademia San Pietro A Maiella; Mon–Thu 9.30am–1pm).

◄ Museo Storico Musicale

Centro Storico Map

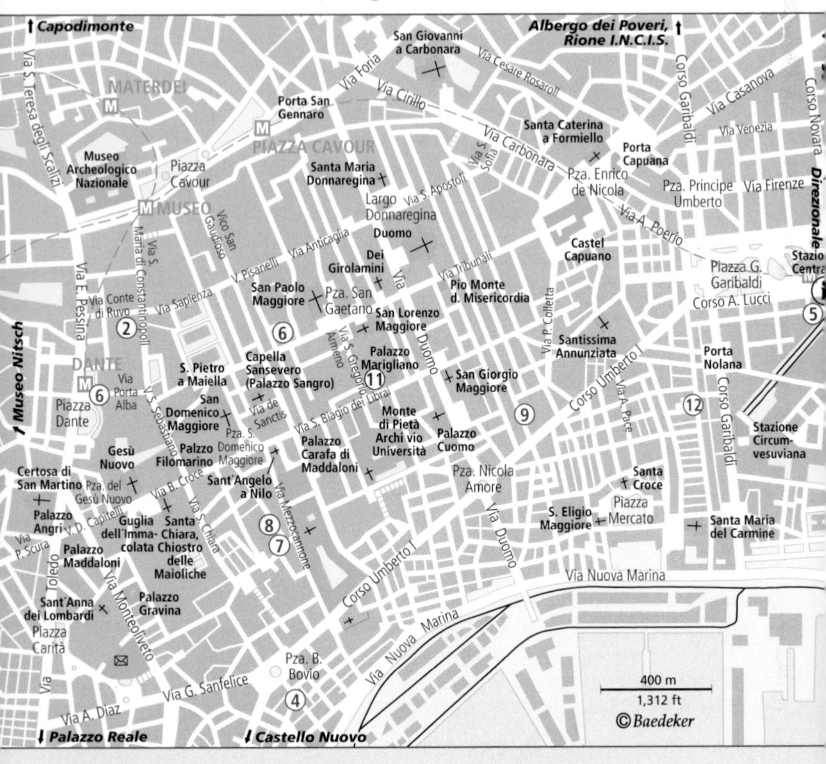

Where to eat
④ Europeo di Mattozzi
⑥ Ristorante Al 53
⑦ Taverna dell'Arte
⑨ Da Michele
⑫ Trattoria da Giovanni dal 1936

Where to stay
② Costantinopoli 104
⑤ Terminus
⑥ Bellini
⑧ Europeo/Europeo Flowers
⑪ Albergo Purgatorio

San Pietro A Maiella

The Gothic Chiesa San Pietro A Maiella is among the city's most important examples of sacred architecture (Via San Pietro A Maiella 4; Mon–Sat 7.30am–noon, 5pm–7.30pm, Sun 9am–1pm). This early 14th-century church is associated with Pietro da Morrone, who spent much time living as a hermit on Mount Maiella in the mountains of Abruzzo before becoming the rather unhappy Pope Celestine V in old age. The House of Anjou financed the construction of the church, which was built between 1319 and 1343. The only remains of a Baroque remodelling are the 17th-century wood ceiling and the altar with beautiful marble inlaid work, by Cosimo Fanzago. Today, the church impresses with the simplicity of its Gothic architecture.

★ **Cappella Pontano**

A rare example of Renaissance architecture in Naples is located adjacent to the large municipal hospital (policlinico) built in 1907. The Cappella Pontano (Via del Tribunali 16; Mon–Sat 9am–1pm) was built between 1490 and 1495 by the philosopher and author Giovanni Pontano, who was also personal secretary to King Alfonso V. The graceful building was very much inspired by antiquity and was erected to house the royal family tomb. The original majolica floor tiles are of particular note. The numerous epigraphs set inside and outside the chapel walls are quotes from Pontano's works: among others, the humanist laments the early death of his wife and three children. In addition, the walls are decorated with Greek and Roman epitaphs from Pontano's personal collection.

! *Baedeker* TIP

Art on the go in Naples

The Naples underground has been a lot more colourful since renowned artists were commissioned to design the new metro stations of Linea 1. The work undertaken for the metro system has also unearthed some archaeological sensations. For example, tunnelling work revealed the remains of a Roman temple and the perfectly preserved hulls from ships once anchored in the ancient harbour. The finds are exhibited in the underground stations that have already been completed. The entire project is due for completion by 2013, and a taster of the »Stazioni dell'arte« can be found at www.metro.na.it.

The **Chiesa Santa Maria Maggiore della Pietrasanta** stands on the remains of an early Christian basilica dating from the first half of the 6th century. The most recent archaeological excavations have also revealed ancient buildings. The present church, a major example of the work by Cosimo Fanzago, dates from 1653–67. Second World War bombing caused permanent damage to the church, and only the façade has remained more or less intact. The campanile (clock tower) to the right of the main façade is the oldest surviving example in Naples. Untouched by any additional structures or rebuilding, it is also a rare piece of **early medieval architecture** in Naples. It is interesting to note how obviously commonplace it was to use architectural spolia during the 10th and 11th centuries, as evidenced in the Roman building fragments set into the clock tower walls.

★  Campanile di Pietrasanta

Via dei Tribunali

Via dei Tribunali leads straight to the Castel Capuano, where the Pretura is the city's most important court building. Its extremely linear approach mirrors the original main street of the city during antiquity, the Decumano Maggiore (though the level has changed).

Palazzo Spinelli di Laurino

On the right-hand side of the road, on the corner with Via Nilo, stands the Palazzo Spinelli di Laurino, one of the typical city palaces of Naples' historic centre. Originally built around 1500, it was substantially altered in 1776. Ferdinando Sanfelice designed the staircase, and Ferdinando Fuga also took part in the remodelling work. The oval courtyard has a novel design.

★★ Santa Maria delle Anime del Purgatorio ad Arco

The much photographed Chiesa Santa Maria delle Anime del Purgatorio ad Arco, by Cosimo Fanzago, is virtually an emblem of Via dei Tribunali (Via dei Tribunali 39; Mon–Sat 10am–1pm; crypt Sat only 10am–1pm). The bronze death's heads by the doorway leading to the staircase are a particularly popular motif for photographs. The foundation of the church in 1604 is said to have been the responsibility of a brotherhood that exists to this day, who dedicated the church to the poor souls burning in hell (purgatorio). It is said that during the 17th century up to 60 services were held here per day! The church is also famous for its cemetery below, where a strange death cult remained active right up until the 1970s. The **Neapolitan obsession with the afterlife** and their apparently heathen rites were brought to an end by the Vatican. Since then, death's heads are no longer »adopted«, i.e. decorated, illuminated and covered with wish lists.

? DID YOU KNOW …?

- Naples is built of volcanic tuff stone. This soft, not particularly weather-resistant stone was already being quarried by the Greek city builders, and giant caves have survived in the labyrinth beneath the centro storico resembling an underground mirror image of the streets above.

Piazza San Gaetano

The Chiesa San Paolo Maggiore and Piazza San Gaetano are located at what was a key point for the city during antiquity, for this is where the Greek agora and the subsequent Roman forum stood. Naples' most important buildings once lined this square or were nearby. The only remains above ground today are the two mighty Corinthian pillars on the façade of San Paolo Maggiore, but urban life has been played out here for at least 2500 years.

★ San Paolo Maggiore

San Paolo Maggiore is an important example of early Neapolitan Baroque (Mon–Sat 9am–1pm, Sun 10am–12.30pm). An early construction dedicated to St Peter and St Paul was erected on the ruins of a Roman Castor and Pollux Temple in the 9th century. The portico of this heathen temple survived in the church façade right up until the earthquake in 1688. Only the columns flanking the church doorway survived after that, although the dual staircase from 1576 does recall the temple podium. To the right of the staircase, there is a door leading to the crypt containing the tomb of St Cajetan. A statue dedicated to him on the piazza was erected in 1737. The present church was built in 1583–1603, designed by Francesco Grimaldi; the aisles were not constructed until 1627. The light-flooded interior is sumptuously decorated. Take a look at the sacristy with pictures by the Neapolitan painter Francesco Solimena (1689–90).

Napoli Sotterranea

To the left of the church is the entrance to a somewhat overrated attraction: the privately-run initiative known as Napoli Sotterranea, which offers guided tours through underground Naples. The mining of volcanic tuff stone left a labyrinthine system of giant caves that served as bomb shelters for the citizens of Naples during the Second World War. The **Greek and Roman cisterns** are located precisely where buildings stood above ground during antiquity. The tour also includes viewing some rather unspectacular remains of the **ancient theatre** (Piazza San Gaetano 68; tours Mon–Fri noon, 2pm, 4pm, Thu also at 9pm, Sat, Sun 10am, noon, 2pm, 4pm and 6pm).

Teatro Romano

Much more recommendable is one of the most recent and spectacular archaeological excavations in the ancient city centre. For some years now the **Roman theatre**, dating back to Augustian times, has been undergoing excavation work between Via Anticaglia, Via San Paolo and Via dei Cinquesanti. In the middle of the centro storico a large part of the cavea (the semicircular spectator area) has come to light. It is now hoped that remains of the scena (the architectural backstage area) will be discovered. The chances to visit the site are still very limited, but regular opening times are being planned. As far as it is possible though, a visit to the excavation is worthwhile. In hardly any other place in today's Naples is antiquity this present (Via San Paolo; ask about visits on location in the centro storico on Piazza del Gesù Nuovo).

✱✱ **San Lorenzo Maggiore**

The most important Gothic church in Naples is the Chiesa San Lorenzo Maggiore, located diagonally opposite San Paolo Maggiore (Via dei Tribunali 316; daily 8am–noon, 3pm–7pm). A few mosaic fragments from the early Christian construction dating from the 6th century can still be seen in the right transept. The present church has its origins in a building constructed in 1270 by Charles of Anjou, and is now considered a masterpiece of French Gothic architecture in Italy. Especially celebrated is the ambulatory built for the Franciscan monks, which is the height of style and architectural finesse. Decades of renovation have restored the plain elegance of the nave (photo p.202) and its nine chapels in the aisles. The most important artwork in the church today is the **tomb of Catherine of Austria**. The wife of Charles of Calabria and daughter-in-law of Robert of Anjou was not even thirty years old when she died in 1323. The sculptor **Tino da Camaino** from Sienna designed the tomb for this Habsburg princess the same year she died. His creation of a free-standing canopy supported by four spiralled pillars standing on lion pediments became the guiding example for such royal tombs for several centuries afterwards.

San Lorenzo Maggiore was also the setting for a meeting that went down in literary history: this is where **Boccaccio** first met **Fiammetta**. Petrarch spent some time living in the Franciscan monastery. Some of the convent's rooms now house the **Museo dell'Opera di San Lorenzo** . Seven metres (23ft) below present ground levels, a **Roman road** has been excavated that once connected the main thoroughfares of the Decumano Maggiore (Via dei Tribunali) and the Decumano inferiore (Via S. Biaggio dei Librai).

✱✱ ◄ Archaeological excavations

SAN LORENZO MAGGIORE

★★ **The most significant Gothic church in Naples lies right in the heart of the historic city centre on Piazza San Gaetano. The building stands around 7m/23ft above the agora of ancient Neapolis. Thus a visit to San Lorenzo is also a journey into the history of the city (www.sanlorenzomaggiorenapoli.it).**

Opening times:
daily 8am–noon and 3pm–7pm (church); Mon–-Sat 9.30am–5.30pm, Sun till 1.30pm only (excavations and museum).

① Architectural history

The nave was constructed on the site of an early Christian building. This older church of St Lawrence dating from the 6th century was built precisely over the agora of ancient Neapolis. There are traces from all building phases to be seen.

② Tombs

There are several grand tombs in the chapels and the choir. These include the tomb of the Habsburg Princess Catherine of Austria (1323, between the first two pillars of the choir, to the right); of Ludovico Caracciolo (1335, in the north transept); and of Charles of Durazzo (1348, in the south transept).

③ Daily life during antiquity

A stairway leads down from the cloister into Greco-Roman antiquity. The Greek agora and later the Roman forum was once around 7m/23ft below the present San Lorenzo church. Over a distance of 54m/59yd, visitors can stroll along a cobblestone cardo, over 2000 years old, lined by shops similar to the ones at Pompeii. For example, there is a bakery complete with a domed oven, a laundry with effluent canals, and an aerarium, where the city's treasure was kept. The Roman brick walls have been dated to the 1st century AD, while the tuff stone blocks are from the 5th century BC and of Greek origin. The cardo ends at the cryptoporticus, the covered market.

④ Museo dell'Opera di San Lorenzo

This door leads to the former Franciscan monastery. In recognition of its importance as the location for the Greek agora, it was the seat of the royal parliament from 1442 onwards. Today, it houses a museum. The model of the Greek agora and its surroundings is particularly worth seeing here. The museum also displays ceramic finds dating from antiquity to the Middle Ages. The third floor shows liturgical vestments and several particularly attractive pastori (Neapolitan crib figurines).

A frieze along the length of the tomb of Catherine of Austria

Fragmen
Museo d
provide a
Christian
earlier 6t

Crib street In front of San Lorenzo Maggiore, to the right, begins Naples' famous street of cribs, **Via San Gregorio Armeno**. Many of the shops double up as workshops, in which entire families are occupied with the production of cribs (pastori). In between the huge host of angels and holy families in every conceivable size, popular Neapolitan characters can also be spotted, such as Totò, Maradona, Padre Pio and Sophia Loren.

✶✶ **San Gregorio Armeno** The most glorious of the city's many Baroque churches is the Chiesa San Gregorio Armeno (daily 9am–1pm; entrance to the cloister is from Via Giuseppe Maffei). The sombre façade hides an interior that continues to be breathtaking. The church origins go back to a convent founded in the 8th century, when Greek nuns arrived in Naples bearing the skull of the Armenian Bishop Gregory. Both the church and the convent were remodelled from 1580 onwards, which is also when the heavy carved wood ceiling in the nave was created. Work on the interior decorations did not end until the 17th century. The cycle of frescoes (1678–79) by **Luca Giordano** portrays the adventurous journey to reach Naples the nuns made with their relics. The second of the city's regular blood miracles takes place at San Gregorio every Tuesday, when the blood of St Patricia miraculously flows. The **campanile** (1716) with its delicate bridge spanning Via San Gregorio Armeno, has become one of the city's emblems. The cloister is not always open to the public as it is still in use by the resident nuns.

✶ **Chiesa dei Gerolamini (San Filippo Nero)** Shortly before Via dei Tribunali joins Via Duomo, the Chiesa dei Gerolamini, also known as San Filippo Nero, stands to the left. The church was founded in 1592 by the order of the Oratory Fathers (Padri dell' Oratorio di San Filippo). The façade from 1780 is a late work by Ferdinando Fuga. The church and adjacent convent, with its cloister, Oratoriana library, and art gallery, was restored to an exemplary standard after sustaining heavy damage during the last war (Mon–Sat 9am–1pm; access from Via Duomo 142–144). The most significant work in the church is the fresco by the entrance: **Luca Giordano's** *Expulsion of the Moneychangers from the Temple* (1684). In a side chapel of the sacristy hangs an altar painting by **Guido Reni** (1620/25) depicting John the Baptist and Christ in an Arcadian landscape. Go through the former convent building to reach the **Biblioteca Oratoriana** – without doubt Naples' finest library. The grand yet welcoming room dates from 1726/36.

Via del Duomo Continuing along Via dei Tribunali, it is just a short walk to Via del Duomo on the left, where the city's cathedral is found. Via del Duomo is part of the original Neapolitan street layout of antiquity. The road was straightened during urban regeneration in the 19th century, when it was lined by stately apartment blocks. Today, it is also Naples' **top location for shops selling wedding apparel**.

Cappella della Santa Maria del Principo: Maria is flanked by San Gennaro and Santa Restituta

✶✶ Duomo di San Gennaro

The Duomo di San Gennaro (Via Duomo 147) is the city's most important church. **2500 years of architectural history** also mark this complex as a monument to Neapolitan urban history.
The façade and the interior have been remodelled and rebuilt after earthquakes so many times that not much remains of the original Gothic church. For example, the present incarnation of the façade in neo-Gothic style was only designed during the redevelopment of Via Duomo, at the end of the 19th century. Only the **doorway** and its figural sculptures originate from the late Middle Ages, though even these have been restored using fragments and individual pieces.

Opening hours:
Mon–Sat
8.30am–12.30pm
4.30pm–7pm
Sun 8am–1.30pm
4pm–7.30pm

The interior of this church fell victim to the tastes of 17th- and 18th-century Baroque. Nevertheless, notable architectural remains from previous epochs survive. Two early Christian churches were integrated into the Gothic building commissioned by Charles of Anjou at the end of the 13th century. Thus the left aisle was originally the Chiesa della Santa Restituta. Founded around AD 320 by Emperor Constantine the Great, the church, with a nave and double aisles, is the **oldest basilica in Naples**. Despite the inevitable Baroque remodelling (1688), the basic design of the church has survived. For example, the recycled pillars still follow the original outline of the Constantinian basilica. In the left aisle, take a look at the **Cappella della**

✶
Chiesa della Santa Restituta

Opening hours:
Mon–Sat
8.30am–noon
4.30pm–6.30pm
Sun 8.30am–1pm

On September 19, 2003, the archbishop of Naples holds the reliquary with the blood of San Gennares. The white cloth is waved as a sign that this year the miracle has happened again and the blood has become liquid.

WONDERS NEVER CEASE

The Neapolitans' love of their patron saint Gennaro is just as unfathomable as the extraordinary regularity with which the blood miracle occurs twice a year.

Gennaro is still the most common male name in Naples. The shortened version, Gennà, is heard on the streets of the Quartieri spagnoli just as much as in the posh cafés around Piazza dei Martiri. **Januarius, the Bishop of Benevento**, died a martyr's death in the Solfatara near Pozzuoli in AD 305. He was beheaded, the lions in the amphitheatre simply refusing to eat the future saint. Afterwards, a relation – other legends insist on a blind woman – caught the bishop's blood in two ampoules, and it is this that has been the **life blood of Naples** ever since.
The first documented mention of the legendary flowing of the blood goes back to 1389, although it is said to have already occurred in 413, when the saint's relics and blood ampoules were taken from Pozzuoli to Naples. The blood has regularly become liquid ever since: on 19 September (the day of martyrdom), and on every last Saturday before the first Sunday in May (in memory of the day the relics were transferred). According to Mark Twain, who witnessed the miraculous ceremony in 1867, it was one of the »most abominable of all religious deceptions« he had ever seen. And those not rooted in the Catholic faith are likely to find the event literally incredible to this day. The miracle in May is dedicated to salvation throughout the world, while the one in September is for the benefit of Naples and its inhabitants.
Yet San Gennaro only became the city's patron saint in the 16th century, rising above numerous other patron saints to become the uncontested **»god of Naples«**. More than anything, it is the miraculous interventions credited to San Gennaro during volcanic eruptions that ensured his status as sole patron saint of Naples. For example, during the famous eruption of Mount Vesuvius in 1631, his blood and skull were taken to the fire-

spouting mountain during two processions. The blood miracle only works its power if both ampoules are brought together. The image of the aversion of the lava flows emanating from the mighty mountain by the power of two small ampoules is one of the greatest unexplained myths of the city.

The blood miracle is always accompanied by a small circle of about thirty women known as the **»parenti«** – »relations of the heart«, as they call themselves. Their knowledge of the complicated sequence of songs and prayer sung, spoken, whispered and shouted can hardly be learnt, but must be internalized over a lifetime of devotion. Their ardency for San Gennaro is a living testament to many generations of the faithful, and the old women themselves are also a striking wonder to behold.

The blood miracle

The liquefaction of the blood in May traditionally occurs after a procession through the historic city centre ending at the church of Santa Chiara. Cardinal Pepe, Archbishop of Naples, then holds the monstrance with the two ampoules close to his breast after a long sermon. The rapt silence of the church filled with thousands of Neapolitans from this chaotic city is already miraculous enough. But when the treasurer of the »tesoro« (as the saint's chapel is known) waves his **white handkerchief**, the unique **miracle** has occurred: the divine sign that has filled Naples with its impulsive energy for centuries. And just for a moment, the swooning joy within the Santa Chiara inspired by the triumph over improbability makes it seem truly palpable.

The May ceremony begins at the San Gennaro chapel in the cathedral and ends at the Santa Chiara church. The September miracle only takes place in the cathedral. Once liquefaction has taken place, the blood relic is displayed to the faithful in the San Gennaro chapel for another eight days.

Santa Maria del Principo, which contains a mosaic from 1322 of the Virgin Mary flanked by St Gennaro and St Restituta.

★ ★ Baptisterio di San Giovanni in Fonte ►

The adjacent **Baptisterio di San Giovanni in Fonte** is the oldest baptistery in the western world and was probably commissioned by Bishop Severus (364–410) and remodelled under Bishop Soter (465–486). A unique feature is the dome mosaic, which displays its deep roots in antiquity. is The scene of the wine miracle during the Wedding of Cana is easily recognizable, as is the encounter between Jesus and the Samaritan woman at the well.

★★ **Archaeological excavations**

The excavations accessed via Santa Restituta are no less interesting than those under the church of San Lorenzo Maggiore. Significant remains of another early Christian basilica – the so-called Stafania – were discovered there. Also, very close to the baptistery, lie several underground Roman storerooms.

What to see in the Duomo

The **Cappella Minutolo**, to the right of the apse, has retained its Gothic design in the ribbed vaulting and frescoes dating from the 14th and 15th century. The imposing **tomb of Cardinal Arrigo Minutolo** by Antonio Baboccio (1402–05) is above the altar. A painting of the Assumption of the Virgin, attributed to Perugino, hangs in the neighbouring **Cappella dell'Assunta**. The figural group in the main choir's chapel also represents the Assumption. The Virgin Mary (1739) surrounded by angels, the work of the Roman sculptor **Pietro Bracci**, was designed to be admired from afar. The gilded coffered ceiling of the nave was created in 1621. To this day, the Cappella del Tesoro di San Gennaro is the **heart of religious Naples**. A Deputazione del Tesoro, which still exists today, was founded as a result of the catastrophic plague epidemic of 1526/28 to fund a magnificent chapel in honour of San Gennaro at the cathedral. The work, under the architectural leadership of Francesco Grimaldi, only began in 1605. The extravagantly embellished early Baroque chapel contains the saint's skull as well as the blood ampoules (►Baedeker Special p.204). The ceiling fresco representing paradise is by Giovanni Lanfranco.

? DID YOU KNOW ...?

- The Duomo di San Gennaro has a very complex architectural history. The left aisle was originally an ancient Roman road, on which stood the two early Christian basilicas of **Santa Restituta** and **San Salvatore** (the remains of present-day Stefania). They were the first churches in Naples. It was not until the construction of the 13th-century Gothic church that the two early buildings, together with the baptistery, were amalgamated into one architectural whole.

★ ★ Cappella del Tesoro di San Gennaro ►

★ **Museo del Tesoro di San Gennaro**

The Treasury Museum (to the right of the basilica's façade) impresses most with its silver bust of St Irene, who blocks an arrow with her right hand while protecting a model of the city of Naples with her left (Tue–Sat 9.30am–5pm, till 2.30pm on Sun and Fri).

Further Sights in the Centro Storico

MADRE

Largo Donnaregina is very close to the cathedral. On the square stands one of the city's newest museums, the Museo d'Arte Contemporanea Donna Regina, more commonly referred to as MADRE. A visit is particularly worthwhile for the building itself: the **Palazzo Donna Regina** was elaborately redesigned by the Portuguese star architect **Alvaro Siza** (Via Settembrini 79; Mon–Fri 10am 9pm, Sat and Sun till midnight; www.museomadre.it). Unfortunately the museum is battling financial difficulties and closure threatens.

Santa Maria Donnaregina Vecchia

The nearby Chiesa Santa Maria Donnaregina Vecchia (early 14th century) is one of the hidden jewels of Naples (Largo Donnaregina; Mon–Fri 8.30am–12.30pm). The **tomb of Charles II of Anjou's wife Queen Mary of Hungary**, designed by **Timo da Camaino** in around 1325/26, is considered one of southern Italy's finest Gothic sculptures. The frescoes in the nuns' choir are also notable.

Museo Diocesano

◄ www.museodiocesanonapoli.it

One of the city's newest museums is also one of its most beautiful. The reason is the recently beautifully restored Chiesa Santa Maria Donnaregina Nuova (17th century) which is worth a visit in itself. The upstairs art gallery overlooks the magnificent nave and contains works by almost all the significant artists working during the golden age of **Neapolitan Baroque**, including Luca Giordano and Francesco Solimena. One of the most beautiful exhibits, though, is the »Collare di San Vincenzo«: this cloak decorated with gold rings, timepieces and a necklace was hung around the shoulders of the saint figure during processions (Largo Donnaregina; Wed–Mon 9.30am–4.30pm, Sun till 2pm).

★★ Pio Monte della Misericordia

Pio Monte della Misericordia is one of the **oldest charitable institutions** in Naples, founded in 1601, and is located on the northeastern stretch of Via dei Tribunali beyond the junction with Via Duomo. (Via dei Tribunali 253; Thu–Tue 9am–2pm). The building was erected in 1658–78. The aristocrats who founded this charity dedicated it to the care of the sick and the poor (Monte means financial capital in this case, and Misericordia means compassion in Italian).Caravaggio's famous altar painting of ***The Seven Works of Mercy*** (1606–07) is still frighteningly realistic. The magnificent painting is inspired by the Gospel of Matthew. The charity is still active today and owns a select collection of paintings that can be viewed in the adjacent gallery.

★ ★ ◄ Caravaggio's Altar Painting

Guglia di San Gennaro

The marble column Guglia di San Gennaro opposite, on Piazza Riorio Sforza, was designed by Cosimo Fanzago and erected to commemorate Naples' miraculous escape from harm during the Vesuvian eruption of 1631 thanks to the intercession of the saint, who has enjoyed the unconditional veneration of all Neapolitans ever since.

Castel Capuano Via dei Tribunali ends at the Castel Capuano, a building that has been **in use without interruption for the past 850 years**. Erected in the mid-12th century by the Norman Duke William I, it was expanded into a fortified residence by his successor, Frederick II, from which time it functioned as the political power base of Naples for several centuries. The Castel Capuano was only reduced to a **court of law** (tribunale), a function it carries out to this day, after the construction of the present-day Palazzo Reale by Pedro di Toledo. Its present form dates back to remodelling in 1857–58.

★ **San Giovanni a Carbonara** The conditions in this quarter near the railway station give little hint that one of the **richest church interiors in Naples** can be found here (Via Carbonara 5; daily 9.30am–noon). The **open staircase** (1708) by the young Ferdinando Sanfelice is magnificent. A fresco dedicated to the Virgin was discovered in the lower church of Madonna Consolatrice in 1620, which was then worshipped for its miraculous powers. The **tomb of King Ladislaus of Anjou-Durazzo** is an outstanding work of art. It was the last Gothic tomb to be constructed in Naples, in 1415, commissioned by the king's sister and heir, Johanna II.

★ **Porta Capuana** The Porta Capuana was restored recently and was part of the Aragonese city walls between 1484 and 1488. The two mighty round towers are **emblems of Naples** and are known as Onore and Virtù (honour and virtue). The Florentine sculptor and architect Giuliano da Maiano designed the marble exterior wall decorated with figural and relief sculptures. Another city gate can be seen at Piazza Porta Nolana along Corso Garibaldi. The round towers Fede and Speranza (faith and hope) are, unfortunately, is a very bad state of repair.

Porta Nolana ►

★★ Spaccanapoli

Running parallel to Via dei Tribunali, the street known as Spaccanapoli (spaccare = divide) was also once an ancient highway. Just under 3km/2mi long, this dead straight road changes its name several times and runs between Piazza del Gesù Nuovo and the Forcella quarter near the main railway station (Via Benedetto Croce, Via S. Biaggio dei Librai, and Via Vicaria Vecchia).

Piazza del Gesù Nuovo is dominated by the monumental façade of diamond-shaped stonework for the church of the same name, and by the Guglia dell'Immacolata. The foundation stone for this

? DID YOU KNOW ...?

- Ever since *Ineffabilis Deus*, a papal bull of 1854, the Catholic world has celebrated the Immaculate Conception (Maria Immacolata) on 8 December. In Naples, tradition demands that the archbishop and mayor lay flowers at the feet of the Madonna della Guglia dell'Immacolata on Piazza del Gesù. In times gone by the city's honourable leaders had to climb up a rickety ladder to cover the 30m/98ft up to the statue. Today, an electrified platform makes the festive ceremony somewhat easier to complete.

The reclining river god, Nile, is the true emblem of the centro storico

34m/112ft-high Baroque **plague column** was laid in 1741. In Italy, these frequently bizarre looking constructions have been known as »macchine« since Renaissance times.

✶
◀ Guglia dell' Immacolata

The Chiesa Gesù Nuovo was once the most important Jesuit church in Naples. It has a complicated architectural history, which can be guessed at from the rather odd façade for a religious building (Piazza del Gesù Nuovo; daily 6.30am–12.30pm, Sun till 1.30pm, 4.30pm–7.30pm). Built in 1455–70, the building was originally designed to be the family palace for the Sanseverinos. The main doorway, with its coat of arms on the inner frame, and the side doorways date from that era. The Jesuits purchased the building in 1584 and proceeded to demolish everything except the façade. After a fire in 1639, the much employed **Cosimo Fanzago** drew up the plans for the interior, which was only completed in the 18th century. Barring a few small renovations, it survives almost intact. An important artwork here is **Francesco Solimena's** fresco *Expulsion of Heliodor from the Temple* (1725) on the inner side of the entrance wall. The left aisle contains a wall altar consecrated by Ignatius of Loyola. The expressive Baroque statues of David and Jeremiah are once more the work of Fanzago. The church was taken over by the Franciscans in 1767. **Giuseppe Moscati** is one of the most recent saints venerated by the Catholic world. His shrine is here in the Santuario Giuseppe Moscati. Born in Benevento in 1880, he died in Naples aged 47.

✶✶
Gesù Nuovo

✶
◀ Expulsion of Heliodor from the Temple

The Baroque interior (1741–47) of the Chiesa Santa Chiara (Via Benedetto Croce; daily 7am–12.30pm, 4pm–7pm) was almost entirely destroyed during a three-day fire in 1943. Restoration work concentrated on recreating the original Gothic interior as much as possible. The church was founded by Robert of Anjou in 1310, though it was not consecrated for another 30 years. Next to San Domenico Maggiore, the Santa Chiara was the most significant work of

✶✶
Santa Chiara

Angevin Gothic in Naples, and it was also the preferred **burial place of the House of Anjou**. The architectural history of the free-standing campanile is documented by a Gothic inscription in the supporting trusses, dating from 1328. A 14th-century doorway through the wall enclosing the entire complex opens onto the small square in front of the main façade. The rose window was reconstructed after the Second World War. Only a very few building sections in the façade still date back to the foundation era of the church. The interior surprises by its dimensions (92 x 30m/302ft x 98ft) and the austere simplicity of the nave. Rows of chapels line the nave to the left and right, each with a plain amphora. The central feature of the altar wall is the trio of princely tombs. The tomb of King Robert of Anjou (1278–1343), also known as Robert the Wise, is of arresting beauty, despite the stone blackened by smoke from a catastrophic fire. The tomb is over 14m/46ft high. Designed by **Tino di Camaino**, it is one of **southern Italy's major works of Gothic sculpture**. To the right of the monumental royal tomb is the **tomb of Charles of Calabria** (around 1332–33), also the work of Tino di Camaino. Charles, Robert of Anjou's son, died at just 31 years old when he suffered a sudden fever during a falcon hunt. The neighbouring tomb is for **Mary de Valois** (Charles of Calabria's wife). It was the final work by Tino di Camainor in 1337, and was completed by his workshop. The **choir of the Poor Clares** is only open to the public on certain days during the Maggio dei Monumenti. It was originally painted by Giotto and his assistants, and the few surviving fragments of paintings have been under study and the subject of restoration work for many years. **Giotto di Bondone** (around 1267–1337), one of the greatest painters of Italian art history, worked in Naples between 1328 and 1334. Already famous during his own lifetime, Giotto was called to Naples by Robert of Anjou, who commissioned him to paint the two most important public buildings of his new royal residence at Naples. Unfortunately, only minimal fragments survive of the great fresco cycles he produced for the Castel Nuovo and the church of Santa Chiara.

✶ Campanile ►

✶✶ Tomb of Robert of Anjou ►

Giotto in Naples ►

✶✶ **Chiostro delle Maioliche**

One of the most enchanting and otherworldly sights in Naples – a veritable **Arcadia of Rococo** – stands in the middle of the historic city centre: the Chiostro delle Maioliche. Originally a Gothic cloister, it was given its present form between 1739 and 1743 (Mon–Sat 8.30am–12.30pm, 3.30pm to 6.30pm, Sun 9am–12.30pm). The redevelopment of the cloister was commissioned by the porcelain-mad Maria Amalia of Saxony, wife of Charles III. The 82 x 78m/269ft x 256ft **cloister garden** was subdivided into four sections by low walls, which were covered in colourful majolica tiles, as were the stone benches and octagonal columns supporting the wood pergolas. The pictures on the tiles show imaginary paradisiacal landscapes inspired by the loveliness of the Bay of Naples. The small Museo dell'Opera exhibits liturgical items, as well as architectural fragments taken from

Museo dell'Opera ►

The central feature of Piazza San Domenico Maggiore is the Guglia di San Domenico

the Gothic interior of Santa Chiara (Mon, Tue, Thu–Sat 9am–12.30pm, 3.30pm–5.30pm, Sun 9am–12.30pm).

◀ Zona Archeologica

The church and monastery stand on the remains of an extensively excavated 900 sq m/9684 sq ft thermal spa area, probably the main thermal pools during the first century AD.

Palazzo Filomarino della Rocca

This palace originally dates from the 14th century, but it has been rebuilt repeatedly and floors have been added. The magnificent entrance portal was designed by Ferdinando Sanfelice. The philosopher, historian and politician **Benedetto Croce** (1866–1952) founded the Istituto Italiano per gli Studi Storici here in 1947. Croce, who wrote his *Manifesto degli Intellettuali antifascisti* as early as 1925, was a leading light of the European resistance against fascism.

★ **Piazza San Domenico Maggiore**

Piazza San Domenico Maggiore is entirely the domain of students from the Università degli Studi di Napoli, also known as the L'Orientale for its Asian Studies faculties, and of the Università Federico II. The square is dominated by the **Guglia di San Domenico**, which was erected after the plague epidemic of 1656. Unlike the exuberantly Baroque Guglia dell'Immacolata on Piazza Gesù Nuovo, this early obelisk and its austere ornamental decorations are still very much of the 16th century.

★ **San Domenico Maggiore**

The construction of the Chiesa San Domenico Maggiore heralded the medieval city's expansion toward the Vomero hill to the west.

The foundation stone was laid in 1289 on the ruins of a former building by Charles I of Anjou, which was incorporated into the new construction. Completed in 1324, the church then functioned as the Dominican seat for almost five centuries, and was also one of the most important churches in Naples. Only a few, but nevertheless notable, remains of this major example of Angevin Gothic have survived the ravages of earthquakes (1455–56) and fires (1506). Its present incarnation goes back to restoration work undertaken in the 19th century (Vico San Domenico Maggiore 18; Mon–Sat 7.15am–-noon 5pm–7pm, Sun 9am–1pm, 5pm to 7pm). The interior of the basilica is dominated by seven pointed arch arcades set over pillars. They have been much restored and were even partly gilded in the 19th century. However, their fundamental design goes back to the original building phase. The wooden ceiling was constructed in 1665, but was also renewed in the 19th century. Notable artworks include the base of the **Easter candelabra** in front of the choir, which came from the workshops of Tino da Camaino; note also the **tomb of John of Anjou** in one of the right-hand side chapels.

Church interior ►

★★ **Cappella Sansevero**

Vico San Domenico Maggiore leads to the nearby Cappella Sansevero. Alessandro De Sangro had the small Marian shrine in the garden of his palace expanded into the present chapel to hold the family tomb in the early 18th century. His son Raimondo later designed the interior, which was much admired by his contemporaries, and is one of the most original interiors of Neapolitan Baroque (Via Francesco De Sanctis 19; Wed–Mon 10am–5pm, Sun till 1.30pm). It is the three sculptures that inspired the most wonder: to the right, next to the main apse stands *Il Disinganno*. This sculpture is the work of the Genoese artist **Francesco Queirolo**, who represented man's »disillusionment« and release from earthly mistakes with a man freeing himself from a net with the help of an angel. To the left stands *Pudicizia* (Modesty), a sculpture by the Venetian artist **Antonio Corradini** (1751). The female figure wrapped in a veil represents untouchable virtue. The apogee of artistry, however, is the *Cristo velato* lying in the middle of the room. Following a design by Corradini, the figure of the dead Christ covered by a translucent veil was created by the Neapolitan sculptor **Giuseppe Sammartino** in 1753. The extraordinary use of the marble material – normally quite brittle – is one of the wonders on display in this chapel. By contrast, the two skeletons in the crypt are macabre and not the work of a great artist but rather the result of a grim experiment. The Prince of Sansevero is believed to have had two of his servants killed by injecting the unfortunate victims with a substance allowing their vein and arterial systems to petrify, even while their bodies died and their flesh decomposed.

★ Il Disinganno ►

Pudicizia ►

Cristo velato ►

Università degli Studi di Napoli

Following the opposite direction, Via Mezzocannone leads past the university, down to Corso Umberto I. The Università degli Studi di

Marble on marble at the Capella Sansevero

Napoli »Federico II« was Europe's first state university, founded by the **Hohenstaufen Emperor Frederick II** on 5 June 1224. With over 100,000 students today, it is one of the largest higher-education establishments in Italy. The university moved to the extensive building complex between Via Mezzocannone and Corso Umberto I in 1880.

◄ Europe's first state university

Diagonally across from Piazza San Domenico Maggiore stands the little Chiesa Sant'Angelo a Nilo. Cardinal Rinaldo Brancaccio had the church constructed close to his family palace in the 14th century, but the building was entirely remodelled in 1709, and the interior is now Baroque (Piazzetta Nilo 23; Mon–Sat 9am–1pm, 4.30pm–1pm, Sun 9am–1pm). The chapel in front of the high altar, to the right, contains the tomb of Cardinal Rinaldo Brancaccio, the most beautiful example of a Renaissance tomb in Naples. **Donatello and Michelozzo** created this monument in their workshop in Pisa before shipping it to Naples in 1428, the year the cardinal died. There is argument over which features can be attributed to which artist, but there is no doubt that Donatello created the relief of the ***Assunzione della Vergine*** (Assumption of the Virgin), because it shows the »relievo schiacciato« technique so typical of Donatello's work. The depth of this flat relief is created not by clever perspective but by delicate nuances in the figures shown. The painting ***San Michele Arcangelo*** by Marco Pino da Siena (1573) hangs above the main altar.

✶ **Sant'Angelo a Nilo**

◄ Cardinal Rinaldo Brancaccio's tomb

★★ **Nile statue** Directly opposite on Largo Corpo di Napoli lies the true **emblem** of the centro storico. The marble sculpture represents the **river god Nile with his Horn of Plenty and Sphinx** and was probably erected by Alexandrian merchants in the first century AD (photo p.209).

! *Baedeker* TIP

Gods and Caffè

Next to the entrance of the bar opposite, a wall altar contains a single hair from the head of Diego Maradona. The great football player has been revered as a god in Naples (along with San Gennaro and Totò) ever since he helped SSC Naples win the UEFA Cup in 1989. Take heed of the bar owner's note hanging next to this curiosity: don't just stare and snap a photo, enjoy an quick cup of excellent coffee next door too!

Historic city palaces on Via San Biaggio dei Librai: the construction of the **Chiesa di Santa Chiara** and its adjacent monastic complex in the 14th–15th centuries turned the area all around the present-day Largo Corpo di Napoli into the favoured residential neighbourhood for the aristocracy. Most of the palaces built then have now been turned into apartment blocks, but even though none are open to the public, it is still worth taking a look at their façades and courtyards. One of the most substantial palaces is the **Palazzo Carafa di Santangelo**, built in 1466 (Via San Biaggio dei Librai 121). An inscription over the doorway recalls the man who commissioned the building: Diomede Carafa (1406–87) was a humanist aristocrat and confidant of King Alfonso I of Aragon. His collection of antiquities was the first of its kind and famous throughout Europe. The recently restored **Palazzo di Capua-Marigliano** (Via San Biaggio dei Librai 39) was first built in 1512–13. Some of its building materials were taken from the Roman theatre at Nola.

★ **Monte di Pietà** Via San Biaggio dei Librai has traditionally been the home of **goldsmiths and jewellers** and, in recent centuries, it has also been where Naples' pawn shops can be found. To put a stop to the shocking usury taking place, in 1579 a handful of aristocrats founded the charity of Monte di Pietà here and set up a lending institute with fixed interest rates.

The foundation commissioned the present palace, whose courtyard is beautifully framed by the vestibule in the building's façade and which contains the **Cappella della Pietà**. The appealing Renaissance façade with its ironic pilasters is decorated by two symbolic sculptures by Petro Bernini (1601). The left wall niche contains **Carità** (Charity) wrapped in a gown, with three naked boys clinging to her imploringly. The right wall niche contains **Securitas** (Security), sleeping peacefully leaning against a pillar. Pietro Bernini (1562–1629), who was much employed as a sculptor in Naples from 1584 onwards, was the father of Lorenzo Bernini, the most outstanding Roman architect and sculptor of the 17th century. It was he who transformed Rome into a Baroque city.

The pieta in the gable is by Michelangelo Naccherino. Today, the Monte di Pietà belongs to the Banco di Napoli Banco di Napoli, which exhibits **sections of its art collection** in the restored rooms of the palace. The exhibition contains mostly religious artefacts (Via San Biaggio dei Librai 114; Sat and Sun 9am–2pm). The former wealth of the charitable foundation can be seen in the fine stucco decorations of the palace, as well as in the majolica flooring and in some of the surviving furniture. The chapel ceiling has a cycle of frescos showing scenes from Christ's Passion by Belisario Corenzio (1601–18).

◄ Banco di Napoli Collection

Before Via San Biaggio dei Librai reaches the authentic but rather run down district of Forcella, it crosses Via Duomo. Palazzo Cuomo there was demolished during expansion work on Via Duomo in 1880, but reconstructed, complete with its Renaissance façade, just 20m/22yrd further on. This palace belonged to the family of the merchant Angelo Cuomo, and was originally built in 1464–90. The interior dates from the 1880–82 reconstruction, though, which was financed by Prince Gaetano Filangieri. He not only paid for the building work, but also donated his **family's art collection** (Museo Civico Filangieri, Via Duomo 288; Tue–Sat 9am–6.30pm, Sun till 1.30pm).

✱ **Palazzo Cuomo**

◄ Museo Civico Filangieri

✱ ✱ National Archaeological Museum

Located at the northern edge of the historic city centre, the Museo Archeologico Nazionale di Napoli is **one of the most famous museums in the world**. Its collection of Greek and Roman art is unique. The building was originally built as a university in 1612 (Palazzo degli Studi). It was extended by Sanfelice in 1748, and further remodelled during a commission from Ferdinand IV, in 1773, when it became the Real Museo Borbonico. The core of the collection, which was once spread over several locations, is made up of the priceless art treasures of the Neapolitan Bourbons, specifically the Farnese collection left by Charles III, whose mother was Elizabeth Farnese. The museum also has finds retrieved from the lost cities around Mount Vesuvius. Since the paintings were taken to the Palazzo Reale di Capodimonte (►p.221), the continuing conversion and expansion to form the Archaeological Museum means that closures of exhibition halls will continue to occur over the next few years while exhibits are rearranged.

Museo Archeologico Nazionale

Opening hours: Wed–Mon 9am–7.30pm, last admission 7pm

To the right, below the staircase leading up to the main entrance, are some of the newest and most interesting exhibition rooms of the museum (now also connected to the new metro stop Museo). Here, finds unearthed during excavation work for the metro can be seen. They originate from the area around Piazza Municipio and from the Roman harbour.

A tour of the museum

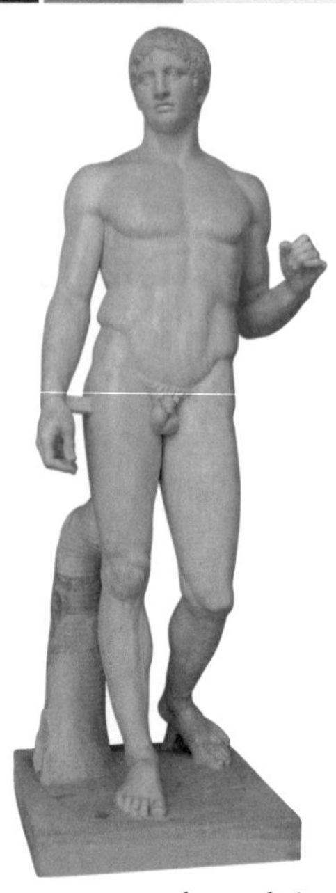

Doryphoros

The large **entrance hall** to the museum can match any of the top establishments in Europe: a well-stocked **bookshop** and an information kiosk – which is almost always manned – is all part of the service. The **Egyptian Collection and the Epigraphy Collection** are in the basement, while the ground floor contains several of the most beautiful sculptures surviving from antiquity, which are usually Roman copies of Greek originals.

A seminal piece of art history stands in the wing to the left of the entrance hall: the marble statue of **Doryphoros** was found in the Great Palestra of Pompeii in 1797. The bronze original has been lost, but we know it was by the Greek sculptor **Polyclitus** (460 to the end of the 5th century BC). The statue of a naked youth carrying a lance signifies a revolution in Greek sculptural art as it represents a development away from the archaic sculptural style embodied in the Kouros (youth) figures, which had both feet firmly planted on the ground. Polyclitus developed the technique known as contrapposto, which created figures resting with most of their weight on one leg, resulting in the pelvis no longer being axial to the vertical statue. The Doryphoros sculpture is surrounded by further copies of Greek statues to create a very photogenic whole, even if it does lack sufficient annotation for individual pieces. Also notable is the delicate relief of **Orpheus and Eurydice**, copied from an original dating from the 5th century BC.

Farnese Collection

Though museum wings opposite are being remodelled as part of a project not due to end before 2010, they remain accessible. Here visitors find the collection of Roman sculptures and busts, as well as the tyrannicides **Harmodius and Aristogeiton**, one of the most significant figural pairs of antiquity. This copy of a bronze original dating from the 5th century BC is another key work of art history, as it was the first time a sculpture displayed to the public at the Athenian agora showed not gods, but real people. The **core of the museum** consists of the Farnese Collection. Rome was in a veritable fever for relics from antiquity during the 16th and 17th century. Aristocrats who had enjoyed a humanist education and even Pope Paul III commissioned targeted archaeological excavations. The pope, born into the mighty House of Farnese and the founder of the Farnese family art collection (► p.221), had his portrait painted by Titian (*Paul III with his Nephews*). The work, one of the most famous portrait paintings in art history, hangs in the Museum at Capodimonte. The **Farnese Bull** was discovered in the Baths of Caracalla in Rome, in 1545, and was the most sensational find of the 16th century next to the Laocoon Group. The much restored and remodelled figural sculpture portrays the Punishment of Dirce, in which Amphion and Zethos, the sons of Antiope, are seen tying Dirce to a wild bull. The drama of this sculpture is an impressive counterpoint to the statue of the reposing **Farnese Hercules** in the same exhibition hall. His legs – once missing, then restored, and then replaced with the originals when they were found – aroused Goethe's interest.

Mezzanine floor

The stairwell leading to the upper exhibition floors was inspired by that of the Roman Parthenon, and contains a statue in honour of the museum founder, Ferdinand IV. Rooms 58–64 on the mezzanine floor are notable for the **mosaics** found in Pompeii and Herculaneum. Two charming scenes from the Pompeian **Villa di Cicerone** show street musicians and three elaborately dressed ladies whose faces and demeanour are particularly expressive. Both works are signed by the artist **Dioscourides**. The mosaic showing the Battle of Alexander was found at the Casa del Fauno on 24 October 1831. Made out of around 3 million pieces, the mosaic measures 2.71 x 5.12m/8.9 x 16.7ft, its unusual size and great artistry underlining its importance as a work of art. There is still argument over whether the scene portrayed is the battle at Issus in 333 BC or the one at Gaugamela in 331 BC, but there is no doubt at all regarding the identity of the protagonists. **Alexander the Great**, King of Macedonia, can be seen charging into the fray from the left edge of the scene, while in the central right section, the great Persian king **Darius III** can be seen fleeing the battle atop his carriage. Alexander the Great's victory was of historic importance and was probably already celebrated in a painting during his lifetime. The mosaic is believed to be a copy of that painting, and was made in the first half of the second century BC. It is thought that it was brought in around 100 BC to Pompeii from eastern Greece, where it was used to decorate the city's wealthiest house.

◄ The Battle of Alexander

Darius III flees before Alexander the Great

Gabinetto Segreto

To protect »public decency«, the Gabinetto Segreto (Secret Cabinet) in room 65 was only ever made available to visitors with a special permit. In recent years, however, a simple reservation at the museum ticket office is enough to permit access. On view in the **Secret Cabinet** are vases and sculptures decorated with erotic scenes that were deemed shocking by the early archaeologists in the 18th century. In addition, there are lucky-charm phalluses in all sizes, as well as frescoes. On the same floor, is Italy's largest numismatic collection, which contains coins dating from antiquity to the time of the Kingdom of the Two Sicilies. Unfortunately, though, it is very often closed due to personnel shortages.

Coin Collection (Halls 51–55) ►

First floor

The exhibition rooms on the first floor, dedicated to Pompeian wall painting, have also been closed for years. A useful adjunct to visiting the ruined cities is, however, a visit to rooms 85 to 89, which contain **domestic artefacts from Pompeii and Herculaneum**. Small bronzes, kitchenware, ceramics and glass give a sense of the everyday luxuries enjoyed in the former Vesuvian cities. Rooms 79 to 84 contain decorative items and a model of the Isis Temple at Pompeii. The cork model of the city of Pompeii (Room 96; 1861/64) is to a scale of 1:100 and is a sad document of the destruction that has taken place in Pompeii over the past 150 years. The bronze statues taken from the Villa dei Papiri at Herculaneum are a highlight of the collection. The villa takes its name from the **papyrus scrolls** discovered there, whose great fragility drove scientists of the 18th and 19th century to despair. A small mechanism developed to un-scroll this carbonized material can be seen in a side room. The **Grande Salone dell'Atlante** is the largest profane space in Naples. The ceiling fresco displays an allegory to the arts and sciences current during the reign of Ferdinand IV. Rays of the midday sun point to the star sign, set into the floor, relevant to the time of year. Other exhibition halls, especially those covering the history of Naples during antiquity and those devoted to the Greek settlement of Pithekoussai on the island of Ischia, are first-rate. Sadly, they too are very often closed due to lack of staff.

Model of Pompeii ►

✶ ✶ Villa dei Papiri ►

Sanità, I Vergini and Capodimonte – Naples' living necropolis

Sanità

Metro stops Museo and Piazza Cavour ►

Within sight of the Archaeological Museum and just behind Piazza Cavour begins the district of Sanità, set between the centro storico and the hills of Capodimonte. One of the most traditional neighbourhoods can be explored here, and although it can seem a bit on the rough side it is also worth visiting for the early Christian catacombs. An evening stroll is not recommended, but the attentive tourist unadorned by jewellery is just as safe here during the daytime as anywhere else in Naples. **Totò**, the movie comedian venerated like a god in Naples, was born here. During antiquity, this area was the location of the **Naples necropoli**.

Frescoes in the catacombs at San Gennaro

The centre of this lively quarter is along **Via dei Vergini**, on which stands one of the most impressive palaces built by the Neapolitan architect **Ferdinando Sanfelice**, the Palazzo dello Spagnolo. The façade and staircase have been perfectly restored. Just a few steps further on, on Via Arena della Sanità, stands **Sanfelice's own palazzo**. Today, it houses numerous families, but a friendly request from the porter will normally allow access to the staircase, which is worth seeing despite its state of decay.

Palazzo dello Spagnolo

The early Baroque Chiesa della Sanità (also known as San Vicenzo) on the square of the same name, is the work of the architect and monk **Giuseppe Donzelli**, also known as Fra Nuvolo, who revolutionized Neapolitan church architecture. The adjacent Dominican monastery was almost entirely destroyed during the construction of the **Ponte della Sanità** at the beginning of the 19th century. The bridge spans the Sanità quarter, which is set in a depression that was still known as the Valley of the Dead during the 17th century (La valle dei morti). It was designed to create a direct connection between the city and the hunting lodge of Capodimonte. While the **paintings by Luca Giordano** alone make a visit to the Chiesa della Sanità worthwhile, the catacombs of San Gaudioso underneath the church are a unique sight. **Gaudiosus, Bishop of Abitina**, escaped his African province with some of his clerics in 439 pursued by King Geiseric's Vandal hordes. He founded his small monastery in the middle of the ancient necropolis before the gates of Naples – the name of I Vergini goes back to that. Gaudiosus died in 482, and his tomb became the central point of an extensive complex of catacombs. The burial place lost its significance in the 9th century, when his venerated remains were removed to the city. Gradually, the annu-

✶✶
Chiesa della Sanità (San Vicenzo)

✶✶
◀ Catacombe di San Gaudioso

Guided tours: daily 9.30am, 10.15am, 11am, 11.45am, 12.30pm

al spring and autumn floods coming down from the surrounding hills submerged the burial site in sand and earth (»Lava dei Vergini«), and it was only after the chance discovery of a 5th–6th-century fresco of the Virgin Mary in 1577 that the catacombs were revived. The fresco, today exhibited in a side chapel of the Sanità church, quickly gained the status of having miraculous powers and gave the church, the quarter and the neighbouring district of Miracoli their names. Access to the catacombs is found directly in front of the high altar. The frescos, some of which are very well preserved, are **unique examples of early Christian art**, and are a match for those of the Roman catacombs in every way. The Dominicans restored the catacombs as a burial place in the 16th and 17th centuries. Several macabre relics of that era can be seen, such as skeletal remains set into the walls and decorated with frescos.

**** Catacombe di San Gennaro**

Tours: daily 9am, 10am, 11am, noon, 2pm

Continuing onwards, it is either possible to walk along very lively streets or, at a more sedate pace, to take the elevator (next to the church of Sanità) up to Corso Amedeo di Savoia. A short stroll leads to the Chiesa dell'Incoronata Madre del Buon Consiglio, and an entrance down to the Catacombs of San Gennaro leads off to the left of this bombastic building (buses: C 64, C 67, R 4, 178). A unique **repository of early Christian painting**, the two levels of the catacombs were used from the 2nd to the 10th centuries. Even if their state of repair is catastrophic, the sheer dimensions are impressive. The »Pompeii of Christendom« (Ferdinand Gregorovius) is in urgent need of extensive restoration to save the structures, frescoes and mosaics, as well as the ceramics lying submerged in the detritus of former graves set in the ground. The bones of Naples' patron saint St Gennaro were brought here from Pozzuoli at the beginning of the 5th century, which led to the catacombs taking on central importance in the city's history. The **Basilica San Gennaro extramoenia** also dates from that time, but due to frequent rebuilding not much of the original building remains. The basilica can only be accessed via the San Gennaro dei Poveri Hospital in the street of the same name. The **bishop's crypt** is therefore the real focal point of the catacombs, where St Quodvultdeus (What God Wants), who was the bishop of Carthage and the metropolitan bishop of all of North Africa, can be seen at the centre of a magnificent mosaic. The highlight of the underground labyrinth is a ceiling fresco dating from the 2nd–3rd century AD: Adam and Eve are depicted among flowers and grotesques. The Teotecnus family tomb, whose daughter Nonnorosa died aged just two-and-a-half years, is a moving sight. Lombards pillaged San Gennaro's remains from the catacombs in 841. Thereafter the catacombs continued to be the burial site for Neapolitan bishops, but lost their significance from the 12th century onwards. The **underground cemeteries** of San Gennaro and San Gaudioso probably originally belonged together, along with the catacombs of San Severo, which have been almost entirely destroyed.

Not far from Sanità is another catacomb, though not from the early Christian era. But the famous Cimiterio delle Fontanelle has finally been reopened (Via Fontanelle 77, Thu – Tue 10am – 5pm).

Cimiterio delle Fontanelle

Via Santa Teresa degli Scalzi leads directly to the Museo di Capodimonte, while Via Foria connects Piazza Museo (Archaeological Museum) with **Piazza Carlo III**. One of the most extraordinary buildings in Naples, the Albergo dei Poveri, lies on this busy square. In its day, this huge building was Europe's largest poor house, commissioned by Charles III and built by Ferdinando Fuga. The newly restored façade hides the fact that the rest of the building is in a state of ruin. Damage during the Second World War and the earthquake of 1980 did considerable damage to the building. A fierce debate raging at present to decide whether or not the site should be revived as a university building. Right next door is the Orto Botanico, one of the very few green spaces in Naples. It was founded as a botanical garden by Joseph Bonaparte and today belongs to the university park. It can only be visited by appointment (Via Foria 223; tel. 0 81 44 97 59, Mon–Fri 9am–2pm).

◄ Albergo dei Poveri

◄ Orto Botanico

★★ Il Museo Nazionale di Capodimonte

This art gallery is unique among the museums of southern Italy: there are no sections closed for restoration, and the presentation of the collection can match that of any of the world's most famous museums. A **self-service restaurant** in a courtyard offers small meals.

◄ Via Miano 2; Buses: C 64, C 67, 178

Opening hours: Thu–Tue 8.30am–7.30pm

Like almost all other Bourbon kings, Charles III had three great passions: hunting, art and architecture. Thus, the construction of the **Palazzo Reale di Capodimonte** in 1738 not only saw the creation of a fine hunting lodge set on Capodimonte hill but also the establishment of a suitable home for the huge royal art collection. The king inherited the Farnese Collection and gathered it from Rome and Parma to his new residence in Naples. Capodimonte can therefore be considered as **Europe's first building designed to be a museum**. At the behest of Queen Maria Amalia, a **porcelain manufactory** was founded at the same time. The large and well tended park is a veritable **green oasis** and the views over the Bay of Naples are just as overwhelming now as they were during the lifetime of Charles III (daily 8am to one hour before sunset). Capodimonte came under the ownership of the House of Savoy after the foundation of the unified Kingdom of Italy, and remained the seat of the Duke of Aosta until 1947. It has been a museum since 1957, but only gained world status as an art gallery in the 1990s after the renovation of the exhibition halls and a new concept for the hanging of its picture gallery. The wealth of masterpieces here is so great that a comprehensive description of the collection is impossible here.

◄ Parco di Capodimonte

1st floor

A tour of the gallery on the first floor immediately begins with one of the most famous paintings by **Titian**: the cryptic portrait of *Paul*

Hunting castle, summer residence and museum: Palazzo di Capodimonto

III and his Nephews. Other art historical treasures are Titian's *Danae* (around 1544) and **Raffael's** *Cardinale Alessandro Farnese* (1509/11). **Masaccio's** *Crucifixion* can be found in room 3. Room 9 has paintings attributed to Raffael's workshop; room 12 contains paintings by **Parmigianino**, including the famous portrait of *Antea* (1531/35), a young woman with a piercing look. **Brueghel's** *Fall of the Blind* (1568) is in room 17.

Several large format paintings by **Guido Reni** are located in room 22. The Royal State Rooms, entirely in the Pompeian style, begin with the Bed Chamber of Francis I. A grand portrait of Charles III by Antonio Sebastiani can be seen in room 32. The king left Naples to become King of Spain in 1759. The portrait of the child Ferdinand IV, above the fireplace, is by **Anton Raphael Mengs**. The next room shows the royal couple of Charles V and Maria Louisa of Spain painted by **Goya**.

Royal State Rooms ▶

Side cabinets ▶

The side cabinets (rooms 35/36) contain **porcelain**, predominantly from the Capodimonte manufactory. Large family portraits of the Bourbons hang in the magnificent room 37. The artist **Angelika Kauffmann** painted the large family of Ferdinand IV in 1783. Directly opposite, already in the more bourgeois style, which was enjoying increasing popularity, hangs a portrait of Francis I and family with a backdrop of the smoking Vesuvius, painted by Giuseppe Cammarano. The festive **ballroom** leads to room 43 and the landscape paintings by **Jakob Philipp Hackert**. Ferdinand IV had his German court artist paint all the major ports, cities and palaces in the Kingdom of the Two Sicilies. Room 52 contains Queen Maria Amalia's porcelain cabinet, which is one of the most beautiful 18th-century decorative rooms ever created in Europe. The fragile artwork was made in 1757–59 and originally decorated a room in the summer residence at Portici. When that residence was converted into the university agricultural college, the porcelain cabinet was dismantled and installed here in 1866. The painting by Louis Nicolas Lamasle in room 54 portrays the sons of Gioacchino Murat, King of Naples (1808–15), visiting the **theatre at Herculaneum**. The theatre, located 27m/88ft underground, still looks the same today, but is not open to the public.

◄ Porcelain cabinet

2nd floor

The second floor is dominated by **13th- to 18th-century Neapolitan painting**. At the entrance to the late medieval collection are two large paintings by **Anselm Kiefer** and nothing could present a more stark contrast with the glittering gold of medieval altar paintings in the following exhibition rooms than these dark contemporary works. The dramatic effect of **Caravaggio's** *The Taking of Christ* (1607/10) in room 78 is best appreciated from a distance, as the artist intended. Rooms 101 and 103 are dedicated to the Neapolitan artist **Luca Giordano**. The 2nd floor also houses a collection of tapestries and a changing exhibition of **prints**, taken from the museum's huge stocks.

The **3rd floor** is dedicated to the late 19th-century Neapolitan school of painting, whose saccharine folksy subjects can become rather tiresome. Of most interest here are the paintings by **Giacinto Gigante**. The collection of **contemporary art** does not appear to follow any specific concept. It includes work by Mario Merz, Sol LeWitt and Janis Kounellis. Andy Warhol's large format *Vesuvius* (1985) – an icon of modern Neapolitan art, seems oddly outdated here.

Baedeker TIP

Bargain hunters beware!

At the southern end of Via Toledo, in front of the Banco di Napoli, hawkers sell copies of European luxury brands, but think carefully before purchasing anything here. Heavy fines, which can quickly match the price of the genuine article, have been imposed on both sellers and buyers since 2005. These African traders are the last and weakest link in the chain of criminal organizations controlled by the Camorra.

Toledo and Piazza del Plebiscito – Royal Naples

✱✱ Via Toledo

Via Toledo is actually the **main street of Naples**. It was constructed in 1536 under Viceroy Don Pedro Alvarez de Toledo, who ruled in the name of the Spanish King Charles V. Much admired as urban innovation at the time, it quickly became a fashionable place for the aristocracy to set up home. Known simply as Toledo, the road connects Piazza del Plebiscito with Piazza Dante.

Via Toledo, Piazza del Plebiscito, Castel Nuovo

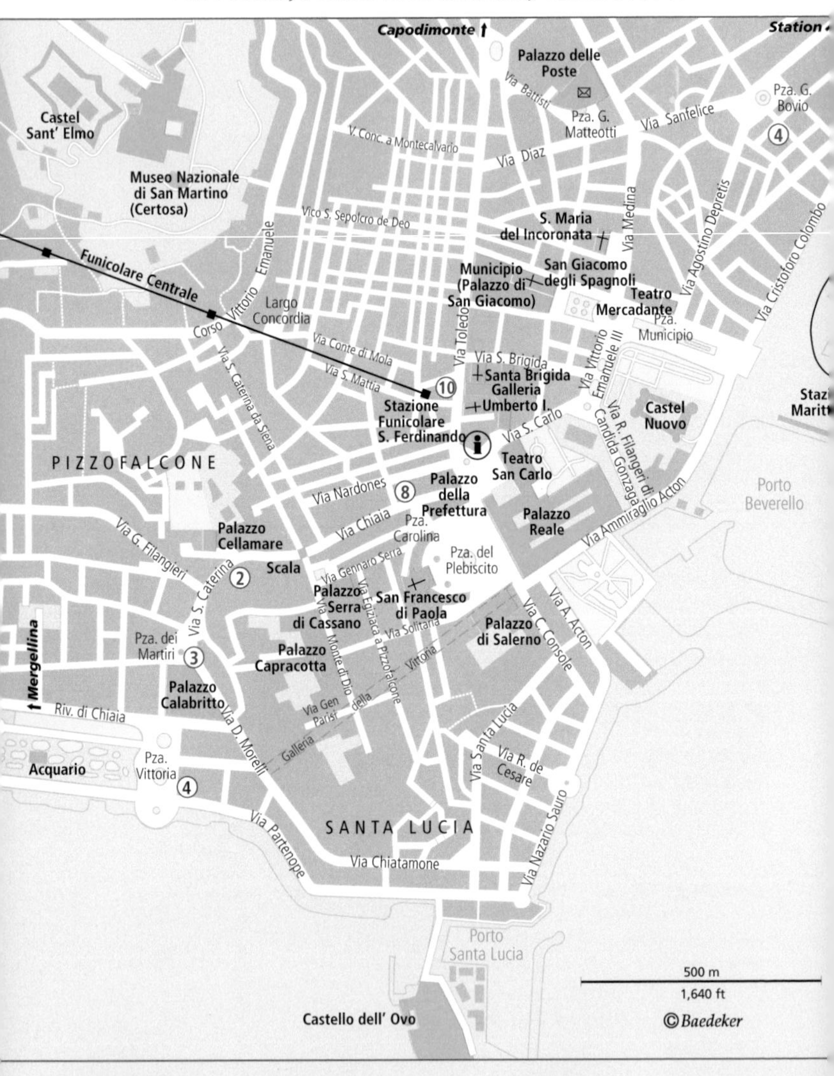

Where to eat
② Stanza del Gusto
③ Terrazza Calabritto
④ Europeo di Mattozzi
⑧ Da Angela
⑩ Gastronomia L.U.I.S.E.

Where to stay
④ Parteno

Opposite Piazza Dante begins the myriad of alleys making up the Montesanto quarter spreading out below the Vomero hill. A stroll around the area is very interesting. From the railway station at Cumana Montesanto trains head for the Campi Flegrei, Pozzuoli and Cumae.

Montesanto quarter

◄ Stazione Cumana

A little to the south of Piazza Dante, the Palazzo Doria d'Angri stands on one of the most exposed junctions of the city centre. A triangular piece of land here, between Via Toledo and Via Sant' Anna dei Lombardi, was purchased by **Luigi Vanvitelli** and his son to build one of the most beautiful palaces in Naples in 1755. Vanvitelli employed the same people responsible for constructing the Royal Palace at Caserta.

* **Palazzo Doria d'Angri**

Via Sant'Anna dei Lombardi and its extension, Via Monteoliveto, lead to several interesting sights.
Piazza Monteoliveto may be one of Naples' smallest squares but, architecturally, it is among the most attractive. The recently restored fountain dates from 1688, and the bronze figure exuding such confidence is of a youthful Charles II of Spain.

Via Sant'Anna dei Lombardi

*

◄ Piazza Monteoliveto

The square is dominated by the façade of the convent that once belonged with the Chiesa Sant'Anna dei Lombardi. The church has one of the most sumptuous interiors in Naples and seems more like a museum than a place of worship (Piazza Monteoliveto 44; Mon–Sat 8.30am–noon). The restoration work needed to repair the severe damage done during the Second World War has yet to be completed. Nevertheless, a visit is extremely worthwhile. Dating from 1411, Sant'Anna dei Lombardi was part of a foundation by the Tuscan Olivetan order. For centuries, it was a favoured burial place for the Neapolitan aristocracy. The Cappella Mastrogiudice (first side chapel to the right) contains the large Annunciation altar from 1489 by the Florentine sculptor **Benedetto da Maiano**. The high-quality work of the right-hand cherub supporting the two garlands has been attributed to Michelangelo Buonarotti. Don't miss the famous terracotta group of the Compianto sul Cristo morto in the **Cappella della Pietà**. The eight life-size figures from 1492 are by **Guido Mazzoni**, and were once coloured with paint. The dramatic expressivity of this Lamentation of Christ was much admired when it was first created. The vault frescoes (1544/45) in the adjacent Sagrestia Vecchia were painted by **Giorgio Vasari**, who was the Olivetan order's official painter from 1537 onwards.

** **Sant'Anna dei Lombardi**

◷

! *Baedeker* TIP

Learn Italian in Naples

There are many Italian language schools, but few are as friendly as the Centro Italiano near the Chiesa Santa Maria La Nova. Small classes and motivated teachers combine with a well thought-out activity programme that make every course an experience. Anyone wishing to learn Italian in one of southern Italy's most exciting cities has come to the right place here (www.centroitaliano.it).

✶ Palazzo Gravina

The somewhat intimidating façade of the Palazzo Gravina was made in 1549 for Ferdinando Orsini, the Duke of Gravina. Extensive 20th-century restoration work has succeeded in recreating the original Renaissance façade quite well. The palace now functions as the seat of the university's architectural faculty, and only the beautiful courtyard survives in its original design (Via Monteoliveto 3; Mon–Sat 9am–7pm).

✶ Palazzo delle Poste e dei Telegrafi

Opposite the Largo Santa Maria La Nova, steps lead up to **Piazza Matteotti**, named after the socialist opposition politician **Giacomo Matteotti**, who was murdered by the fascists in 1924. The Palazzo delle Poste e dei Telegrafi is the city's **main post office**. Designed by the architects Guiseppe Vaccaro and Gino Franzi, it was built in 1933–36. A milestone of 20th-century Italian architectural history, the building is not so much fascist as futurist. Mussolini was responsible for developing and expanding the old quarter of San Giuseppe-Carità, in the heart of Naples, turning it into the city's new administrative centre.

The new development was named Rione Carità, and its architecture is a memorial in stone to his fascist ideology. Piazza Matteotti is lined by further examples of buildings from that era, but the **Palazzo degli Uffici Finanziari** (1937), the **Palazzo della Provincia** (1934) and the **Casa del Mutilato** (1938/40) all seem merely pompous compared to the architectural daring of the main post office. **Piazza Carità** lies behind the Palazzo delle Posto, from which Via Toledo leads down into the city.

Quartieri spagnoli

Naples' **most notorious inner city quarter**, the Quartieri spagnoli, lies to the west of Via Toledo between Piazza Carità and Piazza Duca D'Aosta. These so-called »Spanish neighbourhoods« developed in the mid-16th century, and were built for the Spanish garrisons stationed in Naples. It is true that an evening stroll in the muddle of alleys around here is not recommended. During the day, however, the pulsating life of this district holds a certain charm. The chessboard outline for this area has survived, even if the urbanization that took place within it dates from later building projects in the 18th and 19th centuries. Characteristic for the neighbourhoods of Sanità,

Bassi ►

Montesanto and the Quartieri spagnoli are the so-called bassi, **ground-level one-room apartments**.

Continuing on Via Toledo

The southern section of Via Toledo is lined by the façades of magnificent palaces, which largely date from the 16th and 17th centuries when the Toledo was the city centre's most elegant address. A peek into the courtyards of these urban palazzi, which frequently boast beautiful staircases, is always worthwhile.

The **Palazzo del Banco di Napoli** (Via Toledo 177–178), on the other hand, is another creation of fascist architecture (1939). It backs onto the Palazzo San Giacomo (**Municipio**).

The domed church of San Francisco di Paola, and the Café Gambrinus

The base station for the **Funicolare Centrale** leading up to Vomero is on the pretty Piazza Duca d'Aosta. This was the last of the three cable car services to be inaugurated, in 1928.

Piazza Duca d'Aosta

Almost exactly opposite stands the Chiesa Santa Brigida (1640–1726) on the street of the same name. The church contains several of the most beautiful paintings by the artist **Luca Giordano (1634–1705), who also lies buried here**. For example, in the first side chapel on the right, hangs *St Philip Worshipping the Virgin*, and in the opposite chapel hangs *St Anne*. An early example of Giordano's work can be seen above his tomb in the left transept (1655). It portrays St Nicholas as the Bishop of Myra, liberating a boy kidnapped by Corsairs and returning him to his parents. The dome fresco from 1678 is also by this, the most renowned Neapolitan painter of the 17th century, and shows the apotheosis of St Brigid (daily 7am–12.30pm, 5.30pm–7pm).

✱✱ Santa Brigida

The twin squares of Piazza del Plebiscito and **Piazza Trieste e Trento** formed the true centre of Naples during the Bourbon era. Under the influence of Antonio Bassolino, Piazza del Plebiscito is once again **the city's most beautiful square**. Originally, the Palazzo Reale faced the deprived neighbourhoods below the Pizzofalcone, and it was only King **Gioacchino Murat** who had the square developed into the Foro Murat in 1809. When Murat had to flee in 1815, however, the work came to a standstill. But the return of the Bourbon King Ferdinand IV ensured the project was continued, though under the new name of Foro Ferdinando.

✱ Piazza del Plebiscito, the true centre of Naples

The Chiesa San Francesco di Paola was designed by the architect **Pietro Bianchi** in 1817–1836, and faces the royal palace (Mon–Sat

San Francesco di Paola

7.30am–noon, 3.30pm–6pm, Sun 8.30am–12.30pm). The model for this church was the Parthenon in Rome, while the arcaded walkways were inspired by Palladio's Veneto villas. Following the custom of antiquity, the visitor enters through an atrium before reaching the circular interior with its awe-inspiring dome, 53m/174ft in height and 34m/112ft in diameter. The magnificent pietra dura work (hard stone) of the altar is by **Anselmo Cangiano** and dates from 1641.

Baedeker TIP

Books and much more

The Libreria Treves, one of the city's most historical and friendly bookshops, is located in the right-hand arcades of the Chiesa San Francesco di Paola. The frequent cultural events held here are organized by the Associazione culturale del Plebiscito.

The rectangular **Piazza del Plebiscito** is lined by the Palazzo della Prefettura (1815) to the north and the Palazzo del Principe di Salerno (end of the 18th century) to the south. The two equestrian statues on the piazza by the classical sculptor **Antonio Canova** portray Charles III and Ferdinand I. The nearby Café Gambrinus is among Italy's great historic coffee houses and its status remains unchallenged in Naples. The interior décor is of the best Belle Epoque style. The waiters are suitably arrogant, the cakes superb, the sorbets even better, and the prices are shocking. Nevertheless, a visit to the Gambrinus is a must during any tour of Naples.

✶ Café Gambrinus ►

✶ Palazzo Reale

Opening hours: Thu–Tue 9am–7pm Oct–March till 2pm only

The Royal Palace opposite the Chiesa San Francesco di Paola on Piazza del Plebiscito looks back on an eventful past. The Normans, Hohenstaufen, Anjous and Aragonese had used the fortresses of Castel Nuovo, Castel Capuano and Castel Sant'Elmo as their royal residences in Naples. It was only the Spanish viceroy Pedro di Toledo who ordered that a palace protected by towers be erected on the present-day Piazza Trieste e Trento (demolished in the 19th century). Today the space is filled by the area where the Palazzo Reale adjoins the Teatro San Carlo. The original new residence for the Spanish viceroys was begun in 1600 by the architect **Domenico Fontana**, though a fire in 1837 led to substantial rebuilding and additions. In particular, the southern part of the palace was extended, and the terraced gardens added here today form one of the palace's main attractions for their fabulous views across the Bay of Naples and towards Vesuvius. The most recent remodelling work in 1888 resulted in the addition of **sculptures of some of the most significant Neapolitan rulers** set into several niches in the enclosed arcades: (from left to right) Roger II, Frederick II of Hohenstaufen, Charles I of Anjou, Alfonso I of Aragon, Charles V of Spain, the Bourbon Charles III, Giacchino Murat (Napoleon's nephew), and Vittorio Emanuele of Savoy. The Palazzo Reale was damaged during the Second World War by bombing raids and also later by Allied troops. The palace was restored in the 1950s, and today houses the **Biblioteca Nazionale** as well as various administrative and municipal offices.

A tour of the palace
✶ ✶
◄ Staircase

A magnificent staircase, the architectural highlight of the palace, leads to the state rooms on the upper floor. A tour of the palace begins with the **Teatrino di Corte**, built by Ferdinando Fuga in 1768, on the occasion of the marriage of Ferdinand IV and Maria Carolina of Austria. The ceiling frescoes destroyed during the last World War were recreated in 1954. The sculptures in the wall niches (Minerva, Mercury, Apollo and the Nine Muses) are all made of papier maché. The interiors of the rooms that follow date almost exclusively from the 18th or 19th century, by which time the Palazzo Reale had been reduced to a mere city palace and the actual royal residence moved to Caserta. The doors remain notable and are all in the Pompeian style: richly embellished with grotesques and ornamentation on a gold-leaf base. Some of the stucco ceilings, such as those of the queens' rooms, are also memorable. The silk wall hangings and furniture coverings were produced by the royal manufactory at San Leucio (► p.161). The ceiling fresco in the **Sala del Corpo Diplomatico** by Francesco di Mura is an allegory of the rule of Charles III and his queen Maria Amalia. The **Throne Room** has several portraits by the Neapolitan court artist **Anton Raphael Mengs**. The throne itself dates from 1845, although the 18th-century canopy served duty for Ferdinand IV. The mechanical reading and writing table in room 23 was commissioned by his queen, Maria Carolina. The tendency toward excessive pomp in the rooms is quickly forgiven on seeing the terraces laid out before the south wing. The largest prestigious room is the **Salone d'Ercole**, which takes its name from a copy of the Farnese Hercules that once stood here. The walls are decorated by tapestries containing scenes from the story of Psyche and Amor.

The staircase at the Palazzo Reale

The wooden architectural models of the Palazzo Reale on display in the **Sala delle Guardie** are especially worth seeing. Severely damaged during the Second World War, the **Royal Chapel**, consecrated in 1646, has been elaborately restored. The altar, with its gilded bronze and semi-precious inlaid stones, is the work of Dionisio Lazzari (1672). In the 17th and 18th centuries musicians such as Scarlatti, Pergolesi and Paisiello conducted the Royal Chapel's orchestra, one of the most famous of its day.

La Cappella Reale ►

✶✶ **Teatro San Carlo**

Europe's largest opera house at the time, was supposedly constructed in the record time of eight months in 1737. King Charles III presided over its inauguration in the very same year on the day that celebrated his name, and the Teatro San Carlo went on to play an outstanding role in the history of opera in the 18th and 19th centuries. Operas by Donizetti, Bellini and Rossini were premiered at the San Carlo, and the most famous opera singers performed on its stage. Today, it is not only the artistic shine that has somewhat faded; the San Carlo has also suffered severe financial crises. On the other hand, the concerts by foreign orchestras occasionally still reach global standards. The stage and auditorium burnt down in 1816, but were rebuilt almost immediately. The oldest part of the theatre is its classical entrance facing the Galleria Umberto I. The interior décor of the present auditorium dates from 1841. The opera's dimensions are tremendous: 3000 people can be accommodated on the ground level and a total of six circles (Via San Carlo 93; tours daily 9am–5.30pm).

! *Baedeker* TIP

Theatregoers please note...

An opera or concert here is a real experience, even if the tickets are very pricey. As balcony seats are not numbered, it is worth arriving early. Binoculars are also an advantage, considering the distance between the stage and the balcony seats of the upper levels.

✶✶ **Galleria Umberto I**

The Galleria Umberto I, one of the great iron and glass shopping arcades of the late 19th century, stands opposite the San Carlo. Only slightly smaller than the famous Galleria Vittorio Emanuele in Milan, these arcades are topped by a glass dome 57m/187ft high that was constructed in 1887–91. An entire quarter of the city had to make way for the galleries.

✶✶ Castel Nuovo

Opening hours: Mon–Sat 9am–7pm

Following alongside the small park of the Palazzo Reale, Via San Carlo continues on as far as the Castel Nuovo. The **Castrum Novum** (new castle) was erected in the early years of Angevin rule. Begun in 1279 by Charles I, it was already habitable three years later. Charles II and Robert the Wise commissioned extensions, on which such renowned artists as the architect and sculptor **Tino di Camaino** and the

The elegant Galleria Umberto I

painter **Giotto di Bondone** participated. The castle, which is known locally as **Maschio Angioino**, actually enjoyed its heyday during the rule of the House of Aragon. It was they who kept the most glamorous court of the early Italian Renaissance here, but the castle lost favour once building had started on the Palazzo Reale in 1600. It did, however, retain its role as one of the key defensive positions for the city, along with Sant'Elmo. The main entrance is on the side facing the city to the west.

◄ Triumphal arch

The indisputable effect of the triumphal arch commissioned by Alfonso I of Aragon lies in the juxtaposition of the brilliantly white Carrara marble and the dark stone of the towers that embrace it: the Torre di Mezzo to the left and the Torre della Guardia to the right. The arch is now considered **one of the most important achievements of Renaissance architecture** in southern Italy. The arch was built to commemorate the triumphant entry into Naples by Alfonso of Aragon, on 26 February 1422, after years of violent battles with the House of Anjou. Completed in 1465–66, the arch is really a monumental portal built by master craftsmen from northern and central Italy. The lower section with its Corinthian dual columns is entirely true to the examples of Roman antiquity. The **royal coat of arms** framed by lions and horns of plenty is set into the arch; above it is the relief of the **king's triumphant procession**. The highly individual characterization of the heads was presumably the result of the fact that they are genuine portraits. Examples used in the design for this arch were taken from the Trojan arch in Benevento, and the bridge gate in Capua, commissioned by Frederick II. The famous **bronze doors** (to the right, on the inner wall of the vestibule) concentrate on scenes from victorious battles fought by Alfonso and Ferrante against the House of Anjou. The artist, or rather the craftsman who cast the bronze for these doors, immortalized himself with a self-portrait in the left-hand lower corner.

A tour of Castel Nuovo

The effect created by stepping into the courtyard of Castel Nuovo is still overwhelming, despite its chequered architectural history and frequent near destruction during wars or natural catastrophes, such as the earthquake in 1456 and the great fire in 1919. Steps to the left lead up to the Sala dei Baroni, a **state room** inaugurated by Alfonso of Aragon in 1457. It is still used for meetings of the Neapolitan city council today. A star-shaped dome spans the hall, which is 28m/92ft high and was designed by the Spanish master builder **Guglielmo Sagrera** in 1453. A masterpiece of the late Middle Ages, the hall was completed by his workshop after his death. The entrance to the former royal state rooms is at the **Porta del Trionfo** at the northern end of the front of the castle. The entrance to the Cappella Palatina is next to the stairs leading up to the Sala dei Baroni. The former **Court Chapel** is the only room that has survived from Angevin times in the Castel Nuovo. It has recently been restored to its original design, the Baroque embellishments removed. Only the cycle of frescoes by Giotto is missing: it was damaged beyond repair after the earthquake in 1456, although a few valuable traces can still be seen around the window frames. The **Museo Civico** moved into the castle in 1992, and presents an impressive collection of 19th-century painting.

✶ ✶ Sala dei Baroni ►

? DID YOU KNOW ...?

- The cavity left by a cannon ball in the bronze door is an unsolved mystery. The most likely explanation for the damage, though, is that it happened during the maritime Battle of Rapallo in 1495. The French ships of Charles VIII, sailing with Neapolitan booty, were caught up in battle by ships from Genoa and defeated. It was probably on that occasion that the doors were damaged, but they were later returned to Naples.

✶ **Piazza del Municipio**

Piazza del Municipio became the political centre of the city after the unification of Italy, and Naples is now ruled from the classical **Palazzo San Giacomo**, located on the west side of the square (**Municipio**, city hall). Unfortunately this square, built during urban modernization projects in 1884, is no longer very attractive and suffers from heavy traffic. It has also been a huge building site for several years due to the construction of the new metro route. However, in 2004, those works resulted in sensational archaeological finds. At a depth of 13m/43ft scientists uncovered the remains of the Roman harbour from the 2nd-century AD, a discovery which has led to an entirely

Remains of the Antique port ►

The mighty Castel Nuovo with its twin Renaissance triumphal arches

new understanding of the historic topography of Naples. The remains are due to be left as they are and will, in future, form part of the new metro station, which will double up as a museum.

✶ **San Giacomo degli Spagnuoli**

The Chiesa San Giacomo degli Spagnuoli belongs to the palace of the same name and was once the main church used by the Spanish kings. (Mon–Sat 7.30am–11.30am, Sun 10.30am–1pm). The church was founded by the viceroy Don Pedro de Toledo in 1540, and although the façade was lost when the palace was remodelled into a royal administrative office in 1819–25, the church interior has survived almost unchanged. One of the most important princely Renaissance tombs in southern Italy lies behind the high altar: the tomb of Pedro de Todelo and his wife Maria Ossoria Pimentel. The viceroy himself commissioned it to be created by the most famous Neapolitan sculptor at the time, **Giovanni da Nola**. Sadly, Don Pedro was never buried here because he died during a journey to Florence in 1553 and was buried in the cathedral there. The reliefs on the sarcophagus portray important events during Don Pedro de Toledo's reign, and it is easy to recognize key places such as the Gulf of Pozzuoli, the fortress of Baia, and even a silhouette of Ischia.

✶ ✶ ◀ Tomb of Pedro de Toledo

Other buildings on Piazza del Municipio

The charming **Teatro Mercadante** opened its doors in 1779 with a performance of *L'Infedeltà Fedele* by Cimarosa. The present interior dates from renovation that took place in 1849–51, and the rather inelegant façade was imposed on the building in 1892. The theatre's contemporary events programme maintains high standards, and foreign theatre ensembles frequently guest here. The Stazione

◀ Stazione Marittima

Marittima, **Naples' harbour for ferry passengers**, is exactly opposite the Palazzao San Giocomo. .Mussolini had the building constructed by Cesare Bazzani between 1933 and 1936, with the intention of establishing Naples as the »empire's port«. Today, large cruise ships dock here, while the hydrofoils and ferries for the islands depart from the Molo Beverello.

✶ Piazza Giovanni Bovio

Piazza Giovanni Bovio, also known as **Piazza della Borsa**, is reached by taking Via Agostino Depretis, which runs parallel with Via Medina. The square lies at the heart of Neapolitan life and the pretty Neptune Fountain is the work of Michelangelo Naccherino, Cosimo Fanzago and Pietro Bernini. Corso Umberto I leads from the square to Piazza Garibaldi and the main railway station.

Piazza Garibaldi, Centro Direzionale and the Mercato Quarter

Piazza Garibaldi

The city's largest square (120 x 350m/394 x 1148ft) is also its ugliest and remodelling work has been going on for years. Anyone arriving in Naples by train is therefore engulfed in an inferno of traffic, building sites and illegal street hawkers, and there is little hope that things will improve in the near future. The ambitious plans for green spaces and fountains have come to nothing so far. Originally, the **main railway station** took up the central point of the square, and its frontage was virtually facing the Garibaldi monument. But its ruins were carried off after the Second World War to make way for the present square. The new railway station on the eastern edge of the square certainly has merit. It was designed by **Enrico Tremenzini** and built between 1959 and 1970. The other buildings surrounding the piazza still date from the turn of the 19th century. Access to the underground station of the **Circumvesuviana** is a little way to the south on Corso Garibaldi. Corso Garibaldi is another of those thoroughfares cut into the city centre after 1882, and connects Piazza Carlo III with the old Mercato quarter (►p.235).

Stazione Centrale ►

Corso Garibaldi ►

Corso Umberto I

The dead straight Corso Umberto I runs between Piazza Garibaldi and Piazza Giovanni Bovio, then continues as Via Agostino Depretis to join with Piazza Municipio and the city hall (► p.232). When it was built at the turn of the 19th century, Corso Umberto I, also known to locals as **Rettifilo**, was intended to be one of Naples' finest boulevards, but it is actually **one of the city centre's least attractive streets**.

✶ Centro Direzionale

Piazza Nazionale and the prison of Poggioreale in the environs of Piazza Garibaldi are depressing, although the **high-rise building** of the Centro Direzionale is a highlight of urban planning that is best reached on foot. The design by the Japanese architect Kenzo Tange was realized in 1987 to 1995, and the result is a futuristic office and business sector created out of seven high-rise buildings. The highest of them all is the **Torre Telecom Italia**, which is 129m/423ft high. Its offices are home to Italian Telecom and the Enel electricity company.

★ **Piazza del Mercato**

The Mercato quarter to the west of Corso Garibaldi is one of **Naples' liveliest neighbourhoods**. At its heart is the busy market square of Piazza del Mercato, which is not far from the sea. Unfortunately, however, the square has little relevance to the topography of Naples today, because the destruction during World War Two and haphazard and uncompleted urban regeneration – not to mention the expansion of Via Nuova Marina into a multi-lane highway – have combined to almost totally ruin both the square and its environs.

Piazza del Mercato was originally commissioned by the kings of the House of Anjou in the 13th century, and located outside the city walls. Gradually, it became Naples' most important **market and trading square**. A major fire in 1781 resulted in a new incarnation of the square, which has particular resonance for German-Italian history: this is where, on 29 October 1268, the last legitimate heir of the Hohenstaufen Crown, the young **Conradin of Hohenstaufen**, was executed. Conradin's tomb in the **Chiesa Santa Maria del Carmine** is a special memorial site, as is that of his grandfather's, Frederick II, located at the cathedral in Palermo. The Hohenstaufen dream of a Swabian-Sicilian empire lies buried there.

? DID YOU KNOW ...?

- In July 1647, a merchants' revolt on Piazza del Mercato shook Naples for ten days. It was in protest against the Spanish viceroy's new tax on fruit and went down in the history of European revolutions as the Masaniello Revolt. The 26-year-old fisherman Tommaso Aniello, from Amalfi, emerged as the leader of the revolt, but was murdered by his own people. Just under 150 years later, Masaniello's red Neapolitan fisherman's cap became the favoured head-dress for French revolutionaries.

★ **Santa Maria del Carmine**

The church was built in 1283 on the spot of a previous one, where Carmelite monks venerated the miraculous **»La Bruna« Madonna**. The location was donated to the monks by Charles I of Anjou, and the means to build a church came from his second wife, Margaret of Burgundy, and also from Elizabeth of Bavaria (the widow of Conrad IV), who wished to have a memorial to her beheaded son Conradin. The original church was Gothic, but due to numerous earthquakes and rebuilding its present appearance is Baroque and dates from 1755–66 (Mon–Sat 6.30am–noon, 4.45pm–7pm, Sun 6.30am–1pm, 5pm–7.30pm). The simple statue of the young Conradin between the 4th and 5th chapel on the left was designed by Bertel Thorvaldsen, and gifted by King Maximilian of Bavaria in 1847. The icon to the Virgin Mary known as **La Bruna** hangs behind the high altar in the apse. The 75m/246ft-high **campanile** is the highest in the city and one of Naples' emblems.

★ **Sant'Eligio Maggiore** The Chiesa Sant'Eligio Maggiore on the southwestern corner of Piazza del Mercato was built in 1270 during the rule of Charles I of Anjou. Its austere lack of embellishments is remarkable, and the original cross vault, capitals and isolated frescoes survive intact (Mon–Sat 8am–12.30pm, 5pm–7pm, Sun 8am–1pm).

Vomero

Respectable Naples The 224m/735ft-high Vomero hill offers wonderful views across the Bay of Naples, and is also home to the Museo di San Martino, one of the city's three major museums.Naples' famous **funicolari** connect the city centre with its most bourgeois neighbourhood. The Funicolare Centrale ascends from Toledo, the Funicolare Montesanto arrives from the Quartieri spagnoli, and the Funicolare di Chiaia comes up from Piazza Amedeo. In fact, Vomero was more of a countrified suburb of villas than part of Naples, even as late as the early post-war years of the 20th century. A foreign bank consortium purchased the land there in 1885, and gradually developed the Vomero hill from then onwards. The **most favoured neighbourhood** for the Neapolitan middle class emerged from what were once the two villages of Vomero and Antignano, and the quarter is still home to the most popular addresses in Naples, a respectable alternative to the chaos of the city below. Unfortunately, rampant building speculation during the aftermath of the Second World War damaged the Belle Epoche elegance of the district, but **Piazza Vanvitelli**, **Via Scarlatti** and **Via Bernini** survived with their plush charm intact. Here, the façades decorated with stucco and the small well-tended squares of the Vomero can still be enjoyed to their full effect.

Access ►

★ Prettiest weekly market ► **Largo Antignano** is just a stone's throw from the Piazza Medaglie d'Oro, where the city's most picturesque weekly market can be found. An abundance of the freshest vegetables, fish and fruit are sold here every morning. **Via Scarlatti** is pedestrianized and a lively place to go shopping. There is activity around Piazza Vanvitelli in the evenings, when the centro storico lies abandoned. The classical **Villa Floridiana** was built in the middle of an English Garden for the mistress and later wife of Ferdinand IV, Lucia Migliaccio. The elaborate design of the bubbling fountains that punctuate the winding paths through the park, as well as the fantastic views of the bay, make a visit here a highly rewarding experience.

Porcelain Museum ► These days, the villa belongs to the state and houses the **Museo Nazionale della Ceramica Duca di Martina**, which contains a notable collection of porcelain and ceramics (Via Cimarosa 77; Wed–Mon 8.30am to 1.30pm).

Castel Sant'Elmo The highest point of the Vomero hill is taken up by the Castel Sant'Elmo, which can be reached by walking along Via Tito Angelini or by taking bus V1 (Thu–Tue 9am–6.30pm). The fortress was once a central part of the city's defences and was extended into its present star-shaped design during the reign of Pedro di Toledo. Today, it houses a variety of cultural and scientific institutes.

✱✱ Certosa di San Martino

The charmingly situated former Carthusian monastery of San Martino can also be found on the Vomero hill. It is one of the city's major attractions – not least for the **spectacular view of Naples**. Via dei Tribunali and Via Spaccanapoli, the ancient main roads of the centro storico, can easily be recognized from up here. The monastery was built in the Gothic style between 1325 and 1368 but was rebuilt in the 17th century when it received its almost profligate interior decoration. Secularized during Napoleonic rule, the building has been a **museum** (Piazzale San Martino 5; Thu–Tue 8.30am–7.30pm, Sun. 9am–7.30pm) since 1866. Extensive renovations and a redesign of the collection took place in recent years, and the museum is now dedicated to the **city's history**. The Carthusian order normally prescribes a strictly contemplative life yet, in Naples, the Carthusians allowed themselves a surprising expression of luxury and the **church interior** is a veritable shrine to marble. The walls and floors are covered in precious inlaid stonework, designed mostly by Cosimo Fanzago in 1623–56. The entrance to the sacristy lies behind the main altar beyond two angels by **Giuseppe Sanmartino**. The 16th-century cupboards in the sacristy are decorated with no less than 56 inlaid wood designs. The altar painting to the Virgin Mary in the Capella del Tesoro is from 1637 and is by **Jusepe de Ribera**. The ceiling fres-

◄ Museo di San Martino ⏲

◄ Capella del Tesoro

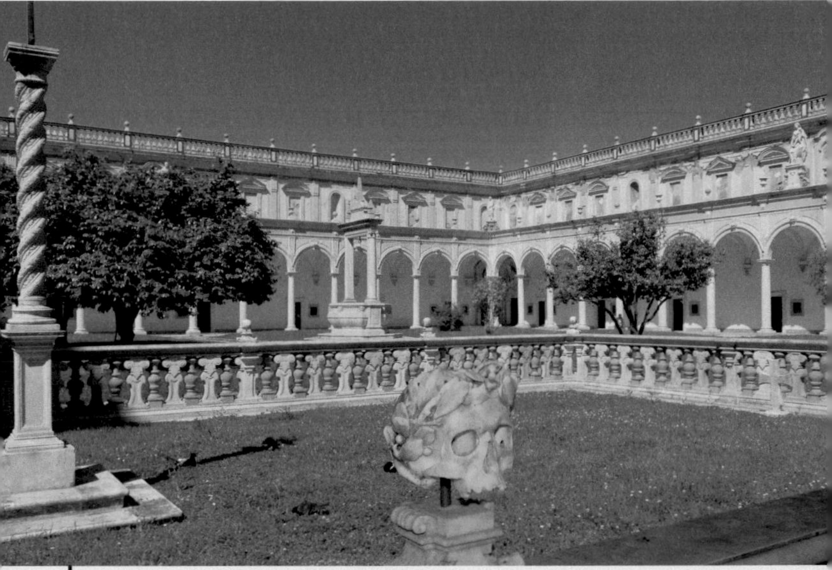

The Large Cloister at the Certosa di San Martino

co portraying *The Triumph of Judith* was painted by **Luca Giordano** in 1704. A long corridor leads from the cloister for the procurators to the larger cloister that once served the monks. The entrance to the Christmas crib exhibition lies on the way. La Presepe Napoletana or the **Neapolitan crib**, is among the most unusual of European crafts to have emerged in the 18th century. Neapolitan folk scenes are incorporated into the traditional Bethlehem scenes with an enormous pleasure in creative detail.

La Presepe Napoletana ►

Large Cloister ►

The monk's Large Cloister lies at the heart of the monastic complex. Its **cemetery** decorated with marble death's heads was the final resting place for the Carthusians, whose individual cells now house displays for the museum, such as paintings associated with the history of Naples. The most famous is the ***Tavola Strozzi*** (room 32), which shows an urban panorama of Naples during the 15th century. An entire room is dedicated to the **Revolt of Masaniello** (room 36). A stroll around the garden terraces built into the hill is very enjoyable.

Garden ►

414 steps down to the city

Via Pedamentina is a stairway with 414 steps leading from the square in front of the museum down to Corso Vittorio Emanuele below. Almost all the buildings along the way are in ruins, and most are uninhabited, so a walk this way should never be undertaken alone and only during daylight hours.

From Pizzofalcone to Posillipo

The lively commercial artery of Via Chiaia leads from Piazza Trieste e Trento towards the classy and sometimes even highly elegant western neighbourhoods of Naples. During antiquity and the Middle Ages this area was far from the city centre, and Chiaia, Santa Lucia and Mergellina were just small fishing villages. Then the Spanish viceroys chose it for their summer retreat.

✶ **Palazzo Cellamare**

The Palazzo Cellamare from the second half of the 16th century was the country home of the Carafa family. Set back from Piazza dei Martiri, the building has been remodelled many times, but enjoyed its heyday during the 18th century when designs by Ferdinando Fuga turned it into the city residence of the Prince of Francavilla.

✶ **Piazza dei Martiri**

Piazza dei Martiri, together with Via Calabritto, lies at the heart of **elegant Naples**. The Monumento ai Martiri Napoletani, commemorating the anti-Bourbon revolts from 1799, 1820, 1848 and 1860, dominates the square. Several significant palaces line the piazza, including the sea-facing **Palazzo Calabritto** designed by Luigi and Carlo Vanvitelli, and the **Palazzo Sessa** at the junction to Via Morelli. One old-fashioned Neapolitan institution is the small and enchanting souvenir shop owned by the **Bowinkel family**, where quality souvenirs have been sold since 1879. Via Calabritto leads down to the palm-lined Piazza Vittoria and to the Lungomare seafront.

Santa Lucia

The much-lauded Santa Lucia, famous from countless travel journals and letters, has long since disappeared . Its demise came with the transformation of Naples after 1870, when it was turned into a »modern« city, along with the elegant coastal development along the Lungomare. The resulting Via Partenope has presented the city's most elegant aspect ever since, with exclusive hotels offering fine views towards Castel dell'Ovo.

★ Castel dell'Ovo

Naples' mysterious and historic fortress is the Castel dell'Ovo (Mon–Sat 8.30am–6pm, Sun 8.30am–2pm). It is set on a small **rocky outcrop** – the Greek Megaris – where Greek seafarers from Rhodes first made land to found Parthnope, the predecessor of Neapolis (»new town«). Pizzofalcone was settled starting from Megaris and, in

Mergellina and Posillipo Map

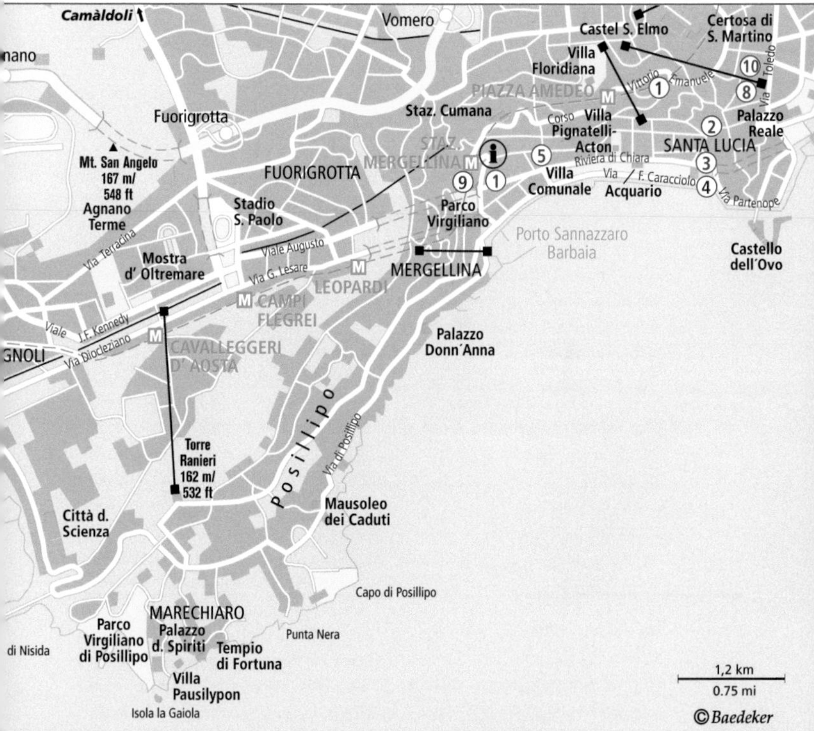

Where to eat

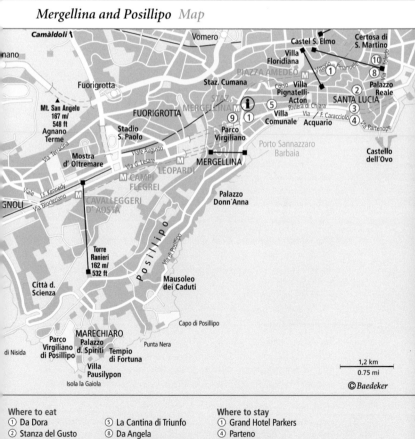

① Da Dora
② Stanza del Gusto
③ Terrazza Calabritto
⑤ La Cantina di Triunfo
⑧ Da Angela
⑩ Gastronomia L.U.I.S.E.

Where to stay

① Grand Hotel Parkers
④ Parteno
⑨ Ostello Mergellina

The oldest castle in Naples: Castel dell'Ovo

Roman times, it was part of the villa and grounds of the general and gourmet Lucio Lucullus. What was once an island (the dam was only constructed at the end of the 19th century), has been **witness to dramatic twists and turns of fate**. The last emperor of the Western Roman Empire, Romulus Augustulus, set foot on Campanian soil here in 476 on his way to exile in Misenium. Under the Normans and Frederick II the strategic island was fortified, and Conradin, the unhappy heir to the Hohenstaufen empire, was incarcerated here prior to his execution. According to local Neapolitan legend, the fortress is associated with **Virgil**, who was revered for his miraculous powers during the Middle Ages. The poet is said to have magically inserted an egg into a bottle, placed the bottle into an iron cage, and hidden it in the foundations of the castle. Mysteriously, this miracle is responsible for the quality of Neapolitan ice cream! The present fortress dates from the 16th century, and was a ruin before being excellently restored to the present Castel dell'Ovo, which functions as a conference centre and as a venue for changing exhibitions. The **Sala delle Colonne** is particularly worth seeing and contains several well-preserved columns from the original Lucullus villa (Mon–Sat 8.30am–6pm, Sun 8.30am–2pm).

? DID YOU KNOW ...?

- Naples' origins are lost in myth: Parthenope, the siren rejected by Odysseus, is supposed to have washed up on the rocks of Megaris. She gave the settlement its first name and archaeological excavations on Pizzofalcone confirm that the first settlement existed here around 650–550 BC.

Borgo Marinari is an **elegant yacht marina**, and Naples' most renowned and expensive fish restaurants serve a mostly luxury hotel clientele here.

◄ Borgo Marinari

Pizzofalcone

The district of Pizzofalcone (Falcon Point), which spreads uphill to the west of Piazza del Plebescito, is only rarely visited by tourists, though it is actually one of the more **charming districts** of Naples. This is the original site of Parthenope. **Monte Echia**, present-day Pizzofalcone, was home to the first Greek settlers, who chose this spot as an ideal place to found a city due to its geographical location above the sea. The settlement was abandoned some time around the 5th century BC, after which Neapolis was founded. There was no more building at Pizzofalcone until the Spanish viceroys began to develop the area. Among the palaces, the Palazzo Serra di Cassano is particularly noteworthy. A major example of the architectural work of Ferdinando Sanfelice (1725/26), it now houses the »Istituto Italiano per gli Studi Filosofici«. It is especially famous for its beautiful stairwell, with its double flight of steps.

◄ Origins of Naples

✱

◄ Palazzo Serra di Cassano

Villa Comunale

After the park at Capodimonte, this is the city's **second largest park**. It is well-kept and popular with Neapolitans, especially at the weekend. Its origins lie with the Spanish viceroys, who had the present-day Riviera di Chiaia paved for the first time. The design that largely survives today was commissioned by Ferdinand IV and based on plans made by Carlo Vanvitelli between 1778 and 1781. The Neapolitan aristocracy soon preferred living along this coastal stretch, between Pizzofalcone and Posillipo, over the cramped and dreary city centre. The **statues** surrounding the park are copies of famous works of antiquity and the Renaissance, and the monolithic **red granite bowl** of the central fountain is said to come from Paestum.

✱

Stazione Zoologica (Aquario)

The Villa Comunale park is dominated by the building of the Stazione Zoologica, known as Aquario for short (Tue–Sat 9am–6pm, Sun 9.30am–7pm). **Europe's first oceanographic research institute** was founded here, after the German scientist **Anton Dohrn** bought a piece of land here in 1870. The plot was originally right by the sea. The architect for this fine building was the German sculptor Adolf von Hildebrand and the institute was open for business by 1874. The **aquarium** was a sensation at the time, its numerous pools introducing the wealth of species from the Mediterranean Sea. A so-called »half-open system« supplies the pools with constant fresh seawater to this day. It comes from 300m/328yd away, pumped from the sea at a depth of 11m/36ft.The frescoes by Hans von Marées in the former library of the zoological research station are a **testament to the fascination with the Bay of Naples**. He painted this vision of a Latin Arcadia in just four months, between July and November 1873. Originally, the room was intended as a concert hall, and the room's proportions and walled divisions were entirely unsuitable for fres-

✱

◄ Frescoes by Hans von Marées

coes; and yet Hildrebrand and Marées created a work of art that has great beauty. The zoological research station is not a museum, but the frescoes can be visited on weekdays by making a request at the ticket office.

Villa Pignatelli

One of the most elegant residences along the Riviera di Chiaia is Villa Pignatelli. Its last owner was the Principessa Rosina Pignatelli, who donated the villa complete with its furnishings and art collection to the city of Naples in 1955 (Riviera di Chiaia 200; Wed–Mon 9am–2pm, last admission 1pm). The neo-classical building was erected by Pietro Valente in 1826 and purchased by the Rothschild family in 1841. However the Rothschilds left Naples after Italy's unification, and Prince Diego Aragona Pignatelli Cortes then bought the villa. Most of the lavish interior décor dates from the second half of the 19th century, and is a unique example of **Neapolitan aristocratic living** of that time. Features surviving from the original construction include a circular **vestibule** and the salottino pompeiano, a charming toilet room decorated with frescoes in the Pompeian style by Guglielmo Bechi. By contrast, the main salons of the ground floor (salotto azzurro, salotto verde, salotto rosso) are in the sumptuous style of neo-Rococo. The museum's particular charm lies in the many personal items from the estate of the Pignatelli family. Also housed in the villa, but not always open to the public, is the art collection belonging to the Banco di Napoli. The Museo delle Carozze, housed in an adjacent building, exhibitsone of the most extensive collections of 18th- and 19th-century carriages in Europe (unfortunately closed at present).

Salottino pompeiano ►

Chiesa dell' Ascensione a Chiaia

The Chiesa dell'Ascensione a Chiaia behind Villa Pignatelli is a work by Cosimo Fanzago (1622–45). The most precious decorations inside are the two paintings by **Luca Giordano**: the portrait of St Anne with the Virgin Mother as a child, hanging above the main altar; and the magnificent Archangel Michael (1657) situated above the right side altar, who charges upon falling devils in a suitably victorious pose (Piazetta Ascensione 15; Mon–Sat 7.30am–noon, 5pm–8pm, Sun 7.30am–noon, 6pm– 8pm).

Piazza Amedeo

Above Villa Pignatelli is the elegant Piazza Amedeo, lined by magnificent **villas in the Italian Liberty style**. A **funicolare** travels up the **Vomero** hill from here (►p 236). Corso Vittorio Emanuele is one of the most beautiful streets in Naples, with breathtaking views opening out onto the Bay of Naples. Its serpentine route runs parallel to the coast between Mergellina and the quarter of Montesanto. Its extension then ends at the National Archaeological Museum (► p.215).

Corso Vittorio Emanuele ►

Mergellina

The former fishing village of Mergellina is now one of the finest neighbourhoods of Naples. The city's wealthy keep their yachts in the former fishing harbour, while hydrofoils to Capri, Procida and Ischia regularly depart from **Porto Sannazaro**A route alongside the Mergellina train station (a newly renovated 19th-century building) leads directly to the **Parco Virgiliano a Piedigrotta** and the presumed location for **Virgil's grave**. This somewhat abandoned area (Via Salita Piedigrotta 20; daily 9am to one hour before sunset) was not only one of the great Neapolitan attractions for 18th- and 19th-century travellers, it was also a much revered place during late antiquity, with the likes of Petrarch having paid their respects to the great poet here. It is, however, questionable whether Virgil really is buried in a grave dating from Augustinian times, though there is no doubt that the poet **Giacomo Leopardi** lies buried in the tomb next door.

◄ Boats for Capri, Procida and Ischia

◄ Tombe dei Poeti

🕑

Posillipo

The hill of Posillipo was once famous for its natural beauty and separates Naples from the Phlegrean Fields (Campi Flegrei). Augustus's general Agrippa had a 705m/771yd **tunnel dug through the Posillipo hill** in order to establish easier access between Naples and the port at Pozzuoli (Puteoli), and also between the city and his military warships stationed at Porto Julius and later at Miseneum. Known as the **Crypta Neapolitana**, this famous construction remained in use until the mid-19th century.

★ **Palazzo Donn'Anna**

One of Europe's most famous ruined palaces is the Palazzo Donn'Anna, which has long fired the imagination of travellers to Naples. The massive and never completed building designed by Cosimo Fanzago is one of the many emblems of Naples. These days, its romantically weathered façade hides luxury flats.

Panoramic route: Via di Posillipo

Continuing in a southwesterly direction, Via di Posillipo becomes an impressive **panoramic route** beyond the palace of Donn'Anna. Many of the park-like private estates along the road have direct access to the sea, and the region exudes an exclusivity that is very distant from the usual Neapolitan clichés.

★ **Marecchiaro**

Despite its run-down appearance, the former fishing village of Marechiaro still retains something of its magic. A long line of steps lead down to the sea from the car park, at the end of Via Marechiaro, and an especially pleasant option is to take one of the frequent fishing boats to the rocks in the sea. Depending on the direction of the wind and the currents, the water quality is perfectly acceptable for swimming here. The coastline between Marechiaro and Nisida was declared a **Parco Sommerso della Gaiola** in 2002, and is now an officially protected area. Numerous Roman remains, such as the ruin of the so-called **Palazzo degli Spiriti**, imply that this coast was once densely populated during antiquity.

Villa Imperiale del Pausilypon

Recent excavations have exposed the extent of what has long been known as the location for the Roman Villa Imperiale del Pausilypon.

? DID YOU KNOW ...?

- Publius Vedius Pollio was a freed slave from Benevento, who achieved great power and wealth. Said to have been particularly cruel, he is an infamous character of Roman antiquity. One much-discussed event rumoured to have taken place is described in great detail in Robert Harris's novel *Pompeii*, where Pollio feeds one of his slaves to the eels in his fish ponds.

It was named Pausilypon (»An End to Pain«) by a certain Publius Vedius Pollio, who is believed to have spread his estate over nine hectares (22 acres), complete with gardens, thermal pools, a vineyard, and fish ponds. After his death, the property came under imperial ownership. Only a small part of this ancient Sanssouci has been exposed; most of it remains buried underground, or has been built over by modern constructions. The size of the former property can be gauged by the extent of the theatre, which once contained 2000 seats (Parco Archeologico del Pausilypon, Access via the Dicesa Coroglio; Tue, Thu, Sat 9am–1pm; appointments advisable: tel. 08 12 30 10 30).

Continuing on Via di Posillipo

None of the historical 19th-century villas along the Posillipo are open to the public, as most of these palatial properties remain private or in the hands of corporations. One that does belong to the state, functioning as the Neapolitan **residence of the Italian President**, is Villa Rosebery. This is where the last Italian king signed his abdication on 9 May 1946. Via di Posillipo ends as the Discesa Coroglio at one of the **most beautiful parks** in the Naples area. Remodelled in recent years, the Parco Virgiliano di Posillipo is not only a green oasis, but also an ideal place to enjoy spectacular views across the Phlegrean Fields, the Gulf of Pozzuoli and the small island of Nisida (Viale Virgilio; daily 7am–10pm; till 8pm during winter).

Villa Rosebery ►

✶ Parco Virgiliano di Posillipo ►

Nisida

The island of Nisida (Nesis = small island), which is connected to the mainland beach at Coroglio by a 300m/328yd dam, has long since lost its relevance to tourism on the Bay of Naples. Yet it did provide an elegant summer retreat for the Neapolitan aristocracy during the 16th century. Today, however, the island is home to the city's **young offenders' institute**. The almost perfectly circular crater island is only 2 sq km/1 sq mi and redolent in history: Brutus and Cassius plotted against Julius Caesar here in the **villa belonging to Lucullus**, of which a few traces remain. The island was established as a prison as long ago as the Bourbon era, and has not been open to the public since.

Bagnoli

Bagnoli, on the other side of the Posillipo hill, is one of **the city's greatest eyesores**. Built in 1907 on what was once one of the most beautiful sections of coast along the Gulf of Pozzuoli, the ILVA steelworks are now **a derelict industrial ruin**. Ambitious plans to revive the area for tourism have so far failed due to lack of funds. The only successful initiative so far is the interactive Città della Scienza, which

Città della Scienza ►

Beautiful villas line Via di Posillipo

has been set among the impressive hulks of industrial wasteland. The **City of Science** is Italy's first attempt to develop a museum where visitors are introduced to the wonders of the natural sciences (Via Coroglio 104; Tue–Sat 9am–5pm, Sun 10am–7pm).

★★ Paestum and Cilento

H/I 6

Region: Campania
Altitude: 18m/59ft
Province: Salerno
Population: 900

Though the Greek temples of Paestum do not lie directly on the Bay of Naples, they have been one of the highlights of any southern Italian journey from as long ago as the days of the Grand Tour. Their historic beauty, the ruins of the surrounding Roman town and the archaeological museum combine to make a visit to Paestum a real experience.

History

Greek colonists from Sybaris, on the southern coast of present-day Calabria, founded Poseidonia towards the end of the 7th century BC. Poseidonia was founded as an outpost – a colony of a colony, so to speak – and the fertility of the earth around the mouth of the river Sele and busy trade with the neighbouring Etruscans meant the settlement soon thrived.

Archaic beauty at Paestum: the Tempio di Cerere, also known as the Temple of Athena

Within just one century, (from the mid-6th century to the mid-5th century BC), the town named in honour of **Poseidon** could afford to build three monumental temples that were even more glorious than the ones in the Greek motherland. Around 400 BC, though, the wealthy town was taken over by a Samnite tribe of Lucanians. There is no evidence among the archaeological finds of a violent takeover, so it is likely that the Poseidonian colony gradually became acculturated with the surrounding Lucanian population. It became a Roman colony during the course of the Roman conquest of Campania in 274/3 BC as was renamed Paestum. Roman veterans settled here were rewarded with land, which also served the purposed of »Romanizing« newly conquered provinces and uniting them with the wider empire. Poseidonia lost its Greek identity, and only the temples and the underground shrine to Hereon were left untouched as a mark of respect to the Gods. A new Roman town with its own public buildings was constructed around the old Greek settlement, however, so a stroll around the archaeological site is an exploration of the **ruined Roman town**.

? DID YOU KNOW ...?

- The driving motivation for Greek colonization of southern Italy was not just a matter of adventure and wanderlust. Considering the infertile lands of mainland Greece, as well as its domestic political conflicts between various city states, it was also a matter of sheer necessity. Homer's opus about the legendary journeys of Odysseus was more than fiction. His verses were, in fact, the early Greek voyages made legend.

Paestum was once famous for its roses. Flowering twice a year, for the longest time they were the city's most important export item. The rose petal oils were used in the production of perfumes and also added to wine. A stone press used for extracting rose oil has survived in the ruins of a shop located on the northern side of the forum. The collapse of the Western Roman Empire also heralded the collapse of Paestum – literally. The Sele river delta became silted up and malaria spread to such a degree that the local population chose to retreat into the nearby hills. It is true that the Athenian temple was converted into an early Christian church, and the city even became a bishopric in the 5th century, but Saracen attacks from the 9th century onwards made the coastal region uninhabitable. In the 11th century, the Norman Duke Robert Guiscard authorized the plunder of Paestum's ruins for use in the construction of the cathedral at Salerno, and then it fell into a kind of Sleeping Beauty slumber for almost a thousand years. It was only after the canals were laid to dry out the Sele delta and the malaria mosquito had been successfully eradicated in the 1920s and 1930s that the inhabitants of Capaccio gradually returned to live near the ruins.

◄ The roses of Paestum

The »rediscovery« of ancient Paestum

The modern SS 18 was originally built in 1740, during the rule of Charles III, to connect Naples with Calabria, which was totally isolated until then. This »Strada delle Calabrie« became one of the kingdom's most important long-distance routes. By chance, it also connected Herculaneum, Pompeii and Paestum: the most significant archaeological ruins in Campania. Via Magna Graecia, which runs parallel to the temples, was built in 1829; it not only cut through the Roman city but also destroyed parts of the amphitheatre. Nevertheless, Paestum was a favourite destination of Grand Tour travellers – even before the lost cities of Vesuvius – not least because of the imaginative engravings by **Giovanni Battista Piranesis**.

? DID YOU KNOW ...?

- In 1740, Charles III's court architect Ferdinando Sanfelice suggested the temples at Paestum ought to be demolished, so their stones and columns might be used to build the Palace of Capodimonte in Naples. »Tutta la quantità di pietre necessaria ...«, he wrote to the king, who thankfully failed to agree to the most beautiful temples of Magna Graecia being turned into a quarry.

20th-century Paestum

In September 1943, Allied troops landed at the Gulf of Salerno and stepped onto what were then the entirely untouched beaches of Paestum. These days, the area of the local Capaccio-Paestum community is characterized by tourism as well as by agriculture. Possibly the best mozzarella in Italy is produced here: **mozzarella di bufala** is made from the milk of water buffaloes, which are emblematic of the local countryside. The small bar next to the entrance to the museum is not only worth visiting for its selection of ice creams; the 20th-century photographs also show the temples during the fascist era,

◄ The best mozzarella

when they were used to stage historical festivals, and during the period when the Allied soldiers arrived here. The temples were added to the **UNESCO World Heritage list in 1998**.

Most recent restoration work

Major restoration work began on the temples after they were added to the UNESCO World Heritage list. The impressive monuments are built of porous shell limestone that has become very brittle after 2500 years of existence. Chemical and structural analysis led to a major restoration project, which at a cost of 25 million euros has now ensured the survival of this unique site.

VISITING PAESTUM

Buffalo at Vannulo farm

INFORMATION

AAST
Via Magna Graecia 889,
84063 Paestum,
Tel. 08 28 81 10 16, fax 08 28 72 23 22
www.infopaestum.it, www.paestum.it.
Friendly information service right by the Archaeological Museum, which also has information on nearby Cilento.

GOOD TO KNOW

Transport
Buses: hourly SITA and CSTP buses to and from Salerno/Piazza della Concordia; CSTP buses continue on into Cilento via Agropoli to Santa Maria di Castellabate, San Marco di Castellabate, Acciaroli and Pioppi (tickets available at Paestum, in the Anna bar; bus schedules also available from AAST).
Trains: regional trains to and from Salerno stop at Stazione F.S. Capaccio-Roccadaspide, from where a taxi or bus will take you to the ruins about 3km/2mi away. Local trains also stop at the Stazione F.S. Paestum, which is 10 minutes walk from the temples (schedules are published in the daily press and are also available from AAST).

Mozzarella
The organic sales outlet Tenuta Vannulo (Via G. Galilei 10, Capaccio Scalo, tel. 08 28 72 47 65; www.vannulo.it) lies alongside the route SS 18 (km 93), a short drive north of Paestum. The freshly »pulled« moz-

zarella di bufala sells out fast every day, and the bar serves delicious ice cream and yogurt made of buffalo's milk.

Sport and outdoors
Paestum overlooks the dunes of a long beach with many beach sections open to the public. The recommended Lido Maremirtilli with camper van parking also lies between Paestum and Agropoli (Linora di Paestum–Capaccio, tel. & fax 08 28 72 23 28; www.maremirtilli.it). The Gorga family also runs the top-class rural tourism business of Il Cannito (►below).

EVENTS

Festa della Madonna del Granato: the ancient rites of Paestum live on in Catholic guise. Pilgrims travel to venerate the Virgin Mary, who holds a pomegranate in her hand, just as Hera once did, on 2 May and 15 August each year. The shrine to the Madonna del Granato stands level with the Belvedere overlooking the Sele plain (side road off route SP 13, shortly before Capaccio).

WHERE TO EAT

► Expensive

① *Nettuno*
Via Nettuno 2
Tel. 08 28 81 10 28
www.ristorantenettuno.it; closed Mon, open only midday
This exquisite restaurant with a view of the temple has been open since the 1920s. It also serves quick and moderately priced menus.

► Moderate

② *Museo*
Via Magna Graecia 921
Tel. 08 28 81 11 35
www.ristorantemuseo.it
Closed Mon; open only midday
Practically historic. Good solid cooking at decent prices.

Capaccio Scalo · ③ *La Pergola*
Via Magna Graecia 1
Tel. 08 28 72 33 77; closed Mon.
Family-run, highly praised establishment with a large garden, specializing in slow cooking, located in the modern part of town, 3.5km/2mi north of Paestum.

► Inexpensive

④ *La Fattoria del Casaro*
Via Licinella 5
Tel. 08 28 72 27 04
www.lafattoriadelcasaro.it
Every morning the caseificio prepares fresh mozzarella, which is sold in the courtyard shop along with other products. Buy it there or try it in the small restaurant attached. The entrance is near to the Ristorante Nettuno.

WHERE TO STAY

► Luxury

Capaccio · ① *Il Cannito*
Via Cannito; tel. 0 82 81 96 22 77
mobile no. 33 33 65 23 24
www.ilcannito.com.
A 15ha/37ac property surrounded by fragrant Mediterranean scrubland, where fine materials and relaxed luxury combine with views of Capri. Meals can be ordered. The temples of Paestum and Cilento's beaches and mountains are all easily reached by car. Very hospitable owner.

► Mid-range

② *Calypso Art Hotel*
Via Mantegna 63
Tel. 08 28 81 10 31
www.calypsohotel.com
March–end Oct. A charming beach hotel that also offers some simple

cheaper rooms, with a good restaurant serving Cilentan cuisine and macrobiotic dishes. 2km/1mi south of the Torre di Paestum. The owners are also full of helpful tips.

③ ***Villa Rita***
Via Nettuno 5
Tel. & fax 08 28 81 10 81;
www.hotelvillarita.it; March–end Oct.
Quiet family hotel in a large park with swimming pool, just a few steps from the archaeological site. The Pisani family also run the recommended Ristorante Nettuno, with views of the temples, in the immediate vicinity.

► **Budget**
Belizzi ·
④ ***Agriturismo La Morella***
Via Fosso Stazione 3
Tel. & fax 0 82 85 10 08
Mobile no. 33 87 15 99 58
www.la-morella.it
A typical masseria on the Sele river plain, with quiet, spacious apartments and attractive guest rooms in the main farmhouse. Fabio Miletto and his wife Anette also rear buffaloes. Good home-cooking available, with ingredients from their own organic garden. About 15km/9mi north of Paestum; directions available on the website.

✶✶ Zona Archeologica di Paestum

Opening hours: daily 9am to one hour before sunset

One of the two entrances to the archaeological site is diagonally opposite the museum. Take a stroll from there along Via Sacra to the Porta della Giustizia. Also impressive, though somewhat dangerous due to the traffic, is a walk along the ancient city wall.

City wall

The 4750m/5200yd-long city wall predominantly dates from Lucanian and Roman times, although its extent is no doubt based on the original Greek foundation of Poseidonia. Today, the **cinta muraria** contains an area of 120ha/300ac, of which only 20ha/50ac are in state ownership. The four city gates date from the early 3rd century BC, when Poseidonia became the Roman Paestum. The city's necropoli were located along the surrounding roads. The most significant tombs found so far are exhibited in the museum. The Porta Sirena, to the west, is particularly impressive. Its access road now ends at the small Paestum train station.

Porta Sirena ►

Athenian temple of Tempio di Cerere

The site is famous for its three temples that form a perfect illustration of the development of Doric temple construction. The temple to the north is known as the Tempio di Cerere, though it was actually **dedicated to the goddess Athena** and erected in around 520/500 BC. A stylobate substructure measuring 14.50 x 32.9m/47.6 x 108ft supports six pillars at each end and 13 along either side, and its equilibrated design is strongly reminiscent of classical forms. The distances between each pillar are precisely calibrated and the interior of the cella is in perfect harmony with the building as a whole, with

Paestum Map

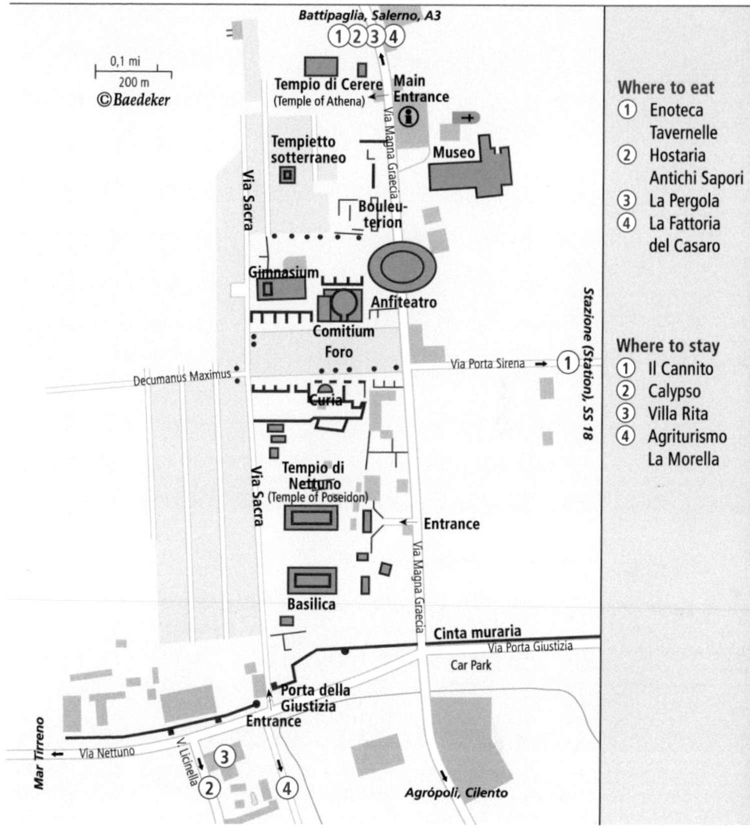

the entasis of the lower columns clearly reduced. The combination of Doric and Ionian columns was an innovation in design done for the first time here in the pronaos (or antechamber) to the sacred interior. Traces of paint indicate that the stucco-covered columns were white, but that the triglyphs were painted blue. The Greek **agora**, the economic and political centre of Poseidonia, was located to the north of the Athena Temple, and two buildings from that era were revealed during excavation work in the 20th century. The circular **Ekklesiasterion** (open-air theatre) was set straight into the rocky ground in around 480/70 BC. Public meetings (ekklesia in Greek) were held here. The highest ruler of the city had dominion over up to 15,000 full citizens. When Poseidonia was taken over by the Romans, the function of this construction became obsolete; it was filled in and a small shrine was placed here instead.

THE DORIC TEMPLE

»The pillar'd shaft, the very triglyph rings; Yea, I believe that the whole temple sings!« Thus wrote Goethe in his *Faust II*, a the lines were probably inspired by the Doric temples at Paestum, which he visited in March 1787.

And yet, in his *Italian Journey*, he had described just these temples, with their »obstruse, conical, closely set masses of columns«, as »oppressive, even horrible«. Just like Goethe in his day, there are plenty of modern visitors who also find the **stocky nature** of the Doric architecture at Paestum unappealing. It fails to live up to the idea of classical antiquity as represented by the austere elegance of Ionic column order or by the acanthus vine-clad Corinthian capitals.

The origins for the design of ancient hall temples is lost in the mists of time. Almost no traces remain of the first constructions built of wood, and it was only with the arrival of the Indo-Germanic tribe of Dorians, who settled the Peloponnese from the 8th century BC, that the age-old wood temple design with surrounding columns was replaced with stone versions. This occurred during the building boom of the 6th century BC.

Origins of Occidental architecture

The **»discovery of the column«** as main support for an architrave, gable, and tiled roof was as much a key moment in architectural history as the much later invention of the dome. Thus the Doric temple marks the beginning of an aesthetic and technical encounter with constructed spaces: in other words, with architecture (Greek arché = beginning; techné

Doric column order

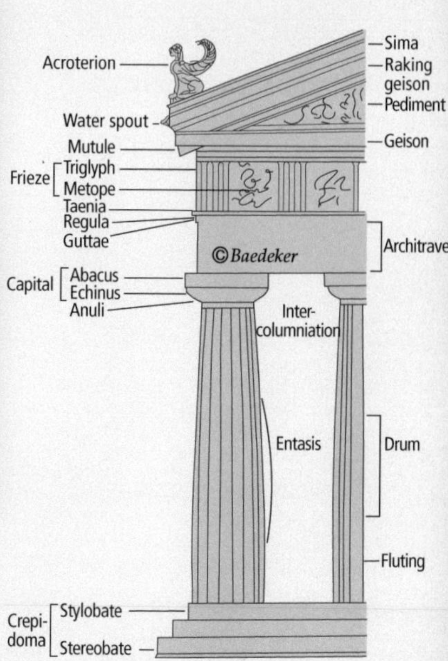

= art, craft). The architectural stylistic canon developed during antiquity formed the guiding principle for the construction of public and prestigious buildings in particular right up until the 19th century.

Construction of a Doric temple

Despite the complexity of column orders and architectural challenges such as the **Doric corner conflict**, the design of a Doric temple is almost simple. A foundation, the **stereobate**, supports the rectangular **stylobat**, whose dimensions decide the size of the temple to be built. The triple-stepped **krepis** rests on the stylobat, which in turn supports the columns which, in Doric temple construction at least, were still built without a base. A notable feature of these crenulated columns, made from so-called barrels, is their **entasis**: just that bulge that Goethe described as cone-like. This feature is particularly prominent in the basilica at Paestum. The 6.45m/21ft-high columns have a base diameter of 1.45m/4ft 9in, which reduces down to just 0.98m/3ft 3in at the top. Because of this feature, the columns of the basilica appear to be sinking under the load they are meant to support.

The **capitals**, designed as a square plate formed by the anuli, echinus, and abacus look a lot like squashed pillows. Yet this intended depression of the supporting elements was designed to make the temple seem less static, and instead almost organic. The effect is further reinforced by the open rows of columns that underline the monumentality of the building. The columns support the unadorned

The Temple of Poseidon, the most recent building among the Trias, exhibits classical construction principles

Colour and antiquity

The European classical era reinterpreted Greco-Roman antiquity in shining white. Yet both the original temples and their sculptures were painted. A few traces of paint were found during recent restoration work of the Temple of Athena, for example. Being the most important buildings for a Greek city's religious and public life, the temples were also designed to display Paestum's might and wealth. The Greek colonists in southern Italy were particularly successful at maintaining their cultural identity by recreating their native architectural customs. Thus the temples of Poseidonia were glowing emblems of the city, their bright colours easily visible from far out at sea.

architrave on which rests the frieze with its alternating plain **triglyphs** and elaborate relief slabs. The **metopes**, **geisons** and **diagonal geison** frame the triangular gable, frequently decorated with sculptures.

The inner sanctum of the temple contained the cella: an enclosed room in which the temple treasure and statue to the temple god was kept. The altar used for offerings was always located outside the building, at a respectful distance from the main façade.

Heroon

The **spiritual centre** of the Greek polis was the heroon, located to the west of the agora. This sacred shrine, facing east just like the temples, was once covered by a rounded earth mound. It was not a grave but rather the place where the founder of the mother city Sybaris was venerated. During Roman times, this feature also lost its function, and the small temple was no longer used for any rituals. A rectangular exterior wall was built, whose eastern side covered the shrine's altar. The heroon was excavated in 1954, when archaeologists found eight honey-filled bronze containers – untouched for 2500 years – alongside an Attican amphora and five iron spears with leather handles (now in the museum).

Shrine to Fortuna Virilis

Shortly before the Roman forum lies a 47 x 21m/154 x 69ft pool that served as the shrine for the fertility cult associated with Fortuna Virilis. During the festival, the city's women took ritual communal baths with a statue of the goddess Venus. The strange posts constructed in the western part of the pool probably supported wooden buildings. The pool, too, was filled in and built over during the Roman era.

Forum, amphitheatre

Just how profound the change from Greek city to Roman colony was is clearly demonstrated by the Roman forum. An area of 60 x 150m/645 x 1614ft in the middle of the Greek city was simply levelled and converted into the forum, surrounded by the most important public buildings. A porticus with Doric columns surrounded the square, which was used for commercial stalls. A capital temple and the circular comitium (place of Roman public meetings) was also constructed along the northern side of the forum. Alongside the south side was the macellum (market hall) and the curia (municipal court). A notable feature in the northeastern corner of the forum is the amphitheatre, which was constructed in the 1st century BC and remodelled in the first century AD. A few seating rows and the tunnel through which the animals entered the arena survive. The road built in 1829 bisected the amphitheatre.

Tempio di Nettuno, Temple of Poseidon

The **most recently constructed of the three Greek temples** is the Temple of Poseidon, located to the south of the forum. Built around 470/50 BC, numerous votive gifts unearthed here prove that the temple was not actually dedicated to Poseidon but to the goddess Hera. The stylobat (24.30 x 59.9m/79.7 x 196.5ft) supports six columns at each end and 14 along each side. Parts of the cella have survived well and, compared to the basilica next door, the incredible technical advances made by Greek builders is remarkable. The proportions of the temple are perfectly calibrated and its mighty size is nevertheless beautifully balanced. A **miraculous achievement of classical architecture**, the temple was built shortly before the construction of the Temple of Zeus in Olympia and served as the stylistic example for Greco-Roman temple building in southern Italy.

Basilica, Temple of Hera

The chunky pillars of the basilica seem rather clumsy in comparison. Located in the southern section of the excavation site, almost by the city wall, this was Paestum's first temple, constructed in 550 BC. It was one of the earliest stone buildings erected for ritual purposes in Greek antiquity and only became known as a basilica in the 18th century. Archaeological finds prove that this temple was also dedicated to the goddess Hera. It has nine columns at either end and 18 along each side, set on a stylobat of 24.5 x 54.3m /80.3 x 178.1ft.

Residental districts of antiquity

A stroll around the ancient residential area to the west of Via Sacra is particularly rewarding because although most of the buildings are reduced to their foundations, there are beautiful floor mosaics to be found in amongst the undergrowth of weeds. Occasionally, there is the marble basin (impulvium) of an atrium to be found. Take a look at the pool of the **Casa con Piscina**, whose proportions alone hint at the lost magnificence of this Roman villa. The strictly linear box-shape design of the streets goes back to the Greek foundation of a colony here. Only a fraction of the settlement has been excavated, however. The east-west axis of the old main road, in the direction of the Porta Marina, now ends in fields.

★★ Museo Archeologico

Opening hours: daily 9am–6.30pm; closed every 1st and 3rd Mon of the month

All archaeological finds discovered in recent decades are exhibited in the Archaeological Museum, which was built next to the excavation site in 1952. The famous metopes (stone relief slabs) from the temple of the **Santuario di Hera Argiva** are exhibited on the ground floor next to the 18th century prints and designs. The shrine to Hera, located 8km/5mi from Paestum, was excavated and studied in the 1930s and the historic metopes portray heroic episodes from the life of Heracles. The bronze containers filled with honey found in the heroon are also on the ground floor. Meanwhile, numerous votives dedicated to Hera (many of them small clay figurines) prove how significant this goddess was for the people of Greek Poseidonia. A striking contrast can be noted between the heavily armed warriors portrayed in the paintings of Lucanian tombs and the joyous mythological scenes on Greek ceramics and on the so-called Tomb of the Diver. The **Tomb of the Diver** was discovered at the southern edge of the city in 1968. A rare example of Greek tomb painting, it is today one of the most popular attractions at the Archaeological Museum. The tomb's paintings, which have been dated to 480/470 BC, portray a so-called **symposium**: this sociable drinking session took place after a festive meal and was the exclusive privilege of men.

? DID YOU KNOW ...?

- A popular game of skill during antiquity was known as kottabos: accompanied by the sounds of lyrical music, men reclining on benches were challenged to flick the last drop of wine from their drinking cups into a bowl placed in the middle of the room (photo p.73).

The departed on his way to the other world (detail from the Tomb of the Diver)

The light-hearted erotic scenes were intended to lighten up the afterlife. The athletic youth portrayed on the tomb cover is diving off a pillar into the water (photo p.40): the pillar of Hercules symbolizes the extent of the inhabited world, as it was known then, surrounded by the oceanus (the ocean). Thus the tuffatore (diver) in this enchanting picture is diving into the beyond without any sense of fear of death, which is simply a gateway from one world to another. The museum's first floor exhibits items relating to Roman Paestum, including sculptures, architectural fragments, and finds from Roman tombs.

✶ ✶ ◂ La Tomba del Tuffatore

Around Paestum

Santuario di Hera Argiva

The ancient historians **Strabo** and **Pliny the Elder** mention the so-called Santuario di Hera Argiva in their writings. Located 8km/5mi from Paestum, at the mouth of the river Sele, its founding is credited to Jason, the legendary leader of the Argonauts. Archaeologists inspired by these literary sources regarding the shrine began excavating there in 1934, discovering that there was indeed truth in the ancient sources. Their work confirmed that colonists from Sybaris first settled at the mouth of the river Sele, constructing two temples before moving on to found Poseidonia. There is virtually nothing of the former settlement to see above ground, though in ground that was still marshy then archaeologists did find a number of **carved metopes**, which are now considered among the finest examples of their kind surviving from Greek antiquity. The originals are now exhibited at the Archaeological Museum at Paestum, but a **multi-media exhibition** on the history of this sacred spot at the Museo Narrante del Santuario di Hera Argiva is also worth seeing. Computer-animated films recreate the heroon and transport the viewer into the legendary world of Heracles (Masseria Procuriali, Via Barizzo Foce Sele 29; Tue–Sat 9am–4pm).

Museo Narrante ►

Capaccio

Capaccio lies at an altitude of 419m/1374ft in the **Monti Alburni** and is the administrative centre for the district of the same name, which also includes Paestum and numerous other small settlements. The hills around here gave refuge to the remaining population of Poseidonia when they fled from the combined threat of malaria and Saracen attacks in the 9th/10th century. A few years ago Capaccio developed a museum dedicated to the **Grand Tour** which explores the obsession with the Bay of Naples. Old prints, maps and drawings document the phenomenon that drew generations of Italy fans to the landscapes and historic ruins here. Pride of place goes to the painting by the German artist Franz Ludwig Catel (1778 – 1856), whose *Veduta di Paestum con i templi* (1838) shows the temples glowing during sunset in the middle of a marshy landscape (Museo Paestum nei Percorsi del Grand Tour, Piazza Vittorio Veneto; Oct–May Tue–Sat 9am–1pm, 3pm–6pm, Sun 9am–1pm, June–Sept Tue–Sat 9am–1pm, 4pm–8pm, Sun 9am–1pm; opening times are subject to change. Check the latest information at www.comune.capaccio.sa.it).

Museo Paestum nei Percorsi del Grand Tour ►

! *Baedeker* TIP

Cilento aktiv

Ob zu Fuß, auf dem Rad, zu Pferd, mit dem Kajak, Gleitschirm oder am Meer: Der handliche Führer »Cilento aktiv – mit Costa di Maratea« (R. Mankau Verlag, Murnau 2007, www.cilento-aktiv.info) von Peter Amann ist eine Einladung, den Cilento sportlich zu entdecken (selbst kulinarische Adressen zur Stärkung fehlen nicht).

✶✶ Cilento

The landscape of the Cilento region, in the southeast of Salerno province, is still something of an insider tip. Of course, its beautiful and occasionally wild coast, the turquoise sea, the sweeping beaches and harbour towns have long been discovered by tourists, but it remains free of the faceless apartment blocks and high-rise hotels seen elsewhere. The surprisingly green interior, meanwhile, contains forested mountains and traditional villages that still live by the old customs.

Cilento landscape

The Cilentan coast stretches almost 100km/62mi from the Gulf of Salerno to the Gulf of Policastro. Inland, the summits of the Monte Alburni characterize the landscape, some reaching as high as 1750m/

VISITING CILENTO

INFORMATION

Parco Nazionale del Cilento e Vallo di Diano
Via Palumbo 16 (Palazzo Mainenti)
84078 Vallo della Lucania, tel. 09 74 71 99 11, fax 0 97 47 19 92 17; www.cilentodiano.it

GOOD TO KNOW

Transport

Buses · Trains · Ferries: SITA buses travel from Salerno via Capaccio Scalo and Paestum to Agropoli; CSTP buses from Salerno go to Paestum, Agropoli, S. Maria di Castellabate, Acciaroli and Pollica. The railway line between Naples, Salerno and Reggio di Calabria follows the Cilento coast, although train stations are frequently located outside towns. The same goes for the rural Battipaglia-Lagonegro railway route that travels through the Vallo di Diano. A more convenient option is to travel by train as far as Salerno or Agropoli and then continue by bus. The Metro del Mare (www. metrodelmare.com; beginning of June to end of Sept) ferries connect the harbours of Cilento with Salerno, the Amalfi Coast, and the Bay of Naples.

Shopping

Bufalina
Corso Matarazzo 155
Santa Maria di Castellabate, tel. 09 74 96 13 56; closed Sun morning.
Well-stocked gourmet shop specializing in Cilento's products.

De Conciliis
Località Querce 1
Prignano Cilento (SS 18 exit Prignano), tel. & fax 09 74 83 10 90
www.viticoltorideconciliis.it
Mon–Fri 9am–1.30pm, 2pm–5pm.
This award-winning family business specializes in the autochtone grape varieties of the Cilento region, focusing on quality rather than quantity.

Family-friendly beach at Marina di Camerota

Sport and outdoors
Water sports: family-friendly beaches are found at Santa Maria di Castellabate, Ascea, Palinuro and Marina di Camerota. The best diving sites are off Punta Licosa, by the Capo Palinuro, and along the Costa degli Infreschi, where there are also diving schools.
The Cilento region is a ***hiker's paradise*** and there is plenty of local information on outfits offering guided tours.

EVENTS

Velia Teatro: Italian-language Greek and Roman comedies are performed in the Velia archaeological zone from the beginning of August to the beginning of September. (information c/o Pro Loco di Ascea, tel. 09 74 97 22 30; www.asceaturis mo.it; www.velia teatro.com).

WHERE TO EAT

► Expensive

Santa Maria di Castellabate · La Taverna del Pescatore
Via Lamia 1,
Tel. 09 74 96 82 93
Closed Mon and Dec–March.
The chic but rustic ambience here is in perfect harmony with the dishes served: even a simple plate of fried squid or cheese-filled sardines are veritable works of art.

► Moderate

Ogliastro Marina · Da Carmine
Via Provinciale
Tel. 09 74 96 30 23; open March–Oct.
Outstanding fish dishes have been served here since 1965, yet the prices are acceptable. Your chosen fish can be grilled, sautéed or »all'acqua pazza«. The terrace is right by the beach, and there is also a small guesthouse attached.

► Inexpensive

San Mauro Cilento · Al Frantoio
Casal Sottano
Tel. 09 74 90 32 43
Daily from June–Sept, and weekends only at other times.
The establishment's advertising slogan is »Laboratorio di Ricerca della Cucina del Cilento Antico« and it is part of the Cooperativa Agricola Nuovo Cilento, which produces olive oil. A large dining hall with wood tables is the setting for traditional country cooking served at very fair prices.

Pioppi · La Caupona
Via Caracciolo
Tel. 09 74 90 52 51
Weekends only mid-Sep–mid-June
Simple and tasty Cilento cooking that inspired the American food scientist Ancel Keys to develop his »dieta mediterranea« in the 1960s. The daily fish catch is on the menu, as are wild vegetables in spring.

WHERE TO STAY

► Luxury

Santa Maria di Castellabate Villa Sirio
Via Lungomare De Simone 15
Tel. 09 74 96 01 62, www.villasirio.it
April–end of Oct
Charming former aristocratic home on the Lungomare. Stylish rooms and sea views (for a supplement). Good restaurant; during summer tables available on the wood veranda overlooking the sea.

► Mid-range

San Marco di Castellabate · Hermitage
Via Catarozza
Tel. 09 74 96 66 18
www.hermitage.it
Quality hotel in a peaceful and elegantly restored farmhouse, about one

mile from the sea. Views of the Mediterranean from the hillside location, swimming pool and tennis court, as well as good cuisine.

Santa Maria di Castellabate · Grand Hotel Santa Maria
Via Velia 15
Tel. & fax 09 74 96 10 01
www.grandhotelsantamaria.it
April–Oct
A recently modernized hotel, originally built in the 1970s, located at a most beautiful section of beach at Santa Maria. The historic centre of the town is just a short walk away. The rooms are spacious and most have sea views. The restaurant serves decent regional home cooking and the breakfast buffet is generous.

Rofrano · Il Centauro
Località Viggiano
Tel. & fax 09 74 98 55 81
www.centaurohotel.com
Modern, family-run hotel and restaurant on the slopes of Monte Centaurino. Popular with the locals for family celebrations. The location is ideal, halfway between the coast and the nature reserve (not far from the SS 18).

► Budget

Pollica-Cannicchio · Agriturismo Il Mulino
Località Monaco
Tel. 34 79 17 41 53 (mobile phone)
www.ilmulinoagriturismo.com.
Housed in a former olive mill, there are five rooms at this friendly agriturismo outfit located 6km/4mi from the seaside resort of Acciaroli. Luisa Bassallo is in charge of the kitchen and uses home-grown ingredients. The fish are caught by her husband.

Contrada Galdo · Terra Nostra
Tel. 33 34 56 02 87 (mobile phone);
www.agriturismoterranostra.it.
?tlsb =-0.03?>This rural tourism establishment alongside the SS 116 between Corleto Monforte and Bellosguardo is a good base for exploring the interior of Cilento. Simple rooms with modern bathrooms. The restaurant serves meals using home-grown organic vegetables.

Baedeker recommendation

Castellabate · Residenz San Leo
Contrada San Leo, Tel. 0049 30 812 01 47
www.cilentissimo.de
Birte Kokocinsky has completely renovated a fieldstone farmhouse and the outbuildings with many good ideas and good taste. Some of the comfortable apartments can be combined for use by families or groups. There is also a view of the sea and a large orchard and vegetable garden where everyone can help himself. The baker Maurizio delivers fresh rolls for breakfast. The neighbour Anna De Marco is always willing to fill up the fridge before arrival.

5742ft. Large sections are protected areas, such as the **Parco Nazionale del Cilento e Vallo di Diano**) and belong to the UNESCO Natural Heritage. The »soft« tourism promoted here, as well as the isolated nature of this region, ensured that the rampant building speculation of the 1960s was unable to do its worst here, unlike in other parts of Campania. Only the once beautiful beaches at the mouth of the river Sele, near Paestum, have lost something of their original appeal.

Seaside resorts
Agropoli ►

Lively Agropoli is the largest resort along the Cilento coast, with a population of around 20,000. It is particularly popular with Neapolitans, especially during the months of July and August, when the historic little walled town gets very busy. It is much quieter a little way to the south, along the coastal route of SS 267. A pretty place to stop off is the 278m/254ft-high Castellabate, which offers beautiful views across Cilento and picturesque alleyways and terraces to explore. The historic centre has been well maintained and this picture-postcard idyll is well and truly on the tourist map. The locals have retreated to the towns by the sea, such as **Santa Maria** and **San Marco di Castellabate**.

✶
Castellabate ►

✶
Velia

The ruined city of Velia, located about 40km/25mi south of Paestum near the seaside resort of **Marina di Ascea**, is one of the lesser known archaeological sites in Campania. The town was founded as Elea by Phocaic Greeks in around 540 BC on a mountain saddle that was once right by the sea. It developed into a thriving trading centre within just two centuries. Always loyal to Rome, Elea became a major southern Italian military post in the service of the fight against Carthage during the Second Punic War (216 BC). The town was elevated to a municipium in 88 BC and renamed Velia. Its decline came after the first century AD, when trade routes moved and long-distance trade was shipped via the port at Puteoli (Pozzuoli) and the new port at Ostia, near Rome. In addition, the geography of the coast changed, so that the town gradually became cut off from the sea. By the time of late antiquity, Velia was reduced to a fishing village and it was finally abandoned by its last inhabitants in the 9th century. The rediscovery Velia, which was referred to in ancient literary sources, happened by accident during the construction of the railway line between Naples and Reggia di Calabria. Archaeological excavations began in the 1920s and continue to this day. During antiquity, Velia achieved renown for the **Eleatic philosophical school** founded by the philosopher **Parmenides** in around 515–445.

Tour ►

Archaeologists believe a necropolis exists under the visitor's car park, which is due to be excavated in the near future. The foundations of buildings in what has been identified as the port area can be seen shortly after the main entrance and before reaching the city walls. The original harbour was northwest of the **Porta Marina**, and the sea defences and quay once washed by the tides are now half submerged in the ground. The best preserved sections are of foundations and walls of **Greek homes**, whose walls made of rocks were once covered in plaster. Compared to the Roman brickwork, they seem almost archaic. Also worth seeing is the Roman bath house dating from the 2nd century AD.

The **Porta Rosa**, discovered in 1964, is an impressive construction and dates from the 4th century BC. An attractive footpath leads up to the acropolis of the original Greek settlement. Once Elea had become an important and wealthy trading town (as early as the 5th

Velia Map

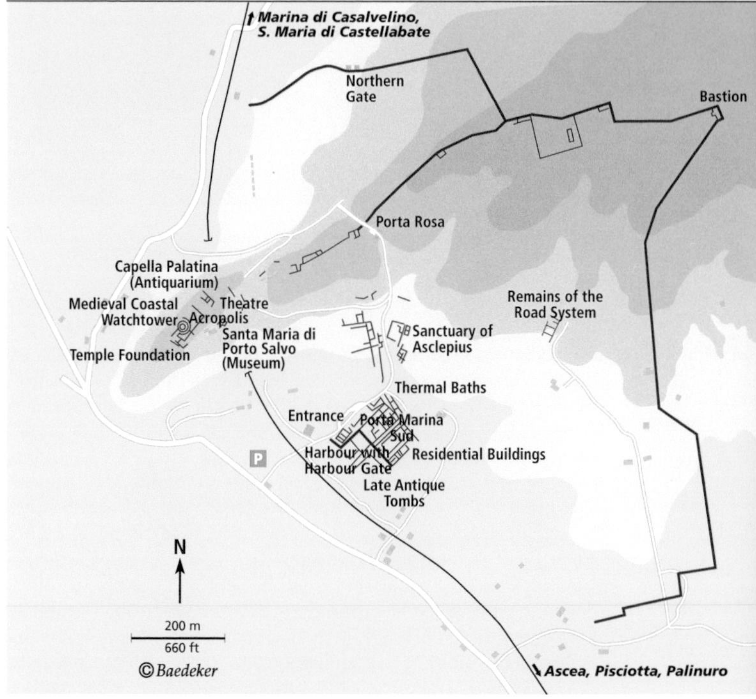

century BC), the town was extended and the acropolis entirely rebuilt. Public buildings and shrines once surrounded it, but the only feature surviving today is the foundation of the Ionic temple. A 13th-century defensive bastion was built over it, using much of the ancient material from earlier settlement periods.

✶ **Palinuro**

Palinuro, to the southwest of Velia, is one of the prettiest towns in Cilento. It is popular for its beaches, among other things. The town is named after the legendary captain working for Aeneas who, according to Virgil, was shipwrecked at the cape here. The attractions of Palinuro include the many **natural grottoes**, such as the Grotta Azzurra and the **Grotta del Sangue**, which can be explored during boat tours. The Cilento coast ends impressively with the Gulf of Policastro, which is reached after passing **Marina di Camerota**, a very popular seaside resort with a beach that almost reaches as far as Palinura.

◄ Marina di Camerota

Inland

The interior of the Cilento region is among the most ancient inhabited areas of Italy. Proof of this lies in the Stone Age bone and

San Giovanni a Piro in Cilento

tool finds discovered in the **caves of the interior**. It is easy to pay a visit to two especially beautiful caves, the **Grotta dell'Angelo** (also called Grotto di Pertosa; follow signs after exits Petina or Polla, off the A 3; www.grottedellangelo.sa.it; April–Oct daily 9am–7pm, November–March 10am–4pm) and the **Grotta di Castelcivita** near Controne (www.grottedicastelcivita.com; guided tours only, mid-March–September daily 10.30, noon, 1.30pm, 3pm, 4.30pm, 6pm; October–mid-March 10.30am, noon, 1.30pm, 3pm). The temperature inside the caves is a constant 16°C/60.8°F throughout the year. A recommended option is to combine a visit to the caves with a scenic drive through the Cilento region: take the SS 166 shortly beyond Paestum to Roccadaspide, then leave it and head in the direction of Controne. After visiting the cave there, the tour continues north into the 600m/1969ft-high **Sicignano degli Alburni** mountains as far as Petina, before descending into the Tanagro valley and to the cave at Pertosa. The SS 166 can then be rejoined via Polla, with its medieval town centre. The town is also the northern gateway to the Vallo di Diano. Beyond the rocky hilltop village of **Corleto Monforte**/ the road continues to **Sant'Angelo a Fasanella**, where the cave of Grotta di San Michele (below the village) was used as a church during the Middle Ages. The village of **Roscigno Vecchio**, south of the SS 166, is a photogenic museum that had to be abandoned by its inhabitants in the early 20th century due to the persistent risk of landslides. They founded a new village of the same name just a short drive higher up. Soon the mountain village of Laurino is reached. The pilgrimage site here for venerating the **Madonna della Neve** can only be reached on foot. A more significant sacred site, however, is the »Holy Mountain« (also known as Monte Gelbison) with its pilgrimage church of **Madonna di Novi Velia**, set at an elevation of 1705m/5594ft. A swift return to Paestum can then be made by returning to the SS 18 via the pretty town of **Vallo della Lucania**. Those wishing to return to the sea should take the SS 447a, a beautiful mountain road that heads south. A detour can be taken from Polla to **Teggiano**. A strategically located settlement that already existed during antiquity, it has maintained its medieval aspect. The route continues to Certosa di San Lorenzo.

✶ ✶ Spectacular caves ▶

Located near the small town of Padula (exit Padula from the A3), Certosa di San Lorenzo is the largest monastic complex in Italy. It was built in 1306 for the Carthusians, who always valued earthly glory as highly as that of heaven. They chose the **Vallo di Diano** in northeastern Cilento because they owned great swathes of land there and, over the course of several centuries, they used their considerable wealth and influence to create this outstanding religious centre, whose architectural style today is very much characterized by the Baroque era. In 1860 the monastery was taken over by the state, which turned it into a cultural centre in 1957. Today, this Carthusian monument is on the UNESCO World Heritage list and a venue for **exhibiting contemporary art**. Many of the works exhibited are by internationally renowned artists, and the pieces have been created specifically for the Certosa.

★ **Certosa di San Lorenzo**

In addition, the **Museo Archeologico di Lucania Occidentale** exhibits archaeological finds from the Roman province of Lucania (daily 9am–7.30pm). The entrance to the Certosa leads into a grand courtyard, with the main building immediately opposite. The magnificent façade dates from around 1720, and the statues between the pillars of the ground floor are of saints Peter, Paul, Bruno and Laurence. Three small cloisters are surrounded by the former apartment for the prior, as well as the refectory, library, and the monastery church. Behind the church stands the **world's largest cloister** (90 x 130m/295 x 426ft), where two storeys lined by arcades once led to the monks' cells. Each cell has its own living and working space plus a small garden, and was intended to live up to the ideal of a hermitage. Yet the Certosa di San Lorenzo was also remodelled in the most extravagant Baroque style during the 17th and 18th centuries, and the magnificent staircase and interior décor of the monastery church remain to this day.

★★ Pompeii

E 4

Province: Napoli
Population: 26,000
Altitude: 16m/52ft

There is probably nowhere else on earth that continues to move its visitors like Pompeii, the ancient city destroyed during a natural disaster that conserved it under a deep layer of volcanic ash. For almost 250 years now, it has provided the great memento mori (remember you shall die) experience of every trip to Italy. When it was rediscovered and excavated for the first time in 1748, it caused a sensation throughout Europe. Its fascination has not waned, even though what visitors see today is merely a fraction of the ruins discovered by the first archaeologists working here.

History of the City

Building history

The modern visitor simply sees ancient buildings, but Pompeii actually had a complex architectural history that went back 700 years by the time it was destroyed. To the surprise of many, Pompeii is not a »sunken« city, but lies on a high plateau, naturally formed by pre-historic lava streams. Nor was the city founded by the Romans; rather it was founded by the Italian Oscan people. Etruscan and Greek influences, and Samnite conquest, in particular, informed the early development of Pompeii, and it was only after the 3rd century BC that Romans were present in Campania. During the Second Punic War, Pompeii was one of the few Campanian cities to remain loyal to Rome, and it was rewarded with a period of great expansion once Hannibal had been defeated. Pompeii and its two ports developed into a major trading centre for towns of the interior, such as Nola or Nuceria. In 80 BC, Pompeii was elevated to the status of a Roman colony. It was renamed Colonia Cornelia Veneria Pompeiana and the Samnite upper classes lost their influence. Once Roman war veterans began to settle here, Pompeii's population increased to between ten and twelve thousand. An additional 5000 people lived in the rapidly expanding suburbs and in the many country villas around the city. A busy industrial and service sector emerged, including numerous textile processing businesses and garum wheat producers, which generated the wealth evident in the elaborately decorated houses and the magnificent public buildings.

? DID YOU KNOW ...?

- Ancient Pompeii had no street names. Instead the thoroughfares had symbols. Today's names of the houses, streets and city gates come from the time of the early excavation work. In some cases the original owners are known through the discovery of seals or inscriptions, and these houses could be named accordingly.

◄ Disasters

A huge **earthquake** shook the entire region in AD 62, and the damage to Pompeii and neighbouring Herculaneum were so great that the initial response was to think of permanent evacuation. Thus, the three-day long **eruption of Mount Vesuvius** on 24 August AD 79 buried a city that was still one large building site. The survivors of that catastrophe and the commissioners sent from Rome waded through ash and discovered the volcano had totally changed the geography of the coastline. Only a few decades later, a pine forest was growing over what was once Pompeii. The hill was known as »Civita« for many centuries, in memory of the city buried there.

◄ Rediscovery

The architect Domenico Fontana built a canal that passed very close to the Temple of Isis in 1592, but the finds discovered at that time were not thought significant. It was only several decades after the chance discovery of Herculaneum that, encouraged by the interest of the new Neapolitan royal couple, Charles III and Maria Amalia, systematic excavations of Pompeii were begun. The first spade was

← *Pompeii continues to hold a fascination for visitors*

wielded on 23 March 1748. What was initially a generalized dig resembling nothing so much as grave looting was turned into a scientific archaeological site in the 19th century. Under the management of **Giuseppe Fiorelli**, it was divided into precise regions and housing blocks zoned for excavation. It was also Fiorelli who devised the technique for filling the hollow spaces left by corpses, which have created the deeply moving plaster casts of Pompeian citizens during their sudden deaths. From that time onwards, all frescoes and other items uncovered were left on site, which made it possible for the ancient city to become the famous »window into the past« and to see it in its proper context. **Amedeo Maiuri** was a director of the archaeological site during the 20th century, and his influence was key. The silt hills left from two centuries of excavation, for example, were only carried off in 1954. 500,000 cubic metres of earth had to be removed before the former vista of the city became visible in its entirety. In fact, two fifths of the city still remains buried, but there are no plans for additional excavation work in the near future.

Pompeian houses

Pompeian houses follow a fixed ground plan: domestic and sleeping quarters (cubiculum) are set around a courtyard (atrium) with a pool at its centre (impluvium). Beyond the atrium, immediately opposite the entrance, the visitor looked towards the reception room (tablinum). Essential to any dwelling was also the altar (lararium) in honour of ancestors and house gods. The peristyle (open porch), which was often developed as an elaborate decorative garden, gradually replaced the kitchen garden (hortus) after the 2nd century BC, a result of Hellenistic influence. Wealthy Pompeian citizens also afforded themselves private thermal baths.

Painting at Pompeii

Archaeologists have identified four consecutive stylistic painting eras which, however, are not always clearly defined as separate. In the **First style** (also known as incrustation style), which lasted until the 2nd century BC, blocks of stucco were either painted or framed in colour to give structure to walls and the impression of marble cladding (Casa del Fauno, Casa di Sallustio). In the **Second style** (also known as the architectural style), which lasted from the 2nd century BC to AD 10, perspective architectural painting decorated walls that were designed like stage sets and created illusions of distance (Villa dei Misteri, Villa Oplontis). In the **Third style** (also known as the ornate style), which lasted until AD 62), scenes from the Greek myths were incorporated into architectural painting, and ornamental decoration increased as did the use of colour (Casa del Criptoportico, Villa dei Misteri). The **Fourth style** (also known as the illusionary style) lasted from AD 40 to AD 79. After the earthquake in AD 62, there was an increased demand for new frescoes, so that this style tends to predominate. It is notable for an almost eccentric exuberance, featuring grotesques, garlands and playfully mannerist architectural painting (Casa dei Vettii, Villa Imperiale).

VISITING POMPEII

INFORMATION

AACST
Via Sacra 1, 80045 Pompeii
Tel. 08 18 50 72 55
www.pompeiturismo.it
The municipal tourist information office is located in the centre opposite the pilgrimage church as well as at the main entrance to the excavations, Piazza Porta Marina 12.

Sopraintendenza Archeologica di Pompei
Porta Marina 12, tel. 08 18 57 53 47
www.pompeiisites.org. An information point at the main entrance to Scavi. Free map, and toilets!

GOOD TO KNOW

Transport
By car: A 3, exit Pompei Scavi. A fee paying car park is located near the main Scavi entrance at Viale delle Ginestre and also near the amphitheatre on Piazza Immacolata. ***By bus:*** EAV from Pompei/Piazza Anfiteatro or Porta Marina via Ercolano on Mt Vesuvius as far as Quota mille (the car park is at an elevation of 1000m/3281ft). CSTP bus no. 50 arrives from Salerno. ***By train:*** the best way to reach Pompeii is on the Circumvesuviana suburban train. Get off the Naples-Sorrento line at the Pompei Scavi-Villa Misteri stop; from there walk to the main entrance of Pompeii at Porta Marina. If travelling on the Naples-Poggiomarino railway line, get off at the Pompei-Santuario station and walk to the side entrance of Pompeii at Piazza Anfiteatro.

Pompeii in private
Several public buildings and private houses in Pompeii, such as the Suburbane Thermal Bath, the Casa del Menandro, the Casa dell'Ara Massima and the Casa degli Amorini Dorati have been restored and are only open to visitors who have made a reservation online at www.arethusa.-net. The crowds can be avoided and there is no extra charge.

Frescoes in Villa dei Misteri

Virtual Pompeii
The website of the Sopraintendenza Archeologica di Pompei (administration of historic monuments) will take you around Pompeii with Google Earth-style precision. Visitors of all ages can discover the historic city in the company of the 8-year-old Caius, and also read detailed descriptions, background articles and tourism tips.

The site includes information on Boscoreale, Herculaneum, Oplontis and Stabia (www.pompeiisites.org).

WHERE TO EAT

► Expensive

① *Il Principe*
Piazza B. Longo 8, tel. 08 18 50 55 66, www.pompeii-restaurant.com
Closed Sun evening and Mon
A restaurant in the centre of modern Pompeii specializing in cuisine inspired by Roman antiquity.

► Moderate

② *Autogrill*
Terme del Foro, tel. 08 15 36 40 98
April–Oct. 8.30am–7.30pm, in winter until 5pm
Snack bar and toilet facilities within the excavation area, near the thermal baths of the forum. The restaurant next door, whose tables are in the shade of the columned courtyard of the palace, is somewhat more upmarket and stylish.

③ *Zi Caterina*
Via Roma 20
Tel. 08 18 50 74 47
Halfway between Piazza Anfiteatro and the Santuario. Pizzas made in a wood-fired oven, including at lunch time.

WHERE TO STAY

► Mid-range

① *Forum*
Via Roma 99
Tel. 08 18 50 11 70
www.hotelforum.it
This hotel is located around 200m/220yd from the Anfiteatro entrance. The renovated rooms are best. Breakfast is served under the lemon trees outside.

► Budget

② *B&B Casa Country Villa Pompei*
Via Traversa Adinolfi 23
Tel. 08 15 36 98 69
www.villapompei.itg. Well-kept modern villa near the Villa dei Misteri; the train stattion for the Circumvesuviana is also within walking distance.

③ *Camping Spartacus*
Via Plinio 127
Tel. 08 18 62 40 78
www.campingspartacus.it
All year round campsite, which also has bungalows, within walking distance to the ruins. Unfortunately the proximity to the Circumvesuviana railway line and the motorway means the site suffers from noise.

Scavi di Pompei · The World's Largest Ruined City as Archaeological Site

Opening hours: Nov–March daily 8.30am–5pm (last admission at 3.30pm) April–Oct daily 8.30am–7.30pm (last admission at 6pm).

A minimum of one day is needed to get to know Pompeii; and good walking shoes and a hat for sun protection is also useful during summer. There is a self-service restaurant and a bar near the forum. The two entrances to the excavation site, at Piazza Anfiteatro and Porta Marina, are both equally overrun, though it is preferable to begin a visit at the **Porta Marina** in order to best understand the ancient city's design. As a general rule, the site empties from around 4pm onwards during high season, and there are always more houses open to the public on weekdays.

The steep ascent towards the **Porta Marina** reminds the visitor just how well fortified the city of Pompeii was. To the left of the city gate lies the **Terme Suburbane**, famous for its erotic frescoes in one of the changing rooms. The site was only excavated in 1985–87, and is open only by appointment. The Porta Marina once led to the harbour, whose historical position is still a matter for debate because the Vesuvian eruption significantly changed the topography of the coast. Pompeii's city walls were more than 3km/2mi long and included twelve watchtowers and seven city gates. Beyond the Porta Marina, to the left, the first shops (tabernae) and eateries (thermopolia) can be seen; travellers once fortified themselves here on arrival in the city. To the right, behind a wall, lie the sparse remains of the **Tempio di Venere**, the Temple of Venus dating from the earliest years of Pompeii's time as a Roman municipium. Right next door, the **basilica** dates from the 2nd century BC. This kind of building was an unfailing component of every Roman town and served as both stock exchange and a court of law. Opposite the basilica stands the **Tempio di Apollo**, which is one of the city's oldest shrines. The design and decorative elements date from the 6th century BC, although the present form of the building goes back to the 2nd century BC. The sculptures of Apollo and Diana are copies, as the originals are exhibited in the Archaeological Museum of Naples.

Public life once played out at Pompeii's forum at the foot of Mount Vesuvius

✱✱ Forum

Beyond the temple, Via Marina soon leads to the forum, which lay at the heart of the city's economic, administrative and religious life from its foundation onwards. The forum is also surrounded by Pompeii's most important public buildings. To the north lies the **Tempio di Giove**, the city's central temple, which is dedicated to Jupiter. It was converted into a **capitolium** after 80 BC, when Juno and Minerva were also worshipped here. Municipal administrative buildings are located opposite the temple, known as the **Edifici Amministrazione Pubblica**. Unlike the forum itself, these buildings were quickly rebuilt after the earthquake of 62 BC. The **Edificio di Eumachia**, on the west side of the forum, was built for a very successful female merchant of the Eumachii family. The inscription on the architrave

Pompeii Excavations

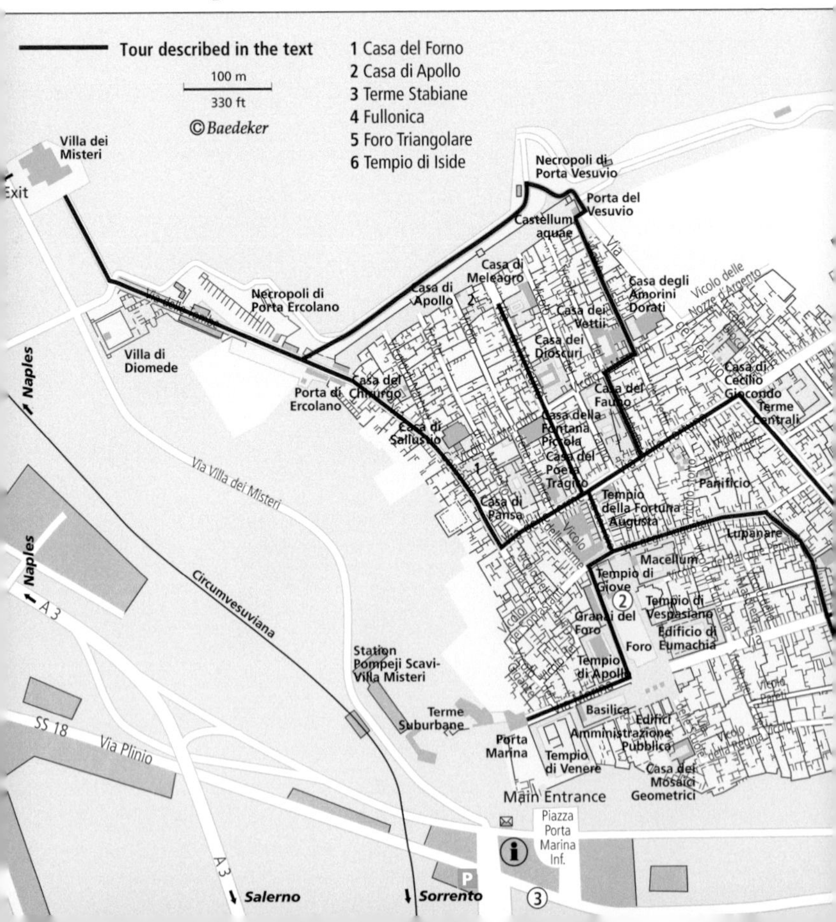

of the portico gives her name as well as her status as priestess. The lady's spacious property here served as the wool market, and probably also as a slave market. The large ceramic containers at the entrance served as containers of urine. The neighbouring **Tempio di Vespasiano** was dedicated to the veneration of the emperor, as was the **Santuario dei Lari Pubblici**, which also served as a place of worship for Pompeii's patron gods. The cult of the emperor was not only limited to worship in temples: almost every public building contained statues of the emperor, as did the **macellum** (market square). The former grain barns are located opposite. Today they are used to house architectural fragments, sculptures and ceramics gathered from all over Pompeii.

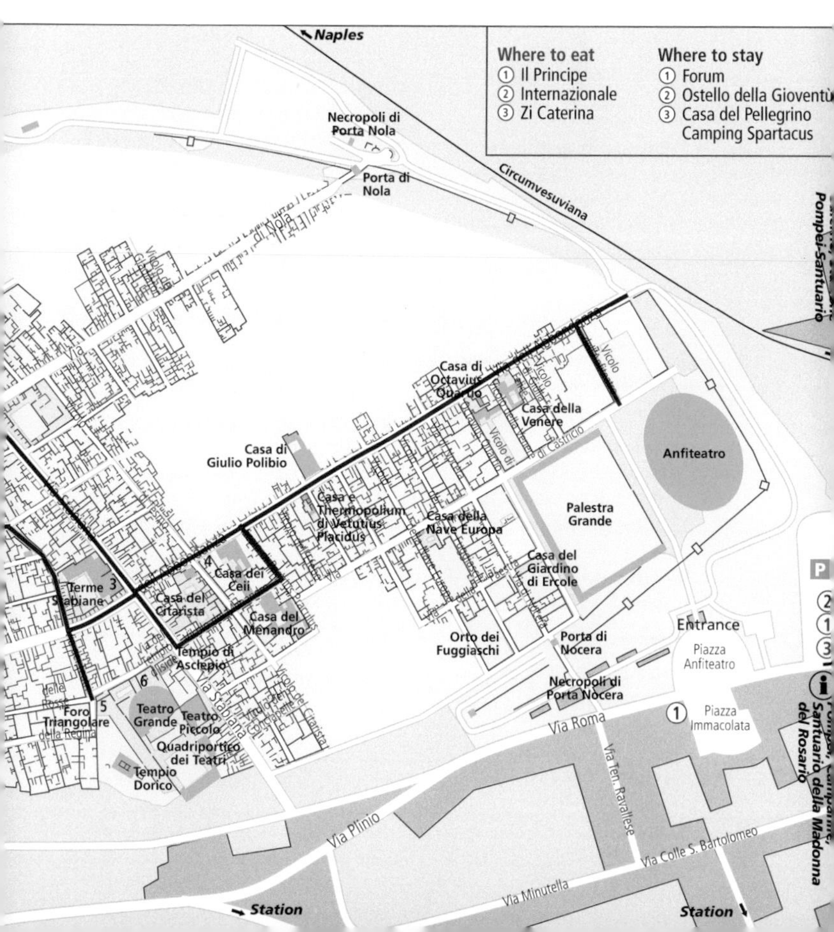

From the forum to Villa dei Misteri

Before entering the fray of the large crowd of visitors all around the forum and Via dell'Abbondanza, it is worth taking a stroll through the quieter neighbourhoods along Via delle Terme and Via Consolare, in the direction of the Porta di Ercolano. To the right, at the end of Via del Foro, is the **Tempio della Fortuna Augusta**, which is one of the many public buildings that was not rebuilt after the earthquake in 62 BC. To the left begins Via delle Terme, and then it is just a few steps to the Vicolo della Fullonica, and the extravagant interior of the Casa del Poeta Tragico. It is particularly famous for its floor mosaic entitled »Cave Canem« (Beware of the Dog!) at the entrance. The **Casa di Pansa** takes up an entire block (insula) along Via delle Terme. Like other aristocratic Pompeian villas, this one was also converted into a series of family apartments after the 62 BC earthquake. Via Consolar leads off diagonally to the right, where the **Casa del Forno** was once one of the largest of the city's 35 renowned bakeries. The mill stone and oven are well preserved. Next door, the **Casa di Sallustio** is one of Pompeii's oldest houses and goes back to the 3rd century BC. Its atrium is impressively large, and it was probably a lack of space rather than money that resulted in the refreshingly original interior design idea of merely suggesting the courtyard by a number of columns. Before reaching the Porta di Ercolano, the path reaches the **Casa del Chirurgo**, on the right, named after the surgical instruments unearthed there. The Roman road towards Herculaneum and Naples once began at the **Porta di Ercolano**. The gate itself was probably constructed in 89 BC, although the original city wall here dates back to the 6th century BC.

✶ Casa del Poeta Tragico ►

? DID YOU KNOW ...?

- ... that urine was an important component for processing wool? Before the wool could be spun and used for weaving, it needed to be cleansed of grease by soaking in large vats of human and animal urine. During the reign of Emperor Vespinian (AD 69–79), urine was also a money-spinner, because a urine tax was imposed to help refill depleted state coffers. When the emperor's son Titus expressed disgust at the money-raising venture, his father had him smell a coin and informed him: »Pecunia non olet!« (»Money does not smell!«). Public toilets in Italy are still known as vespasiani.

✶ **Via delle Tombe**

The **necropolis** outside the city gate along Via delle Tombe/Via di Sepolcri is one of the best preserved of Roman antiquity. Excavation work on the **Via delle Tombe** took place between 1763 and 1770, after which it became one of the great attractions of early tourism to Pompeii. The luxurious country house of **Villa di Diomede** lies almost at the end of the necropolis.

✶✶ **Villa dei Misteri**

A path framed by wild vines leads to Villa dei Misteri (map p.41), a building dating from the 2nd century BC that was completely redesigned after the earthquake. What had been a manorial suburban villa with panoramic views of the sea was converted into a farm. Onions were stored in the former salons and doors were knocked through walls without any regard for the frescoes. Yet this roughshod change of purpose after the catastrophic destruction of the earthquake serves the thesis of some archaeologists that Pompeii fell into the hands of speculators. Despite the vandalism, possibly the **most beautiful cycle of frescoes surviving from antiquity** can still be seen at Villa dei Misteri. A monumental series of wall paintings in the triclinium is set on a background of glowing Pompeian red, with scenes that have yet to be fully understood (photo p.8/9, 269). One possible interpretation is that the scenes illustrate the initiation rite of a young woman into the Dionysisan cult. The artwork was created between 70 BC and 50 BC and is a copy of a Hellenic original.

! *Baedeker* TIP

Pompeii in fiction

Pompeii's fate has inspired poets and writers from time immemorial. Robert Harris' novel *Pompeii* (2003) was a worldwide best seller. Precisely researched and excitingly written, Harris's work tells of life in the ancient city and describes the eruption of Mount Vesuvius on 24 August 79.

✶ **Along the city walls**

Returning back into Pompeii, a small gate in front of the Porta di Ercolano leads to the **Passeggiata fuori le mura**, where a rewarding stroll can be taken along the city walls. It offers unusual perspectives of the ruined city, and is also impressive for the surrounding landscape. The path runs atop an earth mound created from excavation work and runs at the same elevation as the city wall. If time is limited, it is best to return to the ruins at the Porta del Vesuvio.

Castellum Aquae

One of the city's water reservoirs, the Castellum Aquae, lies beyond the **Porta del Vesuvio**. Located at the highest point in the city (42m/138ft above sea level), water was pumped into the three main canals from here. At the time of the volcanic eruption, neither the reservoir nor the canals had been reinstated.

The northwest of Pompeii

✶

◄ Casa dei Vettii

Vicolo dei Vettii leads to two of the most famous houses in Pompeii. The Casa dei Vettii was immediately restored to its original glory after the damage of the earthquake. The owner was from a wealthy family of freedmen and the first-class interior décor was an important way of demonstrating status. Thus the paintings in the Ixion and Pentheus rooms are copies of famous Greek works. The cycle of frescoes in one of the reception rooms adjoining the peristyle is famous, and shows Psyche and Eros in a variety of trades and occupations. These charming portrayals – as appealing as 18th-century cherubs – provide insight into daily life in Pompeii.

✶ **Casa degli Amorini Dorati**

Just a short walk further on is a house whose interior décor is among the most elaborate found in Pompeii. The Casa degli Amorini Dorati has only recently been reopened to the public, and can only be viewed by appointment. The exquisite luxury of this home is unique

Some days, up to 10,000 people make their way through the city. The effect of wind, rain and sun has been equally damaging. More than anything, Pompeii is now a warning of what can happen to a unique example of cultural heritage without the proper care

A WONDER OF THE WORLD DEFILED

Pompeii has only been on the UNESCO World Heritage list since 1997, though the ancient ruined city has long been on the list of the 100 most endangered cultural monuments published by the World Monuments Fund. Inadequate financial resources, an over-stretched Sopraintendenza and over two million visitors per year have devastated Pompeii.

A fitting image to convey the **disastrous condition** of the world's largest archaeological site of a ruined city is the moment in Federico Fellini's film *Roma*, when frescoes discovered during the building of the underground metro fade within minutes of being exposed to oxygen. It took 250 years to turn Pompeii from a wonder of the world into a ruin of what was once a city perfectly preserved underneath ash and lapilli. Only a fraction remains of what visitors were still able to see even 50 to 100 years ago. The dismal sight of Pompeii's Via dell'Abbondanza – once the city's Decumanus – now badly weathered by the combined effects of sun, rain and wind, resembles nothing more than a bombed out city centre after the Second World War.

The earliest excavations were nothing more than **lootings**: houses were robbed of their art treasures and then filled in again. Archaeology as a scientific activity was only established here in the 1860s, and is indelibly associated with **Johann Joachim Winkelmann**. The predecessors of the Sopraintendenza were accused of fraud and the buildings remained unprotected, so that it is only possible to speak of systematic excavations according to scientific standards at Pompeii from 1869 onwards. Looting, corruption and, most of all, the effects of the weather have caused severe damage to the ancient city. In late 2010 the collapse of various buildings made headlines worlwide. The main cause, next to the dilapidation, was the heavy rainfall.

Accelerated decline

The Italian government succeeded with a daring experiment in 1995, when it established the **Lex pompeiana**. Pompeii's Sopraintendenza was granted autonomy to administer all archaeological sites at the Bay of Naples, including Pompeii, as well as control of entrance fees and the pitiable grants available. The stated intention was to free the administrators of Pompeii from the inflexible grip of Italian bureaucracy. According

to superintendent Peitro Giovanni Guzzo, however, 250 million euros would be needed to secure the ancient architecture for future generations. He has saved over 30 buildings from destruction and, being a native of northern Italy, he has also established a reputation for integrity and for being immune to bribes. Unfortunately, with only 700 employees, of which only 12 are archaeologists and 30 conservation specialists, he cannot prevent the **second destruction of Pompeii**.

Pompeii as amusement park

On some days during summer, up to 10,000 people push their way through the fragile ruins. When the crowds are really big, backpacks scrape centuries-old plaster from the buildings, thousands of shoes trample over the ancient mosaic floors in the thermal baths, and inquisitive fingers probe ancient walls. It is true that Pompeii has long ceased to be the great »memento mori« experience it was during journeys to Italy in former times. Rather, **the ancient city has been reduced to the level of an amusement park** – and there is no more lucrative job for the tour guides working here, who do not have to answer to the Sopraintendenza. Their highly desirable jobs are passed on from one generation to the next in the same way as licences for the numerous kiosks selling their abysmal trinkets and souvenirs.

The looting continues

Old photographs show elaborate interiors for houses at Pompeii. These are now empty, if they are even open to the public at all. Every moveable item not stored in the depots of the Archaeological Museum has been stolen. Looters have even broken into the Antiquarium, which has been closed for decades, and incidents with the so-called **»tombaroli«** (looters of ancient monuments) are a regular occurrence. As recently as the spring of 2006, the Neapolitan police discovered a criminal warehouse stuffed with architectural fragments, ceramics, frescoes and small sculptures. All of them appear to have been taken from a 1st-century Roman villa that has yet to be identified. »Many terrible events have taken place in the past, but few can have provided such pleasure for subsequent generations,« wrote Goethe after his visit to Pompeii. These days, however, Pom-

and contains features such as cupids on gold-leaf windows and obsidian mirrors set in the walls. The atrium is also unusual in that its main wall is designed like a stage set. The owners were related to Nero's second wife Poppaea.

★ **Casa del Fauno**

Traces of a formerly underground drains system can be seen along **Vicolo di Mercurio**. A small entrance in the wall then leads into the garden of Pompeii's largest villa – and it is not such a bad idea to approach the Casa del Fauno from behind. The incredible dimensions of the building can be appreciated particularly well that way, and the magnificence of the 3000 sq m/32,280 sq ft property is impressive even in its ruined state. The normal design of a Roman villa is extravagantly magnified. Two of the most famous artworks of antiquity were also found here: namely the mosaic of the **Battle of Alexander** and the Hellenic bronze sculpture of the **dancing fawn** (both works are exhibited in the National Archaeological Museum; photo p.217 and p.9). The proper entrance of the Casa del Fauno is on Via della Fortuna. Continuing the route from there, the Arco Onorario is passed before turning right into Via di Mercurio. The honorary arch was originally dressed in marble and was probably in honour of Nero.

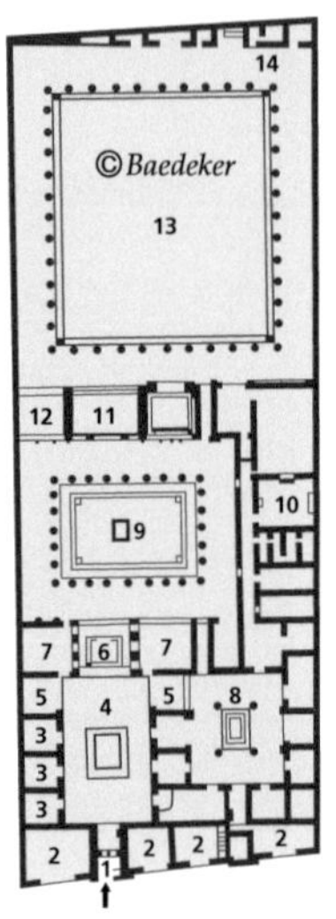

1 Entrance
2 Tabernae
3 Cubicula
4 Tuscan atrium
5 Alae
6 Tablinum
7 Winter and summer triclinium
8 Atrium
9 Small peristyle
10 Kitchen
11 Exedra with Alexander Mosaic
12 Summer triclinium
13 Large peristyle
14 Back door

Houses along Via di Mercurio

To the left stands the **Casa della Fontana Piccola**, which has an attractive fountain decorated with mosaics in the peristyle. Diagonally opposite, at the junction with Vicolo di Mercurio, the **Casa dei Dioscuri** takes up an entire block. The same artist who worked on the Casa dei Vettii was used here, but the majority of its frescoes have been taken to the Archaeological Museum in Naples. The **Casa di Meleagro** lies at the end of the street on the right, and is notable for its unusual feature (in a Pompeian home) of a living and reception room decorated with Corinthian columns. The return walk to the Porta di Nola is along Via della Fortuna. On the way, to the right, take a look at the **Casa della Caccia Antica**, which is a palatial aristocratic home with frescoes portraying hunting scenes. Turning left into Via del Vesuvio at the next junction, the **Casa di Cecilio Giocondo** is reached. The 154 wax tablets that were discovered here provide insight into the business life of a Pompeian banker.

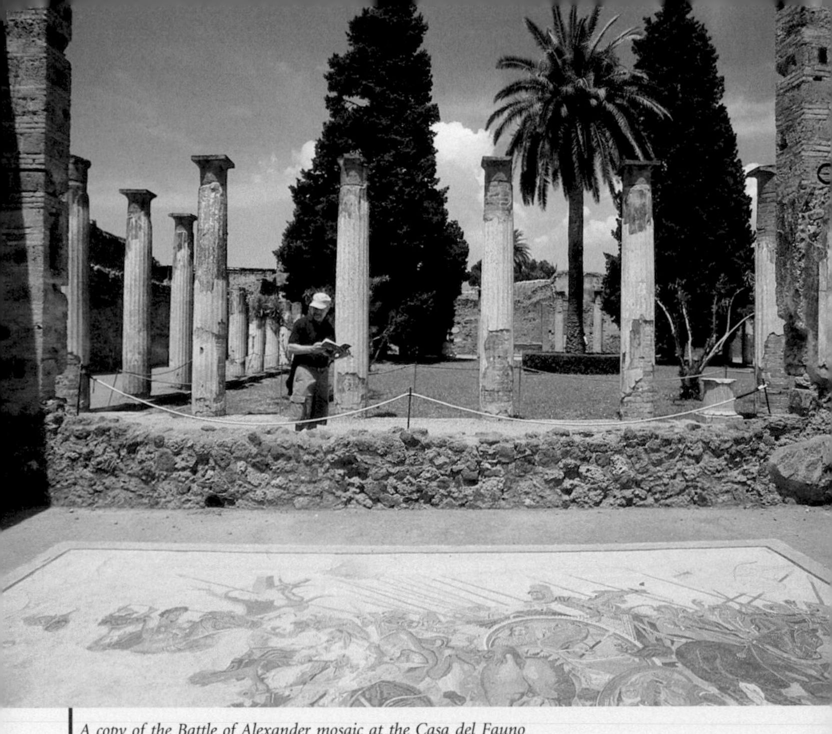

A copy of the Battle of Alexander mosaic at the Casa del Fauno

Pompeian thermal baths

The neighbouring **Terme Centrali** on Via Stabiana are both an ancient building site and a modern ruin: the building complex was only begun after the earthquake of AD 62, but it was never completed. The Terme Stabiane, once the city's largest public bath house, lies at the junction with Via dell'Abbondanza (entrance). The much rebuilt and modernized building goes back to the 4th century BC. The original complex contained a sports ground, a swimming pool, and small rooms with individual tubs. A major refurbishment took place in the 2nd century, when a changing room (apodyterium) was added, as well as a cold-water bathing area (frigidarium), warm-water bathing area (tepidarium), and a hot-water bathing area (caldarium). A particularly notable feature is the hot-air heating system that warmed both the male and female sections of the bath house. The **hypercaustic heating system** here is one of the oldest discovered from this period. Also on view are paintings and coloured stucco dating from the 1st century AD.

✶

◀ Terme Stabiane

Scavi nuovi

On a corner plot opposite the thermal bath house, on Via dell' Abbondanza, lies the **Casa del Citarista**. At 2700 sq m/29,000 sq ft, it is only slightly smaller than the Casa del Fauno. The excavations known as the **Scavi nuovi**, located on the right-hand side off Via dell'Abbondanza between Vicolo del Citarista and Vicolo di Paquius Proculus, are renowned for several important houses, including the Casa del Menandro. The owner of the estate was related to the family of Nero's second wife Poppaea through Quintus Poppaeus. Her wealth can be noted in the overall elegance of this residence, as well as by an unearthed silver service of no less than 118 pieces. The Casa del Menandro can only be viewed by prior appointment.

✶ ✶ Casa del Menandro ►

To the anfiteatro on Via dell'Abbondanza

Via dell'Abbondanza was the city's **central high street**. Shops, eateries and workshops can all be found there. Major restoration work in recent years has secured much of the architecture here, but many of the ancient graffito that was once visible on various façades has now faded into virtual illegibility. The famous mythological scene in which Amphion and Zethus revenge their mother's fate by tying Dirce to a wild bull (►National Archaeological Museum) can be seen in the triclinium (formal dining room) of the **Casa di Giulio Polibio**. A fresco of Venus emerging from a shell that has long been amusing visitors for its disastrous attempt at proportion can be seen at the **Casa della Venere in Conchiglia**, located near the amphitheatre. Next door, the Casa di Octavius Quartio is notable for its magnificent gardens, complete with pools, water channels and ornamental sculptures. The original planting scheme has been recreated, and the owner was identified by a seal ring discovered here. The channel running through the gardens is meant to represent the Nile, as the entire design is inspired by the Egyptian Isis cult.

✶ Casa di Octavius Quartio ►

✶ **Anfiteatro**

One of the oldest amphitheatres of Roman antiquity lies at the end of the Vicolo dell'Anfiteatro. At a time when Rome's theatres were still built of wood, this one was designed and built of stone as early as 70 BC; it set an example that was taken up by many subsequent constructions. 20,000 spectators came to see gladiator competitions here. Unlike at Pozzuoli, there is no basement below the arena, so complicated stage effects were not possible. Great sheets of canvas were once stretched across the oval of the audience area (cavea) to protect it from the sun. The adjacent **Palestra Grande** dates back to the rule of Augustus, and was one of the major sports venues of ancient Pompeii. Arcades line the outside of the building, which contains a swimming pool set in the middle. The extensive cultivation opposite on Vicolo dell' Anfiteatro grows ancient grape varieties, and immediately next door lies the large garden of the **Casa di Giulia Felice**,

? DID YOU KNOW ...?

- Considering the number of inhabitants of the city was less than the 20,000 that could be accommodated at the amphitheatre, we can assume that spectators came from far and wide to see shows here. Records document a bloody riot between Pompeians and visitors from Nocera in the year AD 59. There were numerous fatalities and when the news reached Rome the emperor imposed a ten-year ban on games. The earthquake three years later, however, made all imperial edicts irrelevant.

Pompeii's amphitheatre could hold up to 20,000 spectators

which can be seen beyond the gate. The owner of this house was identified by an inscription on the main façade advertising an apartment here. It seems Giulia Felice needed to rent out parts of her magnificent property after the earthquake disaster.

Theatre district

◄ Foro Triangolare

Immediately beyond the Stabian baths, **Via dei Teatri** turns off to the left and leads to the Foro Triangolare. Of considerable art-historical interest, this triangular square is especially notable for its fine architecture. Originally set outside the city walls, this is also the home of Pompeii's oldest shrine, the **Tempio Dorio**. Now merely a pile of rubble, the former glory of the Doric temple can only be guessed at. A building boom in the 2nd century BC resulted in the square and its neighbouring theatre being completely redesigned and rebuilt. Following the Greek tradition, the Teatro Grande was originally built into a natural hillside and was joined with the Doric temple by a great open-air stairway. The theatre was modernized during the time of Augustus, when the construction was expanded to accommodate around 5000 spectators. Typical stylistic features of Roman theatre building here include the division of the cavea (audience hall) into three sections, each with their own entrance, the proscenium for the stage, and the scenae frons as the stage backdrop. Ringed by Ionic columns, the **Quadriportico dei Teatri** is behind the main theatre and functioned as a kind of art foyer for theatre guests; in the last years of Pompeii, however, it was used as a barracks for gladiators. A

◄ Teatro Grande

small theatre designed to hold around 1000 visitors is right next door: the **Odeion** was built around 80 BC and is said to have had excellent acoustics.

★★ Temple of Isis

Of the two small shrines in the theatre district the Temple of Isis was the most popular. Roman religion was always receptive to foreign gods, not least because it was itself a conglomeration of Greek and Etruscan religions. Unlike Roman gods, the Egyptian goddess Isis promised life after death, and an indication of just how much Pompeians valued her is shown in the fact that the **Tempio di Isis** was the only sacred building to be immediately reconstructed after the earthquake of AD 62. The temple is enclosed by walls, which creates an appealingly intimate space. The so-called purgatorium before the actual temple itself is decorated by beautiful stucco work. Nile water for ritual ceremonies was kept in a cellar underneath the temple. When it was first excavated in 1764, the Temple of Isis was one of the greatest of Pompeii's attractions during the 18th century. However, its wealth of frescoes was removed and taken to the National Archaeological Museum during the early stages of excavation work.

Lupanare

The record time within which the Lupanare was restored just proves what the authorities are capable of when they want to preserve Pompeii's status as a tourist attraction. Even while many other houses are in desperate need of salvage work, this, the city's leading brothel in ancient times, was saved and restored at an astounding pace. It was once one of around thirty such establishments, and its name comes from lupa (she-wolf), the Latin word for prostitute. Pompeii's largest brothel was run by Africanus and Victor: ten small rooms with raised stone bed platforms that once had mattresses on them. The walls were covered in erotic paintings illustrating the services available and giving the names of the prostitutes. Scratched graffito in the rooms also provides the names of many customers.

! *Baedeker* TIP

Pompeii from above

An elevator travels up the 80m/262ft-high campanile which offers extensive views over the archaeological site, modern Pompeii, and the Sarno river plain (May–Oct 9am–1pm, 3.30pm–6.30pm, Nov–April 9am–1pm).

Modern Pompeii

Pompeii is not only Italy's most visited museum, but also an **important Catholic pilgrimage site** for the veneration of the Virgin Mary. The **Santuario della Beata Vergine Del Rosario** (Our Lady of the Rosary) was built in the second half of the 19th century and is visited by 2 million pilgrims annually, who come to worship at the image of the Lady of the Rosary. Pope John Paul II visited Pompeii twice; his last visit took place in autumn 2003. His successor Benedict XVI came in 2008 on an official visit.

★ Pozzuoli and the Campi Flegrei

C 4

Region: Campania
Altitude: Sea level
Province: Napoli
Population: 82,000

The small-town charm of Pozzuoli is best enjoyed at the harbour, where there is a lively morning fish market and ferries departing for the islands of Procida and Ischia. Popular fish restaurants can be found along the Lungomare Yalta (seafront) and around the Temple of Serapis. The town has tried hard to regain some of the shine of its former tourism heyday, and there have been some positive results. The seafront and streets below the Rione Terra boast freshly renovated façades and buildings.

Burning fields

One of antiquity's most famous landscapes is located to the northwest of Naples, where the **Campi Flegrei** (Greek phlegràios = burning) were often the setting for spooky Greco-Roman legends. This

Restoration work in Pozzuoli's historic town centre is far from complete

volcanic landscape covers an area of 65 sq km/25 sq mi, and its hollow-sounding earth with sulphur-spewing crevasses deeply inspired the Greeks, who were very susceptible to the forces of nature. They believed this place was the underground retreat of the Titans after they were defeated by the gods. While the Roman poet Virgil sang the praises of the landscape's mysterious beauty, the magic of the past has been somewhat obliterated by modern 20th-century building. The landscape has also been greatly affected over the past millennia by the effects of **bradyseism** (Greek: brady = slow, seismos = push): the slow but constant up-and-down movement of the earth's surface here.

Rise and fall

The »Town of Just Rule« Dikaiàrchia was founded on what is now the Bay of Naples by Greek colonists in the 8th century BC. The town came under Roman rule in the 4th century BC, and as Puteoli was raised to a colonia in AD 194. With amazing speed this small Greco-Roman town became the most important port of the Roman Empire and quickly turned into an **international centre for merchandizing**, with a population of over 40,000. The processing of grain imports was of particular significance to Rome's food supply, and a huge merchant fleet travelled between Puteoli and the markets of Africa, Egypt and Sicily. This ensured a regular supply of grain to the capital, but also of luxury goods. According to the Acts of the Apostles (Acts 28:13) the **Apostle Paul** disembarked from his ship at Puteoli after a stormy crossing in AD 61 to found an early Christian parish here. The pier, reaching 370m/1214ft out to sea, was considered a masterpiece of engineering and was the town's emblem. It was decorated by statues of the Dioscuri set on pillars and an imperial quadriga (chariot drawn by four horses). These insights into the magnificence of the port's public buildings and its mighty warehouses are predominantly taken from literary sources.The slow route to decline and insignificance began in the 2nd century AD, when a major port was built at Ostia at the mouth of the river Tiber, nearer to Rome, which diverted the major trade routes away from Puteoli. The collapse of the Western Roman Empire, devastation by Goths and, most especially, the relentless effects of bradyseism, eventually turned this global port into a small fishing village. The remaining population retreated to the ancient town centre on the Rione Terra hill, and there was no more significant construction here until the time of the Spanish viceroy Pedro di Toledo in the 16th century. Pozzuoli developed into a small economic centre in the 20th century, particularly after the Second World War. The most important source of work then became fishing and associated food processing, as well as that supplied by the Olivetti family, who erected their factory here. Built in 1951–54, it is not without architectural merit. Pozzuoli is the American base for its NATO troops in the Mediterranean, so there are numerous soldiers stationed here. There is also a training academy for the Italian air force located next to the town.

The rise to a global port ... ►

... and its decline ►

NATO Base ►

VISITING POZZUOLI

INFORMATION

AACST
Via Campi Flegrei 3
80078 Pozzuoli
Tel. 08 15 26 24 19, fax 08 15 26 14 81
www.infocampiflegrei.it
www.comune.pozzuoli.na.it. The monthly information brochure entitled »Benvenuto nei Campi Flegrei/ Welcome to the Phlegrean Fields« can also be read online.

GOOD TO KNOW

Transport · Car
From Naples on the Tangenziale; the Astroni crater and Solfatara can be accessed via the Agnano exit, and Pozzuoli via the Pozzuolio exit; take the Arco Felice exit for Baia and Cumae. Coming from the north, the SS 7 joins the Tangenziale Napoli.

Bus
The no.152 ANM bus travels from Naples (Piazza Garibaldi) to Pozzuoli (Solfatara, amphitheatre, Serapis Temple, port). The EAV bus travels from Naples (Piazza Garibaldi) via Pozzuoli (Solfatara) to Arco Felice, Lucrino, Bacoli, Torregaveta, and all the way to Monte di Procida. An EAV bus from the Lucrino train station also travels to Baia, Bacoli, Miseno, Torregaveta, and the excavation site at Cumae. From *Pozzuoli*, the no. 9 CTP bus travels between Via Roma (harbour, Temple of Serapis), F.S. railway station, Pozzuoli metro station and Solfatara. The no. 12 CTP bus goes from the harbour to Cumae.

Train
Metropolitana 2 Naples–Pozzuoli; Ferrovia Cumaena Naples to Pozzuoli (the station is above the harbour, near the Temple of Serapis).
Ferrovia Circumflegrea Naples–Cuma.

Ferries and hydrofoils
From Pozzuoli, there are car ferries (traghetti) to Procida and Ischia (tickets and information at the harbour; the latest schedules are published in the daily press and by the ferry companies).

Diving
Diving tours to the submerged ruins of Baiae are run by Sea Point (Via Molo di Baia 14, Baia
Tel. 08 18 68 88 68;
www.seapointitaly.it) and Antonio Emanato with Ormeggi Sea World (Via Lucullo 110, tel. 08 18 54 92 53, www.divingseaworld.com). The Centro Subacqueo Ulisse (Via Molo di Baia ¾, tel. 08 13 04 38 24, www.marinesub.it/divingcenter.htm) also organizes diving and snorkelling trips all year.

EVENTS

Festa dell'Assunta: the three-day festival of the Madonna Assunta begins every 15 August. She is the patron saint of the fishermen of Pozzuoli. A popular spectacle during the festival is the »Palo al Mare« competition: a soaped mast pole with a flag at the end is set above the water on the pier, and young men, barefoot and without the use of gloves, must try to reach the flag. Most fall in the water.

WHERE TO EAT

▶ Moderate

① ***Antimo & Diletta***
Via Serapide 37
Tel. 08 15 26 35 16
Closed Sun and Wed
A broad selection of seafood antipasti as well as primi and secondi dishes, all created according to the latest catches fresh from the market. During sum-

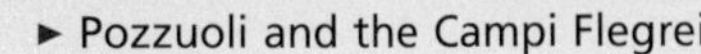

At Antimo & Diletta

mer there is seating outside with views of the Temple of Serapis.

Fondi di Baia · ② Il Casolare di Tobia
Via Pietro Fabris 12
Tel. 08 15 23 51 93, 33 96 70 10 64 (mobile phone); www.datobia.it. Closed Sun evening and Mon. An authentic tavern at the bottom of an extinct crater reached by a leafy footpath near to the API petrol station south of the Castello di Baia. Delicious country cooking, using seasonal fare. Holiday apartments also available.

Baccoli · ③ La Catagna
Via Pennata 26
Tel. 08 15 23 42 18; closed Mon
A slightly out-of-the-way fish restaurant to the north of Porto di Meseno with terrific views over the bay. The owner catches the fish himself and the cuisine depends on his luck with the rod and what's growing in the garden.

④ Sale e Pepe
Via Sacchini 25
Tel. 08 15 26 69 70; closed Sun;
www.ristorante-saleepepe.com
The proximity of the fish market dictates the menu's content.

WHERE TO STAY

► Mid-range

Bacoli · ① Cala Moresca
Via del Faro 44,
Tel. 08 15 23 55 95
www.calamoresca.it.
Charming hotel with an extensive garden at the Miseno Cape. Rooms have balconies and great views towards Procida. Good restaurant, pool and private rocky beach.

Lucrino · ② Villa Luisa
Via Tripergola 50
Tel. 08 18 04 28 70
www.villaluisaresort.it
Well-run establishment with wellness centre, diagonally opposite Camana railway station. Guests are entitled to use the Stufe di Nerone thermal bath. Generous breakfast buffet.

► Mid-range/Budget

Bacoli · ③ Albergo Miseno
Via delle Shoa 21
(formerly Via Miseno)
Tel. 08 15 23 50 00
www.hotelmiseno.it
Family-run establishment by the Porticciolo Casevecchie, a romantic fishing harbour and yacht marina on the edge of the crater. Fish restaurant has open-air seating; car park available in front of the house.

► Budget

④ Camping Internazionale Vulcano Solfatara
Via Solfatara 161
Tel. 08 15 26 74 13
www.solfatara.it; March–Nov
Pleasant, clean and shady campsite in the Solfatara crater (you get used to the sulphur smells!). Bungalows are also available. Pool and sulphur baths. Good train and bus connections to Naples. If coming by car on the Tangenziale Napoli, take exit 11 (Agnano).

What to See in Pozzuoli

★★ **Anfiteatro Flavio**

The most impressive legacy of ancient Puteoli is the **amphitheatre** located right on the main thoroughfare, Corso Terracciano (daily 9am to one hour before sunset). The so-called **Flavian Amphitheatre** was the Roman Empire's third largest after the Colosseum in Rome and the amphitheatre at Capua. Its dimensions of 149 x 116m/489 x 380ft could accommodate 40,000 spectators. The building was probably commissioned by Nero in the 1st century AD, and was completed during the reign of Emperor Vespasian. Four main entrances and twelve side entrances ensured safe entry and exit for the theatre's crowds. The arena and spectator seating was equally well thought out. The arena (75 x 42m/246 x 138ft) was also the venue for

Pozzuoli Map

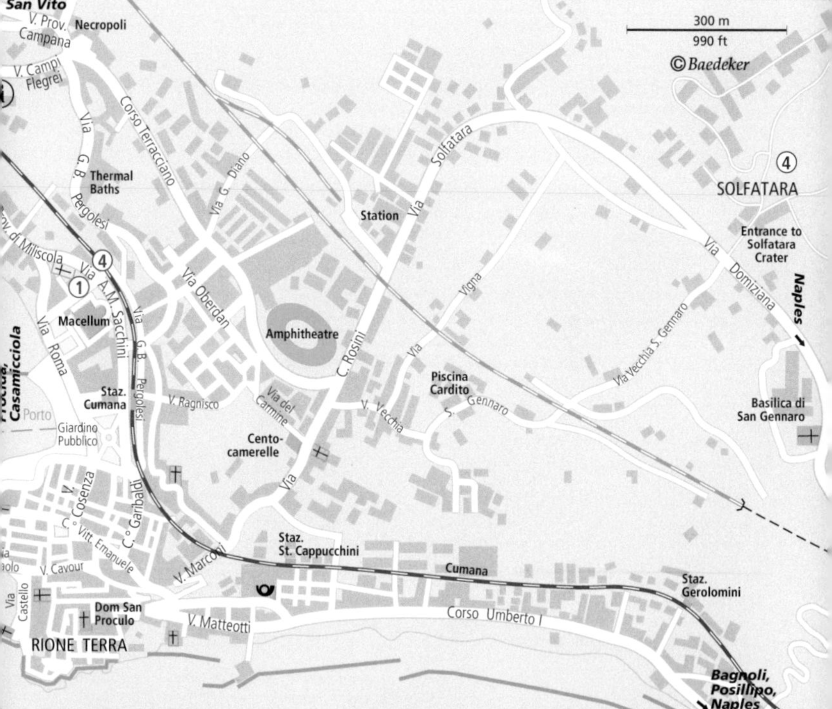

Where to eat
① Antimo & Diletta
④ Sale e Pepe

Where to stay
④ Camping Solfatara

Johann Wolfgang von Goethe in an osteria (drawing by Woldemar Friedrich 1846–1910)

THE GOETHE FAMILY ON HOLIDAY

Next to Rome, Naples was the most important destination on any Grand Tour of the 17th and 18th centuries. Young aristocrats from all over Europe travelled throughout the landscape of classical antiquity.

There can be few lines of German romantic poetry that more effectively inspired hearts and souls – and with such profound results – than the song of Mignon in Johann **Wolfgang von Goethe's** novel *Wilhelm Meister's Apprenticeship*. His »Do you know the land where the lemons grow?« is a question that just about every European can answer in the affirmative. Italy remains the romantic destination it always has been and, in the era of mass tourism and cheap flights, anyone can say »I too, have been to Arcadia.« Goethe's Italian travel journal about his journey in 1786/88 ranks high in world literature. It defined the German image of Italy and to this day is commemorated in many an Italian street. A marble plaque records every spot where the poet passed, visited or stayed the night.

The Grand Tour

Goethe was just one among many – if the most famous – predominantly male students to travel sun-kissed Italy during the era of the Grand Tour. They came for sensual pleasure, and also to complete their classical education. Next to Rome, Naples was considered a great European metropolis and, together with the myth-shrouded Phlegrean Fields, it provided the highlight of every Italian journey. »The most unstable ground under the purest sky,« Goethe recorded in his dairy on 1 March 1787, after his excursion to the volcanic landscape near Pozzuoli.

Barely fifty years earlier, Goethe's father, the imperial councillor **Johann Caspar Goethe**, had explored the same region with scientific rigour, copying Roman inscriptions wherever he went. Due to the many Grand Tour travellers at the time, ancient ruin-filled Pozzuoli was already able to live off tourism in the 18th century, though this did not please Goethe senior. »Those people know a thousand ways to trick the foreign traveller, and get away with it, because no one likes to share the embarrassing news that they have been cheated,« he wrote grumpily. Johann Caspar Goethe returned to Frankfurt with manuscripts, prints, small ancient fragments, and his travel diary, written in Italian, which was even-

tually published as *Journey through Italy in 1740*.

Yearning for Arcadia

The Italian souvenirs spread about the parental house in Frankfurt forever infected the young Johann Wolfgang with a yearning for Italy. Many decades later, when he himself was on his own Italian journey, he wrote: »I forgive anyone who loses his mind in Naples, and fondly recall my father, who was so deeply moved by the indelible impressions left by items I have seen for myself, for the first time, today.«

In 1830, yet another Goethe stood in the Phlegrean Fields, before the very same sights his grandfather and his father before him had visited and described. **August von Goethe** – always overshadowed by his famous father – was somewhat clumsy and prone to stumble through life the worse for alcohol. But he too, admired Pozzuoli and the famous columns of the macellum encrusted with mussels. He wrote back home: »The problem is, one simply cannot understand how the water reached up there.« In 1740, his grandfather Johann Caspar had eaten boiled eggs in front of the **Stufe di Nerone**. Ninety years later, his grandson took a sauna at the ancient bath house wearing nothing but a handkerchief. »It is no small matter travelling here,« August von Goethe mused, »one really has to pull oneself together, not to fall apart. Life gives one a real beating…«

The Goethe family's journeys to the Bay of Naples have gone down in literary history, but they are also a touchstone for the changing perception of this classic landscape from one generation to the next. At the latest, by the time August von Goethe wandered happily from one wine tavern to the next, the era enduring two centuries that had drawn European aristocracy to the Bay of Naples for the Grand Tour was over. Long before the ancient cities of Pompeii and Herculaneum were turned into tourist attractions, early travellers came to admire the seemingly Arcadian landscape of the Phlegrean Fields and the scattering of picturesque ruins from a great past. They left their mark everywhere: their names scratched into stucco or written in soot from burning torches can be seen in many places, including the underground cisterns of the **Piscina Mirabilis**, the **Centro Camerelle**, and on the walls of the **Tempio di Mercurio** at Baia.

popular **venationes**, bloody hunting spectacles involving exotic beasts of prey. Pozzuoli was a major importer of these animals and also supplied the other arenas of the Roman Empire. The unusually well preserved underground caverns are unique: a labyrinth of rooms and passages from which a complicated system of elevators transported both stage sets and animal cages into the arena. The entire excavation site is photogenically dotted by Roman spolia found in Pozzuoli and around the Phlegrean Fields.

★★ **Rione Terra**

Opening hours: It is not known why the excavations are currently closed. But there are plans to reopen them

The archaeological excavations on the historic heights of Pozzuoli are among the most recent in the Campania region. Ordinary Italian life was still going on among the ramshackle Baroque palaces here as late as the 1970s: with eateries and fluttering lines of washing lining the streets, people went about their everyday business. But strong bradyseismic movements in 1970 and the earthquakes of 1980 and 1983 finally forced the authorities to insist on a complete and final evacuation of the historic town centre of Pozzuoli. 2600 years of continuous habitation was thus ended, and Rione Terra was reduced to a ghost town. Archaeological work began in 1993, and has since uncovered the main street of the Roman town, along with shops, warehouses, bakeries, and a large amount of earthenware. The **heart of Roman Puteoli** lies beneath the ruined 16th- and 17th-century Baroque town, and a stroll along the underground glassed-over pathways and along ancient cobblestones is highly memorable. Artworks found here include unbroken marble statues, which are now displayed in the Archaeological Museum dedicated to the Phlegrean Fields, located in the fortress at Baia (►p.295). The windowless **slave accommodation** once ventilated by lead pipes (still visible) is impressive, and there is still a great deal more excavation and restoration work to be done at Rione Terra. For example, the most significant building of all, the Cathedral of St Proculus, is not open to the public yet. The Baroque church burnt down in 1964, revealing the imposing **remains of the Capitol Temple**, which dates back to Augustinian times.

Cathedral of St Proculus ►

★ **Macellum, Temple of Serapis**

The macellum, known as the Temple of Serapis, is located below Rione Terra in a small archaeological park that is not open to the public but is easy to see from above. Initial excavations during the time of Charles III revealed a statue of the Egyptian god Serapis, a discovery that led to the erroneous identification of the building as a temple. In fact, this was the Roman macellum or **food market**, similar to the one preserved in Pompeii. The main entrance to this »ancient supermarket« once faced

! *Baedeker* TIP

Fish restaurants with reasonable prices

A few very good and well-priced fish restaurants can be found right next to the Temple of Serapis. Few things could be more romantic on a summer's evening than dining close to the illuminated ruins.

The food market at Puteoli: Tempio di Serapide

the sea, on the west side, and a total of 32 tabernae (small shops) lined the walls around the rectangular courtyard. Right in the middle of the courtyard, it is still possible to spot the **tholos**: a small circular building once surrounded by 16 Corinthian pillars. Also notable are the well preserved latrines in the corners of the east side of the main building. The effects of bradyseismic activity can be appreciated clearly here. Along with sections of the coast, the macellum sank 4m/13ft below sea level in the 3rd century AD. Evidence for this phenomenon can be seen in the traces of mussels on the three monumental pillars. The building then gradually rose out of the sea, only to sink once more in the 16th century, when it sagged down to a level of 5m/16ft below sea level. At present, movement is also downwards. During the 19th century, a thermal bath was constructed within the ruins.

◀ Bradyseism

Around Pozzuoli

Solfatara

The other merely dormant volcano of Campania is Solfatara, also known as **»Le petit Vesuv«**, which has long been a major attraction of the Campi Flegrei (Via Solfatara 161; daily 9am till one hour before sunset). Like Mount Vesuvius, Solfatara is a dangerous place, though that is all the two volcanoes have in common. Their appearances could not be more distinct. The relatively young Solfatara rises only 98m/321ft above sea level and emerged after an eruption about 5000 years ago. The crater spreads out in the form of an elliptical plateau, with dimensions of 770 x 580m/2526 x 1902ft, and looks a lot like a moon landscape. Sulphuric fumes steam from cracks in the earth – known as fumaroles – and after rain, the mixture of sulphu-

Hot and sulphurous: Solfatara

ric ground water with washed clay materials creates bubbling **miniature volcanoes**. The volcano's fearful beauty not only impressed the Greeks. Precise radar equipment on board the Envisat satellite has alerted modern scientists to the fact that the pressure of the immense underground magma chambers is pushing the crater floor up again, raising it by 2.8cm/1.1in annually.

✶ **Oasi Naturalistica del Monte Nuovo**

Monte Nuovo, to the west of Pozzuoli, is Europe's youngest mountain, whose dubious fame rests on the fact that it was created during a natural catastrophe. Over a period of a few days in 1538 (from 28 September to 6 October), the earth exploded, obliterating the village of Tripergole and devastating Pozzuoli. When the clouds of ash had finally settled, a new mountain had appeared in the Phlegrean Fields. Today, this 134m/440ft-high volcanic cone is a protected landscape greened by scrubland (Via Virgilio, Arco Felice-Pozzuoli; daily 9am to one hour before sunset; Sun and Fri 9am–1pm). Next to Monte Nuovo, the volcanic Astroni crater forms one of the **last surviving sections of unspoilt nature** in the Phlegrean Fields. The 247ha/610ac area of woodland with its many bird species makes for tranquil walking far from the madding crowds of Naples. Note, however, that due to its isolated nature, lone walkers are not granted entry. From the 15th to 19th century, the Astroni crater served as the private hunting grounds of royalty (Riserva Naturale Cratere degli Astroni, Via Agnano Astroni 468; daily 9.30am–4.30pm).

✶ Astroni crater ▶

Lago d'Averno

To the right, on the way to Baia, lies the Lago d'Averno, a small, pretty lake with a belvedere above it, which also offers magnificent views of the Phlegrean landscape. The Greeks believed the **entrance to the underworld** was located here: in their day, the lake was surrounded by a dense forest, where poisonous clouds hanging over the water could make birds fall dead from the sky.

Entrance to the underworld ▶

No wonder Homer and Virgil both set the entrance to the underworld at the Lake Averno, and both Odysseus and Aeneas descended into the world of the dead from here. The Romans, who admired all things Greek, were however always a little more pragmatic. They turned the lake into a **military harbour** in 37 BC, connecting it to the sea via canals that also linked it with the smaller Lake Lucrino. As Portus Julius, it then functioned as a support base for the Roman war fleet until the construction of the nearby port at Misenum. Roman brickwork can be seen from the belvedere down by the left-hand shore of the lake, which has been identified as the remains of a thermal bath.

★ **Stufe di Nerone**

The famous Stufe di Nerone can be found at the end of a shaft dug into the rock shortly before reaching Baia. A visit to this modern spa is still a rewarding experience, not least for the high quality of the warm thermal waters (Via Stufe di Nerone 37; Mon, Wed, Sat 8am–8pm, Tue, Thu, Fri 8am–11pm, Sun and holidays 8am–3pm).

Baia, Baiae

★

◄ Parco Archeologico

The palaces, villas and thermal pools of ancient Baiae, which was once **the Roman Empire's most luxurious spa and bathing resort**, have largely disappeared into the sea due to the effects of bradyseism. Unlike Pompeii, where visitors are elbow to elbow in its streets and houses, the ruins of Baia are usually almost empty (Via Fusaro 37; Tue–Sun 9am till one hour before sunset). Yet there are some magnificent domed buildings preserved here. The **Tempio di Mercurio** – so frequently portrayed in 17th and 18th century engravings – is among the earliest examples of Roman dome architecture

Pozzuoli and Campi Flegrei Map

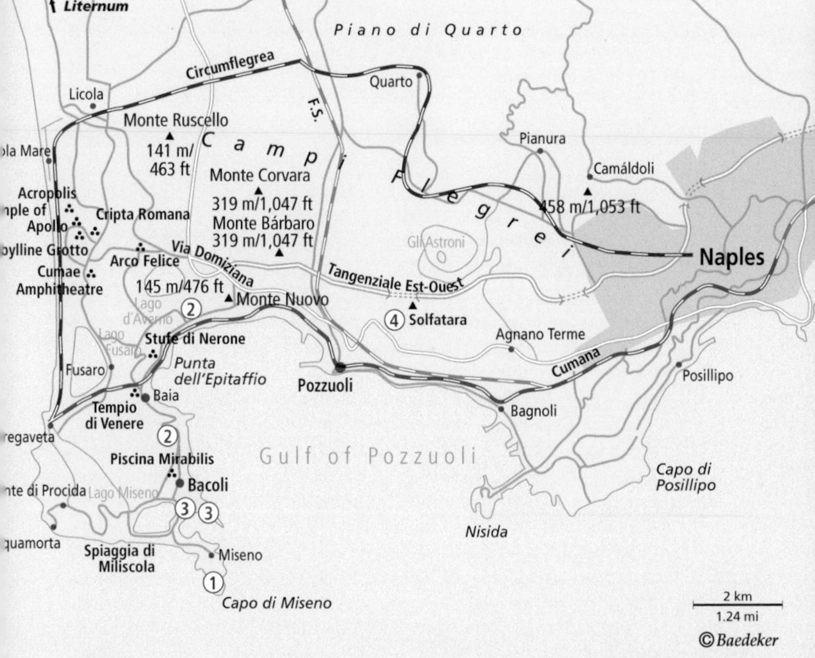

Where to eat
② Il Casolare di Tobia
③ La Catagna

Where to stay
① Cala Moresca
② Villa Luisa
③ Albergo Miseno
④ Camping Solfatara

Looking over the excavations towards the Castello Aragonese at Baia

(the one at the Pantheon in Rome was constructed a whole century later). With diameters of up to 29.5m/96.8ft, this type of construction was made possible by the development of particularly light yet durable cement made of pumice stone and Puteolan earth, known as opus caementicium. The monumental size of the ruins led to the mistaken idea, during the Middle Ages, that this was a heathen temple. In fact, the Tempio di Diana and Tempio di Venere (outside the archaeological park) were both **secular buildings** and made up the most sophisticated thermal spa complex of their time. The spa at Baia was in service from the 2nd century BC until the Middle Ages, though rebuilding, additional constructions and demolition work has now made unequivocal identification difficult. Also, bradyseismic movement of the seabed resulted in a large section of the magnificent complex sinking into the sea in the 4th century AD. Underwater archaeology is therefore a rewarding activity here and a sensational discovery was made in the form of the grottoes of the nymphaeum at a depth of 7m/23ft in 1982–83. The sculpture of Odysseus and his companions preparing to blind Polyphem found there is now exhibited at the Archaeological Museum in the fortress of Baia. **Glass-bottomed boat tours** are offered at Baia harbour, although their val-

Tempio di Diana, Tempio di Venere ▶

ue is limited (even during quiet seas), due to the heavy boat traffic churning up sand and frightened fish that obscure the view of submerged ruins.

✱ **Museo Archeologico dei Campi Flegrei e Castello Aragonese**

The Archaeological Museum is located in the elaborately restored 16th-century fortress (Via del Castello 39; Tue–Sun 9am–7pm) and exhibits a fantastic new presentation of finds from the Phlegrean Fields such as the **sculptural group found at the nymphaeum**. The work is displayed in a recreation of the grotto in which it was found. Also on display are the **statues of emperors Vespasian and Titus** discovered at Misenum in 1968. Their suitably aged heads are strikingly at odds with their athletic youthful bodies. The views from the museum terrace overlooking the Gulf of Pozzuoli are unforgettable.

◄ Views

✱ **Bacoli**

Like Baia, Roman Bauli (Bacoli, pop. 27,000) was not originally a town but a collection of elegant villas. Today, however, it is the domain of predominantly Neapolitan holidaymakers, who fill the town each summer. Agrippina's supposed tomb is near the harbour, but the much-altered building is certainly not the tomb of the emperor's mother. More likely, it was a small theatre (odeon) belonging to a villa. Not to be missed in Bacoli are the Roman cisterns. The **Cento Camerelle** or »Hundred Chambers«, are located in a two-storey underground building which once formed the water supply system for a villa that no longer exists (currently closed due to danger of collapse, reopening not before 2015). Another memorable sight is the nearby **Piscina Mirabilis**. The giant chamber, 70m/230ft long and 35m/115ft wide, seems more like an underground cathedral than an ordinary water reservoir. The barrel vaulting is supported by 48 pillars. Up to 12,600 cubic metres of water could be stored here, pumped out by a hydraulic mechanism, to supply the nearby **naval base at Misenum**. The place takes its name from a comment by **Petrarch**, who is supposed to have described the reservoir as »mirabile« (wonderful). The keep can be found in the first house on the left, at the beginning of Via Piscina Mirabilis 9 (admission free – tip welcome!).

Capo Miseno

Capo Miseno – the ancient Misenum – is famous for being the spot from which Pliny the Elder watched the Vesuvian eruption of AD 79. The two letters written by his nephew Piny the Younger, describing what happened, are the only written record of an **eye witness account of the catastrophe**. The nearby beach of **Spiaggia di Miliscola** becomes a chaotic bathing paradise for the extended families of Neapolitan holidaymakers during summer. Meanwhile, the **Grotta della Dragonara**, a Roman cistern cut into the rock of the Misenean Cape, is closed for restoration. The route to Cumae leads past **Lago di Fusaro**, where people have been cultivating mussels since antiquity. The elegant hunting lodge of **Casino Reale** was commissioned by Ferdinand IV and built over a bridge by Carlo Vanvitelli.

✶✶ Cumae

Ancient Cumae holds a pivotal place in European cultural history. The first Greek settlers made the Italian mainland here in around 730 BC, arriving from the Island of Euboea. They arrived fired up by Homer's legends, having already founded a trading post at Pithekoussai on the island of Ischia, and were determined to conquer new lands. The god Apollo himself is said to have shown those pioneers the way, in the body of a dove. »Follow the god« was one of the oracles proclaimed at Delphi, and thus the Greek settlers followed the brightest of their gods and landed on the coasts of southern Italy. They brought with them not only the alphabet, but also the tried and tested socio-political model of the polis: the autonomous Greek city state. The chequered history of this ancient town is brought to us through ancient literary sources and also from archaeological excavation work done in the 1930s. Due to its legendary past, the small town of Cumae enjoyed great status during the Roman era as well, and spread between the hilltop castle and the Arco Felice. Renewed archaeological work has been taking place here for several years.

Parco Archeologico di Cuma ►

The **archaeological park** at Cumae is rarely visited, despite its lovely setting, which makes its beauty an all the more enjoyable pleasure (daily 9am to one hour before sunset). Right at the beginning of the excavation area, on the castle mound, the first sight is the **Crypta Romana**, which was the light shaft for a mighty tunnel that led through the acropolis all the way to the Roman forum on the plain to the east of the castle hill. On the opposite side of the hill, meanwhile,

Antro della Sibilla ►

the Antro della Sibilla provides a spectacular sight: a 131m/143yd-long **trapezoidal passage cut into the rock** parallel to the hillside. Discovered in 1932, it was at first tempting to identify it as the legendary seat of the Cumaean Sibyl. Though an Apollonian oracle was said to have existed here from the 7th century onwards, the impressive tunnel is in fact a Greek defence passage known as a **dromos**, and dates from later centuries. Based at their fortress in Cumae, the Greeks won decisive battles against the Etruscans. The location for Sibyl's legendary grotto, meanwhile, remains a mystery. The remains of two 6th-century BC temples can be found on top of the castle mound. Due to their superb elevated position, they must have been visible from far out to sea in their time. Via Sacra leads up to the Temple of Jupiter from the Temple of Apollo. Both temples were converted into Christian churches early on, but the surviving fragments are still impressive. The **Arco Felice** is believed to have been constructed as a triumphal arch during the reign of Emperor Domitian (AD 81–96), and Via Domitiana, constructed in AD 95, passed through it en route between Rome and Pozzuoli.

? DID YOU KNOW ...?

- Various works of literature feature the Cumaean Sibyl, including Virgil's *The Eclogues* and *The Aeneid*, Ovid's *Metamorphoses* and Petronius's *The Satyricon*. Christians believed that the Cumaean Sibyl's prophesy of the coming of a saviour described in Virgil's fourth eclogue foretold the birth of Jesus Christ.

★ Procida

C 4

Region: Campania
Area: 4 sq km/1.5 sq mi
Population: 10,700
Province: Napoli
Altitude: up to 92m/302ft

The smallest island in the Bay of Naples is no doubt the most famous »insider tip« for Campania. Yet outside the high season Procida appears virtually untouched compared to Ischia or Capri. Sedate island life continues here, despite the tourism – which is by no means unwelcome.

History

Within sight of the Phlegrean Fields, the island of Procida has volcanic origins that spanned a slow process beginning about 55,000 years ago and ending 17,000 years ago. Extinct and partly submerged craters can still be recognized along the coast. The island was probably already inhabited during the **Bronze Age**, and its name indicates that a Greek settlement must have existed here. Notable traces of Roman occupation have not survived. The easily defended plateau on the northeast side of the island was used in the 9th century to build a keep, which was expanded into the **Terra Murata** fortress in the 16th century. From then on, the island's development was dictated by the arrival of the youthful King Charles III on the throne of Naples. A hunting royal, he found the accessible island ideal, and turned it into his personal hunting grounds. Capri was used for hunting quail and Nisida for rabbit, but Procida was reserved for larger game, which was released onto the island especially. The islanders themselves were not permitted to hunt, and were prohibited from owning shotguns, dogs or even cats. In return, they received royal favours in the form of shipping rights for wood and coal. Traditional trades, such as boat building and chandlery, have their origins here, and the island was also used for training sea captains. Successful seafarers built themselves fine houses here that characterize the island's architecture to this day. Up until 1907, the **Monte di Procida** on the peninsula of Miseno also belonged to the municipality of Procida. From 1957, the island was the first in the Bay of Naples to receive an underground drinking water pipe from the mainland. Procida also once served as a **prison island**: from 1830 to 1988, it was first used for political prisoners by the Bourbons, and later authorities used it to incarcerate criminals from the Neapolitan criminal underworld.

? DID YOU KNOW ...?

- Procida has been the setting for two films inspired by literature: the atmospheric harbour of Corricella was used as the backdrop for several scenes in the remake of Patricia Highsmith's classic thriller *The Talented Mr Ripley* (1999, Anthony Minghella), and some of the landscape shots for the successful *Il Postino* (1994, Michael Radford) were also filmed here, when Procida stood in for Capri.

VISITING PROCIDA

INFORMATION

AACST Pro Loco di Procida
Stazione Marittima
Tel. 08 18 10 19 68
www.ischiaprocida.it
www.procida.net

Graziella Travel
Via Roma 117
Tel. 08 18 96 91 90
This extremely competent travel agent right by the harbour acts as unofficial tourist office.

GOOD TO KNOW

Transport
Ferries/hydrofoils: ferries (traghetti) depart from Pozzuoli and Naples/ Porta Calata di Massa; hydrofoils (aliscafi) depart from Naples/Molo Beverello and Naples/Mergellina; there are ferries and hydrofoils to Ischia Porto and Casamicciola. The latest schedules are published in the daily press by the AACST and the ferry companies.

Car · Taxi · Bus: the island suffers greatly from the weight of local traffic and is so small that it can be crossed on foot in half an hour. Public transport is well organized and there are plenty of taxis too. The central bus station is near the ferry arrivals at Marina Grande.

Sport and outdoors
Procida is very small, so it can certainly be explored on foot, although the narrow roads, missing pedestrian paths and honking traffic do take some getting used to. The best beaches lie to the west. During summer, numerous beach lidos operate along the broad Spiaggia di Ciraccio. Continuing east, the sandy coves embraced by strangely weathered tuff stone cliffs can be reached either by swimming to them or on foot along Via Salette. The landscape beyond the Punta Serra, known as the Cala del Pozzo Vecchio, is also spectacular. Boat hire outfits at the Marina di Chiaiolella make it easy to explore Procida's coastline from the sea, even without holding a sailing licence. Initial instructions are short and to the point, prices are acceptable, and the fun is priceless.

EVENTS

The *Processione dei Misteri* sets off at the crack of dawn on Good Friday, beginning at the Abbazia di San Michele Arcangelo. Life-size figures of the crucified Christ and the Virgin in mourning are carried through the narrow lanes by men in white robes and blue capes. The procession is followed by the so-called misteri sculptures, which portray the Passion of Christ. On 8 May and 29 September, there are also processions and fireworks in celebration of Procida's patron saint, San Michele Arcangelo.

WHERE TO EAT

► Expensive

Gorgonia
Via Marina Corricella 50
Tel. 08 18 10 10 60
June–Sep daily; Sat and Sun only in April, May and Oct.
First-rate fish restaurant with tables on the pier during summer.

► Moderate

Lo Scarabeo
Via Salette 10, tel. 08 18 96 99 18
May–Sep daily; Sat and Sun only during winter.
Rustic establishment set in a lemon grove, in the rural northeast of the

The fishing harbour at Marina Corricella

island. Signora Paola's specialty is Coniglio alla cacciatore (rabbit).

Fishbone
Piazza Marina Chiaiolella 29
Tel. 08 18 96 74 22
March–Nov, closed Mon
Good fish restaurant serves the catch of the day.

WHERE TO STAY

The travel agent Procida Holidays offers choice apartments in tastefully restored fishermen's houses along the Corricella. www.isolaprocida.it

► Mid-range

Casa sul Mare
Via Salita Castello 13
Tel. & fax 08 18 96 87 99
www.lacasasulmare.it
A small boutique hotel in the north-east of the island, housed in an 18th-century palace located above the Corricella, and offering panoramic views. Tastefully decorated rooms with terraces and sea views. Free beach shuttle.

► Budget

Solcante
Via Serra 1
Tel. & fax 08 18 10 18 56
www.solcante.it
A beautiful old country estate turned hotel in the quiet northeast of the island. The Spiaggia del Pozzo Vecchio is within walking distance.

What to See on Procida

Terra Murata

The **urban centre** of Procida lies at the **northern end of the island** around the harbour of Sancio Cattolica, the Terra Murata, and the Corricella quarter. Apart from the lively harbour and famously picturesque pastel-coloured seafront houses, the main attraction on the island is the hill-top »walled earth« or **Terra Murata**. The Terra Murata was commissioned by Alfonso d'Avalos in the 16th century, when the castle hill was fortified and walled in to offer protection to the islanders during Saracen raids. From the 17th century onwards, they also found refuge in the Sancio Cattolico quarter. The area is only partly inhabited these days and makes a rather forlorn impression, but a revival is in the pipeline. The walk up the hill is worthwhile, not least for the **panoramic views**. Equally rewarding is a visit to the Chiesa di San Michele Arcangelo (Via San Michele 1; daily 9.45am–12.45pm, 3pm–6pm, Sun mornings only). The Baroque church was built on the remains of a 13th-century church; in the interior, take a look at the votive gifts and the paintings by **Luca Giordano** and his pupil **Nicola Russo**. For example, the painting of the archangel Michael locked in battle with Lucifer, set into the richly embellished ceiling, is believed to be by Giordano. One of the four paintings ascribed to his pupil Russo is perhaps even more striking: located in the apse, the archangel Michael descends from heaven to assist the islanders against the Saracens, with Procida and the island of Ischia clearly recognizable in the background.

✶

San Michele Arcangelo ►

La Marina di Corricella

The winding lanes and seafront of the Marina di Corricella make up the archetypal romantic fishing harbour. Just a few bars and restaurants dot the quay, where the scent of fish is a permanent feature. The German travel writer and Italy connoisseur **Eckart Peterich** once described Mediterranean architecture thus: »Dice thrown together to create both charming and mysterious towns and villages topped by domes or flat roof terraces; generously arched loggias and sweeping outdoor staircases; and everything almost always painted a sparkling white – blinding in the sunshine and silvery white in moonshine – either glowing above the black-blue sea or set in the shimmering bluish evergreen of trees and bushes«. It was a description inspired more than anything by Procida's harbour of Sancio Cattolico, which he considered to be the most beautiful example of »Mediterranean Island style«. The true origin of the architecture characterizing the islands in the Bay of Naples is disputed. Byzantine or Arab influences have been suggested, but Peterich is probably correct in believing the origins go back much further.

Island style ►

Marina di Chiaiolella

During summer, plenty of motor boats lay anchor off the idyllic fishing harbour of Marina di Chiaiolella in the southwest of Procida, and it is also popular for the **beautiful sandy beaches** nearby. As there are not many beaches on the island, this is Procida's most visited spot.

Vivara

The tiny protected island of Vivara (Riserva Naturale) has only been linked to Procida by a dam since the 1950s. Archaeological excavations have revealed a Stone Age settlement here. The island makes for beautiful walks in almost complete solitude. Procida's tourist information office can provide information on the irregular opening times for the island reserve.

★★ Ravello

F 5

Region: Campania
Province: Salerno
Altitude: 350m/1148ft
Population: 2500

Also known as »La Città della Musica« due to the annual music festival held in the gardens of Villa Rufolo, Ravello, perched high above Amalfi, is perhaps the most enchanting place on the Bay of Naples.

Città della Musica

The oriental fairy-tale beauty of Ravello is best enjoyed on an overnight visit rather than on a day trip. Set about 350m/1150ft above the sea, both its architecture and the views across the Gulf of Salerno are impressive.

History

Judging by the archaeological finds, the mountain saddle above the Valle del Dragone was probably already settled during Roman times. Perhaps sections of the coastal population fled enemy invaders by taking refuge in the safety of these remote hills after the Roman Empire collapsed. But the real story of Ravello begins with that of Amalfi. Wealthy aristocrats of that maritime city state once lived in splendid isolation up in Ravello; yet the place was more than just an

View of the Amalfi Coast from Villa Rufolo

Amalfi suburb of villas. The town had its own merchant fleet and even provided considerable commercial competition to its more important neighbour. By the time Ravello became a bishopric in 1086, Amalfi's heyday was already in the past, and so the history of the two towns is characterized by a strange ambivalence coloured by conflicting business interests and close family ties. Despite pillaging by seafarers from Pisa that took place well into the 13th century, Ravello succeeded in maintaining its wealth, and only declined into a fairytale ghost town after a plague epidemic in the 17th century. Most of the population, which had been estimated at 30,000 as long ago as the 13th century, died in that epidemic.

Ravello and its visitors

Ravello's beauty is unique in the world, successfully combining the atmosphere of a fashionable summer resort with its status as an architectural jewel. The town is both serious and dreamy, and although some of its hotels are among the most luxurious in all of Italy, Ravello is still capable of enchanting understatement. Even the publicity-shy **Greta Garbo** spent her holidays here, and the number of VIP guests is legion. **Richard Wagner** was inspired to the music of *Parsifal* by the gardens of Villa Rufolo (»Klingsor's magic garden has been found!«); and the same villa also makes an appearance in Boccaccio's *Decamerone*. Hillary Clinton visited her compatriot Gore Vidal at his »La Rondinaia« villa during her attendance at a G7 Summit. Vidal lived in Ravello for over thirty years, and only moved back to North America in 2005.

VISITING RAVELLO

INFORMATION

AAST
Via Roma 18 bis, 84010 Ravello
Tel. 0 89 85 70 96, fax 0 89 85 79 77
www.ravellotime.it
www.ravello.it – Free good city map and hiking map

GOOD TO KNOW

Transport
By car: the serpentine SS 373 turns off the SS 163 up to Ravello, continuing in the direction of Pompeii and Naples via Valico di Chiunzi (A 30).
Fee-charging car park available below Piazza Vescovado.
By bus: orange municipal buses regularly travel between Ravello, Scala and Amalfi.

Shopping
Camo: Giorgio Filocamo is the local coral king of Campania (Piazza Duomo 9, tel. 0 89 85 74 61).
His own designs are displayed alongside historical pieces, and there is also a well-stocked little museum with coral carvings and cameos.

EVENTS

Festival Musicale di Ravello
A society event with relatively accessible prices. Originally, it was purely a Wagner festival, but these days it presents a variety of musical and dance offerings from Italian and international artists. The festival takes place between April and October each year. Open-air performances are normally

held in the gardens of Villa Rufolo. In July, there are symphony concerts; in August, there is jazz on the cathedral square; in September, there is chamber music. Dates and advance tickets are available via AAST Ravello and at www.ravellofestival.com).

WHERE TO EAT

► Expensive

① ***Rossellini's***
Via San Giovanni del Toro 28
Tel. 0 89 81 81 81
March–end of Oct
Even if the holiday budget does not stretch to a night at the Palazzo Sasso, you might consider splashing out at the excellent hotel restaurant.

② ***Villa Maria***
Hotel restaurant (►see below). A gorgeous terrace with stunning views and a choice cucina amalfitana; vegetables come from the hotel gardens.

③ ***Garden***
Via Boccaccio 4, tel. 0 89 85 72 26
Good Campanian home cooking with a large selection of wines is offered at this family restaurant in a superb location. There are also ten pretty rooms at mid-range prices. Only 500m/550yd from the cathedral square.

► Moderate

Campinola di Tramonti · ④ Cucina Antichi Sapori
Via Chiunzi 72
Tel. & fax 0 89 87 64 91
Mobile no. 34 75 94 33 89
www.cucinaantichisapori.it
Elaborate mountain cuisine at acceptable prices. Good selection of wines. Located on the road between Maiori and the Valico di Chiunzi.

Ravello Map

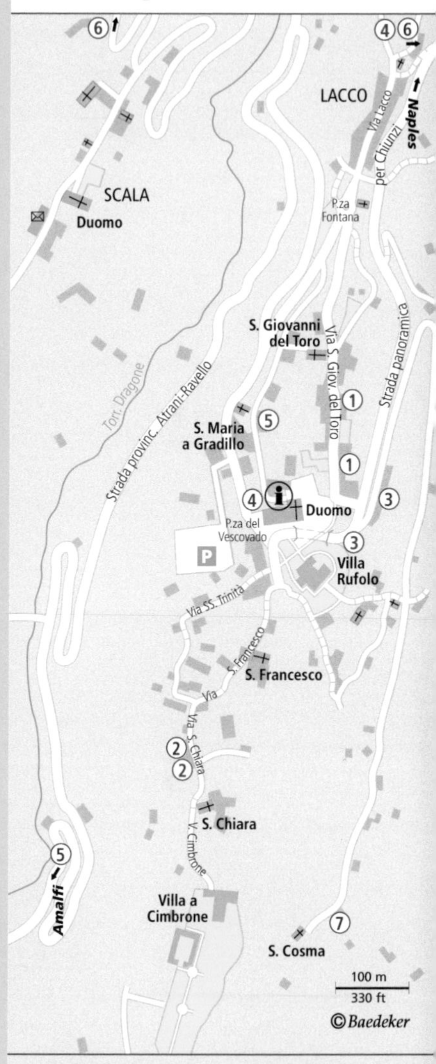

Where to eat
① Rosselini's
② Villa Maria
③ Garden
④ Cucina Antichi Sapori
⑤ Cumpà Cosimo
⑥ Da Lorenzo

Where to stay
① Palumbo
② Villa Maria
③ Da Salvatore
④ Toro
⑤ Villa San Michele
⑥ B&B Farfalle e Gabbiani
⑦ B&B Il Giardino dei Limoni

⑤ *Cumpà Cosimo*
Via Roma 44
Tel. 0 89 85 71 56
Closed Mon.
Homemade pasta and vegetable dishes, as well as meat from the in-house butchery. A little overpriced.

Scala · ⑥ *Da Lorenzo*
Via Fra Gerardo Sasso 21
Tel. 0 89 85 82 90
Sat and Sun only; June–Aug normally open daily – advisable to call first
Relaxed fish restaurant with attractive terrace and views across Ravello, also popular with the locals.

WHERE TO STAY

► Luxury

① *Palumbo*
Via San Giovanni del Toro 16
Tel. 0 89 85 72 44, www.hotelpalumbo.it
Five-star luxury hotel with lots of atmosphere in the Moorish rooms of the medieval Palazzo Confalone. Shuttle service to private beach complete with fish restaurant.

② *Villa Maria*
Via Santa Chiara 2
Tel. 0 89 85 72 55
www.villamaria.it
Views across the Dragone valley towards the sea from the terrace, the garden, and most of the rooms. The owner also runs the nearby Hotel Giordano, whose car park and pool can be used by guests staying here as well.

► Mid-range

③ *Da Salvatore*
Via della Repubblica 2
Tel. & fax 0 89 85 72 27
www.salvatoreravello.com
Jan–Nov
The owner of the restaurant of the same name offers rooms with small terraces and coastal views.

④ *Toro*
Via Roma 16
Tel. & fax 0 89 85 72 11,
www.hoteltoro.it;
Mid-March–mid-Nov.
Run by the same family for the past four generations, this is a charming albergo in a central location just a few steps from the cathedral. The graphic artist H.M. Escher also once stayed here (his signature is in the guest book).

Località Castiglione · ⑤ *Villa San Michele*
Via Carusiello 2
Tel. & fax 0 89 87 22 37
www.hotel-villasanmichele.it
End Feb–Nov.
Charming albergo set in the midst of cliffs and a beautiful garden. Located below the SS 163 between Amalfi and the turn-off to Ravello. Good food as well.

► Budget

Campinola di Tramonti · ⑥ *B&B Farfalle e Gabbiani*
Via Casa Pepe
Tel. & fax 0 89 85 64 69
Mobile no. 32 08 37 38 69
www.farfalleegabbiani.it
Welcoming rooms in the Tramonti valley, the largest wine-growing area on the Amalfi Coast. Life still moves at a more relaxed pace here in the hinterland of the Costa Divina.

⑦ *B&B Il Giardino dei Limoni*
Via Casanova 3
Tel. & fax 0 89 85 35 39
Mobile no. 33 98 63 31 63
www.giardinodeilimoni.com
Located below Ravello, with beautiful views towards Minori and Maiori. The bus stop is just under a mile away.

What to See in Ravello

★ **Duomo di San Pantaleone**

The unique location of Piazza del Duomo makes it one of the most beautiful squares in Italy. Mighty pine trees frame views of the Mediterranean unmatched elsewhere on the Bay of Naples. The Duomo di San Pantaleone dates from the 12th century, and the predecessor building from the 11th century is documented as having been the first bishop's church here. Its remodelling in the Baroque style was reversed to a certain degree in the 20th century. An outstanding feature are the bronze doors, and there is an interesting comparison to be made with those on the cathedral at Amalfi. A good hundred years lie between the creation of the two sets of doors, and the development of the engraving techniques used is clear to see: the sections of the Amalfi doors are merely engraved, while the Ravello ones have become veritable relief plates. The master craftsman responsible for the Ravello doors was **Barisano**, who came from Trani (present-day Bari) in Puglia. He also created the doors for the cathedral at Bari and those for the church in Monreale near the Sicilian capital of Palermo. The cathedral's magnificent **pulpits** are no less impressive. The smaller one dates from 1130, and its mosaics illustrate the

★★ ◄ Bronze doors

Some of the relief plates on the doors of the cathedral at Ravello

miracle of Jonas. The larger pulpit is the work of the Puglian sculptor Nicola di Bartolomeo, and rests on six pillars carried by lions and lionesses. It was commissioned by Ravello's wealthiest family in 1272. Small portrait heads of the commissioning couple, Nicolo and Sigelgaita Rufolo, can be seen on the side of the stairway up to the pulpit. The remains of Ravello's patron saint **St Pantaleon** are kept in the Baroque chapel to the left of the main altar. The cathedral museum is located in the crypt and exhibits predominantly medieval architectural fragments and sculptures. A visit is worthwhile for the bust of Sigalgaita Rufolo alone, said to be the work of the same sculptor who made the large pulpit (cathedral: daily 8.30am–1pm, 4pm–7pm; museum: daily 9am–1pm, 2.30pm–5pm).

Museo del Duomo ►

★★ Villa Rufolo

Just a few steps from the cathedral stands Villa Rufolo, a vision of other-worldliness set in an exotic garden. This creation, seemingly inspired by *One Thousand and One Arabian Nights*, was built towards the end of the 13th century, when the Rufolo family were at the height of their power (Matteo Rufolo was banker to the Neapolitan royal House of Anjou). After the demise of the House of Rufolo, the property changed hands many times, and was reduced to ruins by 1851. However the English botanist Francis Neville Reid fell in love with the place, taking ownership and reconstructing it. Today, the villa is the headquarters of an institute dedicated to the protection of historic monuments. Just a few of its rooms can be visited, along with the Moorish courtyard and a small museum containing numerous architectural fragments. The fairy-tale property is entered via a suitably idiosyncratic gate adorned with numerous spolia set into its walls. The real attraction today, though, is the **garden** with its superb views overlooking the coast (Piazza Vescovado; daily 9am–8pm, till 6pm during winter).

★★ Villa Cimbrone

No less fantastical than Villa Rufolo, and a lot more eccentric, is Villa Cimbrone. It was bought by the English millionaire Ernest William Beckett in 1904, who purchased the property when it was occupied merely by the ruin of a 14th-century palazzo. A great deal of money and imagination went into rebuilding the ruin, and Beckett also used the exceptional location to surround his villa with an enchanting landscape garden. Medieval spolia, replicas of ancient statues and all kinds of architectural curiosities reflect the early 20th-century obsessions of its former owner. The spectacular cliff-top setting for the **»Villa Rondinaia«** was Beckett's choice for his daughter's home which, after Gore Vidal moved out in 2005, became a hotel. Villa Cimbrone itself is also a hotel now, and therefore only open to guests. However, the garden with its famous »Terrace of Infinity« is open to the public (Via Santa Chiara; daily 9am–6pm).

Terazza dell' Infinito ►

The neighbouring **Chiesa di San Francesco** goes back to the 13th century and legend has it that St Francis of Assisi rested on a stone by the façade during his visit to Ravello in 1222.

In the garden of Villa Cimbrone

What to see in the Toro quarter

The favoured residential neighbourhood in medieval times was the **Toro quarter**, which can be reached by walking uphill to the right of the cathedral. Several palazzi there are now historic hotels, such as the **Palumbo** or the **Caruso Belvedere**. The views from the Palumbo restaurant are just as dizzying as the prices! On the other hand, the views from the nearby **Belvedere Principessa di Piemonte** are free.

✶ ◀ San Giovanni del Toro

The nearby 12th-century Chiesa San Giovanni del Toro has a pulpit decorated with mosaics and 13th-century frescos, but as the church now functions as a concert hall, it is not always open to visitors.

The third Romanesque church to see in Ravello is the **Chiesa Santa Maria a Gradillo**, whose impressive dome is matched by a beautiful campanile. The interior contains fragments of floor mosaics and numerous columns with spolia. Despite being Christian churches, both San Giovanni del Toro and Santa Maria a Gradillo recall oriental mosques, a testament to the Arab and Norman influence in southern Italy's history. In spring 2010 the spectacular **auditorium** designed by the Brazilian architect Oscar Niemeyer was opened in Ravello. it will be used all year round for concerts.

Around Ravello

✶ **Scala**

The best way to visit Scala, set opposite Ravello, is as part of a hike in the Dragone valley, which separates the two towns. They look back on a lengthy common history, and it is said that both Amalfi and Ravello were founded from an initial base at Scala. The origins of this small town go back to the 6th century. It was a bishopric from

987 to 1603, and also played a role in maritime trade during the 11th and 12th centuries. Its 12th-century cathedral of **San Lorenzo** dates from Scala's heyday, and has a particularly notable crypt with a 13th-century wood sculpture of the crucifixion above the altar.

Minuta Minuta lies even higher up than Scala. A delightful stepped path descends to Amalfi via the neighbouring village of Pontone from the 12th-century **Chiesa dell'Annunziata** at Minuta (notable 12th-century frescoes).

★ Salerno

G 4

Region: Campania
Altitude: Sea level
Province: Salerno
Population: 146,000

Salerno lies on the gulf of the same name between the green hills of the Monti Picentini and the sea, with a medieval fortress watching over both. The capital of Campania's largest province, Salerno is the most important economic and transport hub of the region next to Naples.

A city in transition Like Naples, Salerno has seen a prolonged period of decline characterized by decades of rampant building speculation while its historic city centre fell yet further into ruin. It was also severely damaged by the earthquake in 1980. However the city has also been reviving since the early 1990s: it is a major port as well as the gateway to the Amalfi Coast and the Cilento region.

History Thanks to its strategic location between the Amalfi Coast and the plain of Paestum, the port of Salerno has been a major transport and trading centre throughout its history. Yet due to the ravages of natural catastrophes and, more recently, the destruction wrought by the Second World War, few traces remain of its close to 3000-year history of human settlement. Archaeological excavation in the Fratte quarter has revealed traces of a **Samnite and Etruscan settlement** called Irna, which is believed to go back to the 6th century BC (Museo Archeologico di Fratte, Via San Francesco Spirito; daily 9am to one hour before sunset, Sun 9am–1pm). Irna was a centre for ceramics and also an important trading post between the Greek settlements at Paestum and Velia, as well as for the Etruscans coming to Campania from the north. The **Romans** re-founded the city in 197 BC, when Salernum became the military base and administrative centre for the ancient region of **Lucania**. The present Via Tasso was once the Roman Decumaenus Maggiore. The forum is believed to have been underneath Piazza Abate Conforti, while the Chiesa dell'Addolorata is built over the foundations of the capitol temple. The

Salerno in the Middle Ages ►

Salerno: major port and gateway to the Amalfi Coast and the Cilento region

city enjoyed its heyday during the Middle Ages when the Norman King Robert Guiscard elevated Salerno to the capital city of his southern Italian kingdom in 1076. The city's reputation was further bolstered by the **Scuola Medica Salernitana**, which had already been founded in the 10th century and was promoted above all by the Hohenstaufen kings. But Salerno lost out to Naples from the 13th century onwards. During the early 19th century, major industries settled in Salerno, using it as their first base in southern Italy. In particular, the Swiss came to Salerno to found textile processing plants. The factory workers were also brought mostly from Switzerland, forming a German-speaking colony in Campania. Salerno's 21 textile factories were still employing around 10,000 workers in 1877 – compared to only 4000 in Turin, despite the move of most economic activity to northern Italy which occurred after unification.

Salerno today

Salerno was occupied by the Germans during the Second World War and, in September 1943, it was heavily bombed by the Allies: 80% of all buildings were damaged and the harbour was reduced to rubble. Yet due to immigration from poorer provinces the population doubled in the post-war years and, like the rest of the Bay of Naples area, the purpose-built housing developed at that time did nothing to improve the aesthetic views of the city. However, there is probably no other city in Campania that is trying harder to undo the damage of past urban planning horrors and to bring the city up to 21st century standards. The historic city centre has been successfully renewed and it is now full of life once more. The Catalan star architect **Oriol Bohigas** has played a key role in the urban regeneration plan for Salerno. It includes plans for a new harbour, and the commission to design it has gone to the renowned architect **Zaha Hadid**.

VISITING SALERNO

INFORMATION

AACST
Lungomare Trieste 7/9
84123 Salerno
Tel. 0 89 22 49 16
www.aziendaturismo.sa.it

EPT
Piazza Vittorio Veneto
84125 Salerno
Tel. 0 89 23 14 32
www.eptsalerno.it
This friendly information office at the railway station piazza provides guidance on the city and the province of Salerno.

GOOD TO KNOW

Transport
By car: there are large pay parking lots, identified by a blue »P«, near the city centre at Piazza Alvarez/Molo Manfredi, Piazza Manzini/railway station, Piazza della Concordia/Porto Turistico and around the historic city centre.

By bus: CSTP buses to Pompeii depart from Piazza Vittorio Veneto/railway station, and SITA buses travel to the Amalfi Coast and Naples airport. SITA buses to Naples/main railway station stop along Corso Garibaldi, in front of the bar Cioffi. CSTP buses to the Cilento region via Paestum depart from Piazza della Concordia/Porto Turistico. Tickets available in bars and tobacconists.
By train: there are good connections from the main railway station at Piazza Vittorio Veneto to Naples, Rome, Avellino and Benevento. Local trains also go to Cilento via Paestum.

By ferry/hydrofoil: ferries operate between April and Oct; Alicost sails from Molo Manfredi to Amalfi, Positano and Capri; Metro del Mare sails from the Molo Manfredi to Naples and Pozzuoli via Sorrento; also to Capri and Cilento; Cooperativa Sant'Andrea travels from the Porto Turistico to the Amalfi Coast. Ships stop in Vietri, Cetara, Maiori, Minori, Amalfi, Positano and Sorrento.

Shopping
Moda italiana can be found in the pedestrian zone along Corso Vittorio Emanuele. Upmarket boutiques, jewellers and tailors line Via dei Mercanti in the historic city centre. Those with a sweet tooth have been heading for the treats at Pasticceria Pantaleone since 1868.
Three generations of the same family have supplied London bankers, men of the world and priests with handmade bowler hats, borsalinos and round curates' hats at Antica Cappelleria di Russo Giosuè (Via Duomo 41, mobile no. 32 90 69 11 13).

Sport and outdoors
Beautiful beaches, pristine waters and hiking paths can be found along the nearby coast of Cilento (►p.258) and around the Amalfi Coast (►p.118).

EVENTS

*Salerno Porte Aperte:*During May, Salerno opens the doors to monuments and buildings normally closed to the public. Schools »adopt« individual monuments and offer tours, and there is often a varied cultural programme to match (www.comune.-salerno.it).
San Matteo: Salerno's patron saint, the Apostle Matthew, is celebrated with processions and a giant firework display on 21 September each year.

Salerno Map

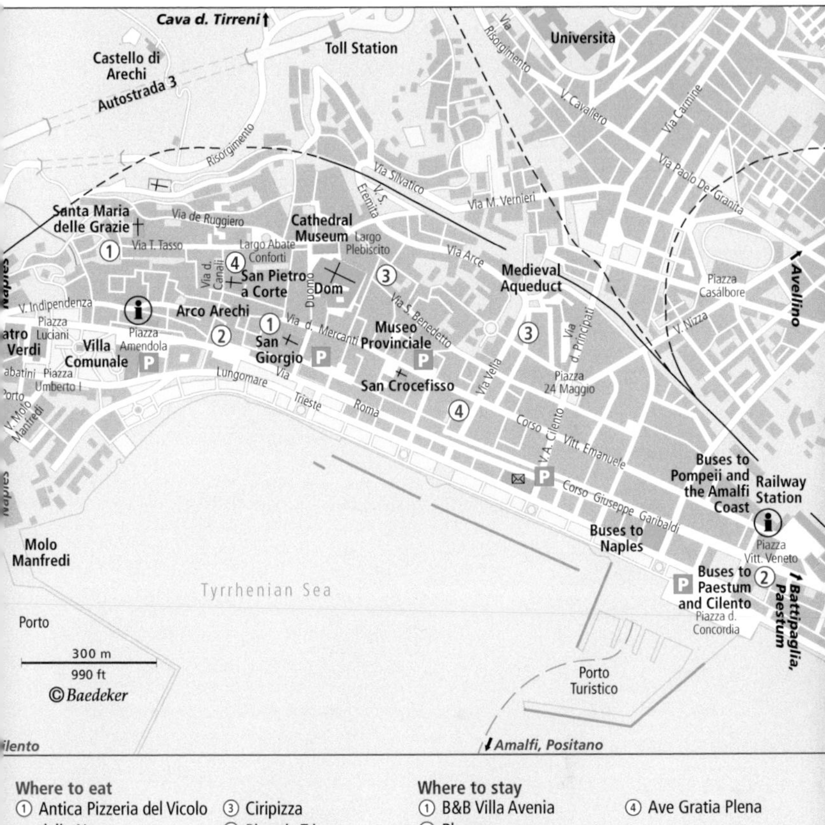

Where to eat
① Antica Pizzeria del Vicolo della Neve
② Santa Lucia
③ Ciripizza
④ Pizzeria Trianon

Where to stay
① B&B Villa Avenia
② Plaza
③ Il Convento San Michele
④ Ave Gratia Plena

WHERE TO EAT

► Moderate

① *Antica Pizzeria del Vicolo della Neve*
Vicolo della Neve 24, tel. 089 22 57 05; www.vicolodellaneve.it; closed Wed, evenings only. The city's oldest trattoria, hiding in a narrow alleyway in the city centre (below Via di Mercanti), is a well-known insider tip.

② *Santa Lucia*
Via Roma 182,
(corner with Via Porta di Mare)
Tel. 0 89 22 56 96; closed Mon.
This restaurant has been an institution for two generations. The tasty fish dishes are also very popular with the regulars from the theatre world. A B & B with the same name is located above the restaurant.

► **Inexpensive**

③ ***Ciripizza***
Via Fieravecchia 41
Tel. 0 89 23 39 40, closed Mon
Locals swear by the pizzas from the wood-fired oven, made only with the best ingredients. The only problem is the lack of parking spaces nearby.

④ ***Pizzeria Trianon***
Piazza Flavio Gioia 22
Tel. 0 89 25 25 30; closed Sun.
A branch of the most famous pizzeria in Naples, offering outdoor seating on the piazza during summer.

WHERE TO STAY

► **Mid-range**

① ***B&B Villa Avenia,***
Via Porta di Ronca 5/Via Tasso 83
Tel. 0 89 25 22 81
Mobile no. 34 03 61 18 13
www.villaavenia.com; closed Nov.
Comfortable rooms with good beds in a regal palazzo a short way from the Giardini della Minerva. Opulent breakfasts are served on the garden terrace; facilities include a wellness centre with sauna.

② ***Plaza***
Piazza Vittorio Veneto 42
Tel. 0 89 22 44 77
www.plazasalerno.it. Very central location at the end of the pedestrian zone. The best hotel of those that can be recommended around the railway station.

③ ***Il Convento San Michele***
Via Bastioni 8, tel. 08 92 75 36 02
www.ilconventosanmichele.it. This former medieval convent behind the cathedral was elaborately restored and has been turned into a comfortable and stylish hotel. Facilities include a restaurant, wine bar and car park.

► **Budget**

④ ***Ave Gratia Plena***
Via dei Canali, tel. 0 89 23 47 76
www.ostellodisalerno.it. There is no age limit at this youth hostel located at the northern edge of the city centre near Piazza Amendola. The rooms are plain, but the beds and bathrooms are good. Housed in a restored convent, the Baroque cloister makes for an amazing place to socialize and the small roof terrace offers views across the old centre of Salerno.

What to See in Salerno

Overview

Despite its proximity to the southern Italian capital, Salerno feels nothing like Naples. The centro storico here is full of life at night, while the seafront of the Lungomare Trieste is a pleasant place for the evening passeggiata. Via dei Mercanti, an extension of the elegant Corso Vittorio Emanuele, leads into the historic centre, where the most significant attractions can be found, and on to Via Roma.

★ **Duomo di San Matteo**

At the heart of the historic centre lies the Duomo di San Matteo, a fine **Romanesque church** (Piazza Alfano 1; Oct–May daily 7.30am–noon and 4pm–7pm, June–Sept 7.30am–noon, 4pm–8pm). The building was constructed between 1076 and 1085, during the rule of Robert Guiscard; the campanile dates from the 12th century. Despite a Baroque remodelling after earthquake damage in the 18th century, a good amount of the original Romanesque architecture and interior survives due to careful restoration work undertaken after the 1980 earthquake. A Baroque open staircase leads up through the 12th-century Lion Portal and into the atrium. A dual set of arcades rest on pillars taken from ancient Paestum. The **bronze doors**, decorated using the typically Byzantine engraving method, were made in Constantinople in 1099 and are comparable with those at Amalfi and Atrani.

The cathedral's interior is a mixture of Romanesque and Baroque stylistic elements. For example, the ceilings of the nave and aisles are decorated with Baroque stucco, while the transept has the original open wooden ceiling going back to the Romanesque period. During a Baroque remodelling, the spolia columns dividing the nave and aisles were thickened to become massive pillars, but are now slim once more. The floor around the altar is Romanesque, though the marble once decorated buildings in ancient Poseidonia (Paestum). A mosaic in the apses depicts scenes from the life of St Matthew, some of which date back to the 11th and 13th centuries. A notable feature of the church is the marble inlaid technique for the pulpits; note too the Easter candelabras dating from the 12th to 13th century. To the right of the high altar lies the **Cappella delle Crociate**, where **Pope Gregory VII** was buried in 1085. He is perhaps best known for the

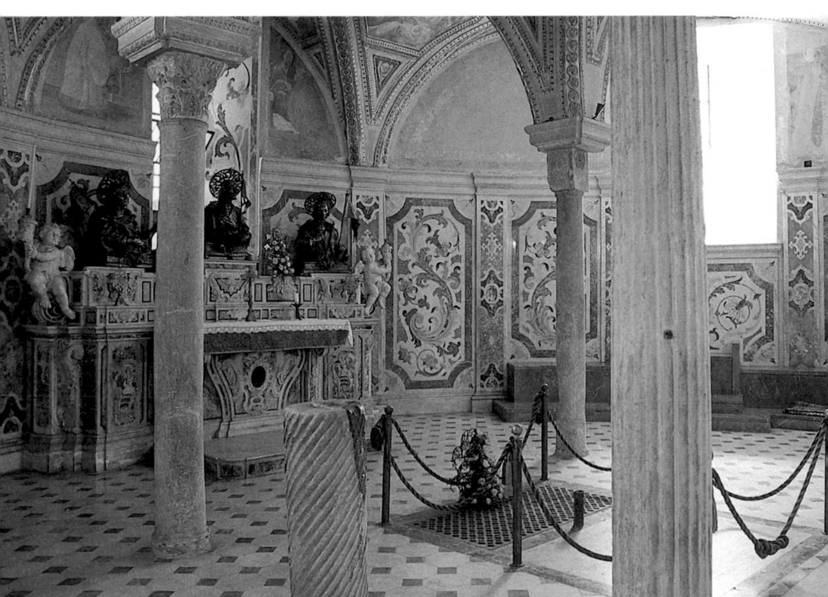

A jewel of Italian inlaid marble art: the crypt in the cathedral at Salerno

part he played in the dispute with Emperor Henry IV known as the Investiture Controversy. The remains of the Apostle Matthew are kept in the magnificent Baroque crypt, richly embellished by inlaid marble. The cathedral museum contains one of the world's largest collections of medieval diptychs made of ivory (Piazza Plebiscito; daily 9am–6.30pm).

Museo Diocesano ►

Pinacoteca The painting gallery in the Palazzo Pinto exhibits works from the Renaissance until the first half of the 20th century (Tue–Sun, 9am–8pm).

Museo della Scuola Medica Salernitana Only closed by Gioacchino Murat in 1812, the history of this world-famous medical school is documented in the former church of San Gregorio. (Via dei Mercanti 72; daily 9am–1pm, 4pm–7pm, Sun until 1pm).

✶ SS Crocifisso The exuberant Baroque façade of the small Chiesa del SS Crocifisso on Via dei Mercanti actually hides an interior that is almost entirely 10th century. Characteristic of the Romanesque style here is the open wood-beam ceiling, and the many spolia columns that were presumably brought from Paestum.

Other sights The 8th-century **Arco Arechi** at the western end of Via dei Mercanti is all that remains of a Lombard residence. The nearby **Chiesa San Pietro a Corte** (Vicolo Adalberga) was the palace chapel belonging to the same Lombard, and later Hohenstaufen, complex. The only other remains today are the much altered buildings of the present Palazzo Frascione (Vicolo dei Satori). The **Museo Archeologico Provinciale di Salerno** (Via San Benedetto 38; Tue–Sun 9am to 7.30pm) exhibits archaeological finds, while an impressive section of a medieval aqueduct (8th/9th century) can be seen nearby on Via Acre.

✶ Castello Arechi This building, first erected by the Lombard Prince Arechi atop Byzantine foundations, was later extended by Salerno's other rulers. The strategic importance of the location for securing the Bay of Naples and its interior is underlined by the phenomenal views. The newly restored fortress now houses a **local history museum** (daily 9am–2pm, 4pm until 1 hour before sunset); the fortress is reached via a stepped pathway coming up from the city centre or by bus.

Around Salerno

Nocera Present-day Nocera superiore (pop. 24,000), located around 20km/12mi northwest of Salerno, was a flourishing market town known as Nuceria in antiquity. But once trade routes took different paths to reach the Vesuvian plain in the early 12th century, the market town also needed to relocate, and thus modern Nocera inferiore was founded (pop. 46,000).Excavations at Nocera superiore have revealed

Nocera superiore ►

traces of a Roman past. For example, sections of a necropolis road have been found complete with monuments that can match those at Pompeii. A theatre has also been discovered. The most significant building in town today is the **Chiesa Santa Maria Maggiore**, also known as **La Rotonda**. This beautiful 7th-century circular building has very impressive features, such as the font surrounded by 15 dual columns. The floor exhibits mosaic fragments from a previous building, dated to the 6th century (Battisterio di Santa Maria Maggiore, Via Santa Maria Maggiore; view by appointmentonly; tel. 081 93 15 28).

Pontecagnano
◄ Museo Archeologico

The expansion of Etruscan culture into southern Italy is the subject of the new museum at Pontecagnano Faiano, 15km/9mi southeast of Salerno. The archaeological finds here include vases and containers, an 8th-century BC equestrian mask, urns in the shape of log cabins, and various everyday items. Excavated at the necropolis in Pontecagnano, they illustrate the extensive trading relationships this pre-Roman culture already had (Via Lucania; Tue–Sun 9am–1.30pm). The archaeological park, which is still being excavated, doubles up as the municipal park (Parco Eco-Archeologico di Picentia, Via Stadio).

★ Sorrento · Sorrento

E 5

Region: Campania
Altitude: 50m/164ft
Province: Napoli
Population: 16,500

Like Capri, Sorrento and the villages of the Sorrentine peninsula have long held a magnetic charm for European travellers. The dream of a Mediterranean Italy of blue skies and sea and fragrant vegetation becomes reality here. And Sorrento is still lovely, despite the excesses of all-inclusive mass tourism, which the visitor should accept with good grace.

History

Sorrento and the Sorrentine peninsula were already a popular summer retreat during antiquity. Magnificent Roman villas once dotted the natural rocky plateau offering terrific panoramic views – though almost nothing of them remains today. Only the ancient roads and the classical system of decumaeni and cardines (the street plan on a rectangular grid) can still be clearly recognized, despite modern building. The present Via Tasso runs where once the Decumaenus Maximus ran, while Via S Cesareo/Via Fuoro used to be the Cardo Maximus. The forum was once located beneath the cathedral and surrounding streets. The origins of the town, however, are Greek, and the cliff itself has been settled since the early Stone Age. Greek expansion on the Bay of Naples was accelerated by victory over the Etruscans at the maritime Battle of Cumae (474 BC), although Sorrento, too, came under the influence of the Samnites – in common with almost all towns in Campania – before being elevated to a Roman municipium after the wars of 90/89 BC. It was settled by Roman war veterans.

During the post-Roman era, Sorrento was heavily contested by invaders coming from the north, despite being virtually impossible to take from the sea. Sorrento briefly became an independent maritime city state in the 10th century, but was soon incorporated into the kingdom of **Roger II**. From then on it remained a part of the Kingdom of the Two Sicilies until 1860. A constant threat for the coastal settlements here was attack by Saracen or Turkish pirates, and after a particularly bad attack a fortified wall was built in 1558. It followed the ancient city wall and surrounds the present historic town centre.

Dream destination of the Grand Tour

Sorrento was synonymous with a southern Italian Arcadia as early as the beginning of the 18th century – more so than any other place on the Bay of Naples. Entire generations of wealthy Englishmen spent the winter here, living in the luxurious hotels and enjoying the mild climate. The exuberant lemon and orange groves of Sorrento are famous to this day. In addition to the beautiful scenery, early tourism made Sorrento a hot spot for the European aristocracy. For example, the **Hotel Bellevue Syrene**, opened in 1824, was one of Italy's top hotels. Travellers did not just stay here when they were passing through. Many lived here during leisurely long-term visits.

VISITING SORRENTO

INFORMATION

AACST di Sorrento
Via Luigi De Maio 35
80067 Sorrento, tel. 08 18 07 40 33, fax 08 18 77 33 97
www.sorrentotourism.it
www.comune.sorrento.na.it. Accommodation listings, free hiking maps and a monthly bilingual brochure entitled »Surrentum«, complete with city map and tips.

AACST di Vico Equense
Via Filangieri 100
80069 Vico Equense
Tel. & fax 08 18 01 57 52
www.vicoturismo.it
Useful information material and hiking map for the Monte Faito.

AACST di Castellammare di Stabia
Piazza Matteotti 34
80053 Castellammare di Stabia, tel. & fax 08 18 71 13 34; www.stabiatourism.it

GOOD TO KNOW

Transport
By bus: the bus terminal is located in front of the Circumvesuviana station in Sorrento. SITA buses travel around the Sorrentine peninsula and along the Costiera Amalfitana. Curreri buses run six times daily from Sorrento to Naples airport (tickets on the bus), travelling via Vico Equense and Castellamare di Stabia. Sorrento has orange municipal buses. Travel schedules and tickets available from kiosks, in bars, and from tobacconists;

Marina Grande in Sorrento

timetables are also published in the daily press.
By train:
Sorrento is the last stop on the Circumvesuviana, travelling via Vico Equense, Castellammare di Stabia, Pompeii and Herculaneum to Naples.
Ferries/hydrofoils:
Sorrento's ferry port is at Marina Piccola, reached either on foot via steps and a very busy road, or by taking a bus from the city centre. Ferries (traghetti) and hydrofoils (aliscafi) depart for Capri, Ischia and Naples. During summer, there are additional ferries to Castellammare and the Amalfi Coast. The Capri boats are in very high demand during summer and advance purchase of tickets is advisable. The latest schedules are published in the daily press and by the AAST and also advertised at the harbour.

Shopping

The pedestrianized Corso Italia is the main shopping street in Sorrento. In the historic city centre Via Cesareo and its extension Via Fuoro run parallel to it. Food stores and bakeries can be found here, as well as limoncello factories, antique shops and souvenir joints.
One old-established local handicraft is the production of ***inlay work***. To learn the difference between kitsch and art, imitation and the real thing, it is a good idea to visit the Museobottega della Tarsialignea (Via S. Nicola 28; April–Oct Tue–Sun 9.30am–1pm, 3pm–6pm, Nov–March 9.30am–-noon, 4pm–8pm).
The distillery Nastro d'Oro (Piazza S. Croce 5) in Termini produces liqueurs and limoncelli to rival many others.

Sport and outdoors

Sorrento only has one narrow sandy beach, so local firms have built long jetties out to sea to make up for the lack of sunbathing room. To the northwest of Sorrento – easily reached by municipal bus followed by a short walk – lie the emerald green natural

Bagno de la Regina

pools of the *Bagno della Regina Giovanna* located at the Capo di Sorrento. The most beautiful beaches on the Sorrentine peninsula are at *Marina del Cantone*, where footpaths or taxi boats can be taken to reach tranquil rocky coves along the *Baia di Jeranto*.

EVENTS

Sorrento offers an impressive *Good Friday procession*. The brotherhoods dressed in white hooded capes set off before dawn, singing their way through the streets. A procession of boats and a firework display celebrate the local *patron saint of San Antonio Abate* at Marina del Cantone on the evening of 13 June. As part of the *Estate Musicale*, classical concerts are held in the cloisters of San Francesco in Sorrento in July and August.

WHERE TO EAT

▶ Expensive

Sant'Agata sui due Golfi · ① Don Alfonso 1890
Corso S. Agata 13
Tel. 08 18 78 00 26
March–Dec, closed Mon. Star-rated temple for gourmets. The ingredients used for the innovative Campanian cuisine are all supplied from the in-house organic farm. The wine cellar leaves nothing to be desired. Advance reservations essential.

Marina del Cantone · ② Quattro Passi
Via A. Vespucci 13/N
Tel. 08 18 08 12 71
www.ristorantequattropassi.com
March–Oct, closed Mon and Tue evening.
The other star-rated restaurant on the Sorrentine peninsula, with a friendly ambience. Outdoor seating under the green pergola during summer. Also offers cookery courses and rooms.

Vico Equense · ③ Torre del Saracino
Via Toretta 9
Tel. 08 18 02 85 55
Closed Sun evening and Monday,
www.torredelsaracino.it
One of the region's best fish restau-

rants, located below the old watchtower at the Marina di Equa.

► Moderate

④ ***Trattoria S. Anna – da »Emilia«***
Via Marina Grande 62
Tel. 08 18 07 27 20; closed Tue
Authentic harbour trattoria in Sorrento, with wooden terrace over the sea. The food is delicious and the prices are very reasonable.

► Inexpensive

Termini · ⑤ Miracapri
Via Roncato 13
Mobile no. 36 83 06 08 63
The restaurant used to be called »Aspiett nu poc« and was located in Nerano. As the name implies, you had to be patient, but the wait is still worthwhile, not least for the generous antipasti and the pizzas from the wood-fired oven. Enjoy the view of Capri until the food comes.

WHERE TO STAY

► Luxury

① ***Bellevue Syrene***
Piazza della Vittoria 5
Tel. 08 18 78 10 24
www.bellevuesyrene.it
Once upon a time, there was an aristocratic villa here, and the Bellevue Syrene has been welcoming writers, artists and wealthy visitors since 1820. The restaurant is in the style of an elaborately decorated Pompeian villa. Private beach.

② ***Parco dei Principi***
Via Rota 1, tel. 08 18 78 46 44
www.hotelparcoprincipi.com
End of March–end of Oct. A 1960s-style symphony in blue created by the architect Gio Ponti (1891–1979), the hotel is set in the middle of a 27ha/67ac park right on the steep shore. Pool and elevator to private beach.

► Mid-range

③ ***La Badia***
Via Nastro Verde 8, tel. 08 18 78 11 54
www.hotellabadia.it
Mid March–end of Oct
A former monastery, this hotel is in the middle of an olive grove on the road to Sant'Agata (15 minutes' walk from the village; buses). Attentive management, attractive and quiet rooms, and a good restaurant.

Baia di Recommone · ④ La Conca del Sogno
Via S. Marciano 9
Tel. & fax 08 18 08 10 36
www.concadelsogno.it
Easter–end of Oct.
Refined guesthouse with restaurant located at a remote and dreamy cove, complete with views towards the Amalfi Coast. A good spot for honeymooners! Can be reached on foot in 15 minutes from Marina del Cantone or by water taxi. Vehicle access is via the private road belonging to the »Villaggio Syrenuse« campsite.

Sant'Agnello · ⑤ Seven Hostel
Via Iomella Grande 99
Tel. & fax 08 18 78 67 58
www.sevenhostel.com
Accomplished transformation of an old villa into a modern, sparkling clean hostel that is open to guests of all ages. Great roof terrace; cool bar.

► Budget

Massa Lubrense · ⑥ Agriturismo La Lobra
Via Fontanella 17
Tel. & fax 08 18 78 90 73, www.lalobra.it
A child-friendly property set in lemon and olive groves, and with its own vegetable gardens. Located on the road between Massa and the Marina della Lobra. Excellent restaurant. Boat tours can be arranged.

What to See in Sorrento

Piazza Torquato Tasso

Sorrento's city centre is Piazza Torquato Tasso, which is bisected by the very busy Corso Italia. The square contains two statues: one to the city's patron saint of St Anthony, and the other to the poet Torquato Tasso, the city's most famous son.

✶ **Museo Correale**

Just a short walk from Piazza Tasso, the Museo Correale di Terranova is among the most interesting museums in the Bay of Naples area (Via Correale 50; Wed–Mon 9am–2pm). The ground floor of the museum is dedicated to the **family history** of the Correales di Terranova, who have lived in Sorrento since the early 15th century. In addition, there is an exhibition of ancient architecture and sculpture found in the Sorrento region, while the first floor shows 16th-century paintings by Neapolitan artists.
The second floor focuses on veduta by the Scuola di Posillipo, but the real treasure at this museum is the **porcelain** collection, which contains items from all of Europe's major manufactories. Equally impressive is the collection of 18th-century furniture, with its intricate inlaid designs that reflect a strong local tradition in this craft, which is still practiced today. The library contains valuable first editions of works by **Torquato Tasso**, as well as the poet's autographs.

? DID YOU KNOW ...?

- The Grand Hotel Execlsior Vittoria is a legend among the world's luxury hotels. Richard and Cosima Wagner are among the many illustrious guests who stayed here; they entertained Friedrich Nietzsche here, and the seeds for their final rift were sown in this lovely Sorrento setting. Enrico Caruso was also a regular at the Excelsior, and the piano on which the tenor once played still stands in the Caruso Suite.

More sights

Sorrento's real attraction is the wealth of **stupendous views** over the sea, although the two medieval palaces on Via della Pietà (parallel to the corso) are also worth noting. The 13th-century **Palazzo Veniero** and the nearby 15th-century **Palazzo Correale** both display beautiful pointed arch windows and elegant decorations on their façades.

SS Filippo e Giacomo ▶

Built on the foundations of the Roman forum, Sorrento's cathedral of SS Filippo e Giacomo (Largo Arcivescovado/Corso Italia) dates from the second half of the 15th century, though it was erected on the foundations of an earlier 11th/12th-century church, of which almost nothing remains. Only the arched passage with its ancient spolia columns in the campanile survives from the earlier church. The Gothic-style church façade was constructed in 1913–26. The genius Italian poet of the late Renaissance **Torquato Tasso** spent his childhood in Sorrento. The house where he is supposed to have been born is today the Imperial Hotel Tramontano, on Via Vittorio Veneto. Two rooms associated with the poet's family are open to the public.

The cloister of the former Franciscan monastery is much more appealing than the cathedral. Originally founded by the Benedictines in the 8th century, the monastery housed Franciscan monks from the 15th century onwards. The 14th-century Gothic-Moorish cloister is similar to those at Amalfi and Ravello. The adjacent cloister gardens are now open to the public as **Villa Comunale**, and the beautiful views here make it easy to forget the tourist hustle and bustle of Sorrento.

✶ **San Francesco cloister**

The Sedile Dominova on Piazza Reginaldo Guiliani is a much-photographed sight in Sorrento. During the 15th century, the building served as meeting place for the Sorrento council, but today its loggia looking out onto two streets hosts a club for card players. The 18th-century frescoes of this semi-public space are magnificent, though the card tables and coffee house chairs make the overall impression more homely.

✶ **Sedile Dominova**

The remains of a 5th-century BC **Greek city gate** are passed on the way to the Marina Grande which, though much restored, still survives in large sections. Near the cathedral, it is also possible to see an up to 500m/547yd stretch of the medieval city wall. Down by the

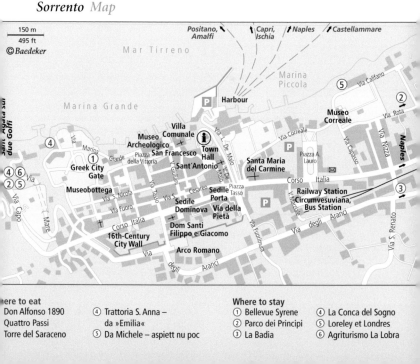

Marina Grande

Sorrento Map

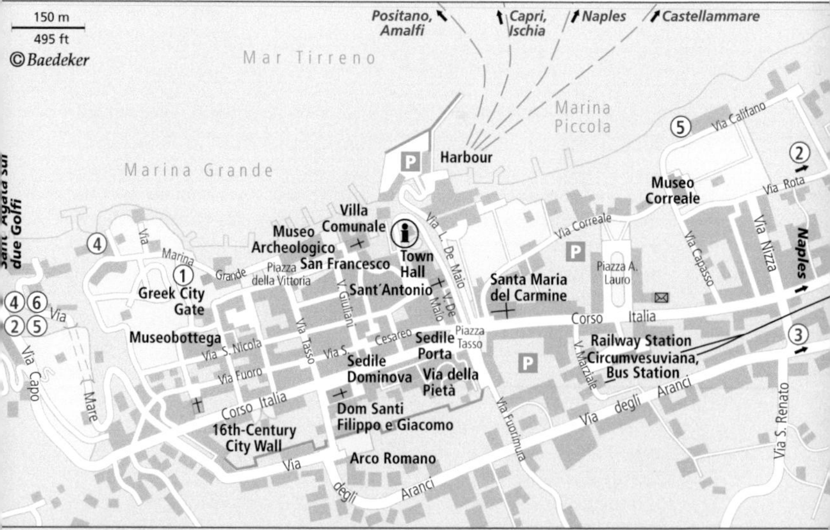

ere to eat
Don Alfonso 1890
Quattro Passi
Torre del Saraceno
④ Trattoria S. Anna – da »Emilia«
⑤ Da Michele – aspiett nu poc

Where to stay
① Bellevue Syrene
② Parco dei Principi
③ La Badia
④ La Conca del Sogno
⑤ Loreley et Londres
⑥ Agriturismo La Lobra

Marina Grande **fishing harbour** there are outstanding views of the tuff stone plateau Sorrento was built on, falling steeply into the sea. The famous hotels that enchant their visitors with their views today stand where the Romans once had their holiday villas.

✶ Sorrentine Peninsula

Penisola Sorrentina

The landscape of the Sorrentine peninsula, with its superb views across the Bay of Naples and towards the islands of Capri, Ischia and Procida, is considered a natural wonder. It also contains the mountain chain of Monti Lattari, embraced by the Amalfi Coast on one side and the Castellammare di Stabia on the other. The mountains are a geological offshoot of the Apennines, and include the summits of Monte Sant'Angelo Tre Pizzi (1444m/4738ft), Monte Faito (1131m/3711ft), Monte Cervigliano (1204m/3950ft) and Monte Cerreto (1316m/4318ft). To the southwest, beyond Vico Equense and Positano (on the Amalfi Coast side), the Lattari mountains quickly flatten out. The original point of the peninsula was Capri, but today it ends with the Punta Campanella.

? DID YOU KNOW ...?

- According to the ancient legend, the Sorrentine peninsula was home to the seductive Sirens, who tempted passing seafarers to their deaths on the treacherous cliffs with their songs. Only Orpheus and Odysseus withstood the temptations of these female beings, which were half-bird and half-human. Orpheus drowned the sound of their singing with his own voice, while Odysseus had himself tied to his ship's mast and his companions' ears sealed with wax. It was the Siren Parthenope who was the mythical founder of Naples.

Castellammare di Stabia

A tour of the Sorrentine coast can begin at Castellammare di Stabia. This lively little town with 67,000 inhabitants looks back on a great past, though its present status is more complex. The place was a popular seaside resort in the 1960s and 1970s, but severe pollution of the river Sarno, which empties into the sea nearby, has destroyed its appeal as a bathing resort. Yet ancient **Stabiae** was famous for its thermal baths and there are still 28 different thermal springs here. Sadly, the modern spa is not very inviting (Nuove Terme Stabiane; www.termedistabia.com). In fact, Castellammare is mostly worth visiting for its archaeological site.

Ancient **Stabiae** was an Oscan and Samnite foundation, allied to Rome from the mid-4th century BC, and then conquered by Sulla in 89 BC. The Roman aristocracy appreciated the magnificent panoramas to be enjoyed from the cliffs above the sea here, and quickly established the place as a popular summer resort. Unlike Pompeii or Herculaneum, the town was rebuilt after the eruption of Vesuvius in AD 79, developing into the port of Nuceria (Nocera). By the second century AD it was the main port for exports from the fertile hinterland between Vesuvius and the Lattari mountains. Later, the place reappears in the literary sources as the Lombard »Castrum ad Mare di

View from the Punta Campanella into the Baia di Ieranto

Stabiis«, though its present appearance of faded seaside resort and industrial town has its origins in the rule of Ferdinand IV, who had shipyards built here in 1785. Always in competition with its prettier neighbour of Sorrento, Castellammare enjoyed its tourist heyday in the 19th century.

The town is centred on Piazza Giovanni XXIII. The **Cattedrale di Santa Maria Assunta e di San Catello** was erected in the late 16th century but remodelled in 1875–93. The **Chiesa del Gesù** (1615) opposite is an eclectic building composed of a mixture of Baroque and ancient stylistic elements. The altar painting of the Madonna del Soccorso is by **Luca Giordano**. It is worthwhile to take a trip by cable car (opposite the Circumvesuviana station of Castellammare di Stabia) up to the summit of the 1131m/3710ft-high Monte Faito. The view across the Bay of Naples is incomparable on a fine day. There are also some hiking paths departing from the mountain cable car station, located at an elevation of 1102m/3615ft.

✶ ◄ Monte Faito, View

Villa Quisisana

Villa Quisisana lies above town on the SS 145, which really lives up to its name as the **Strada Panoramica**. The Neapolitan king Robert of Anjou had a building formerly belonging to Frederick II converted into his royal summer residence in 1310. Further major rebuilding works were undertaken during the era of the Bourbon kings, and the present exterior dates back to the 1820s. The villa was a luxury hotel between 1879 and the end of the 1960s, and has now been restored to its former glory once more. The long period of restoration ended in 2010 and the complex will be used as a cultural centre.

★★ Ville romane di Stabia

The excavation site for **three Roman villas** dating from the 1st century BC can be found on the slopes of the Varano hill above the town. **Villa Arianna** and **Villa B** seem to belong to each other and underline just how built-up the Stabian coast was during antiquity. Like Villa dei Papiri in Herculaneum, these luxurious summer residences were built into the coastal hillsides as a series of terraces. Despite the extensive damage, the wall frescoes of Villa Arianna are still enchanting, while the 30m/98ft pool of **Villa San Marco** indicates the opulence once enjoyed here (the villa was damaged during the 1980 earthquake). The pleasure of exploring here is also greatly enhanced by the fact that the place is largely deserted (Via Passeggiata Archeologica; daily 8.30am–7.30pm, Nov–March till 5pm only).

Gragnano, Lettere

Continuing along the Strada Panoramica on the northwestern side of the **Monti Lattari**, there are a number of places that are no great sights in themselves, but nevertheless exude a certain charm. **Boccaccio** was a fan of the landscape's appeal and, in particular, of the elegant villas, now almost all disappeared, where the Angevin aristocracy once passed their summers. One of the best-known places along here today is **Gragnano**, a major centre for pasta production. Top-quality products of the Italians' staple food have been produced here since the 17th century, and Gragnano's flour mills were once powered by the clear spring waters coming down off the Lattari mountains. Nearby **Lettere** was a popular little hillside summer resort until the early 20th century for Neapolitans looking to escape the heat. In fact, the forested Lattari mountains were the favoured spot for luxurious country summer living (or »villeggiatura«) long before the creation of the Miglio d'Oro or the discovery of the islands in the Bay of Naples. These days, the region's towns and villages, such as Gragnano, Cásola di Napoli, and Santa Maria la Carità, are better known as centres of small-scale textile production, where countless family firms produce the bulk of the Italian swimwear that is exported all over the world.

Pasta centre ►

★ Vico Equense

This jolly little town is packed with Italian holidaymakers during the summer months. The beaches along the Marina di Equa are ideal for bathing, while the mountainous hinterland makes for excellent walking and hiking. Ancient Aequa was already settled before the Romans came and along with Etruscan necropoli numerous Oscan and Samnite finds have been revealed, including several beautiful examples of Greek red and black painted ceramics. The latter can be seen in the **Antiquarium Aequano** (Corso Filangieri, Palazzo Municipale, Mon–Fri 9am–1pm). The unfortified town set on a tuff stone plateau was ransacked many times by the Goths in the 6th century and the Saracens in the 9th century, so that by the time of Charles II of Anjou, a decision was made to construct a fortress. **Castello Giusso** was built above the town at the end of the 13th century (privately owned). Vico (vicus in Latin means collection of houses), and later

Castle and bathing beach at Vico Equense

Vico di Sorrento, became summer residences for the Angevin kings, and the dramatically situated **Chiesa dell'Annunziata** (Via Vescovado) was also founded by Angevin royals. Despite a Baroque remodelling, fragments of the original Gothic church can still be spotted, though the façade dates from the late 18th century. The town centres on **Piazza Umberto I**, which has a pretty dolphin fountain. There are only a few architectural remains recalling Vico Equense's era as a summer residence for the royal houses of Anjou and Aragon, but some Gothic portals and window designs can be seen. A Renaissance courtyard that has survived the ravages of time can be seen at no. 3 Via Michele Natale. Finally, at the **Museo Mineralogico Campano** (Via San Ciro 2; Tue–Sun 9am–1pm, during summer 4pm–7pm), visitors can see models of prehistoric animals and peruse over 3500 mineral fossils.

Inland of Vico Equense

Pleasant excursions can be made into the mountainous interior all along the 20km/12mi Via Raffaele Bosco. This is a landscape that was already settled by war veterans during the reign of Augustus, but after Saracen attacks in the 9th century the coastal population retreated into the hills, founding agrarian villages where time seems to

! *Baedeker* TIP

Ancient luxury

A pretty walk can be made to the ruins of a Roman villa dating from the 1st century AD. It is located at the Punta del Capo to the west of Sorrento beyond the suburb of Capo di Sorrento. Thanks to descriptions found in writings by the poet Statius, archaeologists have been able to identify the villa as the former residence of a wealthy merchant called Pollius Felix. The former elegance of the estate can easily be imagined while strolling around the property: the villa, landscaped gardens and natural views were beautifully integrated to create a complete work of art. A model of the property can be seen at the museum in Piano di Sorrento.

have stood still. The idyllic villages along this unique panoramic route line the road like pearls on a necklace. The oldest settlement is **Massaquano**, where the late Gothic **Cappella di Santa Lucia** was built to house the tomb of Bartolomeo Cioffi in 1385. The outstanding painted decorations are in the tradition of Giotto. Nearer Sorrento, the villages have grown together. Yet, despite several 20th-century urban planning disasters and the heavy traffic, this is also where the magic of the Sorrentine peninsula comes into its own: pristine white villas set in green parks, lemons glowing in the sunshine, and a sheer blue sky and ocean horizon make for great Mediterranean views. The **Museo Archeologico Georges Vallet** was opened in Piano di Sorrento in 1999. The much-frequented summer seaside resort makes for a lively setting to the museum's classical Villa Fondi, which is worth seeing in its own right. The park, complete with a reconstructed Roman nymphaeum, is also beautiful (Via Ripa di Cassano 14; Tue–Sun 9am–1pm, 4pm–7pm).

Piano di Sorrento ►

Sant'Agata sui due Golfi

✶ ✶

View ►

This small village located around 6km/4mi from Massa Lubrense on the road between Sorrento and Positano owes its name to a view: for both the Bay of Naples and the Gulf of Salerno can be seen from the belvedere at the **Monastero del Deserto**. The monastery's favourable position and views made it a much-praised attraction during the era of the Grand Tour, and new life is being breathed into it now by the Benedictine sisters of the convent at San Paolo in Sorrento, who have been working to save it from dereliction. The Baroque parish church of Santa Maria delle Grazie contains a main altar with surprisingly intricate marble inlaid decoration, which is credited to Dionisio Lazzari (around 1654).

Massa Lubrense

The true magic of the Penisola Sorrentina unfolds beyond Massa Lubrense (pop. 13,000) to the south of the peninsula. The tourism mainstream is left behind here, and the crowds of Sorrento are forgotten in a rural landscape ideal for beautiful walks. The name of this little medieval town is taken from the Latin word for shrine or temple (delubrum) and is a reference to the cult of the Sirens or a possible shrine to the goddess Minerva. The town centres on the idyllic **Piazza Vescovado**, with wonderful views out over the bay. A notable building is the Chiesa Santa Maria delle Grazie, built in

1512–36 and restored in 1760, which has a lovely 18th-century majolica floor. An attractive stroll can be made down to the **Marina della Lobra**, a popular yacht marina during the summer months.

✶✶ Punta Campanella

The undisputed highlight of a hike around the southwestern tip of the peninsula is the Punta Campanella. A path lined by exuberantly flowering vegetation during spring heads out of the small village of Termini, located at the foot of Monte San Costanzo. The home of the Sirens, this landscape is deeply embedded in myth and legend: Odysseus is said to have erected a shrine to Athena here (it was turned into a temple to Minerva by the Romans). The strait between the island of Capri and the tip of the peninsula was greatly feared by ancient seafarers, and the goddesses had to be petitioned for protection and aid with prayer and sacrifices. Those ancient shrines once stood where now the lighthouse looks out to sea. The 15th-century Chiesa di San Costanzo, at the top of the 498m/1634ft-high **Monte San Costanzo**, also stands on the foundations of an ancient temple.

★★ Vesuvius · Vesuvio

E 3/4

Region: Campania **Province:** Napoli
Altitude: 1281m/4202ft

Naples' much admired local mountain is also Europe's most dangerous volcano. Vesuvius is by no means extinct, despite the fact that the last major eruption took place over 40 years ago. Vulcanologists believe a serious eruption is possible at any time.

3D ► p.18

The particular danger posed by Mount Vesuvius lies in its geological structure as a highly explosive stratovolcano (strata = levels), as well as in the fact that it is so densely populated. The volcano's characteristic silhouette, with its dual cones, was caused by the AD 79 eruption, which blew the summit off neighbouring Monte Somma. The new crater collapsed and the present shape of Vesuvius was formed in the remaining caldera. It has dominated the vista of the Bay of Naples as a »double-headed volcano« (with the remains of Monte Somma at 1132m/3714ft) ever since. The ascent of Mount Vesuvius takes a challenging half and hour, but the reward is being able to look into the crater (around 200m/656ft deep, with a diameter of 600m/1967ft) and enjoy breathtaking views of the Bay of Naples. A network of footpaths was established with the foundation of the **Parco Nazionale del Vesuvio** in 1991 (entrance fee). The path to the crater begins near the central car park.

The eruption of AD 79

The earthquake in AD 62 was a harbinger of the catastrophe that engulfed »Campania Felix« 17 years later. The eruption on 24/25 August 79 was the **first natural catastrophe to be recorded in writing in human history**. The two letters written to the historian Tacitus by **Pliny the Younger** provide a detailed account of the eruption, especially of the 30km/19mi-high towering cloud of ash that rose from the exploding summit of Monte Somma. His uncle, **Pliny the Elder**, did not survive the eruption, suffocating on the beach at Stabiae.

Historic eruptions

around 25,000 BC	Volcanic activity commenced at Monte Somma.
around 8000 BC	So-called Ottaviano eruption
around 1740 BC	Avellino eruption: Bronze Age settlements around Avellino, 35km/22mi from Naples, were smothered.
24/25 August AD 79	Plinian eruption: Pompeii and Herculaneum are destroyed.
202–1139	Eleven documented eruptions
1631	4000 people die during an eruption. San Gennaro's blood ampules are carried to Mount Vesuvius during a large procession.
1794	Torre del Greco is destroyed.
1906	The last major eruption claims 500 human lives. The streets of Naples are lined by a layer of ash over 1m/3ft high. The volcano's cone collapses into itself and its total height is diminished by 200m/656ft.
1944	The most recent eruption of Mount Vesuvius, during which the small towns of Massa di Somma and San Sebastiano were destroyed. The volcano's characteristic plume of smoke – Il Pennacchio – has not risen into the sky since then.

Volcanology One of the first volcanologists was the English ambassador at the royal court in Naples, **Lord William Hamilton**. Not only was he an obsessive collector of Greek ceramics, he was also fascinated by Mount Vesuvius, and his three-volume *Observations of the Volcanoes of the Two Sicilies* (1776) is a detailed study of all the volcanoes located on the Bay of Naples. His passion was shared by **Goethe**, who ascended Vesuvius several times during his visit to Naples, and also carried numerous volcanic minerals back to his home in Weimar. These days, Vesuvius is one of the most researched and observed volcanoes in the world, and daily observations are taken at the **Osservatorio Vesuviano** and at its associated measuring stations. Scientific data is collated and analyzed to detect the tiniest changes in temperature inside the crater, as well as to register the changing chemical

On the dormant volcano Mount Vesuvius

composition of any gas being expelled. The highly sensitive measuring instruments record around 200 small earth tremors per year – so small that no other means would detect them. Yet these measurements prove that Vesuvius is only dormant, not extinct. Concern was raised by volcanologists at the University of Naples in 2001 when a huge underground magma lake was detected, stretching from the volcano all the way to the Phlegrean Fields. This clearly underlines the potential danger here that applies not only to Mount Vesuvius itself, but includes the Solfatara in the Campi Flegrei. Founded by Ferdinand II in 1841, this research institute is now more of a museum than a scientific base. The main work of modern scientists takes place at the labs in Fuorigrotta. Nevertheless, visitors get a vivid introduction to the world's volcanoes at the exhibition that was installed here in 2000 (»Vesuvio: 2000 anni di osservazione«). In addition to pictures, maps and photographs, there are impressive computer simulations. Webcams also provide real time views into the craters of Vesuvius, Etna, Vulcano (Aeolian Islands) and Stromboli. Vesuvius's daily conditions can be accessed at www.ov.ingv.it (Via Osservatorio; Sat and Sun 10am–2pm). That Mount Vesuvius will erupt again is beyond doubt – only the »when« is in question. Scientists claim there would be two to three weeks' time prior to a potential eruption to evacuate settlements in the areas particularly endangered. This so-called »red zone« is inhabited by around **600,000 people**. Once entirely rural, this is a region transformed into dormitory suburbs for Naples by building speculation and the »abusivo« of the post-war years. Today, the Italian government is trying to persuade

★ ◄ Osservatorio Vesuviana

VISITING VESUVIUS

INFORMATION

Parco Nazionale del Vesuvio
Via Palazzo del Principe (Castello Mediceo), 80044 Ottaviano
Tel. 08 16 65 39 11, fax 08 18 65 39 08
www.epnv.it, www.vesuvioinrete.it
The information kiosk at the Quota mille (car park) also provides the hiking map entitled »I sentieri del Parco Nazionale del Vesuvio«.

TRANSPORT

By car: A 3 exit Ercolano or Torre del Greco. The highland Vesuvius route leads past the old observatory and ends at the Quota mille car park at and elevation of 1000m/3280ft. The narrow country roads at the foot of the volcano lead through a densely populated area and require a great deal of patience.
By taxi: there are taxis and minibuses from the Ercolano/Circumvesuviana stations to the Quota mille car park (tel. 08 17 39 36 66; www.vesuvio express.it).
By bus: Vesuviana Mobilità travels from Naples/Molo Beverello/Piazza Garibaldi to Pompeii/Piazza Anfiteatro/ Porta Marina via Ercolano/Stazione Circumvesuviana on Vesuvius, and onwards to the Quota mille car park.
By train: use the Circumvesuviana, whose main route between Naples and Sorrento includes stops at Portici, Ercolano, Pompeii and Torre Annunziata. Additional services run between Naples and Baiano (Nola and Cimitile stations), and Sarno; timetables are published in the daily press.

EVENTS

Somma Vesuviana celebrates the *Festa di Sant'Antonio Abate* every 17 January, when celebratory evening fires are lit on the streets and squares. The medieval district of Borgo Casamale celebrates the *Festa delle Lucerne* every four years (2010, 2014, etc.), when the Madonna della Neve is carried through streets lit by hundreds of little oil lamps.

WHERE TO EAT

► Moderate

Ercolano · Casa Rossa 1888 al Vesuvio
► Herculaneum, p.164

Somma Vesuviana · La Lanterna
Via Colonello G. Aliperta 8
Tel. 08 18 99 18 43
www.lanternadisomma.it
closed Mon
Tourists only rarely venture to the »back« of Mount Vesuvius, where Luigi Russo's colourful restaurant makes an excellent culinary finale to a tour of the volcano. During evenings, the pizza oven is also fired up.

► Moderate/Inexpensive

Ercolano · Kona
Via Osservatorio 14, tel. 08 17 77 39 68
Closed Mon and Dec–Jan
A friendly tavern with views, located above the Casa Rossa. Pasta dishes, local cheeses, fresh fish, and seasonal vegetables.

WHERE TO STAY

► Mid-range/Budget

San Sebastiano al Vesuvio · Bel Vesuvio Inn
Via Panoramica Fellapane 40
Tel. 08 17 71 12 43
www.agriturismobelvesuvioinn.it
An 18th-century summer villa located at the base of the lava flow of 1944. Rooms have views of the volcano or the sea. The restaurant serves dishes using its own farm products.

the inhabitants of the 17 municipalities affected to move away. Their »Vesuvia« (»Away from Vesuvius«) project is a major undertaking and includes financial incentives, for the scenario of a future eruption of Vesuvius is without precedent and rightly feared. In view of the blocked roads during the daily evening rush hour in the Vesuvian suburbs, however, any evacuation plan is likely to remain utopian!

Baedeker TIP

Virtual Vesuvius

The websites of the Swiss volcanologists Jürg Alean, Roberto Carniel and Marco Fulle (www.stromboli.net) and the Università Roma Tre (http://vulcan.fis.uniroma3.it/) are good places to get some background knowledge on volcanology in general and up-to-the-minute information on Vesuvius and the Phlegrean Fields.

Archaeological Sites on Vesuvius

No inhabitant of ancient Pompeii would recognize the landscape around the volcano today. Both Vesuvius and the coastline have changed. But the region has long been a popular place to live, as it was in the 18th century and also during antiquity. Anyone who could afford it built a summer villa here. For example, the family of Octavian (later Emperor Augustus) built an estate on the northern slopes of Vesuvius near the present village of Ottaviano. Most of the ancient villas were only rediscovered and excavated in the 19th and 20th centuries.

✶✶ Villa Oplontis

◄ 3 D p.332
Text continues on p.334

Unfortunately, the depressing little town of **Torre Annunziata** (pop. 60,000) is a Camorra stronghold, and one of the worst places to live on the Bay of Naples. Unemployment and pretty crime are its greatest problems. Yet tourists need not worry, and even in this dreary place, visitors are welcomed with typically Italian grace. In fact, a visit here is highly recommended, because one of Campania's finest attractions can be found in the town: the imperial Villa Oplontis (Via Sepolcri, 10 minutes' walk from the Circumvesuviana station). Despite only having been partly excavated, **Poppaea's villa** is still the largest and most luxurious Roman villa to be seen around the Bay of Naples. Whether **Poppaea Sabina** really was the owner of this huge property has not been definitively established. Yet Nero's mistress and then wife (murdered by him in AD 65) was closely related to the family of Quintus Poppaeus, who lived in nearby Pompeii. The likelihood of her ownership is also reinforced by the finds unearthed here, such as wine amphores decorated with her name. The villa was built in the first century AD and was possibly uninhabited at the time of the Vesuvian eruption, due to damage caused by the preceding earthquake. This is probably the reason why no interior furnishings have been discovered, although a large depot of sculptures was found. An entire wing of the villa remains buried underneath the road, but its dimensions are still staggering. A labyrinth of elegant

VILLA OPLONTIS

★★ **A magnificent Roman villa was discovered in Torre Annuziata in the 1960s. Going by the method of wall construction and the paintings, the villa was constructed on land sloping down to the sea in the middle of the 1st century AD. Its former sea views have been lost for good, however.**

Opening times:
Nov–March daily 8.30am–5pm, April–Oct daily 8.30am–7.30pm

① Atrium
The large atrium with central pool (impluvium) was presumably once used as the reception hall. The decorations in the Second style are among the largest surviving examples in existence. At the back, three halls lead to further rooms. The last one has no back wall, a columned porticus opening to the garden instead.

② Bathing area
The bathroom (caldarium) has under-floor (hypocaustic) heating and decorated double walls (photo p.334). To the right of the caldarium is the entrance to the kitchen and a large stairway which once led to the floor above.

③ Dining and banqueting hall
The triclinium was also elaborately decorated in the so-called architectural style. Popular motifs were windows, columns, and arches, as well as wall openings with views onto gardens or landscapes with statues, human figures, animals, plants and all kinds of other features.

④ Banqueting hall
The composition of this room, for which excavation is yet to be completed, exhibits the Second style and indicates a shrine to Apollo.

⑤ Porticato
The painting in this area recalls a stage with no backdrop.

⑥ Natatio
A garden (hortus) adjoined the 100m/328ft-long swimming pool flanked by dozens of plinths for statues.

Visitors today enter this shining example of a Roman luxury villa via the garden.

salons, gardens, dining rooms and bedrooms, as well as a pool of Olympic proportions, indicate imperial living at its best.The tour begins with a descent to the still extensive gardens that once offered distant perspectives across the Campanian landscape. A particularly attractive feature is the suite of rooms lining the **atrium**. In addition to the bathing rooms, there are various dining rooms with several high-quality frescoes featuring compositions such as fruit bowls covered in translucent veils. Frescoes using elaborate three-dimensional perspectives frame a shrine to Apollo in the large reception hall. Unlike at Pompeii and Herculaneum, where the frescoes are suffering from the effects of weather, the painting at Villa Oplontis is in remarkably good condition. Thanks to the relatively recent discovery of the building, the most modern techniques of preservation could be used during its restoration. The east wing contains additional elaborate suites of rooms, with a series of windows and passages that allow views through the entire suite. The pool, almost 100m/328ft long, was once lined by sculptures, while the **garden** still contains the remains of root systems from the original planting of oleander bushes. At the time of their submerging in ash, they were already over a hundred years old and had been pruned and shaped by gardeners into actual trees.

Tour ►

? DID YOU KNOW ...?

- The 13th-century copy of the Tavola Peutingeriana is the only map surviving from Roman antiquity. 11 parchment sheets show the entire Roman Empire as it was during the 4th century AD, and thanks to its annotations we know that the present Torre Annunziata was once ancient Oplonti. The map is named after its one-time owner, the German scientist and humanist Konrad Peutinger (1465–1547).

Boscoreale

Seven Roman villas were excavated in Boscoreale (4km/2.5mi northeast of Pompeii) at the end of the 19th century and the beginning of the 20th century. Sadly, nothing remains of their former interiors, as frescoes and art treasures were removed to museums all over the world. The illegal sale of the **Tesoro di Boscoreale**, a 109-piece silver service, by the owner of the property containing the **Villa della Pisanella** was one of the great scandals of the era. However, the **Villa Regina**, discovered and restored in 1977, has been opened to the public as an example of a country estate. This **villa rustica** once produced wine. Evidence is provided by the 18 storage containers (dolia) unearthed here, which alone were capable of storing a total of 10,000l/2650gal of wine. The building itself is plain, but sits in a huge pit that really brings home the extent of the inundation caused by Vesuvius. The adjoining Antiquario di Boscoreale presents a permanent exhibition on life around the volcano in antiquity, as well as models, drawings and finds from villas no longer standing in Boscoreale (Nov–March, daily 8.30am to 3.30pm, April–Oct daily 8.30am–6pm).

★ Antiquario di Boscoreale ►

What to See on the Northern Slopes of Vesuvius

Life on the volcano

The northern slopes of Vesuvius are dotted by several settlements that believe their patron saint will protect them from the volcano: San Sebastiano al Vesuvio, Sant'Anastasia, Somma Vesuviana and San Giuseppe Vesuviano. No house insurance can be taken out here and no gas pipes connect homes to the Neapolitan network of supplies.

Sant'Anastasia

Sant'Anastasia contains the notable church of Madonna ad Arco, before which one of Campania's largest processions is held each Easter Sunday. A steep and dusty road that makes an excellent hiking path leads from **Somma Vesuviana** up the volcano, although it is nicer to walk through medieval walled Borgo Casamale. The views are unique and the many restaurants and trattorias here are very busy during summer weekends. **San Giuseppe Vesuviano** has a tradition of small-scale textile production, although the family businesses here are struggling to compete with China these days. The streets are lined by shops decorated with lanterns bearing Chinese scripts, but Campania's textile markets are still supplied from here.

? DID YOU KNOW ...?

- Norman Lewis described witnessing an eruption by Vesuvius in his book »Naples 44«, where the arrival of the lava streams at the small town of San Sebastiano al Vesuvio are recorded thus: »A house, cautiously encircled and then overwhelmed, disappeared from sight intact, and a faint, distant grinding sound followed as the lava began its digestion.«

Nola

Already settled in prehistoric times, the former size and importance of Nola (pop. 33,000) can only be guessed at by the extent of its historic centre, which roughly mirrors that of antiquity. The great attraction here are the early Christian basilicas in outlying Cimitile. But during the Roman era, Nola was a major trading and agricultural centre for southern Italy, enjoying its heyday during the 2nd century BC due to its loyalty to Rome. Virgil owned a country estate here, as did the family of Emperor Augustus. Yet almost nothing remains above ground to indicate Nola's illustrious past. Only a third of the 1st century BC **anfiteatro** has been excavated, and it is only open to the public during the seasonal Maggio dei Monumenti. A great deal of Roman spolia can be found throughout the town, however. The highly attractive **Palazzo Orsini** on Piazza Giordano Bruno (the poet and philosopher was born in Nola in 1548) is entirely constructed from ancient building materials. The church of **San Felice** was erected on the site of a Roman temple. The present neo-Baroque building was constructed in 1870 after a fire. The bronze of Emperor Augustus (a copy) on the town square was placed here during the fascist era. Finds dating from the Bronze Age and the Roman era can be seen at the Archaeological Museum (Via Sen. Cocozza; Tue–Sun 9am–7pm).

✱ ◄ Museo Archeologico

The lively folk festival of the Festa degli Gigli in Nola

★★ **Festa dei Gigli** Ever since AD 431, a lively folk festival has been held on the first Sunday after 22 June each year. According to a moving legend, the town was pillaged by Alaric in AD 409, who also kidnapped a large part of the population, including a young boy. The boy's mother pleaded for help from **Paolino, the Bishop of Nola**. The bishop offered to stand in as hostage for the child and was promptly sold into slavery to Africa (or Turkey, depending on the source). However, after a series of miracles and after many years, Paolino was able to secure his freedom and returned to Nola, where a jubilant population embraced him. He was later canonized, and the impressively elaborate festival in his honour continues to be held each year to this day.

Villagio Preistorico di Nola Archaeologists believed they had discovered a second, much more ancient Pompeii when they excavated a Bronze Age site near Nola in 2002. This village was smothered by an eruption of Monte Somma about 3800 years ago in a natural catastrophe that has preserved Bronze Age life just as well as the later Vesuvian eruption froze an era 1900 years later. Plans are underway to open the excavation site to the public.

★ **Cimitile** Extensive ancient necropoli were once located to the north of Nola, which is also where the early Christian tomb of St Felix can be found. A number of churches were built around the tomb and, during the 4th and 5th centuries, the area was Italy's most important pilgrimage site next to Rome. Today, Cimitile has around 7000 inhabitants; its name recalls the ancient cemetery (Latin: ceometerium). The architectural remains of the Basiliche Paleocristine and its surviving frescoes constitute **significant traces from early Christian times**. The core of this complex of ruins is made up by the tomb of St Felix, already honoured by Paulinus (daily 9am–1pm, 3.30pm–7.30pm, Sun 9am–1.30pm). The adjacent **campanile** (renewed in the 13th century), is considered to be the earliest in Christendom. To the north of the tomb of St Felix lies the **Basilica Nova**, which was also commissioned by Paulinus, and the 3rd-century **Basilica dei Martiri**, which is considered of equal art-historical importance as the tomb. Its frescoes, including a representation of Adam and Eve in a somewhat divine pose, are examples of early Christian art. A similar fresco can be seen in the catacombs at San Gennaro in Naples.

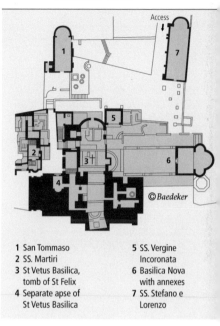

Cimitile Plan

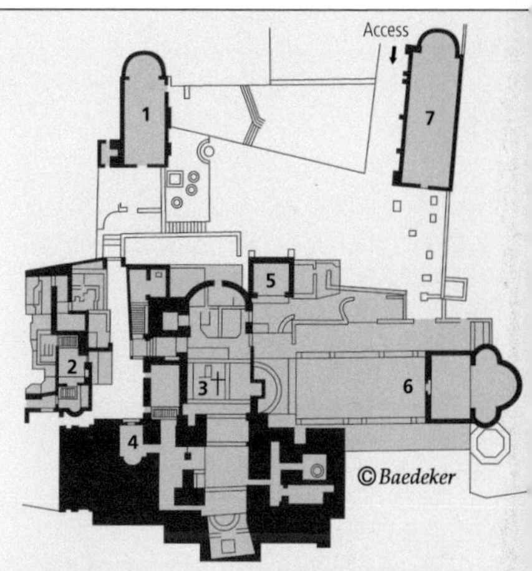

1 San Tommaso
2 SS. Martiri
3 St Vetus Basilica, tomb of St Felix
4 Separate apse of St Vetus Basilica
5 SS. Vergine Incoronata
6 Basilica Nova with annexes
7 SS. Stefano e Lorenzo

Vulcano Buono

Finally, the Il Vulcano Buono Shopping Centre opened in 2008 is also an attraction. Built from designs by the star architect Renzo Piano, southern Italy's **largest shopping mall**, with over 150 shops, is a »copy« of Mount Vesuvius on a scale of 1:50 (Via Boscofangone; www.vulcanobuo no.it).

Glossary of Art & Architecture

Abacus Square slab above the echinus, with which it forms the bell of the capital in the Doric order (►diagram p. 341)
Abaton, Adyton The sanctuary/holiest part of a temple, entered only by priests
Agora Marketplace, centre of a town's public life
Acanthus Prickly herb whose spiny leaves were used as model for ornamentation of Corinthian and Byzantine (Justinian) capitals
Acropolis Upper city, usually an elevated temple region
Acroterion Figure or ornament on roof ridge and gables (►diagram p. 341)
Ambo Desk for the reading of liturgical texts or pulpit for the sermon
Antis Colonnade in front of the protruding cella wall of a temple
Antis temple Temple with columns between the antis walls on the narrow front side
Apotheosis Deification of a human being
Apse Space at the end of a church, usually half-circular
Architrave Horizontal stone beam lying across the top of pillars
Arena Ellipse-shaped area for fighting in an amphitheatre
Arcade 1. An arch supported by columns or pillars 2. A continuous row of such arches
Atrium 1. Main space of a Roman house 2. Forecourt of an early Christian basilica
Atrium house Roman house arranged around an open inner courtyard (atrium); the cubiculum (space for sleeping and repose) and tablinum (reception area) open onto the atrium. The centre of the atrium was formed by the impluvium, in which rainwater was collected.
Baptisterium Baptismal church
Basileus King
Basilian Designation for orthodox monks whose rule goes back to the church father Basil the Great (approx. 330–379).
Basilica 1. King's hall (Stoá basiliké; usually with several aisles), place for trading and/or law court
2. Basic form of Christian church building developed in the fourth century AD, with a nave and two or four aisles
3. Title of honour bestowed on a church by the pope, regardless of its architectural type
Bema 1. Orator's platform
2. Altar space of a Christian church
Blind arcading, blind arch Arcade or arch affixed to the front of a wall for aesthetic reasons
Boss 1. Roughly hewn stone of a wall
2. Projection of a keystone used in the formation of a junction/intersection, aided by ropes and pulleys
3. Protective covering of hewn stones, worked off after completion of the junction
Bouleuterion Seat of the city council

Campanile Free-standing bell-tower of Italian churches

Capital Head of a column or pillar (►diagram p. 341)
Cardo North-south axis of a Roman city, at right angles to the decumanus
Caryatid Female figure used instead of a column to support an entablature
Cathedra Bishop's throne
Cathedral Church with bishop's throne, episcopal church
Cavea Shell-shaped rows of seating in a theatre (cf. Koilon)
Cella Interior space of a temple
Central building Building with main axes of equal length, for instance octagon or rotunda
Chamfer Cuboid link between capital and arch
Cherubim Angels, heavenly guardians with four, or sometimes six, wings
Choir Space between nave or transept of a Christian church and its main apse
Choir arch, triumphal arch Arch separating the nave or transept from the choir
Chthonic Belonging to the earth, subterranean, designation for divinities such as Persephone
Classical column orders

In the **Doric order** the column shaft with 16 to 20 fluting channels, narrowing towards the top, stands directly on the stylobate above the three steps of the substructure. Characteristic is the entasis (bulge) of the columns which soften the cold severity of the building, as does the frequently attested curve of the substructure. The Doric capital of forward-curving ring (echinus) and square slab (abacus) supports the architrave entablature with frieze above, of etched triglyphs and smooth or sculpted metopes. The gable triangle (tympanum or pediment) is framed by horizontal garland moulding and diagonal eaves and usually continues the composition of the gable figures. Ornamentation in the form of reliefs is found on the metopes and pediment. Where limestone was used rather than marble, it was covered with a smooth layer of stucco and the building was coloured, with blue and red dominant, alongside white.

The **Ionian order** prefers more slender, softer forms as compared to the Doric. The columns convey this impression partly because they stand on a base and narrow bars between the fluting emphasize the vertical character. The characteristic element of the Ionic capitals is the snail-shaped volute roll at either end. The frieze is brought round, above the three-part architrave, without triglyphs.

The **Corinthian order** matches the Ionic, except for the capitals. The ornamentation of the Corinthian capital is formed by large, lobed acanthus leaves, which surround the round body of the capital. Tendrils climb up to the corners of the concave abacus. The Corinthian order was widely used especially during the time of the Roman Empire; at this time a composite capital combining Ionic and Corinthian forms also arose, and increasingly lavish systems of decoration were developed.

Colossal order Pillars or columns extending over several storeys
Columbarium Burial place, usually beneath ground level, with niches one above the other to house the urns

Column basilica Basilica supported by columns
Composite capital See Classical column order
Corner contraction The reduction of the distance to the the corner columns of the Dorian temple to resolve the Dorian corner conflict, in which the axis of the corner triglyph does not match up with the column axis
Crepidoma Three-step substructure of a temple (krepis = "shoe"; ►diagram p. 341)
Cross-cupola church Byzantine type of church architecture with a central cupola above the intersection of crossing arms of equal length
Crossing space Square space arising from the intersection of nave and transept in a church
Crypt Part of church below ground level
Cryptoporticus Winding, covered passage dug into the earth
Curvature Gentle incline of the uppermost step of the temple substructure (crepidoma) towards the centre
Decumanus East-west axis of a Roman Castrum and a Roman town, running at right angles to the cardo
Echinus Originally cushion-shaped, later curved circular protuberance; forms the Dorian capital with the abacus above it (►diagram p. 341)
Entasis Bulge of the column in its lowest third (►diagram p. 341)
Epiphany Appearance of a divinity
Epistyle Beams lying across the top of columns in a temple; a frieze on the upper outer side (►diagram p. 341)
Exedra Space, usually semicircular, with benches
Fluting Vertical furrow on pillar shaft (►diagram p. 341)
Forum Main open place, or square, and political centre of a Roman town
Frieze Decorated area over the architrave of a temple; consisting of metopes and triglyphs in the Doric order, running smooth or sculpted in the Ionic (►diagram p. 341)
Geison Cornice or eaves of a temple roof. The eaves geison forms the lower edge of the roof on the long sides. In the gable space the figures stand on the horizontal geison beneath the raking geison that follows the slope of the roof (►diagram p. 341).
Gigantomachy Battle between gods and giants
Greek cross Cross with four arms of equal length
Gymnasium Area for sporting activity and for education generally (from Greek "gymnós" = naked)
Heraion Sanctuary of the goddess Hera
Heroon Cult place or burial place of a hero
Hieron Sanctuary
Hippodamic Principle Principle of town planning with straight streets crossing at right angles; named after Hippodamos of Miletus (5th century BC)
Hippodrome Racecourse for horses and chariots, consisting of two tracks running in opposite directions, separated by the spina
Hypogaum Subterranean vault, cult space

Classical Orders of Architecture

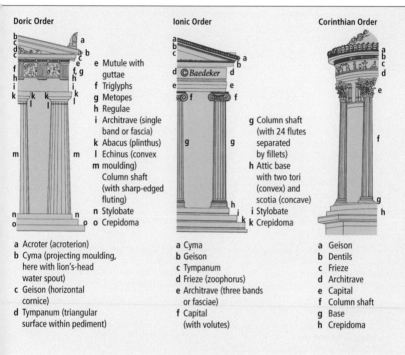

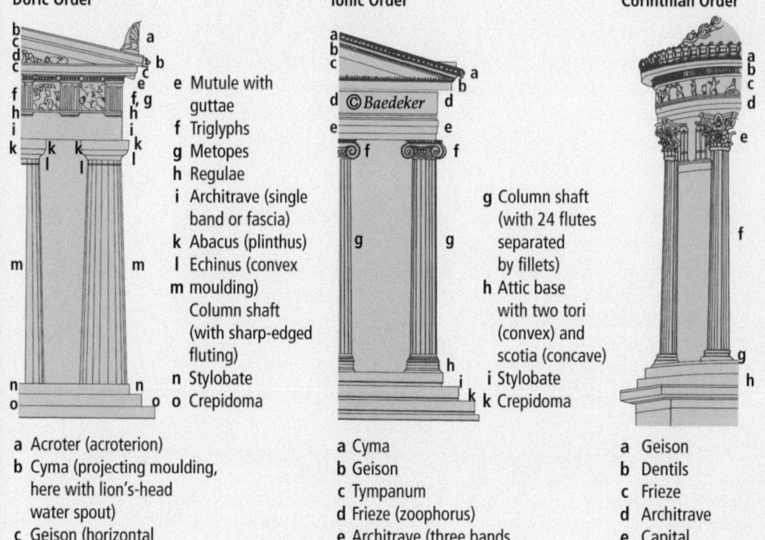

Hypocaust Under-floor heating system for baths or dwellings

Iconostasis Picture screen in the Byzantine church, separating the congregational space from the altar space

Incrustation Covering of a wall with precious material, esp. marble

In situ On site; in this place

Intercolumniation Light space between two columns

Kline Reclining bed

Koilon Shell-shaped seating space in a theatre (►cavea)

Kore Girl, statue of a girl; name for Persephone

Kyma Ancient ornament. The three "classic" forms are Dorian, Ionian and Lesbian.

Latin cross Cross with one long and three shorter arms

Lesena Flat pilaster, structuring the surface of a wall

Lunette Crescent-shaped space above windows and doors

Meander Winding ornament, called after the river Maiandros in Asia Minor (modern Turkish Büyük Menderes)

Megaron Main room of Mycenaean palaces; also regarded as the basic form of a Greek temple

Metope Square slab between the triglyphs on the frieze of a Doric temple; smooth or with relief work (►diagram p. 341)
Monopteros Round temple without naos (cella)
Naos Temple, interior of temple (cella)
Narthex Porch of a Byzantine church
Necropolis City of the dead, burial place, cemetery
Nymphaeum Area dedicated to the nymphs; a richly ornamented fountain
Odeon, Odeion Roofed building for musical performances
Octagon Eight-sided building
Olympion Holy sanctuary of Olympian Zeus
Orchestra Chorus dance space; round or semicircular space between stage and auditorium in the theatre
Palaestra Building for sporting activities (incl. wrestling)
Pantocrator Lord of all, lord of the world (Christ)
Peripteros Temple surrounded by columns, portico temple
Peristyle Colonnade, colonnaded hall or courtyard
Pilaster Pillar set against a wall
Pillar basilica Basilica with aisles separated by pillars; counterpart to the column basilica
Piscina Baptismal font in baptistery; artificially constructed fish-breeding pond in a Roman villa
Polis Economically self-sufficient and politically autonomous Greek city-state
Polychromy Variegated colour of ancient sculptures and temples
Polygonal Constructed from multi-edged stones
Polyptychon Winged altar with more than two wings
Portico Colonnaded hall
Pronaos Temple porch
Prostylos Temple with colonnaded porch
Rustica Stone wall with rough (»rustic«) surface
Sima Gutter eaves of temple, with lion heads as gargoyles (►diagram p. 341)
Spolia Reused fragments of older buildings
Stadium 1. Length measure: 600 ft = approx. 185 m
2. Running track of this length
3. Running track with embankment or seating for viewers
Stalactite vault Islamic vaulting with ornamentation that hangs down in clusters
Stele Free-standing pillar, usually with inscription, often with relief work
Stoa Colonnaded hall
Stylobate Uppermost step of temple substructure; base on which columns stand (►diagram p. 341)
Temenos Sacred space
Theatre 1. The Greek theatre consists of a construction at the rear (scena), the front part of the stage (proscenium) and the round or semi-circular orchestra, around which the rather more than semi-circular cavea with rows of seats is arranged, utilizing a natural hollow between hills.
2. The Roman theatre has a similar basic form, but the backdrop (scenae frons) is raised as high as the upper edge of the auditorium, which

reaches right up to it, built over the side entrances of the chorus; in this way an enclosed space, without roof, is created. The orchestra is semicircular, the acting platform is raised at a later date to rest on a podium. The auditorium is usually supported by substructures in which the entrances are located.

Thermae Baths in a private house or as public facility, consisting of changing-room (apodyterium), cold water bath (frigidarium), lukewarm air bath (tepidarium), hot water bath (caldarium), floor heating (hypocaustum) and further rooms for relaxation

Thermopolium Eating house, simple inn

Thesaurus Treasure, treasure-house

Tholos Round building

Tracery Geometrical decoration of the Gothic period, for instance on window breasts and parapets

Triclinium Dining room in a Roman house

Triglyph Stone slab with two incisions; separating the metopes of the Doric order (►diagram p. 341)

Triumphal arch 1. Single or double-arched monumental gate in Roman antiquity 2. Choir arch of a Christian basilica

Tympanum 1. Flat triangular gable of Greek temple (►diagram p. 341) 2. Arch space above church portal

Volute Spiral element of the Ionian capital (►diagram p. 341)

Yoke Space between two axes of columns

INDEX

a

'A juta a Montevergine **128**
Abbazia della Santissima Trinità (Cava dei Tirreni) **124**
Acciaroli **261**
Adelswaerd-Fersen, Jacques d' **136**
Aequa **324**
Agerola **126**
Agrippina **59**
agriturismo **66**
Agropoli **262**
air ambulance services **75**
air transport **70**
Albergo di Pover **49**
Alfonso V **28**
Allers, Christian Wilhelm **137**
Amalfi **118**
Amalfitana **123**
Amelio, Lucio **54, 56, 159**
Anacapri **147**
Anjou **28**
Antonio Bassolino **21**
Apennines **15**
Arco Felice **296**
area codes **93**
area in sq km/sq mi **17**
arrival **68**
art and culture **38**
Astroni crater **292**
ATM machines **91**
Atrani **126**
Atripalda **134**
Augustus **26**
Avellino **134**

Bacoli **295**
Badia di S. Maria di Olearia **125**
Baia **293**
Baia di Jeranto **318**
Baiae **293**
banks **91**
Barisano **305**
Baroque **47**
Bartolomeo, Nicola di **306**
basiliche paleocristiane (Cimitile) **44**
Bassolino, Antonio **20, 37, 59**
bathing spots **71**
Bauli **295**
beach holidays **71**
beaches **71**
Beckett, Ernest William **306**
bed & breakfasts **66**
Benevento **42, 127**
Beuys, Joseph **56**
Boccaccio **46**
Bomerano **126**
Bonaparte, Joseph **31**
Boscoreale **334**
bradyseism **15, 16, 44, 284**
Bruno, Giordano **335**

c

Camaino **46**
Camorra **32, 36**
Campania Artecard **93, 191**
Campanian Apennines **15**
Campi Flegrei **283**
camping **68**
canzoni **52**
Capaccio **258**
Capo di Sorrente **326**
Capo Miseno **295**
Capri **135**
Capua **44, 154**
car theft **99**
Caracciolo, Giovanni Battista **48**
Caravaggio **48, 207**
carceri vecchie **154**
Casa del Fauno **42**
Casa della Venere **42**
Casamicciola **181**
Case di Pietra (Ischia) **183**
Caserta **155**
Casertavecchia **161**
cash machines **91**
Casino Reale **295**
Cásola di Napoli **324**
Cassa per il Mezzogiorno **36**
Castellabate **262**
Castellammare di Stabia **322**
Castello Aragonese (Baia) **295**
catacombs **44**
Cava dei Tirreni **124**
Cento Camerelle **295**
Centro Italiano **225**
Charles III of Bourbon **30, 155**
chemists **81**
Chiaolella **300**
children **72**
churches (opening times) **92**
Cilento **258**
Cimitile **336**
Circumvesuviana **171**
Città Spectacolo **128**
climate **101**
coach travel **69**
Colonna, Vittoria **181**
Conca dei Marini **126**
concerts **76**
Conradin **28**
coral carvings **302**
Corleto Monforte **264**
Costiera Amalfitana **123**
credit cards **91**
cucina italiana **79**
cult of Mithras **151**
Cumae **296**
currency regulations **91**
customs regulations **70**
cycling **95**

Dicaearchia **26**
Diefenbach, Karl Wilhelm **144**
Don Carlos **30**
Donzelli, Giuseppe **48**
Douglas, Norman **57**
driving licence **70**

eating habits **79**
economy **20**
Elboeuf, d' **165**
electricity **74**
emergency **74**
ENIT **82**
Ente per le Ville Vesuviane **171**
environment **16**
environmental protection **16**
Ercolano **163**
Etruscans **25**
euro **91**
Eurolines **69**
events **75**
exchange rate **91**

Fango **182**
Fanzago, Cosimo **48**
fauna **16**

Ferdinand I
(formerly Ferdinand IV) **31**
Ferdinand II **31**
Ferdinand IV **30**
Ferdinandopoli **161**
Ferragosto **101**
Fersen, Jacques
d'Adelswaerd **136, 146**
Festa dei Gigli **336**
Festa delle Lucerne **330**
Festa di S. Vito **119**
Festa di Sant'Antonio
Abate **330**
Festival delle Ville
Vesuviane **164**
Festival Musicale
di Ravello **302**
festivals **75, 76**
Fiorelli, Giuseppe **268**
fishing **23, 96**
flora and fauna **16**
folk festivals **75**
Fondazione Amelio **56**
Fontana **183**
Fontana, Domenico **48**
food and drink **79**
Forio **183**
Fra Nuvolo **48**
Francis I **31**
Francis II **31**
Frederick II **27**
Fuorigrotta **329**
Futurism **53**

g

Galli islands **127**
Garbo, Greta **302**
Garibaldi **31**
garum **119**
getting there **68**
Giardini Poseidon (Ischia) **184**
Gigante, Giacinto **52**
Gioia, Flavio **122**
Giordano, Luca **48**
Giotto **46**
Goethe, Johann Wolfgang
von **51, 288, 328**
Gragnano **22, 324**
Grand Tour **50, 258, 288**
Greene, Graham **57**
grid **74**
Grimaldi, Francesco **47**
Grotta dello Smeraldo **126**
Grotta di Castelcivita **264**
Grotta di Pertosa **263, 264**

h

Hackert, Jacob Philipp **51, 159**
Hamilton, Sir William **51, 328**
health **81**
health insurance **71**
Herculanense Museum **171**
Herculaneum **163**
hiking **95**
hire cars **99**
history **24**
holiday apartments **67**
holidays **75**
horse-riding **96**
hotel categories **66**
hotels **66**
hypercaustic heating **279**
hypocauston **41**

i

Iervolino, Rosa Russo **20, 21**
industry **22**
internet addresses **83**
Irpinia **133, 134**
Ischia **172**
Ischia Ponte **181**
Ischia Porto **174**
Italian cuisine **79**

k

Kauffmann, Angelika **51**
Koch, Josef Anton **51**
Kopisch, August **51, 139**
Krupp, Friedrich Alfred **136,
143**

l

La Canocchia **154**
La Mortella (Ischia) **184**
Lacco Ameno **181**
Lago d'Averno **292**
Lago di Fusaro **295**
Language **83**
Laurino **264**
Lauro, Achille **37**
Leopardi, Giacomo **172**
Lettere **324**
Leuciana Festival **157**
Lewis, Norman **57**
Li Galli **127**
Liberty **53**
literature **88**
Lord Nelson **30**
Loren, Sophia **60**
Lorraine, Emanuel-Maurice
de **165**
Lucania **308**
Luna Convento **126**

m

Maddaloni **162**
Madonna della Neve **264**
Madonna di Novi Velia **264**
mafia **36**
Maggio dei Monumenti **37**
Magna Graecia **26**
mail **93**
Maiori **125**
Maiuri, Amedeo **268**
Malaparte, Curzio **53, 57**
Maltese, Giovanni **183**
Marées, Hans von **52**
Maria Carolina of Austria **61**
Marina del Cantone **318**
Marina di Ascea **262**
Marina di Camerota **71**
Massa Lubrense **326**
Massaquano **326**
matres matutae **155**
mayor **20**
meals **79**
media **91**
Mengs, Anton Raphael **51**
Miglio d'Oro **171**
Minori **126**
Minuta **308**
Misenum **295**
Mitreo Film Festival **152**
mobile phones **93**
Mommsen, Theodor **155**
money **91**
Monte Alburni **261**
Monte di Procida **297**
Monte Epomeo **172, 174, 176,
183**
Monte Faito **323**
Monte Gelbison **264**
Monte Nuovo **292**
Monte San Costanzo **327**
Monte Solaro **138**
Monte Tifata **155**

Monte Vergine **134**
Monte Virgo **161**
Montevergine **134**
Monti Alburni **258**
Monti del Matese **15**
Monti Lattari **123, 324**
Morante; Elsa **57**
Morelli, Domenico **52**
motorway tolls **96**
mozzarella **23**
Munthe, Axel **57**
Murat, Gioacchino **31**
Museo dell'Opera di San Lorenzo **200**
Museo Narrante del Santuario di Hera Argiva (Paestum) **258**
museums **92**
music festivals **76**
Mussolini **36**

n

Naples 185
– Albergo dei Poveri **221**
– Aquario **241**
– archaeological excavations under San Lorenzo **199**
– Bagnoli **244**
– Banco di Napoli Collection **215**
– bassi **226**
– Battle of Alexander **217**
– Bernini, Pietro **214**
– Bondone, Giotto di **210**
– Borgo Marinari **241**
– Café Gambrinus **228**
– Cappella Pontano **197**
– Cappella Sansevero **212**
– Carthusian monastery of San Martino **237**
– Casa del Mutilato **226**
– Castel Capuano **208**
– Castel dell'Ovo **239**
– Castel Nuovo **230**
– Castel Sant'Elmo **236**
– Centro Direzionale **234**
– Certosa di San Martino **237**
– Chiesa dei Gerolamini **202**
– Chiesa dell'Ascensione a Chiaia **242**
– Chiesa della Sanità **219**
– Chiesa della Santa Restituta **203**
– Chiesa di Santa Chiara **214**
– Chiesa Gesù Nuovo **209**
– Chiesa San Domenico Maggiore **211**
– Chiesa San Francesco di Paola **227**
– Chiesa San Giacomo degli Spagnuoli **233**
– Chiesa Sant'Angelo a Nilo **213**
– Chiesa Sant'Anna dei Lombardi **225**
– Chiesa Santa Brigida **227**
– Chiesa Santa Chiara **209**
– Chiostro delle Maioliche **210**
– Cimiterio delle Fontanelle **221**
– Circumvesuviana **234**
– Città della Scienza **244**
– city hall **232**
– Coin Collection **218**
– Complesso Archeologico di San Lorenzo Maggiore **199**
– Conradin of Hohenstaufen **235**
– Coroglio **244**
– Corso Umberto I **234**
– Corso Vittorio Emanuele **242**
– Cristo velato **212**
– Croce, Benedetto **211**
– Crypta Neapolitana **243**
– Dohrn, Anton **241**
– Duomo di San Gennaro **203**
– Fanzago; Cosimo **237**
– ferry port **234**
– Fra Nuvolo **219**
– funicolari **236**
– Gabinetto Segreto **218**
– Galleria L'Accademia di Belle Arti di Napoli **195**
– Galleria Umberto I **230**
– Giordano, Luca **223, 227**
– Giotto di Bondone **210**
– Guglia dell'Immacolata **208**
– Guglia di San Gennaro **207**
– Hotel de Londres **233**
– I Vergini **218**
– La presepe napoletana **238**
– Largo Antignano **236**
– Largo Corpo di Napoli **214**
– Lungomare **238**
– main post office **226**
– main railway station **234**
– Marechiaro **243**
– Marées, Hans von **241**
– Masaniello **238**
– Matteotti, Giacomo **226**
– Megaris **239**
– Mengs, Anton Raphael **229**
– Mercato quarter **235**
– Mergellina **242**
– Monte di Pietà **214**
– Montesanto quarter **225**
– Moscati, Giuseppe **209**
– Museo Civico (Castel Nuovo) **232**
– Museo Civico Filangieri **215**
– Museo del Tesoro di San Gennaro **206**
– Museo dell'Opera **210**
– Museo dell'Opera di San Lorenzo **199**
– Museo delle Carozze **242**
– Museo di San Martino **237**
– Museo Diocesano Napoli **207**
– Museo Nazionale della Ceramica Duca di Martina **236**
– Museo Nitsch **194**
– Museo Storico Musicale **195**
– Museum of Contemporary Art **207**
– Napoli Sotterranea **198**
– National Archaeological Museum **215**
– Nisida **244**
– Orto Botanico **221**
– Palazzo Calabritto **238**
– Palazzo Carafa di Santangelo **214**
– Palazzo Cellamare **238**
– Palazzo Cuomo **215**
– Palazzo degli Spiriti **243**
– Palazzo degli Uffici Finanziari **226**
– Palazzo del Banco di Napoli **226**
– Palazzo del Principe di Salerno **228**
– Palazzo della Prefettura **228**
– Palazzo della Provincia **226**

– Palazzo delle Poste e dei Telegrafi **226**
– Palazzo dello Spagnolo **219**
– Palazzo di Capua-Mariglian **214**
– Palazzo Donn'Anna **243**
– Palazzo Donna Regina **207**
– Palazzo Doria d'Angri **225**
– Palazzo Filomarino della Rocca **211**
– Palazzo Gravina **226**
– Palazzo Municipale **233**
– Palazzo Reale **228**
– Palazzo San Giacomo **232**
– Palazzo Serra di Cassano **241**
– Palazzo Sessa **238**
– Palazzo Spinelli di Laurino **197**
– Parco Archeologico del Pausilypon **244**
– Parco Sommerso della Gaiola **243**
– Parco Virgiliano **243**
– Parco Virgiliano di Posillipo **244**
– Piazza Amedeo **242**
– Piazza Bellini **195**
– Piazza Carità **226**
– Piazza Carlo III **221**
– Piazza Dante **194**
– Piazza dei Martiri **238**
– Piazza del Gesù Nuovo **208**
– Piazza del Municipio **232**
– Piazza del Plebiscito **227, 228**
– Piazza della Borsa **234**
– Piazza Duca d'Aosta **227**
– Piazza Garibaldi **234**
– Piazza Giovanni Bovio **234**
– Piazza Matteotti **226**
– Piazza Medaglie d'Oro **236**
– Piazza Monteoliveto **225**
– Piazza San Domenico Maggiore **211**
– Piazza San Gaetano **198**
– Piazza Trieste e Trento **227**
– Piazza Vanvitelli **236**
– Piazza Vittoria **238**
– Pizzofalcone **241**
– porcelain and ceramic collection (Villa Floridiana) **236**
– Porta Capuana **208**
– Porto Sannazaro **243**
– Posillipo **243**
– Quartieri spagnoli **226**
– Rettifilo **234**
– Rione Carità **226**
– San Filippo Nero **202**
– San Gaudioso Catacombs **219**
– San Gennaro Catacombs **220**
– San Giovanni a Carbonara **208**
– San Gregorio Armeno **202**
– San Lorenzo Maggiore **199**
– San Paolo Maggiore **198**
– San Pietro A Maiella **196**
– San Severo Catacombs **220**
– San Vicenzo **219**
– Sanfelice, Ferdinando **219**
– Sanità **218**
– Sanmartino, Giuseppe **237**
– Sant'Eligio Maggiore **236**
– Santa Lucia (quarter) **239**
– Santa Maria del Carmine **235**
– Santa Maria delle Anime del Purgatorio ad Arco **198**
– Santa Maria Donnaregina Nuova **207**
– Santa Maria Donnaregina Vecchia **207**
– Santa Maria Maggiore della Pietrasanta **197**
– Spaccanapoli **208**
– St Gaudiosus **219**
– statue of the Nile **214**
– Stazione Centrale **234**
– Stazione Cumana Montesanto **225**
– Stazione Marittima **234**
– Stazione Zoologica **241**
– Teatro Mercadante **233**
– Teatro Romano **199**
– Teatro San Carlo **230**
– thermal spa (Chiostro delle Maioliche) **211**
– Torre Telecom Italia **235**
– Totò **218**
– Università degli Studi di Napoli »Federico II« **213**
– university **211**
– Via dei Tribunali **197**
– Via di Posillipo **243**
– Via San Gregorio Armeno **202**
– Via Sant'Anna dei Lombardi **225**
– Via Scarlatti **236**
– Via Toledo **223**
– Villa Comunale **241**
– Villa Floridiana **236**
– Villa Imperiale del Pausilypon **243**
– Villa Pignatelli **242**
– Villa Rosebery **244**
– Virgil's grave **243**
– Vomero **236**
– weekly market (Largo Antignano) **236**
– Zona Archeologica (Chiostro delle Maioliche) **211**
natural environment **15**
nature reserves **16**
newspapers **91**
Niemeyer, Oskar **309**
Nocera **314**
Nola **335**
Norman Douglas **146**
Nureyev, Rudolf **127**

opening hours **92**
opus caementicium **41, 294**
Osservatorio Vesuviano **328**
Ottaviano **331**

p

Padre Pio **62, 132**
Padula **265**
Paestum **245**
Pagano, Giuseppe **139**
Paladino, Mimmo **132**
Palazzo delle Poste **53**
Palinuro **263**
Palio delle Quattro Antiche Repubbliche Marinare **119**
Parco del Cilento e Vallo di Diano **16**
Parco Nazionale del Cilento e Vallo di Diano **261**
Parco Nazionale del Vesuvio **16, 327**
parking **99**
Parmenides **262**

Parthenope **26**
Parthenopean Republic **30**
Pedro di Toledo **28**
Penisola Sorrentina **322**
Petrarch **46**
petrol **97**
pets **70**
pharmacies **81**
Philip V **30**
Phlegrean Fields **283**
Piano di Sorrento **326**
Pietrelcina **132**
Piscina Mirabilis **295**
Pithekoussai **173, 182**
Pitloo, Anton Sminck van **51**
Pliny the Elder **328**
Pliny the Younger **328**
Plüschow, Wilhelm von **137**
Pompeii **42, 265**
Ponte della Sanità **31**
Pontecagnano Faiano **315**
Pontone **308**
population **20**
Positano **126**
post offices **93**
Pozzuoli **283**
Praiano **126**
prices **93**
Procida **297**
Punta Campanella **327**

r

radio **91**
rain **101**
Ravello **301**
refuse collection **20**
Reggia di Portici **171**
Reid, Francis Neville **306**
Resina **163**
restaurants **79**
Ribera, Giuseppe (José) **48**
Richter, Ludwig **51**
Rione Carità **53**
Roscigno Vecchio **264**

s

Salerno **308**
Salerno Porte Aperte **310**
Samnites **25**
San Giuseppe Vesuviano **335**
San Leucio **161**
San Marco di Castellabate **262**
San Matteo **310**
San Sebastiano al Vesuvio **335**
Sanfelice, Ferdinando **49**
Sant Angelo in Formis **161**
Sant'Agata de Goti **133**
Sant'Agata sui due Golfi **326**
Sant'Anastasia **335**
Sant'Angelo (Ischia) **184**
Sant'Angelo a Fasanella **264**
Santa Maria **262**
Santa Maria Capua Vetere **150**
Santa Maria la Carità **324**
Santuario di Hera Argiva **257**
Santuario di Monte Vergine **134**
Scala **307**
Scuola di Posillipo **51**
Sentiero degli Dei **126**
Settembrata Anacaprese **141**
Settembre al Borgo **157**
shopping **94**
Sicignano degli Alburni **264**
Solfatara **291**
Solimena, Francesco **48**
Somma Vesuviana **335**
Sommer, Giorgio **52**
Sorrentine peninsula **322**
souvenirs **94**
Spartacus **150**
spas and thermal baths **71**
Spiaggia di Miliscola **295**
sport **95**
SS 163 **123**
St Pantaleon **306**
Stabiae **322**
stamps **93**
Stufe di Nerone **293**
symposium **256**

t

Tange, Kenzo **56**
Tasso, Torquato **320**
Taxi del Mare **69**
Teatri di Pietra **152**
Teggiano **264**
telephone **93**
television **91**
temperatures **101**
Termini **327**
thermal springs **71**
Tiberius **26**
time **96**
Torre Annunziata **331**
Torre del Greco **172**
torri saraceni **172**
Torri saraceni **125**
Totò **62**
tourism **23**
tourism offices **82**
towing **97**
traffic regulations **97**
travel documents **70**
Trenitalia **100**
Tripergole **292**

u

unemployment figures **20**
Uniconapoli ticket **188**

v

Valle dei Mulini **124**
Vallo della Lucania **264**
Vallo di Diano **265**
Vallone di Furore **126**
Vanvitelli Luigi **157**
Vanvitelli, Carlo **49, 156**
Vanvitelli, Luigi **49, 155**
Velia Teatro **260**
venationes **290**
Vesuvius **327**
Via Traiana **131**
Vico Equense **324**
Vidal, Gore **57, 302, 306**
Vietri sul Mare **124**
Villa dei Misteri **42**
Villa dei Papiri **40**
Villa della Pisanella **334**
Villa La Colombaia **184**
Villa Oplontis **331**
Villa Quisisana (Castellammare di Stabia) **323**
Villa Regina **334**
Villa Regina (Boscoreale) **41**
villa rustica **41**
villa urbana **41**
Virgil **63**

Visconti, Luchino **57, 184**
volcanism **15**

w

Wagner festival **302**
Wagner, Richard **302**
Warhol, Andy **56**
water sports **96**
when to go **101**
Wilde, Oscar **136**
wine growing **23**
wines **80**

y

youth hostels **66**

LIST OF MAPS AND ILLUSTRATIONS

Sightseeing highlights **3**
Naples in Europe **21**
Mount Vesuvius (3 D) **18**
Climate **86**
Table of distances **97**
Circumvesuviana **99**
Tours **105**
Tour 1 **107**
Tour 2 **108**
Tour 3 **109**
Tour 4 **110**
Tour 5 **112**
Tour 6 **113**
Benevent **129**
Capri **144/145**
 Villa Jovis **147**
Capua **153**
Herculaneum **167**
Ischia **178/179**
Naples
 Overview **Boxed map of city centre on separate large map**
 Metro **189**
 Centro storico **196**
 San Lorenzo Maggiore (3 D) **200**
 Via Toledo, Piazza del Plebiscito und Castel Nuovo **224**
 Mergellina and Posillipo **239**
Paestum **251**
 Doric column order **253**
 Velia **263**
Pompeii **272/273**
 Villa dei Misteri **41**
 Casa del Fauno **278**
Pozzuoli **287**
 Campi flegrei **293**
Ravello **303**
Salerno **311**
Sorrent **321**
Mount Vesuvius
 Villa Oplontis (3D) **332**
 Cimitile **337**

Overview **back cover inside**

PHOTO CREDITS

akg-images 28/29, 55
Peter Amann 10, 12 (above), 53, 72, 137, 222, 277, 240, 279, 292, 318, 323, 336
Dumont Bildarchiv/W. Fabig 8/9, 155, 173, 213, 271, 313
Dumont Bildarchiv/R. Kiedrowski 4, 12 (below), 13, 45, 102/103, 142, 149, 229
Huber 19 (Bernhart), 245 (Ripani)
IFA-Bilderteam 11 (Center), 309 (Jon Arnold),
Interfoto 18 (above left, Bärbel; above right, Sammlung Rauch)
Rainer Kiedrowski 139, 180, 299
laif/Zanettini 18
Mauritius 77 (Cubolimages), 317 (Hiroshi Higucchi)
picture-alliance/akg-images 18 (below left), 50, 289
picture-alliance/CM Dixon 18 (below right)
picture-alliance/dpa 34, 60, 205
Wolfram Schleicher front cover inside, 1, 2, 6, 7, 9, 11 (above, below), 12 (center), 14, 17, 22, 23, 24, 33, 38, 40, 43, 48, 58, 61, 62, 64/65, 65, 73, 85, 95, 100, 103, 105, 106, 111, 113, 114, 116/117, 117, 119, 121, 123, 125, 131, 133, 150, 151, 156, 160, 162, 165, 170, 186, 191, 195, 200, 201 (right, above left, below left), 202, 203, 209, 211, 216, 217, 227, 231, 233, 237, 246, 248, 254, 257, 259, 264, 266, 269, 281, 283, 291, 286, 294, 301, 305, 307, 325, 329, 332, 333 (3 x), 334, back cover inside and outside
Andreas Schlüter 219

Cover photo: Panther Media / Avenue Images

PUBLISHER'S INFORMATION

Illustrations etc: 141 illustrations, 39 maps and diagrams, one large map
Text: Andreas Schlüter, Peter Amann
Editing: Baedeker editorial team (Robert Taylor)
Translation: Robert Taylor
Cartography: Christoph Gallus, Hohberg; Franz Huber, Munich; MAIRDUMONT/Falk Verlag, Ostfildern (map)
3D illustrations: jangled nerves, Stuttgart
Design: independent Medien-Design, Munich; Kathrin Schemel

Editor-in-chief: Rainer Eisenschmid, Baedeker Ostfildern

1st edition 2012

Based on Baedker Allianz Reiseführer »Golf von Neapel« 3. Auflage 2011
Copyright: Karl Baedeker Verlag, Ostfildern
Publication rights: MAIRDUMONT GmbH & Co; Ostfildern

The name Baedeker is a registered trademark. All international rights reserved. No part of this publication may be copied, stored in a retrieval system, or transmitted in any form by any means, electronic, mechanical, recording or otherwise, except brief extracts for the purpose of review, and no part of this publication may be sold or hired, without the written permission of Karl Baedeker Verlag GmbH.

Printed in China

BAEDEKER GUIDE BOOKS AT A GLANCE

Guiding the World since 1827

- Andalusia
- Australia
- Austria
- Bali
- Barcelona
- Berlin
- Brazil
- Budapest
- Cape Town • Garden Route
- China
- Cologne
- Dresden
- Dubai
- Egypt
- Florence
- Florida
- France
- Gran Canaria
- Greek Islands
- Greece
- Iceland
- India
- Ireland
- Italian Lakes
- Italy
- Japan
- London
- Madeira
- Mexico
- Morocco
- Naples • Capri • Amalfi Coast
- New York
- New Zealand
- Norway
- Paris
- Portugal
- Prague
- Rome
- South Africa
- Spain
- Thailand
- Turkish Coast
- Tuscany
- Venice
- Vienna
- Vietnam

DEAR READER,

We would like to thank you for choosing this Baedeker travel guide. It will be a reliable companion on your travels and will not disappoint you.
This book describes the major sights, of course, but it also recommends the most beautiful beaches as well as hotels in the luxury and budget categories, and includes tips about where to eat or go shopping and much more, helping to make your trip an enjoyable experience. Our authors ensure the quality of this information by making regular journeys to the Amalfi Coast and putting all their know-how into this book.

Nevertheless, experience shows us that it is impossible to rule out errors and changes made after the book goes to press, for which Baedeker accepts no liability. Please send us your criticisms, corrections and suggestions for improvement: we appreciate your contribution. Contact us by post or e-mail, or phone us:

▶ **Verlag Karl Baedeker GmbH**
Editorial department
Postfach 3162
73751 Ostfildern
Germany
Tel. 49-711-4502-262, fax -343
www.baedeker.com
www.baedeker.co.uk
E-Mail: baedeker@mairdumont.com